PAUL

HarperOne Titles by N. T. Wright

The Day the Revolution Began

Simply Good News

Surprised by Scripture

The Case for the Psalms

How God Became King

Simply Jesus

Scripture and the Authority of God

The Kingdom New Testament

After You Believe

Surprised by Hope

Simply Christian

The Meaning of Jesus (with Marcus Borg)

Other Titles by N. T. Wright

Christian Origins and the Question of God series:

The New Testament and the People of God

Jesus and the Victory of God

The Resurrection of the Son of God

Paul and the Faithfulness of God

PAUL

A Biography

N. T. WRIGHT

HarperOne
An Imprint of HarperCollins*Publishers*

HarperOne

FIRST EDITION

Designed by Michelle Crowe

Maps by Beehive Mapping

Library of Congress Cataloging-in-Publication Data

Names: Wright, N. T. (Nicholas Thomas), author.
Title: Paul: a biography / N.T. Wright.
Description: FIRST EDITION. | San Francisco : HarperOne, 2018. | Includes bibliographical references.
Identifiers: LCCN 2017027846 | ISBN 9780061730580 (hardcover)
Subjects: LCSH: Paul, the Apostle, Saint.
Classification: LCC BS2506.3 .W749 2018 | DDC 225.92 [B]—dc23
LC record available at https://lccn.loc.gov/2017027846

---

18 19 20 21 22 LSC 10 9 8 7 6 5 4 3 2 1

In loving memory of Carey Alison Wright
October 12, 1956–June 3, 2017

CONTENTS

PART THREE: THE SEA, THE SEA

LIST OF MAPS

PREFACE

THE APOSTLE PAUL is one of a handful of people from the ancient world whose words still have the capacity to leap off the page and confront us. Whether we agree with him or not—whether we *like* him or not!—his letters are personal and passionate, sometimes tearful and sometimes teasing, often dense but never dull. But who was he? What made him tick? And why did his seemingly erratic missionary career have such a profound influence on the world of ancient Greece and Rome and thereby on the world of our own day?

Any worthwhile answer must presuppose the detailed historical and theological study of his letters in debate with ongoing scholarship. I have tried to do this in *The Climax of the Covenant* (1991/1992), *Paul and the Faithfulness of God* (2013), the collection of essays entitled *Pauline Perspectives* (2013), and the survey of modern (largely Anglophone) research *Paul and His Recent Interpreters* (2015).[1] But the biographer's questions are subtly different. We are searching for the man behind the texts.

Like most historians, I try to include all relevant evidence within as simple a framework as possible. I do not regard it a virtue to decide ahead of time against either the Pauline authorship of some of the letters or the historicity of the Acts of the Apostles (on the grounds, perhaps, that Luke was writing long after the events, inventing material to fit his theology). Each generation has to start the jigsaw with all the pieces on the table and to see if the pieces can be plausibly fitted together to create a prima facie case. In particular, I make two large assumptions: first, a South Galatian address for Galatians; second, an Ephesian imprisonment as the location of the Prison Letters. In the former I am following, among many others, Stephen Mitchell, *Anatolia: Land, Men, and Gods in Asia Minor,* vol. 2, *The Rise of the Church.*[2] In the latter I am indebted to many, including an older work by a St. Andrews predecessor, George S. Duncan, *Paul's Ephesian Ministry: A Reconstruction.*[3] I have found that these hypotheses make excellent sense of the historical, theological, and biographical data. References to primary sources are found in the notes at the end, but I have not usually cluttered things up with endless references to Acts itself.

A small note on style. Despite protests, I keep the lowercase *s* in "(holy) spirit," because that conforms to my own translation, which I use here[4] (translations of Old Testament quotations are either my own or from the NRSV), and particularly because when Paul wrote the Greek word *pneuma,* he did not have the option of a distinction between upper and lower case. His letters were in any case written initially to be read out loud. The word *pneuma* had to make its way in a world where it had different shades of philosophical and religious meaning without the help of visible markings. This itself makes an important point about Paul, who told and lived a Jesus-shaped Jewish message in a confused and contested world.

I am grateful to several friends and colleagues who have read all or part of this book in draft and have offered suggestions, corrections, additions, and clarifications. They are not responsible for the errors that remain. I think particularly of Simon Kingston, Scot McKnight, Mike Bird, Mike Gorman, Max Botner, Craig Keener, Andrew Cowan, John Richardson, and Jonathan Sacks.

The publishers have been uniformly helpful and encouraging; I'm thinking of Mickey Maudlin, Noël Chrisman, and their coworkers at HarperOne, and Sam Richardson, Philip Law, and their coworkers at SPCK. I am once again grateful to my colleagues and students at St. Andrews for their encouragement and enthusiasm, and to my dear family for their unfailing support. The book is dedicated to the beloved memory of my late sister-in-law, Carey Wright, who like Paul gave love and joy unstintingly to those around her.

Tom Wright
Ascension Day, 2017
St. Andrews

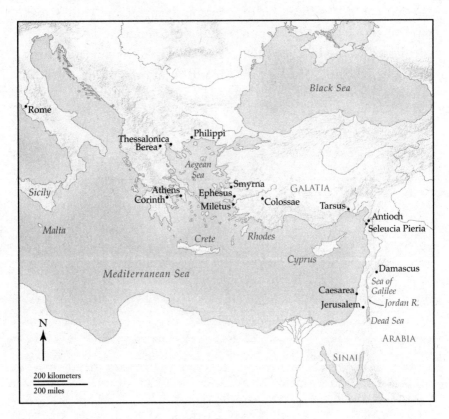

Paul's World

Introduction

HUMAN CULTURE HAS normally developed at the speed of a glacier. We moderns, accustomed to sudden changes and dramatic revolutions, need to remind ourselves that things have not usually worked this way. Slow and steady has been the rule. Occasional inventions that suddenly transform human life for good or ill—the wheel, the printing press, gunpowder, the Internet—are rare.

That is why the events that unfolded two thousand years ago in southeastern Europe and western Asia are still as startling in retrospect as they were at the time. An energetic and talkative man, not much to look at and from a despised race, went about from city to city talking about the One God and his "son" Jesus, setting up small communities of people who accepted what he said and then writing letters to them, letters whose explosive charge is as fresh today as when they were first dictated. Paul might dispute the suggestion that he himself changed the world; Jesus, he would have said, had already done that. But what he said about Jesus, and about God, the world, and what it meant to be genuinely human, was creative and compelling—and controversial, in his own day and ever after. Nothing would ever be quite the same again.

Consider the remarkable facts. Paul's letters, in a standard modern translation, occupy fewer than eighty pages. Even taken as a whole, they are shorter than almost any single one of Plato's dialogues or Aristotle's treatises. It is a safe bet to say that these letters, page for page, have generated more comment, more sermons and seminars, more monographs and dissertations than any other writings from the ancient world. (The gospels, taken together, are half as long again.) It is as though eight or ten small paintings by an obscure artist were to become more sought after, more studied and copied, more highly valued than all the Rembrandts and Titians and all the Monets and Van Goghs in the world.

This raises a set of questions for any historian or would-be biographer. How did it happen? What did this busy little man have that other people didn't? What did he think he was doing, and why was he doing it? How did someone with his background and upbringing, which had produced saints and scholars but nobody at all like this, come to be speaking, traveling, and writing in this way? That is the first challenge of the present book: to get inside the mind, the understanding, the ambition (if that's the right word) of Paul the Apostle, known earlier as Saul of Tarsus. What motivated him, in his heart of hearts?

That question leads immediately to the second one. When Saul encountered the news about Jesus, his mind was not a blank slate. He had been going full tilt in the opposite direction. More than once he reminds his readers that he had been brought up in a school of Jewish thought that adhered strictly to the ancestral traditions. As a young man, Saul of Tarsus had become a leading light in this movement, the aim of whose members was to urge their fellow Jews into more radical obedience to the ancient codes and to discourage them from any deviations by all means possible, up to and including violence. Why did all that change? What exactly happened on the road to Damascus?

This poses a problem for today's readers that had better be mentioned at once, though we will only be able to address it bit by bit. The term "Damascus Road" has become proverbial, referring to any sudden transformation in personal belief or character, any "conversion," whether "religious," "political," or even aesthetic. One can imagine a critic declaring that, having previously detested the music of David Bowie, he had now had a "Damascus Road" moment and had come to love it. This contemporary proverbial usage gets in the way. It makes it harder for us to understand the original event. So does the language of "conversion" itself. That word today might point to someone being "converted" from secular atheism or agnosticism to some form of Christian belief, or perhaps to someone being "converted" from a "religion" such as Buddhism or Islam to a "religion" called "Christianity"—or, of course, vice versa. Thus, many have assumed that on the road to Damascus Saul of Tarsus was "converted" from something called "Judaism" to something called "Christianity"—and that in his mature thought he was *comparing* these two "religions," explaining why the latter was to be preferred. But if we approach matters in that way we will, quite simply, never understand either Saul of Tarsus or Paul the Apostle.

For a start, and as a sign that there are tricky corners to be turned, the word "Judaism" in Paul's world (Greek *Ioudaïsmos*) didn't refer to what we would call "a religion." For that matter, and again to signal challenges ahead, the word "religion" has itself changed meaning. In Paul's day, "religion" consisted of God-related activities that, along with politics and community life, held a culture together and bound the members of that culture to its divinities and to one another. In the modern Western world, "religion" tends to mean God-related individual beliefs and practices that are supposedly separable from culture, politics, and community life. For Paul, "religion" was woven in with all of life; for the modern Western world, it is separated from it.

So when, in what is probably his earliest letter, Paul talks about "advancing in Judaism beyond any of his age,"[1] the word "Judaism" refers, not to a "religion," but to an *activity:* the zealous propagation and defense of the ancestral way of life. From the point of view of Saul of Tarsus, the first followers of Jesus of Nazareth were a prime example of the deviant behavior that had to be eradicated if Israel's God was to be honored. Saul of Tarsus was therefore "zealous" (his term,[2] indicating actual violence, not just strong emotion) in persecuting these people. That is what he meant by *Ioudaïsmos*. Everything possible had to be done to stamp out a movement that would impede the true purposes of the One God of Israel, whose divine plans Saul and his friends believed were at last on the verge of a glorious fulfillment—until, on the Damascus Road, Saul came to believe that these plans had indeed been gloriously fulfilled, but in a way he had never imagined.

Saul, therefore, poses a double question for the historian in addition to the many questions he poses for students of ancient culture, ancient "religion," or ancient faith. How did he come to be a world changer? He was, we may suppose, a surprising candidate for such a role. He was a teacher of Jewish traditions, perhaps; a reformer, quite possibly. But not the kind of activist who establishes in city after city little cells of unlikely people, many of them non-Jewish, and fires them with a joyful hope that binds them together. Not the kind of philosopher who teaches people not just new thoughts, but a whole new way of thinking. Not the kind of spiritual master who rethinks prayer itself from the ground up. How did it happen? And, beyond the initial impact, why was Paul's movement so successful? Why did these little communities founded by a wandering Jew turn into what became "the church"? That's the first set of questions we are addressing in this book.

The second set gives this a radical twist. How did Saul the persecutor become Paul the Apostle? What sort of transition was that? Was it in any sense a "conversion"? Did Paul "switch religions"? Or can we accept Paul's own account that, in following the crucified Jesus and announcing that Israel's God had raised him from the dead, he was actually being loyal to his ancestral

traditions, though in a way neither he nor anyone else had anticipated?

These questions doubtless puzzled Paul's contemporaries. That
would have included other followers of Jesus, some of whom regarded him with deep suspicion. It would have included his fellow
Jews, some of whom reacted as violently to him as he himself had
to the early Jesus movement. It would certainly have included the
non-Jewish population in the cities he went to, many of whom
thought he was both mad and dangerous (and a Jew to boot, some
would have said with a sneer). Wherever he went, people must
have wondered who he was, what he thought he was doing, and
what sense it made for a hard-line nationalist Jew to become the
founder of multiethnic communities.

These questions do not seem to have puzzled Paul himself,
though, as we shall see, he had his own times of darkness. He had
thought them through and arrived at robust and sharp-edged
answers. But they have continued to challenge readers and thinkers ever since, and they confront in particular a modern world
that has been confused about many different aspects of human
life, including those sometimes labeled by that tricky word "religion." Paul confronts our world, as he confronted his own, with
questions and challenges. This book, a biography of Paul, is an
attempt to address the questions. I hope it will also clarify the
challenges.

★ ★ ★

These were not the questions that first goaded me into reading
Paul seriously for myself. No matter. Once you start reading him,
he will lead you to all the other questions soon enough. Studying
Paul in my teens with like-minded friends (there were many different styles of cultural rebellion in the 1960s, and I'm glad this
was one of mine), I tended to focus on basic theological issues.
What precisely was "the gospel," and how did it "work"? What
did it mean to be "saved" and indeed to be "justified," and how

might you know that this had happened to you personally? If you were "justified by faith alone," why should it then matter how you behaved thereafter? Or, if you were truly "born again," indwelt by the spirit, oughtn't you now be leading a life of perfect sinlessness? Was there a middle way between these two positions, and if so, how did it make sense? Was faith itself something the individual "did" to gain God's approval, or was that just smuggling in "good works" by the back door? Did Paul teach "predestination," and if so, what might that mean? What about the "spiritual gifts"? Just because Paul spoke in tongues, did that mean we should too? Paul was clearly worried, in his letter to the Galatians, that his converts might get circumcised; granted that none of us felt any pressure in that direction, what was the equivalent in our world? Did it mean that Paul was opposed to all "religious rituals," and if so, what did that say about church life and liturgy and about baptism itself?

These questions swirled around in our eager young minds as we listened to sermons, got involved in church life, and wrestled with the texts. We were reading Paul in the light of fairly typical concerns of some parts of the church in the 1960s and 1970s, but of course what we wanted to know was not what this or that preacher or professor thought, but what Paul himself thought. We believed (in a fairly unreflective manner) in the "authority" of scripture, including Paul's letters. What we were after, therefore, was what Paul himself was trying to say. We were, in other words, trying to do ancient history, though we didn't think of it like that and might have resisted the idea if we had. (This was the more ironic in my case, in that Ancient History was part of my undergraduate degree.) Paul's words, inspired, so we believed, by God, were charged with the grandeur of divine truth, and their meaning was to be sought by prayer and faith rather than by historical inquiry, even though, of course, those words themselves, if one is going to understand them, require careful study precisely of their lexical range in the world of the time.

Paul's letters existed for us in a kind of holy bubble, unaffected by the rough-and-tumble of everyday first-century life. This enabled us blithely to assume that when Paul said "justification," he was talking about what theologians in the sixteenth century and preachers in the twentieth had been referring to by that term. It gave us license to suppose that when he called Jesus "son of God," he meant the "second person of the Trinity." But once you say you're looking for original meanings, you will always find surprises. History is always a matter of trying to think into the minds of people who think differently from ourselves. And ancient history in particular introduces us to some ways of thinking very different from those of the sixteenth or the twentieth century.

I hasten to add that I still see Paul's letters as part of "holy scripture." I still think that prayer and faith are vital, nonnegotiable parts of the attempt to understand them, just as I think that learning to play the piano for oneself is an important part of trying to understand Schubert's impromptus. But sooner or later, as the arguments go on and people try out this or that theory, as they start reading Paul in Greek and ask what this or that Greek term meant in the first century, they discover that the greatest commentators were standing on the shoulders of ancient historians and particularly lexicographers, and they come, by whatever route, to the questions of this book: who Paul really was, what he thought he was doing, why it "worked," and, within that, what was the nature of the transformation he underwent on the road to Damascus.

★ ★ ★

Another obvious barrier stood between my teenage Bible-reading self and a historical reading of Paul. I assumed without question, until at least my thirties, that the whole point of Christianity was for people to "go to heaven when they died." Hymns, prayers, and sermons (including the first few hundred of my own sermons) all pointed this way. So, it seemed, did Paul: "We are citizens of heaven," he wrote.[3] The language of "salvation" and "glorification," central to Romans, Paul's greatest letter, was assumed to mean the same thing: being "saved" or being "glorified" meant "going to heaven," neither more nor less. We took it for granted that the question of "justification," widely regarded as Paul's principal doctrine, was his main answer as to how "salvation" worked in practice; so, for example, "Those he justified, he also glorified"[4] meant, "First you get justified, and then you end up in heaven." Looking back now, I believe that in our diligent searching of the scriptures we were looking for correct biblical answers *to medieval questions*.

These were not, it turns out, the questions asked by the first Christians. It never occurred to my friends and me that, if we were to scour the first century for people who were hoping that their "souls" would leave the present material world behind and "go to heaven," we would discover Platonists like Plutarch, not Christians like Paul. It never dawned on us that the "heaven and hell" framework we took for granted was a construct of the High Middle Ages, to which the sixteenth-century Reformers were providing important new twists but which was at best a distortion of the first-century perspective. For Paul and all the other early Christians, what mattered was not "saved souls" being rescued *from* the world and taken to a distant "heaven," but the *coming together* of heaven and earth themselves in a great act of cosmic renewal in which human bodies were likewise being renewed to take their place within that new world. (When Paul says, "We are citizens of heaven," he goes on at once to say that Jesus will come *from* heaven not to take us back there, but *to transform the present world* and us with it.) And this hope for "resurrection," for new bodies within a newly reconstituted creation, doesn't just mean rethinking the ultimate "destination," the eventual future hope. It changes everything on the way as well.

Once we get clear about this, we gain a "historical" perspective in three different senses. First, we begin to see that it matters to try to find out what the first-century Paul was actually talking about over against what later theologians and preachers have assumed he was talking about. As I said, history means thinking into other people's minds. Learning to read Paul involves more than this, but not less.

Second, when we start to appreciate "what Paul was really talking about," we find that he was himself talking about "history" in the sense of "what happens in the real world," the world of space, time, and matter. He was a Jew who believed in the goodness of the original creation and the intention of the Creator to renew his world. His gospel of "salvation" was about Israel's Messiah "inheriting the world," as had been promised in the Psalms. What God had done in and through Jesus was, from Paul's perspective, the launching of a heaven-and-earth movement, not the offer of a new "otherworldly" hope.

Many skeptics in our own day have assumed that Christianity is irrelevant to the "real world." Many Christians have agreed, supposing that if they are going to insist on the "heavenly" dimension, they have to deny the importance of the "earthly" one. All such split-world theories, however well meaning, miss the point. Though Paul does not quote Jesus's prayer for God's kingdom to come "on earth as in heaven," the whole of his career and thought was built on the assumption that this was always God's intention and that this new heaven-and-earth historical reality had come to birth in Jesus and was being activated by the spirit.

Third, therefore, as far as Paul was concerned, his own "historical" context and setting mattered. The world he lived in was the world into which the gospel had burst, the world that the gospel was challenging, the world it would transform. His wider setting—the complex mass of countries and cultures, of myths and stories, of empires and artifacts, of philosophies and oracles, of princes and pimps, of hopes and fears—this real world was not an incidental backdrop to a "timeless" message that could in principle have been announced by anyone in any culture. When Luke describes Paul engaging with Stoics, Epicureans, and other thinkers in Athens, he is only making explicit what is implicit throughout Paul's letters: that, in today's language, Paul was a *contextual* theologian. This doesn't at all mean that we can relativize his ideas ("He said that within his context, but our context is different, so we can push him to one side"). On the contrary. This is where Paul's loyalty to the hope of Israel comes through so strongly. Paul believed that in Jesus the One God had acted "when the fullness of time arrived."[5] Paul saw himself living at the ultimate turning point of history. His announcement of Jesus in *that* culture at *that* moment was itself, he would have claimed, part of the long-term divine plan.

So when we try to understand Paul, we must do the hard work of understanding his context—or rather, we should say, his contexts, plural. His Jewish world and the multifaceted Greco-Roman world of politics, "religion," philosophy, and all the rest that affected in a thousand ways the Jewish world that lived within it are much, much more than simply a "frame" within which we can display a Pauline portrait. Actually, as any art gallery director knows, the frame of a portrait isn't just an optional border. It can make or mar the artist's intention, facilitating appreciation or distracting the eye and skewing the perspective. But with a historical figure like Paul, the surrounding culture isn't even a frame. It is part of the portrait itself. Unless we understand its shape and key features, we will not understand what made Paul tick and why his work succeeded, which is our first main question. And unless we understand Paul's Jewish world in particular, we will not even know how to ask our second question: what it meant for Paul to change from being a zealous persecutor of Jesus's followers to becoming a zealous Jesus-follower himself.

★ ★ ★

The Jewish world in which the young Saul grew up was itself firmly earthed in the soil of wider Greco-Roman culture. As often in ancient history, we know less than we would like to know about the city of Tarsus, Saul's hometown, but we know enough to get the picture. Tarsus, a noble city in Cilicia, ten miles inland on the river Cydnus in the southeast corner of modern Turkey, was on the major east–west trade routes. (The main landmass we think of today as Turkey was divided into several administrative districts, with "Asia" as the western part, "Asia Minor" as the central and eastern part, "Bithynia" in the north, and so on. I will use the simple, if anachronistic, method of referring to the whole region by its modern name.)

Tarsus could trace its history back two thousand years. World-class generals like Alexander the Great and Julius Caesar had recognized its strategic importance; the emperor Augustus had given it extra privileges. It was a city of culture and politics, of philosophy and industry. Among those industries was a thriving textile business, producing material made from goats' hair, used not least to make shelters. This may well have been the basis of the family business, tentmaking, in which Saul had been apprenticed and which he continued to practice. The cosmopolitan world of the eastern Mediterranean, sharing the culture left by Alexander's empire, flowed this way and that through the city. Tarsus rivaled Athens as a center of philosophy, not least because half the philosophers of Athens had gone there a hundred years earlier when Athens backed the wrong horse in a Mediterranean power play and suffered the wrath of Rome. But if the Romans were ruthless, they were also pragmatists. Once it was clear they were in charge, they were happy to make deals.

One deal in particular was struck with the Jews themselves. Everybody else in Saul's day, in regions from Spain to Syria, had to worship the goddess Roma and *Kyrios Caesar,* "Lord Caesar." Augustus Caesar declared that his late adoptive father, Julius Caesar, was now divine, thus conveniently acquiring for himself the title *divi filius,* "son of the deified one," or in Greek simply *huios theou,* "son of god." His successors mostly followed suit. The cults of Roma and the emperor spread in different ways and at different speeds across the empire. In the East, Saul's home territory, they were well established from early on.

But the Jews were relentless. They wouldn't go along with it. They could and would worship and pray to only one God, the God of their ancestors, whom they believed was the only "god" worthy of the name. The ancient Israelite prayer in Greek, which they all now spoke, made a sharp contrast between "Lords." *Kyrios Caesar?* No, they declared, *Kyrios ho theos, Kyrios heis estin,* "The LORD our God, the LORD is one."[6] There is one *Kyrios* and only one. So what was to be done? Would the Romans force the Jews to compromise, as some earlier conquering empires had tried to do? Some Jewish leaders proposed to Rome that, instead of praying *to* Caesar, they would pray *to* their One God *for* Rome and its emperor. Would that be enough? Yes, said Caesar, that will do. A special pragmatic privilege. Live and let live. That was the world in which young Saul had grown up.

We don't know how long his family had lived in Tarsus. Later legends suggest various options, one of which is that his father or grandfather had lived in Palestine but had moved during one of the periodic social and political upheavals, which, in that world, always carried "religious" overtones as well. What we do know about them is that they belonged to the strictest of the Jewish schools. They were Pharisees.

The word "Pharisee" has had bad press over many years. Modern research, operating at the academic and not usually the popular level, has done little to dispel that impression, partly because the research in question has made things far more complicated, as research often does. Most of the sources for understanding the Pharisees of Saul's day come from a much later period. The rabbis of the third and fourth centuries AD looked back to the Pharisees as their spiritual ancestors and so tended to project onto them their own questions and ways of seeing things. Ironically for those who try to locate Paul within his own Pharisaic context, his writings themselves offer the best evidence for that context in the period prior to the Roman-Jewish war of AD 66–70.

Paul's evidence must no doubt be taken with a pinch of salt

because of his newfound faith in Jesus; some later Jews have questioned whether he had ever been a Pharisee at all. But the other great first-century source on Pharisees, the Jewish historian Josephus, requires equal caution. Yes, he says quite a lot about Pharisaic movements in the period, but everything he says is colored by his own stance. Having been a general at the start of the war, he had gone over to the Romans and had claimed moreover that Israel's One God had done the same thing, an alarmingly clear case of making God in one's own image. So all the evidence requires careful handling. Despite this, however, I think it is clear that Saul and his family were indeed Pharisees. They lived with a fierce, joyful strictness in obedience to the ancestral traditions. They did their best to urge other Jews to do the same.

This was never going to be easy in a city like Tarsus. Even in Jerusalem, with a mostly Jewish population and with the Temple itself, the building where heaven and earth came together, right there in its recently restored beauty there were cultural pressures of all sorts that could draw devout Jews into compromise. How much more had this kind of challenge existed in the Diaspora, the "dispersion" of Jews around the rest of the known world, a process that had been going on for centuries. Cultural pressures and different responses to them were the stock in trade of Jewish life as families and individuals faced questions such as what to eat, whom to eat with, whom to do business with, whom to marry, what attitude to take toward local officials, local taxes, local customs and rituals, and so on. The decisions individual Jews made on all of these questions would mark them out in the eyes of some as too compromised and in the eyes of others as too strict. (Our words "liberal" and "conservative" carry too many anachronistic assumptions to be of much help at this point.)

There was seldom if ever in the ancient world a simple divide, with Jews on one side and non-Jews on the other. We should envisage, rather, a complex subculture in which Jews as a whole saw themselves as broadly different from their non-Jewish neighbors.

Within that, entire subgroups of Jews saw themselves as different from other subgroups. The parties and sects we know from Palestinian Jewish life of the time (Sadducees, Pharisees, Essenes, and a nascent militantly "zealous" faction) may not have existed exactly as we describe them, not least because the Sadducees were a small Jerusalem-based aristocracy, but intra-Jewish political and social divisions would have persisted. We who today are familiar not only with the complexities of Middle Eastern culture and politics but also with the Western challenge of multicultural living (a bland homogeneity or a dangerous mix of particular identities?) can imagine something of what a city like Tarsus must have been like.

We can't be sure how many Jews lived in Tarsus in Saul's day. There were, quite possibly, a few thousand at least in a city of roughly a hundred thousand. But we can get a clear sense of how things were for the young Saul.

If there are parallels between today's complex societies and that of a city like ancient Tarsus, there is one radical difference, at least when seen from the modern Western perspective. In the ancient world there was virtually no such thing as private life. A tiny number of the aristocracy or the very rich were able to afford a measure of privacy. But for the great majority, life was lived publicly and visibly. The streets were mostly narrow, the houses and tenements were mostly cramped, there was noise and smell everywhere, and everybody knew everybody else's business. We can assume that many of the Jews in Tarsus would have lived close to one another, partly for safety (Jews, absenting themselves from official public "religion" including the celebrations of the imperial cult, were regularly seen as subversive, even though they tried in other respects to be good citizens) and partly for ease of obtaining kosher food. The questions of where one stood on the spectrum between strict adherence to the ancestral code, the Torah, and "compromise" were not theoretical. They were about what one did and what one didn't do in full view of the neighbors. And about how the neighbors might react.

All this obviously involved the workplace as well. We know from Paul's mature life and writings that he engaged in manual work. "Tentmaking" probably included the crafting of other goods made of leather or animal hair in addition to the core product of tents themselves. (We may think of tents as camping gear for leisure use, but in Paul's world then, as in parts of the world today, many people moved from place to place for seasonal work, and even people who stayed put would depend on canvas awnings and shelters to enable them to work under the hot sun.) This probably means two things.

First, Saul was probably apprenticed to his father in this family business. We don't know whether the father was himself a Torah scholar, though it seems likely that Saul's deep familiarity with Israel's scriptures and traditions, however much they were nurtured in his subsequent Jerusalem education, had begun at home. But being a Torah student or teacher was not a salaried profession. Rabbis in Saul's day, and for centuries afterward, earned their living by other means.

Second, the market for tents and similar products would be wide. One might guess that likely purchasers would include regiments of soldiers, but travel was a way of life for many other people as well in the busy world of the early Roman Empire. It seems improbable that a Jewish tentmaker in a city like Tarsus would be selling only to other Jews. We can safely assume, then, that Saul grew up in a cheerfully strict observant Jewish home, on the one hand, and in a polyglot, multicultural, multiethnic working environment on the other. Strict adherence to ancestral tradition did not mean living a sheltered life, unaware of how the rest of the world worked, spoke, behaved, and reasoned.

Reasoning, in fact, is one thing the mature Paul was particularly good at, even if the density of his arguments can still challenge his readers. Everything we know about him encourages us to think of the young Saul of Tarsus as an unusually gifted child. He read biblical Hebrew fluently. He spoke the Aramaic of the Middle East (the mother tongue of Jesus and quite possibly Saul's mother tongue as well) in addition to the ubiquitous Greek, which he spoke and wrote at great speed. He probably had at least some Latin.

This multilingual ability doesn't mark him out in and of itself. Many children in many countries are functionally multilingual. In the longer perspective of history, in fact, it is those who know only one language who are the odd ones out. But the mature Paul has something else of which fewer people, even in his world, could boast. He gives every impression of having swallowed the Bible whole. He moves with polished ease between Genesis and the Psalms, between Deuteronomy and Isaiah. He knows how the story works, its heights and depths, its twists and turns. He can make complex allusions with a flick of the pen and produce puns and other wordplays across the languages. The radical new angle of vision provided by the gospel of Jesus is a new angle on texts he already knows inside out. He has pretty certainly read other Jewish books of the time, books like the Wisdom of Solomon, quite possibly some of the philosophy of his near contemporary Philo. They too knew their Bibles extremely well. Saul matches them stride for stride and, arguably, outruns them.

What is more, whether Saul has read the non-Jewish philosophers of his day or the great traditions that go back to Plato and Aristotle, he knows the ideas. He has heard them on the street, discussed them with his friends. He knows the technical terms, the philosophical schemes that probe the mysteries of the universe and the inner workings of human beings, and the theories that hold the gods and the world at arm's length like the Epicureans or that draw them into a single whole, *to pan,* "the all," like the Stoics. It's unlikely that he has read Cicero, whose book *On the Nature of the Gods,* from roughly a century before his own mature work, discussed all the options then available to an educated Roman (this does not, of course, include a Jewish worldview). But if someone in the tentmaker's shop were to start expounding Cicero's ideas, Saul would know what the conversation was about. He would be able to engage such a person on his own terms. He is thus completely at home in the worlds of both Jewish story and non-Jewish philosophy. We may suspect that he, like some of his contemporaries, somewhat relishes the challenge of bringing them together.

Reading some of his letters, in fact, one might almost think that he had been a childhood friend of someone like the philosopher Epictetus, a down-to-earth thinker determined to get philosophy out of the classroom and into the street. He uses well-known rhetorical ploys. When he tells the Corinthians that human wisdom is useless, he sometimes sounds like a Cynic; when he talks about virtue, a casual listener might, for a moment, mistake him for a Stoic. When he writes about the difference between the "inner human" and the "outer human," many to this day have supposed him to be some kind of Platonist—though what he says about resurrection and the renewal of creation then becomes a problem. The mature Paul would not have been afraid of giving impressions such as these. He believes, and says explicitly here and there, that the new wisdom unveiled in Israel's Messiah can take on the world and incorporate its finest insights into a different, larger frame. The "good news" of the Messiah opens up for him the vision of a whole new creation in which everything "true, attractive, and pleasing"[7] will find a home.

But the messianic "good news" meant what it meant, first and foremost, within the Jewish world of the first century. Whole books could be written about every aspect of this, not least as it relates to the young Saul of Tarsus, but we must be brief. Saul grew up within a world of story and symbol: a single story, awaiting its divinely ordered fulfillment, and a set of symbols that brought that story into focus and enabled Jews to inhabit it. If we are going to understand him, to see who he really was, we have to grasp this and to realize that for him it wasn't just a set of ideas. It was as basic to his whole existence as the great musical story from Bach to Beethoven to Brahms is to a classically trained musician today. Only more so.

The story was the story of Israel as a whole, Israel as the children of Abraham, Israel as God's chosen people, chosen *from* the world but equally chosen *for* the world; Israel as the light to the Gentiles, the people through whom all nations would be blessed; Israel as the Passover people, the rescued-from-slavery people, the people with whom the One God had entered into covenant, a marriage bond in which separation might occur but could only ever be temporary. There are signs all across the Jewish writings of the period (roughly the last two centuries before Paul's day and the first two centuries afterward) that a great many Jews from widely different backgrounds saw their Bible not primarily as a compendium of rules and dogmas, but as a single great story rooted in Genesis and Exodus, in Abraham and Moses. Saul's Bible was not primarily a set of glittering fragments, snapshots of detached wisdom. It was a narrative rooted in creation and covenant and stretching forward into the dark unknown.

It had become very dark indeed in the centuries leading up to Saul's day. Whether people read Isaiah, Jeremiah, or Ezekiel, whether they followed the line of thought through the books of Kings and Chronicles, or whether they simply read the Five Books of Moses, the "Torah" proper, from Genesis through to Deuteronomy, the message was the same. Israel was called to be different, summoned to worship the One God, but Israel had failed drastically and had been exiled to Babylon as a result. A covenantal separation had therefore taken place. Prophet after prophet said so. The One God had abandoned the Jerusalem Temple to its fate at the hands of foreigners.

Wherever you look in Israel's scriptures, the story is the same. Any Jew from the Babylonian exile onward who read the first three chapters of Genesis would see at a glance the quintessential Jewish story: humans were placed in a garden; they disobeyed instructions and were thrown out. And any Jew who read the last ten chapters of Deuteronomy would see it spelled out graphically: worship the One God and do what he says, and the promised garden is yours; worship other gods, and you face exile. A great many Jews around the time of Paul—we have the evidence in book after book of the postbiblical Jewish writings—read those texts in that way too; they believed that *the exile—in its theological and political meaning—was not yet over.* Deuteronomy speaks of a great coming restoration.[8] Isaiah, Jeremiah, and Ezekiel all echo this theme: the words of comfort in Isaiah 40–55, the promise of covenant renewal in Jeremiah 31, the assurance of cleansing and restoration in Ezekiel 36–37. Yes, some Jews (by no means all) had returned from Babylon. Yes, the Temple had been rebuilt. But this was not, it could not be, the restoration promised by the prophets and by Deuteronomy itself.

Through those long years of puzzlement, the complaint of the ("postexilic") books of Ezra and Nehemiah sounded out: "We are in our own land again, but we are slaves! Foreigners are ruling over us."[9] And slaves, of course, need an Exodus. A new Exodus. The new Exodus promised by Isaiah. This was the hope: that the story at the heart of the Five Books—slavery, rescue, divine presence, promised land—would spring to life once more as the answer *both* to the problem of covenantal rebellion in Deuteronomy 27–32 *and* to the parallel, and deeper, problem of human rebellion in Genesis 1–3. The former would be the key to the latter: when the covenant God did what he was going to do for Israel, then somehow—who knew how?—the effects would resonate around the whole world.

At the center of this longing for rescue, for the new Exodus, stands one text in particular that loomed large in the minds of eager, hopeful Jews like Saul of Tarsus. Daniel 9, picking up from Deuteronomy's promise of restoration, announces precisely that idea of an *extended exile:* the "seventy years" that Jeremiah said Israel would stay in exile have been stretched out to *seventy times seven,* almost half a millennium of waiting until the One God would restore his people at last, by finally dealing with the "sins" that had caused the exile in the first place. The scheme of "seventy sevens" resonated with the scriptural promises of the jubilee—this would be the time when the ultimate debts would be forgiven.[10] Devout Jews in the first century labored to work out when the 490 years would be up, often linking their interpretations of Daniel to the relevant passages in Deuteronomy. This was the long hope of Israel, the forward-looking narrative cherished by many who, like Saul of Tarsus, were soaked in the scriptures and eager for the long-delayed divine deliverance. And many of them believed that *the time was drawing near.* They knew enough chronology to do a rough calculation. And if the time was near, strict obedience to the Torah was all the more necessary.

The Torah loomed all the larger if one lived, as did the young Saul, outside the promised land and hence away from the Temple. The Torah, in fact, functioned as a movable Temple for the many Jews who were scattered around the wider world. But the Temple remained central, geographically and symbolically. It was the place where heaven and earth met, thus forming the signpost to the ultimate promise, the renewal and unity of heaven and earth, the new creation in which the One God would be personally present forever. We don't know how often Saul traveled to the homeland with his parents for the great festivals. Luke describes Jesus, aged twelve, being taken from Nazareth to Jerusalem for Passover, and we know that tens of thousands of Jews gathered from all over, both for that festival and for others such as Pentecost, the feast of the giving of the Torah. It is thus quite probable that the young Saul acquired at an early age the sense that all roads, spiritually as well as geographically, led to the mountain where David had established his capital, the hill at the heart of Judaea where Solomon, David's son, the archetypal wise man, had built the first Temple. The Temple was like a cultural and theological magnet, drawing together not only heaven and earth, but the great scriptural stories and promises.

The Temple was therefore also the focal point of Israel's hope.

The One God, so the prophets had said, abandoned his house in Jerusalem because of the people's idolatry and sin. But successive prophets (Isaiah, Ezekiel, Zechariah, Malachi) had promised that he would return one day. That list is significant, since the last two prophets named, Zechariah and Malachi, were writing *after* some of the exiles had returned from Babylon, after they had rebuilt the Temple and restarted the regular round of sacrificial worship. We will never understand how someone like the young Saul of Tarsus thought—never mind how he prayed!—until we grasp the strange fact that, though the Temple still held powerful memories of divine presence (as does Jerusalem's Western Wall to this day for the millions of Jews and indeed non-Jews who go there to pray, though they do not think that the One God actually resides there now), there was a strong sense that the promise of ultimate divine return had not yet been fulfilled.

If this seems strange, as it does to some, consider this. Two of the greatest scenes in Israel's scriptures are moments when the divine glory filled the wilderness Tabernacle and then the Jerusalem Temple with a radiant presence and power.[11] Isaiah had promised that this would happen once more, indicating that this would be the moment when Jerusalem would be redeemed at last and Israel's God would establish his kingdom in visible power and glory.[12] At no point do any later Jewish writers say that this or anything like it has actually happened. The closest you might come is the glorious double scene in Sirach 24 and 50, written around 200 BC. In the first, the figure of "Wisdom" comes from heaven to dwell in the Temple; in the second, the high priest himself appears to be an almost visible manifestation of Israel's God. But this rather obvious piece of propaganda for the aristocratic high-priesthood of the time cut little ice after the various crises that then followed. No, the point was that *it hadn't happened yet.* The God of Israel had said he would return, but had not yet done so.

Saul of Tarsus was brought up to believe that it *would* happen, perhaps very soon. Israel's God *would* indeed return in glory to establish his kingdom in visible global power. He was also taught that there were things Jews could be doing in the meantime to keep this promise and hope on track. It was vital for Jews to keep the Torah with rigorous attention to detail and to defend the Torah, and the Temple itself, against possible attacks and threats. Failure on these points would hold back the promise, would get in the way of the fulfillment of the great story. That is why Saul of Tarsus persecuted Jesus's early followers. And that is why, when Paul the Apostle returned to Jerusalem for the last time, there were riots.

All this, to pick up an earlier point, is many a mile from what we today mean by "religion." That is why I often put that word in quotation marks, to signal the danger of imagining that Saul of Tarsus, either as a young man or as a mature apostle, was "teaching a religion" in some modern sense. Today, "religion" for most Westerners designates a detached area of life, a kind of private hobby for those who like that sort of thing, separated by definition (and in some countries by law) from politics and public life, from science and technology. In Paul's day, "religion" meant almost exactly the opposite. The Latin word *religio* has to do with "binding" things together. Worship, prayer, sacrifice, and other public rituals were designed to hold the unseen inhabitants of a city (the gods and perhaps the ancestors) together with the visible ones, the living humans, thus providing a vital framework for ordinary life, for business, marriage, travel, and home life. (A distinction was made between *religio,* official and authorized observance, and *superstitio,* unauthorized and perhaps subversive practice.)

The Jewish equivalent of this was clear. For Saul of Tarsus, the place where the invisible world ("heaven") and the visible world ("earth") were joined together was the Temple. If you couldn't get to the Temple, you could and should study and practice the Torah, and it would have the same effect. Temple and Torah, the two great symbols of Jewish life, pointed to the story in which devout Jews like Saul and his family believed themselves to be living: the great story of Israel and the world, which, they hoped, was at last reaching the point where God would reveal his glory in a fresh way. The One God would come back at last to set up his kingdom, to make the whole world one vast glory-filled Temple, and to enable all people—or at least his chosen people—to keep the Torah perfectly. Any who prayed or sang the Psalms regularly would find themselves thinking this, hoping this, praying this, day after day, month after month.

Surrounded by the bustling pagan city of Tarsus, the young Saul knew perfectly well what all this meant for a loyal Jew. It meant keeping oneself pure from idolatry and immorality. There were pagan temples and shrines on every corner, and Saul would have a fair idea of what went on there. Loyalty meant keeping *the Jewish community* pure from those things as well. At every stage of Israel's history, after all, the people of the One God had been tempted to compromise. The pressure was on to go with the wider world and to forget the covenant. Saul was brought up to resist this pressure. And that meant "zeal."

Which brings us at last to the biographical starting point that the later Paul mentions in his letters. "Zealous?" he says, "I persecuted the church!"[13] "I advanced in *Ioudaïsmos* beyond many of my own age and people," he says, "I was extremely zealous for my ancestral traditions"[14] Where did this "zeal" come from? What did it mean in practice? If this is what made the young Saul tick, what was the mechanism that kept that ticking clock running on time? And what did it mean, as he himself puts it in his first letter, to exchange this kind of "zeal" for a very different kind?[15] Addressing those questions brings us to the real starting point of this book.

PART ONE

Beginnings

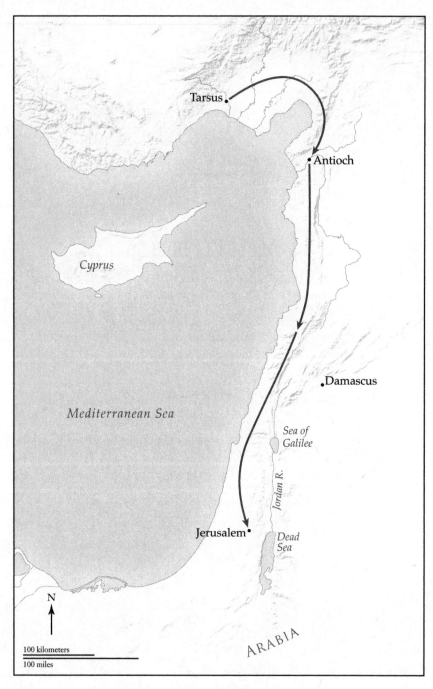

Tarsus to Jerusalem

I

Zeal

I T BEGINS WITH an ancient tale of sex and violence.

We glimpse the little boy, precocious beyond his years, soaking up the stories of his ancestors, reading them for himself without realizing how unusual it was for a small boy to read big books in the first place. There are certain activities—music, mathematics, and chess, for instance—in which quite young people can become prodigies. In Jewish families, studying the Torah can be like that: the young mind and heart can drink it all in, sense its drama and rhythms, relish the ancestral story and promise. The youngster can get to know his way around the Five Books of Moses the way he knows the way around his own home. All the signs are that Saul of Tarsus was that kind of child. We sense the quiet delight of his parents at his youthful enthusiasm.

It wasn't simply a matter of head knowledge. Far from it. Jewish life was and is centered on the rhythm of prayer. We see young Saul learning how to strap the *tefillin,* small leather boxes containing key scripture passages, to the arm and the head as Moses had commanded for male Jews when praying the morning service. We see him reciting the Psalms. He learns how to invoke the One God without actually saying the sacred and terrifying Name itself, declaring allegiance three times a day like a young patriot saluting the flag: *Shema Yisrael, Adhonai Elohenu, Adhonai Echad!* "Hear, O Israel: the LORD our God, the LORD is one!" Saul may be young, but he has signed on. He is a loyalist. He will be faithful.

Little Saul soon learns to look forward to the great festivals such as Tabernacles or Hanukkah, commemorating great moments from the nation's history. Especially he would enjoy Passover, with its wonderful story and its strange, evocative meal ("Why is this night different from all other nights?" he had asked when he was the youngest in the family). He reads *that* story, the freedom story, in the book later generations would know as Exodus, the "coming out" book. This was the story of what had happened, of what would happen. This was what the One God did when his people were enslaved—he overthrew the tyrants and set his people free, bringing them out of Egypt and leading them to their "inheritance," their promised land. Saul drinks it all in. This is *his* story, the story he will make his own. It will happen again: a new, second Exodus, bringing full and final freedom. He will play his part in the long-running drama.

The trouble was, of course, that God's people seemed bent on wandering off in their own direction, again and again. That's where the sex and the violence came in. It always seemed to go that way. They wanted to be like the *goyim,* the nations, instead of being distinct, as they had been summoned to be. That's what the food laws are all about: *others* eat all kinds of things, including blood; *Jews* eat only the "clean" foods, with careful procedures in place for how animals are killed and cooked. That's what circumcision was supposed to say: *others* regard sex as a toy, but for *Jews* it's the glorious sign of the ancient covenant. *Others* have no rhythm to their lives; *Jews* keep the Sabbath, delighting in the weekly anticipation of God's promised future, the day when God's time and human time would come together at last. Again and again the ancient Israelites had forgotten these lessons, and bad things had happened. And now, in the recent memory of the

Jewish people of Saul's day, many Jews had forgotten them again, had compromised, had become like the *goyim*. And that is why some Jews, and he among them—one of the first solid things we know about young Saul—followed the ancient tradition of "zeal." Violence would be necessary to root out wickedness from Israel.

The tradition of "zeal" is part of the freedom story. Young Saul learned that story early on, that it was God's people against the rest of the world, the nations, the *goyim,* and the *goyim* usually won. There were brief flashes of glorious history: David beating the Philistines, Solomon teaching wisdom to the whole world. That's how it was supposed to be. But clinging to this story meant struggling to retain hope in the face of experience. Long ages of disappointment and disaster seemed to be the norm: ten tribes lost, and the remaining two dragged off into captivity, weeping by the waters of Babylon.

Why did it happen? The prophets made it clear. It was because Israel sinned. That was the deal God established in the first place: "Now that I've rescued you, stay loyal to me and you'll live in the land. Turn away from me, worship other gods, and I'll kick you out." Just like Adam and Eve in the Garden.

But, as Saul's father would no doubt explain Sabbath by Sabbath, the *goyim* were still a threat. They still ran the world their own way. They didn't believe in Israel's God. They had invented a thousand little gods of their own; and they went to and fro, this way and that, trying to pay them all off, doing their best to placate them. And the more you read the old stories, the more you would see how the *goyim* would try to pull loyal Jews away from the Name, from the One God. And "we"—by which Saul's father wouldn't just mean "we Jews" but "we *perushim,* we Pharisees"— "we have to know the Torah, we have to say the loyalty prayer, we have to stay pure. And we must be ready to act when the time comes."

Young Saul knows precisely what this means. He knows the freedom story, the Five Books. Reading through these ancestral traditions, turning them over and over in his mind, he would find long passages where nothing much happens: regulations for sacrifices, lists of names, detailed law codes. These passages are powerful in themselves. Once you get to know and love them, they have a kind of incantatory quality. But a boy wants action, and suddenly here it is.

First there is the strange story of Balaam.[1] As the people of Israel come near the end of their journey through the wilderness, they arrive at the territory of Moab, on the east bank of the Jordan. They are within sight of the promised land. This is bad news for Balak, the king of Moab. He hires Balaam, a soothsayer, to curse Israel. At first Balaam refuses, but the promised reward eats into his soul, and he gets on his donkey to go and comply. The donkey, however, sees what Balaam does not. The angel of the Lord stands in the way, drawn sword in hand; the donkey swerves off the road, lies down, and refuses to go on. Balaam loses his temper and beats the poor animal, whereupon it speaks to him with a human voice. Balaam's eyes are opened, and he recognizes his lucky escape. So, instead of cursing the Israelites, he blesses them—much, of course, to Balak's annoyance.

It's a great story, almost worthy of Grimms' fairy tales. But the real thrust of the story, the point Saul's tradition celebrates, is yet to come. It focuses on an incident that will spark a youthful vocation. And it offers a promise that echoes another, more ancient promise that Paul the Apostle will make central to his theology.

It begins with Balaam's problem: no curse, no fee. Well, perhaps there was another way. Send in the girls. Plenty of the Israelite men, tired of desert wandering and strict sexual morality, were only too happy to take a Moabite girlfriend—which meant not only disloyalty to the One God and his Torah (as well as to their own wives), but also worshipping Moabite deities and following their practices. Idolatry and immorality went together, as they always did. Israel was supposed to be the One Bride of the One God, in an unbreakable marriage bond. Breaking human marriage bonds was a sign and symptom of the breaking of the divine covenant.

What happened next shaped the imagination of many generations. Things got out of control. The people were running wild. A plague broke out—heaven-sent retribution, it seemed—but they didn't care. One man brought his Moabite girl into his tent, in full view of Moses and everybody else.[2] That did it. Phinehas, one of Aaron's sons, took a spear, followed the man into the tent, found the pair already in the act, and killed them both with a single thrust.

That was the defining moment of "zeal." It had immediate results: the plague stopped; the rebellion was over. And Phinehas, the hero of "zeal" from then on, received the remarkable promise of a perpetual personal covenant. His family would be priests forever.

One of the old psalms, referring delicately to the incident (the psalm says only, "Phinehas intervened" or possibly "Phinehas interceded"), has a turn of phrase indicating this everlasting covenant established between God and Phinehas. "Phinehas intervened," says the song, "*and that has been reckoned to him as righteousness.*"[3] The Hebrew word for "righteousness," *tzedaqah,* indicates a relationship: a committed, covenanted relationship. "God reckoned it (Phinehas's zealous action) as righteousness" means that this action was the hallmark of the covenant between God and his family: a covenant of perpetual priesthood. Zeal was the outward badge of the unbreakable relationship.

Young Saul would have known the sentence anyway, because it is what Genesis says about Abraham. God made sweeping but seemingly impossible promises to Abraham. Abraham believed them, and then and there God took him into a covenant, a binding agreement. Genesis sums this up with the same phrase: "And the LORD reckoned it to him as righteousness"[4] Abraham's faith, in other words, was the hallmark of the covenant that God established with him. It was the sign, the badge, of his covenant membership. The resonances between Abraham and Phinehas are obvious to anyone who knows the texts well, but this isn't just a matter of our saying so. The two passages occur in close proximity in one of the primary "zeal" texts of Saul's day, 1 Maccabees.[5] We imagine the young boy, eager for God and the law, storing all this away for future reference. He will be zealous for God and Torah. Perhaps God will use him as part of the great moment of covenant renewal. "It was reckoned to him as righteousness." Nobody could have guessed at the further meanings that key sentence would acquire in the new world that lay just around the corner.

Saul of Tarsus grew up knowing this story. We imagine the young boy, knowing well enough how the *goyim* on the streets of Tarsus behaved, simultaneously repelled and fascinated by the thought of God's people carrying on like that, and then simultaneously excited and challenged by the thought of Phinehas's zeal. Sex and violence grab the imagination. When Paul the Apostle describes himself in his earlier life as being consumed with zeal for his ancestral traditions, he was looking back on the Phinehas-shaped motivation of his youth.

Phinehas, though, wasn't the only role model for "zeal." The other principal one is found in the books of Kings, and we imagine young Saul devouring those stories as well. After the great days of David and Solomon things had gone from bad to worse. Most of the Israelites had started to worship Baal, a Canaanite fertility god. Like worshipping the Moabite divinities, Baal worship took certain practices for granted: fertility rituals, naturally, and then child sacrifice, the latter perhaps dealing with the results of the former. Step forward the prophet Elijah.[6] He lured the Baal worshippers into a contest that Israel's God won, and he had the whole lot killed. Once again, great zeal and a great victory.

Later traditions couple Elijah with Moses when it comes to prophetic status. But when it comes to "zeal," as in 1 Maccabees 2, Elijah is coupled with Phinehas. When these later traditions see things that way, they are not simply celebrating ancient memories. They are calling a new generation to meet new challenges. When Paul the Apostle refers to his earlier "zeal," we catch the echoes of Elijah as well as of Phinehas. And, as we shall see, the Elijah story has its own darker side as well.

Putting Phinehas and Elijah together explains a good deal of the violent zeal to which Paul later confesses. But there was an extra element pushing him in the same direction. Folk memory, kept fresh through the winter festival Hanukkah, celebrated the zealous acts of Judas Maccabaeus ("Judah the Hammer") two centuries before Saul's day. The Syrian megalomaniacal king Antiochus Epiphanes (the word "Epiphanes" means "the divine manifestation") tried to do to the Jewish nation what, as Saul's father would remind him, the *goyim* always tried to do—choke the life out of the Jewish people and overthrow once and for all their perverse and antisocial belief in the One God. Only in this way could Antiochus turn the Jews into docile members of his own empire. So, with massively superior military force, he desecrated the Jerusalem Temple itself, establishing pagan worship and customs on the site. What were the Jewish people to do?

Many of them were prepared to compromise (just like their ancestors in the wilderness, Saul would have reflected). They went along with the new regime. But one family, like Phinehas, decided to act. The books of the Maccabees tell of zeal for Israel's God, zeal for God's Torah, zeal for the purity of Israel, and all of it rooted in the story that stretched back to Abraham and included Phinehas and Elijah among its key moments.[7] If this was Israel's story, this is how a loyal Israelite should now behave when faced with the same problem. Judas Maccabaeus and his brothers went to work, a little revolutionary group against the powerful pagan empire. Against all probability, they succeeded. They beat off the Syrians, reconsecrated the Temple, and established, for a century or so, an independent Jewish state. Zeal worked. It demonstrated utter loyalty to the One God. It brought freedom. And for those who suffered or died in the struggle, a new vision of the future shimmered on the horizon: resurrection. The One God would make a new world, and he would raise his people, particularly his loyal and zealous people, to new bodily life in that new creation.[8] Zeal would have its ultimate reward in the kingdom of God, on earth as in heaven.

These stories would have resonated powerfully in Saul's devout Jewish home. The Jewish communities in Turkey and in many other parts of the Roman Empire lived relatively peacefully alongside their *goyische* neighbors. But they could never tell when the *goyim* would try it again or what diabolical means they might find to undermine the covenant loyalty the Jews owed to the One God. They had to be ready. Saul came from a family who knew what that meant. It meant *Ioudaïsmos:* as we saw, not a "religion" called "Judaism" in the modern Western sense, a system of piety and morality, but the active propagation of the ancestral way of life, defending it against external attacks and internal corruption and urging the traditions of the Torah upon other Jews, especially when they seemed to be compromising.

That was the air breathed by the young Saul, growing up in the early years of the Common Era. The best guess has him a little younger than Jesus of Nazareth; a birth date in the first decade of what we now call the first century is as good as we can get. As for his family, we find later that he has a sister and a nephew living in Jerusalem; there may well have been more relatives there, although Tarsus was probably still the family home. Anyway, it was to Jerusalem that he went, most likely in his teens, his head full of Torah and his heart full of zeal. *Shema Yisrael, Adhonai Elohenu, Adhonai Echad.* One God, whose never-to-be-spoken Name was replaced in the great prayer by *Adhonai,* which went into the ubiquitous Greek as *Kyrios.* One God, One Torah; One Lord, One People, called to utter loyalty. And with that loyalty went the one hope, the Passover hope—freedom, especially freedom from the rule of foreigners. A whole new world, with Israel rescued from danger once and for all. A new creation. A new Eden.

This wasn't just a dream. This was the right time for it all to happen. We don't know whether the synagogues in Tarsus would have taught young Saul the hidden secrets inside the prophetic writings, secrets about how he could tell when the One God would act, secrets about how he might even experience the vision of this God for himself, patterns of prayer and meditation through which one might gain a glimpse of the heavenly realities, an advance sight of what was to come one day. It was all there in scripture if one only knew not only where to look, but how to look. There were teachers in Jerusalem who would leave the zealous young student in no doubt about all this. Saul would pick up, either at home or in Jerusalem or both, the increasing excitement as people searched the prophetic writings, particularly the book of Daniel, finding plenty of hints that the time was now ripe and plenty of suggestions as to how they might pray their own way into that future.

Paul's teacher in Jerusalem would have made sure he was steeped in the ancestral traditions. Gamaliel was one of the greatest rabbis of the period. Under his guidance, Saul would have studied the scriptures themselves, of course, and also the unwritten Torah, the steadily accumulating discussions of finer points that would grow as oral tradition and be codified nearly two hundred years later in the Mishnah. But among the many different interpretations of the Torah at that time, there was a divide that was getting wider and wider and that would result, over the next century, in two radically different beliefs about what loyalty would mean at such a time of crisis. Saul was shaped as a young man by these debates. The side he took was not the side advocated by his great teacher.

Gamaliel, at least as portrayed in Acts, advocated the policy of "live and let live." If people wanted to follow this man Jesus, they could do so.[9] If this new movement was from God, it would prosper; if not, it would fall by its own weight. If the Romans wanted to run the world, so be it. Jews would study and practice the Torah by themselves. This, broadly speaking, had been the teaching of Hillel, a leading rabbi of the previous generation.

But all the signs are that Gamaliel's bright young pupil from Tarsus wasn't satisfied with this approach. His "zeal" would have placed him in the opposing school, following Hillel's rival Shammai, who maintained that if God was going to establish his reign on earth as in heaven, then those who were zealous for God and Torah would have to say their prayers, sharpen their swords, and get ready for action. Action against the wicked pagans; yes, when the time was right. Action against renegade or compromising Jews: yes indeed, that too. Remember Phinehas. Later Jewish traditions insisted that there was a sharp break between the Hillelites and the Shammaites, but that reflects (among other things) the bitter times around the two great crises, the Roman-Jewish war of AD 66–70 and the Bar-Kochba rebellion of AD 132–35, not to mention the tense, uneasy years in between. In Saul's day it was much more feasible for different views to be debated, for a student to disagree with a teacher. Gamaliel believed in living and letting live. Saul believed in zeal.

I thought of the young Saul of Tarsus in November 1995, when the then prime minister of Israel, Yitzhak Rabin, was assassinated by a student called Yigal Amir. Rabin had taken part in the Oslo Accords, working out agreements toward peace with the Palestinian leadership. In 1994 he shared the Nobel Peace Prize with his political rival Shimon Peres and with the Palestinian leader Yasser Arafat. He also signed a peace treaty with Jordan. All this was too much for hard-line Israelis, who saw his actions as hopelessly compromising national identity and security. The news media described the assassin as a "law student," but in Europe and America that phrase carries a meaning different from the one

it has in Israel today and the one it would have had in the days
of Saul of Tarsus. Amir was not studying to be an attorney in a
Western-style court. He was a zealous Torah student. His action
on November 4, 1995, was, so he claimed at his trial, in accordance with Jewish law. He is still serving his life sentence and has
never expressed regret for his actions. The late twentieth century
is obviously very different from the early first century, but "zeal"
has remained a constant.

As I watched the television broadcasts that November afternoon, my mind shuttled back and forth between modern Jerusalem and the Jerusalem of Saul's day. In that earlier Jerusalem a
young man called Stephen had been stoned to death—illegally,
since under Roman rule only the Romans could carry out the
death penalty. Saul of Tarsus, a zealous young Torah student, had
been there, watching, taking it all in, looking after the coats of
the men throwing rocks, who were ceremonially cleansing the
city of the poison that Stephen had been uttering.

What was that poison? It had to do with the Temple, which
meant it had to do with God himself. The Jerusalem Temple was
"the house," or "the place": the place where Israel's God had
promised to put his name, his presence, his glory, the place the
One God had promised to defend. The place where heaven and
earth met, where they were linked, where they enjoyed a glorious though highly dangerous commerce. The place where, a year
or two before, a Galilean self-styled prophet not much older than
Saul himself had caused a stir with a symbolic demonstration.
That had seemed, at the time, to have been intended as a warning of divine judgment: Israel's God would use the pagan nations
to destroy Israel's most cherished symbol. By Saul's reckoning,
of course, that was totally out of order. Everybody knew that it
would be the other way around, that the One God would judge
the wicked pagans and vindicate his people, Israel. In any case,
the authorities had caught up with the demonstrating prophet,

handed him over to the Roman authorities, and seen him killed
in the most shameful way imaginable, making it clear once and
for all that he was a blaspheming imposter. Whoever heard of a
crucified Messiah?

But now the followers of this Jesus were claiming that he had
been raised from the dead. They were talking as if heaven and
earth were somehow joined together in *him,* in this crazy, dangerous, deluded man! They were speaking as if, by comparison
with this Jesus, the ancient institutions of Israel were on a lower
footing. The Temple itself, Stephen was saying, was only a temporary expedient. God was doing a new thing. And, yes, the
present generation was under judgment for rejecting Jesus and
his message. Stephen, on trial for his life, made matters worse.
"Look!" he shouted. "I can see heaven opened, and the son of
man standing at God's right hand!"[10] Heaven and earth open
to one another, and this Jesus holding them together in prayer?
Blasphemy! The court had heard enough. Stephen was rushed
out of the city and crushed to death under a hail of rocks. Saul
approved. This was the kind of action the Torah required. This
was what "zeal" was supposed to look like.

From that moment, the young man saw what had to be done.
Several of the Jesus-followers had left Jerusalem in a hurry after
Stephen's death, frightened of more violence, but they had continued to spread the poison. Wherever they went, they established
groups, little revolutionary cells, and propagated this new teaching, putting Jesus in the center of the picture and displacing the
ancient Israelite symbols, up to and including the Temple itself.
From Saul's point of view, if the compromisers in the old biblical
stories had been bad, this was worse. This could set back the coming kingdom. This could call down further divine wrath upon
Israel.

Saul therefore set off as a new Phinehas, a new Elijah. The
scriptural models were clear. Torah and Temple—the One God

himself—were under attack from this new movement. With his Bible in his head, zeal in his heart, and official documents of authority from the chief priests in his bag, young Saul set off in the firm hope that he too would be recognized as a true covenant member. "It was reckoned to him as righteousness." Phinehas then; Saul now.

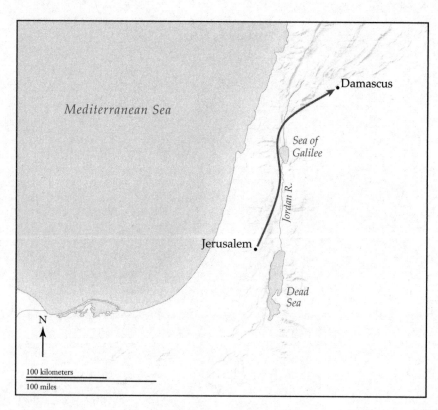

Jerusalem to Damascus

2

Damascus

A BLINDING LIGHT; a voice from heaven. A Caravaggio masterpiece. The persecutor becomes the preacher. The Feast of the Conversion of St. Paul is celebrated on January 25 every year in many Western churches, including my own. The event has become a cultural metaphor. Traditions, on the one hand, and proverbial usage, on the other, conspire together to make what happened to Saul of Tarsus both famous and obscure. The incident, narrated three times (with interesting variations) in the book of Acts, is clearly vital: from Paul's own brief autobiographical remarks in his letters it is obvious that something fairly cataclysmic happened to him that day. But what exactly happened? And what did it mean?

A century after Freud, we are all amateur psychologists. The "road to Damascus," a byword for millions who have only the sketchiest idea where Damascus actually is, has been a honey trap for psychological speculation—and for psychological reductionism. What was going on in Saul's mind and heart that day? What transformed the zealous persecutor into the zealous apostle?

Theories have come and gone. Saul's vision was "really" the moment when his "twice-born" personality kicked in. No, it was when his residual guilt at Stephen's stoning came back to haunt him. No, it was what might be expected when the tension between the inner lusts of a young man and the outer demands of strict holiness finally exploded. Actually, it was an epileptic fit. Or maybe he was just dehydrated in the midday sun, and so on, and so on. Anything rather than face the question from the other end. Supposing . . . supposing it was more than this?

Theories of this kind are, in fact, a bit like what happens when people who have never seen a neon sign are suddenly confronted with one—but in the script of a foreign language. They spend their time wondering how on earth it lights up like that, without even realizing that the sign is saying something. The whimsical English poet John Betjeman puts it like this:

> *St. Paul is often criticised*
> *By modern people who're annoyed*
> *At his conversion, saying Freud*
> *Explains it all. But they omit*
> *The really vital part of it,*
> *Which isn't how it was achieved*
> *But what it was that Paul believed.*[1]

Betjeman, as it happens, doesn't do a very good job of explaining "what it was that Paul believed," but he is right about the main point. To ask "how it was achieved" might or might not require that we study Paul's psychology, but it is ultimately the wrong question. In any case, historical psychology may be an amusing armchair sport, but it is next to useless in real historical investigation.

A moment's thought will make this clear—and it's an important point at the start of a biographical investigation. Any trained pastor or counselor, let alone any actual psychiatrist, knows perfectly well that human beings are deep wells of mystery. We can still be surprised, perhaps shocked, when a friend of many years or even a spouse allows us a small glimpse of unsuspected inner depths, what some cultures call the "heart" and others the "soul." Even when the counselor is trusted completely, sharing the same cultural assumptions and spiritual values, it will almost always be much harder than one might have supposed to get to the root of the personality, the deep springs of motivation, the dark agonies that produce sleepless nights or dysfunctional days. How much more impossible is it with someone who lived two thousand years ago in a culture very different from our own.

In addition to being impossible, that sort of study is fortunately unnecessary for biography, as indeed for history in general. This doesn't mean that we cannot study human motivation. We are not restricted to talking only about "what happened" at the level picked up by a camera or tape recorder. The historian and biographer can study, and should study so far as possible, the levels of motivation that *are* available, not least the implicit narratives that run through a culture or through the mind of a political leader or an isolated individual.

Something like that was attempted before the buildup to the invasion of Iraq by American and British forces and their allies in 2003. Two enterprising American writers produced a survey of the popular cultural figures (in movies, TV shows, and comic strips) listed as favorites by presidents over the previous century.[2] Again and again the presidents favored Captain America, the Lone Ranger, and similar characters' scripts, in which heroes act outside the law to restore peace to beleaguered communities. The narrative seemed worryingly familiar. That wasn't psychoanalysis, but it was a study of motivation. We can in principle inspect the implicit narratives that drive people to particular actions.

This has been done, to take another example, by historians of World War I. As historians, we cannot psychoanalyze the leaders of Germany, Russia, Poland, Serbia, France, and the other countries involved, or even the stiff-upper-lipped British foreign secretary at the time, Sir Edward Grey. Nor should we try. But historians can in principle probe the way in which the statements and actions of such people reveal a sense of purpose, an understanding of national identity and duty, a *narrative* of past wrongs needing to be put right, and a sense, in some cases, of the arrival of a historic moment that ought to be seized. We can, in other words, study why so many people in so many countries all came to the conclusion, around the same time, that what Europe needed was a good brisk war. This isn't psychology. It is the historical study of how and why humans make the choices they do.[3] History is not just about events, but about motivations. Motivations, no doubt, float like icebergs, with much more out of sight than above the waterline. But there is often a good deal visible above the water, often including a strong implicit narrative. We can study that.

When, therefore, something shakes someone to the very core, so that that person emerges from the cataclysm in some ways the same but in other ways radically different, there are, no doubt, many explanations that could be given. Such explanations ought not to cancel one another out. What we can try to do, and will now try to do in the case of Saul of Tarsus on the Damascus Road and thereafter, is to take what we know of our subject before the event and what we know of him after the event and place these apparently contrasting portraits within the rich cultural and spiritual Jewish world of his day, replete as it was with various forms of the controlling Jewish narrative. We must look carefully to see what emerges, not only about the event itself, whatever it was, but about the way in which the "zeal" of the eager young Torah student emerged in a different form as "zeal" for what he called the "good news," the *euangelion,* the gospel, the message about Jesus—the fulfillment, shocking though it seemed, of the ancestral hope.

Some saw it at the time, and many have seen it since, as one narrative replacing another. The word "conversion" itself has often, perhaps usually, been taken that way. But Saul—Paul the

Apostle—saw it as the same narrative, now demanding to be understood in a radical, but justifiable, new way. The narrative in question was the hope of Israel.

If I say that Saul of Tarsus was brought up in a world of hope, many readers may misunderstand me. "Hope" and "optimism" are not the same thing. The optimist looks at the world and feels good about the way it's going. Things are looking up! Everything is going to be all right! But hope, at least as conceived within the Jewish and then the early Christian world, was quite different. Hope could be, and often was, a dogged and deliberate choice when the world seemed dark. It depended not on a *feeling* about the way things were or the way they were moving, but on *faith,* faith in the One God. This God had made the world. This God had called Israel to be his people. The scriptures, not least the Psalms, had made it clear that this God could be trusted to sort things out in the end, to be true to his promises, to vindicate his people at last, even if it had to be on the other side of terrible suffering.

"Hope" in this sense is not a feeling. It is a virtue. You have to practice it, like a difficult piece on the violin or a tricky shot at tennis. You practice the virtue of hope through worship and prayer, through invoking the One God, through reading and reimagining the scriptural story, and through consciously holding the unknown future within the unshakable divine promises. Saul had learned to do this. Paul the Apostle, much later, would have to learn the same lesson all over again.

In Saul's world, those unshakable promises were focused on one great story, with one particular element that would make all the difference. The great story was the ancient freedom story, the Passover narrative, but with a new twist. The One God had liberated his people from slavery in Egypt, and he would do the same thing again. But they weren't in Egypt now. Their slavery, in Saul's day, was more complicated. For a start, nobody in the ancient stories had ever suggested that Israel's time in Egypt was a punishment for wrongdoing. But Israel in Babylon was a different story. Read the prophets—it's hard to miss. Young Saul, as we saw, would easily have made the connection between Adam and Eve being exiled from the Garden of Eden and Israel being exiled from the promised land. Adam and Eve listened to the voice of the snake and no longer did their job in the Garden, so off they went, into a world of thorns and thistles. The Israelites worshipped the idols of Canaan and no longer did justice, loved mercy, or walked humbly with the One God, so off they went to Babylon.

In neither case (Adam and Eve, on the one hand, and Israel, on the other) could this be the end of the story. If it was, the One God would stand convicted of gross incompetence. The story of Israel, starting with Abraham himself, had always been, and in Saul's day was seen to be, the start of a rescue operation, the beginning of a long purpose to put humans right and so in the end to put the whole world right again. The human project, the humans-in-the-garden project, had to get back on track. But if the rescue operation (Abraham's family) was itself in need of rescue, what then? If the lifeboat gets stuck on the rocks, who will come to help, and how?

By Saul's day it was clear that the Abraham project, the Israel vocation, had indeed gotten to the point where it needed rescuing. As we saw earlier, some Jews had come back from Babylon, while others were scattered all over the known world. But the cry went up from generation to generation, between the time of the Babylonians and the time, four centuries later, when Roman soldiers marched through the sacred land: *We are still in exile.* "Exile" wasn't just geographical. It was a state of mind and heart, of politics and practicalities, of spirit and flesh. As long as pagans were ruling over the Jews, they were again in exile. As long as they were paying taxes to Caesar, they were in exile. As long as Roman soldiers could make obscene gestures at them while they were saying their prayers in the Holy Place, they were still in exile. And, since the exile was the result of Israel's idolatry (no devout Jew would have contested the point, since the great prophets had made it so clear), what they needed was not just a new Passover, a new rescue from slavery to pagan tyrants. They needed *forgiveness*.

That was the glad news the prophets had spoken of, the word of comfort at every level from the spiritual to the physical. That is why the famous opening of the central poem in the book of Isaiah stresses comfort: "Comfort, O comfort my people, says your God."[4] When the king pardons a jailed criminal, the criminal is set free. When the One God finally puts away the idolatry and wickedness that caused his people to be exiled in the first place, then his people will be free at last, Passover people with a difference.

That was the ancient hope, cherished not only by Saul of Tarsus but by thousands of his fellow Jews. By no means were all of them as "zealous" as Saul was. Few, perhaps, had his intellectual gifts. But they were mostly aware, through scripture and liturgy, of the ancient divine promises and of the tension between those promises and the present realities. One way or another, it was a culture suffused with hope. Hope long deferred, but hope nonetheless.

That is the great story in which Saul and his contemporaries were living. That is the narrative they had in their heads and their hearts. That story gave shape and energy, in a thousand different ways, to their aspirations and motivations. It explains both hope and action. This is not psychoanalysis. It is history.

★ ★ ★

The particular element that brought all this into sharp focus, and indeed into blinding focus on the road to Damascus, concerned Israel's God himself. It wasn't just Israel that had gone into exile. According to the prophets, Israel's God had abandoned Jerusalem, had departed from the Temple, leaving it open to invasion and destruction. But the prophets didn't leave it at that. They promised a great restoration. Two of Israel's greatest prophets, Isaiah and Ezekiel, focused these long-range promises on the assurance that the One God, having apparently abandoned his people to their fate, would return. "Flatten the hills and fill in the valleys," shouts Isaiah. "Roll out the red carpet for God to come back!"[5] The watchmen on Jerusalem's walls will shout for joy as, in plain sight, they see him returning to Jerusalem.[6] A new Temple would appear, declared Ezekiel, and the divine glory would come to dwell there as it had in the wilderness Tabernacle at the climax of the freedom story, the book of Exodus.[7]

All this meant that the symbolism at the heart of all ancient temples would come true at last. Temples were built to hold together the divine realm ("heaven") and the human realm ("earth"). Jerusalem's Temple, like the wilderness Tabernacle before it, was designed as a small working model of the entire cosmos. This was where the One God of creation would live, dwelling in the midst of his people. When the Temple was destroyed, this vision was shattered, but the prophets declared that God would one day return. Malachi, one of the last of the ancient prophets, several generations after the return of some Jews from Babylon, insists to the skeptics that "the Lord whom you seek *will* suddenly come to his temple."[8] Rumors of an endless absence were wrong. He would return. But the people had better be prepared . . .

So how could one prepare? What should a devout Jew be doing in the meantime? Well, one should keep the Torah for a start. As we saw earlier, for many Jews even in this period (i.e., before the final destruction of the Temple in AD 70) the Torah had become like a portable Temple: wherever they were, in Rome or Babylon, in Greece or Egypt, if they prayerfully studied the Torah, then it might be *as if they were in the Temple itself.* The divine presence would be there, not with flashing glory, not with a pillar of cloud and fire, but there nonetheless.

There were patterns and disciplines of prayer, too, through which that glorious moment might be anticipated by a devout Jew (and young Saul was nothing if not a devout Jew). There were ways of prayer—we hear of them mostly through much later traditions, but there are indications that they were already known in Saul's day—through which that fusion of earth and heaven might be realized even by individuals. Prayer, fasting, and strict observance of the Torah could create conditions either for the worshipper to be caught up into heaven or for a fresh revelation of heaven to appear to someone on earth, or indeed both. Who is to say what precisely all this would mean in practice, set as it is at the borders of language and experience both then and now? A vision, a revelation, the unveiling of secrets, of mysteries . . . like the Temple itself, only even more mysterious . . .

There was a centuries-old tradition of Jewish sages longing for this kind of thing and in some cases being granted it. Such stories go all the way back to the narratives of Israel's patriarchs. Abraham has a strange, disquieting vision of the divine presence as a burning cooking pot, passing between the halves of sacrificial animals and establishing the covenant.[9] Jacob, running away for his life, dreams of a ladder reaching down from heaven to earth.[10] Joseph interprets dreams for Pharaoh's servants and then for Pharaoh himself, before suddenly finding that his own boyhood dreams are fulfilled as well in ways he could never have imagined.[11] Closer to the first century, there was Daniel. Daniel, like Joseph, interpreted dreams for a pagan king; then, like Jacob, he had his own visions of heaven and earth in dangerous but glorious interchange.[12]

These memories informed the minds of those first-century Jews who found themselves in the long, puzzling interval between the time when the One God had abandoned the Temple and the time when he would return in glory. Heaven and earth would come together at last. But how? And when? Interim answers were given in various writings. Seers, mystics, and poets wrote of dreams and visions whose subject matter was the rescue of Israel and the final saving revelation of the One God. Often these took the literary form of "dream plus interpretation," fused together to provide the "revelation" (in Greek *apokalypsis*) of things normally hidden. This was the world in which Saul of Tarsus, heir to these traditions, practiced his fierce and loyal devotion to Israel's God. This was how to keep hope alive, perhaps even to glimpse its fulfillment in advance.

Once again, locating him within this world is a matter not of psychology, but of history. We are trying to think our way into the mind of a zealous young Jew determined to do God's will whatever it cost, eager to purge Israel from idolatry and sin, keen to hasten the time when God would come back and rule his world with justice and righteousness. What could be more appropriate than for such a young man to seek through prayer and meditation to inhabit for himself those strange old traditions of heaven-and-earth commerce, to become, in his own mind and heart and perhaps even body, part of that heaven-and-earth reality, a visionary whose inner eye, and perhaps also whose outer eye, might glimpse the ultimate mystery?

You will see where this is going (though Saul, of course, did not). But there is one more element to add to the mix before we get there. In later Jewish tradition—again we must assume that such traditions have deep historical roots, though they are now lost to our view—one central text for meditation of this sort, for heaven-and-earth mysticism if we want to call it that, was the opening of the book of Ezekiel. In one of the strangest scenes in all scripture, the prophet sees the heavenly throne-chariot upon which the One God goes about his business. He describes it with immense caution, starting down below with the whirling and flashing wheels and the strange four-faced creatures (angels? who can say?) that inhabit them. (Even reading the text can make you giddy. Some of the later rabbis tried to keep people from reading it until they were at least forty years old.)

Slowly, gradually, the prophet works his way up from the living creatures and the whirling wheels to the throne itself; then, from the throne to the figure sitting on the throne. Here he hardly dares say what he seems to see: "something that seemed like a human form."[13] The prophet falls on his face as though dead. He is, however, commanded at once to stand up to receive his prophetic vocation, though this in its way is just as frightening as the vision itself. Perhaps such a vocation can only be undertaken by someone who has seen such a sight.

This passage in Ezekiel became a focal point of meditation for devout Jews of Saul's time and later. Contemplating such an awe-inspiring scene might, they hoped, bring into personal focus, ahead of the long-awaited visible return of God to Jerusalem, that fusion of heaven and earth that was the very raison d'être of the Temple itself. This wouldn't just be about one person having what we moderns might call "a glorious spiritual experience." A throne vision, a Temple vision, would be about heaven and earth coming together; in other words, it would have to do with the long-awaited renewal of creation itself—the ultimate prophetic vision.

The more I have pondered what happened to Saul of Tarsus on the road to Damascus, holding together (as a historian must) the somewhat formalized accounts in the book of Acts and the brief, cryptic references in Paul's own letters, the more I have wondered whether Saul had been practicing this kind of meditation. It was the kind of thing one might well do during the long, hot hours on the journey from Jerusalem to Damascus. In Caravaggio's famous painting, Saul is riding a horse; historically, a donkey seems a good deal more likely. This would also produce an oblique echo of the story that began with Balaam on his donkey and ended up with Phinehas's moment of zeal.

As we reflect on what Paul the Apostle came to say about the incident much later, it would make perfect sense to suppose that he had been meditating upon Ezekiel's vision and seeking, if he could, to glimpse for himself what the prophet had seen. (I assume he was well under the prescribed age of forty. But I also assume that the attempted prohibition was a later restriction, designed precisely to protect young hotheads from danger.) Perhaps Saul was praying the *Shema*, "Hear, O Israel: the LORD our God, the LORD is one," praying it as a mantra, repeating it to the rhythm of his breathing, to the steady movement of the beast beneath him. Pray and watch. Watch and pray. Stay loyal to Israel's God. Stand up for his kingdom. Pray and watch. Start with the living creatures and the whirling wheels, and perhaps ascend from there . . .

In his mind's eye, then, he has the four-faced creatures and the wheels. He focuses on them. He sees them. He ponders them. Will he dare to go further? Upward, with prayer and quickening pulse, to the chariot itself. Was it his imagination? Was he actually seeing it? Were his eyes open, or was it just his heart's eyes opened to realities normally invisible? Nobody who has had that kind of experience is likely to give a scientific answer to such questions, but such questions are in any case left behind when heaven and earth are coming together. Upward again, then, to the lower parts of what seems to be a figure on the throne, some kind of human form. Saul of Tarsus, head full of scripture, heart full of zeal, raises his eyes slowly upward once more. He is seeing now, eyes wide open, conscious of being wide awake but conscious also that there seems to be a rift in reality, a fissure in the fabric of the cosmos, and that his waking eyes are seeing things so dangerous that if he were not so prepared, so purified, so carefully devout, he would never have dared to come this far. Upward again, from the chest to the face. He raises his eyes to see the one he has worshipped and served all his life . . . And he comes face-to-face with Jesus of Nazareth.

To explain what this meant in the language of psychology would be like trying to copy a Titian with a child's crayons. To understand the explosion that resulted, we need history, we need theology, we need a strong sense of the inner tensions of the first-century Jewish world and the zealous propagators of Jewish culture. This moment shattered Saul's wildest dreams and, at the same split second, fulfilled them. This was—he saw it in that instant—the fulfillment of Israel's ancient scriptures, but also the utter denial of the way he had been reading them up to that point. *God the Creator had raised Jesus from the dead, declaring not only that he really was Israel's Messiah, but that he had done what the One God had promised to do himself, in person.* Saul had been absolutely right in his devotion to the One God, but absolutely wrong in his understanding of who that One God was and how his purposes would be fulfilled. He had been absolutely right in his devotion to Israel and the Torah, but absolutely wrong in his view of Israel's vocation and identity and even in the meaning of the Torah itself. His lifelong loyalty was utterly right, but utterly misdirected. He had a zeal for God, but had not understood what the One God was up to. Everything was now focused on the figure from whom there streamed a blinding light, the figure who now addressed Saul as a master addresses a slave, the figure he recognized as the crucified Jesus of Nazareth. Heaven and earth came together in this figure, and he was commanding Saul to acknowledge this fact and to reorient his entire life accordingly.

So when Christian tradition speaks of the "conversion" of Saul, we need to pause. In our world, as we saw earlier, we normally apply that term to someone who "converts" from one "religion" to another. That was not the point. Not for one second did Saul cease to believe in the One God of Abraham, Isaac, and Jacob. It was just that . . . well, what had happened was . . . how could he put it? Twenty years or so later he would write of glimpsing "the glory of God in the face of Jesus the Messiah."[14] That was one way of putting it. There would be other ways too. This wasn't about "religion," whether in the ancient or the (very different) modern sense. It was about Jesus. About Jesus as the point at which—exactly as the martyr Stephen had claimed—heaven and earth were now held together, fused together; it was about Jesus as being, in person, the reality toward which the Temple itself had pointed.

It is easy, in our culture, to get this seriously wrong. People still speak of Paul and the groups of Jesus-followers who sprang up through his work as offering a new kind of "religion" comparable to or in competition with something called "Judaism." This is misleading on several counts. There was nothing called "Christianity" in the first century, only groups of people who believed that Jesus of Nazareth was Israel's Messiah and the world's rightful Lord. There was nothing corresponding to what we now call "Judaism" in the first century (the word then, as we saw, had an active force meaning "the zealous propagation of the Jewish way of life"), only the many communities of Jews around the world, praying to Israel's God, studying the scriptures, focusing on Temple and Torah.

What drove Paul, from that moment on the Damascus Road and throughout his subsequent life, was the belief that Israel's God had done what he had always said he would; that Israel's scriptures had been fulfilled in ways never before imagined; and that Temple and Torah themselves were not after all the ultimate realities, but instead glorious signposts pointing forward to the new heaven-and-earth reality that had come to birth in Jesus. Paul remained to his dying day fiercely loyal to Israel's God, seen in fresh and blinding focus in Jesus. Neither Paul nor his communities were engaged in "comparative religion." They were not saying, "We've tried one way of being religious, and now we think we have a better one." Nobody thought like that in the first century, certainly no Jew. They were focused on what we might call *messianic eschatology:* the belief that the One God had acted climactically and decisively in, and even *as,* Israel's Messiah. A shocking, blinding reality. The reality that would change the world.

They led Saul by the hand and brought him into the city.

★ ★ ★

If you look up "Straight Street" in Damascus (on Google Earth, say), you will be directed to Bab Sharqi. It is part of an ancient Roman road running east to west across the heart of the old city. Bab Sharqi is now the eastern half of a longer street, with the

Jewish quarter lying on its southern side. Somewhere in that district Saul of Tarsus was taken, stone blind, to a lodging where he stayed, shocked and stunned, for three days. He didn't eat; he didn't drink; he couldn't see; but he prayed. Of course he prayed. "Hear, O Israel . . ."

But what would that great prayer mean now? What form would loyalty to the One God now take? Paul would, of course, continue to invoke the One God as the God of Israel. But what if Israel's purposes had been fulfilled in one man, the anointed king? And what if Israel's God had done *in person,* in the person of this man, what he said he would do, defeating death itself and launching his new creation? What would the word "God" itself now mean? What would the word "Israel" now mean? (This question was faced by many Jewish groups of the period, from the Covenant Sect at Qumran to the eager groups supporting various potential "messiahs" over the next century or so, each claiming an exclusive inside track on the divine purposes.) Saul, knowing the Psalms and prophets and, behind them all, the great story of creation and the Exodus, prayed and prayed.

On the third day there was a knock at the door. The little group of Jesus-followers in Damascus, some of them perhaps refugees from the persecution in Jerusalem, had known that Saul of Tarsus was coming to get them, to drag them off to prison or even death. One of that group, Ananias, had a vision. (People today sneer at such things, but that is often mere prejudice. Many people in various cultures still speak of strange senses of direction or even command, unexpected promptings that, when followed, produce unexpected results.) He was to go and lay his hands on Saul so that he could see again. Ananias naturally recoiled. Was the Lord asking him to walk into a trap, into a lion's den? No. As so often—it becomes a recurring theme in early Christian storytelling—when something has to be done, it will be done through an obedient, but quite likely nervous and worried disciple. So off he goes.

Jesus had told him three things about Saul. First, he was praying. People have sometimes suggested that "praying" was itself a
sign that Saul had had a new "religious experience," like a secular
atheist in today's world meeting God and praying for the first time;
but that of course is nonsense. Saul had prayed all his life and was
now praying with a new focus and a new perplexity. Second, Saul
was to be a "chosen vessel" through whom the message would go
out to the world. Third, Saul would have to suffer for Jesus's sake.
But Ananias didn't say that to Saul. That was for Jesus himself to
make clear. Ananias had other words and other actions. Together
they introduce several themes that will shape Saul's life and work.

"Brother Saul," he began. *Brother?* Yes. From the very start—
from the teaching of Jesus himself—the members of this strange
new group regarded one another as "family" in a world where
"family" meant a lot more than it does in most Western cultures today. Even before Saul has been baptized, Ananias recognizes him as part of what anthropologists call a "fictive kinship
group." Of course, at this point all the Jesus-followers were Jews,
so there was already a sense of extended kinship within which
this new reality had come to birth. But quickly, not least through
the work of Saul himself, this kinship would be extended to a
much wider company, creating serious problems on the way but
always making the same strong affirmation. "There is no longer
Jew or Greek; there is no longer slave or free; there is no 'male
and female'; you are all one in the Messiah, Jesus."[15] Paul wrote
those words at least fifteen years later. But the truth they express
was already contained within Ananias's opening greeting.

Ananias explained to Saul that Jesus had sent him so that Saul
would be able to see again and so that he would receive the holy
spirit. Who knows what those words did to Saul after his three days
of turmoil and blindness? Whatever was going on inside him, the
outward evidence was clear: something like scales fell from his eyes
(another proverbial phrase; had the blinding light caused some sort
of a scab?), and he could see. We in the modern world do not put

much stock in "miracles." But when we are faced with events that seem to fall in no other category, we speak of miracles as though they are caused by a "supernatural" power from outside the world that "invades" the chain of "natural causes." It may sometimes feel like that. But a more biblical account would recognize the strange, steady work of God within so-called natural causes as well, so that the sudden and shocking new event is held within a larger continuum of ultimate divine causation.

In any case, the early followers of Jesus knew very well that, just as Jesus himself had gone about healing people, so they too were entrusted with this gift—not all the time and never simply at their own whim, but with a lasting and powerful effect that carried its own evidential weight. Writing his letters some years after this, Paul would refer to the same kind of healing power working through him and through others—just as he would also refer to illnesses, his own and those of others, that were not healed, or not in the way one had hoped. The mystery remained, but the power remained too.

So then Ananias baptized the puzzled Saul. As in some of the other occasions in Acts, this happened at once, as soon as the person came to believe in the crucified Jesus as the risen Lord. There was no period of waiting, teaching, or preparation. That would come in due time. Baptism, looking back to Jesus's own baptism and past that to the crossing of the Red Sea in the Passover story, marked out the new family, the new Passover people.

Jesus himself had used the image of baptism to speak of his approaching death. Paul would later make it clear that this dramatic plunging into water and coming up again spoke in powerful and effective symbolic language about the dying and rising of Jesus and about the new world that had come to birth through those events. To be baptized was therefore to die and rise with Jesus, to leave behind the old life and to be reborn into the new one. Insofar as it marked out members of the family, it functioned somewhat like circumcision for a Jew, except of course that women were included as well. Equally, it was a bit like a slave being branded (so that the slave was now under a new master), though of course slaves and free alike were baptized. The important thing was that, having been baptized, one now belonged to the Messiah. Saul was now a "Messiah man," shaped in the pattern of the Jesus who had summed up the divine purposes for Israel.

Something else happened at the same time: Saul received Jesus's own spirit. The fourth and last point of immense significance in Ananias's visit to Straight Street is that Saul was promised the gift of the spirit, and everything in his subsequent life and writings indicates that he believed this had happened then and there. The story in Acts doesn't say that Saul spoke in tongues or prophesied. The idea that things like that had to happen for the spirit's gift to be genuine is a much later fiction. What Acts offers instead is the remarkable statement that Saul went at once to the synagogue in Damascus and announced that Jesus was the son of God (a theme to which we shall return in due course). There was a new power coupled with a new sense of direction.

Paul's powerful, spirit-driven proclamation of Jesus as "son of God" can hardly be called "preaching," if by "preaching" we mean the sort of thing that goes on in churches week by week in our world. This was a public announcement, like a medieval herald or town crier walking through the streets with a bell, calling people to attention and declaring that a new king had been placed on the throne. This was, indeed, how the word "gospel" would be heard right across the Roman world of the day: as the announcement of a new emperor. Paul's proclamation was not, then, a fresh twist on the regular teaching work of the local Jewish community. He wasn't offering advice on how to lead a more holy life. He certainly wasn't telling people how to go to heaven when they died. He was making the all-time one-off announcement: Israel's hope has been fulfilled! The King has been enthroned! He was declaring that the crucified Jesus was Israel's long-awaited Messiah.

But what happens when half the people in the town don't want this new king? Saul discovered the answer to that all too soon, not that he would have been particularly surprised. The local Jewish community in Damascus was shocked at the sudden turnaround of this hotheaded young man, transformed from persecutor to proclaimer. Not just shocked; they were deeply offended (as of course Saul himself had been) at the suggestion that Israel's history would reach its climax in a crucified messiah. Not all Jews in this period, so far as we can tell, believed in a coming messiah in the first place. Those who did hope for such a figure envisaged the messiah as a warrior hero. He would be a new David; he would overthrow the wicked pagans, restore the Temple to make it fit for Israel's God to come back to at last, and establish a worldwide rule of justice and peace. Jesus of Nazareth, as everybody knew, had done none of those things. Saul of Tarsus could produce all the scriptural "proofs" he liked from his long years of study. But the synagogue in Damascus was not going to be convinced.

★ ★ ★

Up to this point, we have been following the story of Paul on the road to Damascus and then in the city itself more or less as we find it in the book of Acts. But Paul, in a later writing, injects another episode into the mix at this point. This extra episode, when properly understood, strongly reinforces our developing picture of the hotheaded young zealot suddenly stopped in his tracks. He went away, he says, to Arabia.[16] What was that all about? Why did he go? What did it mean? How does it help us to see not only what motivated Saul from the beginning, but also what was involved in his sudden transition from persecutor to apostle? What does it contribute to our effort to understand the man whose subsequent writings would shape a worldwide movement and, in a measure, the world itself?

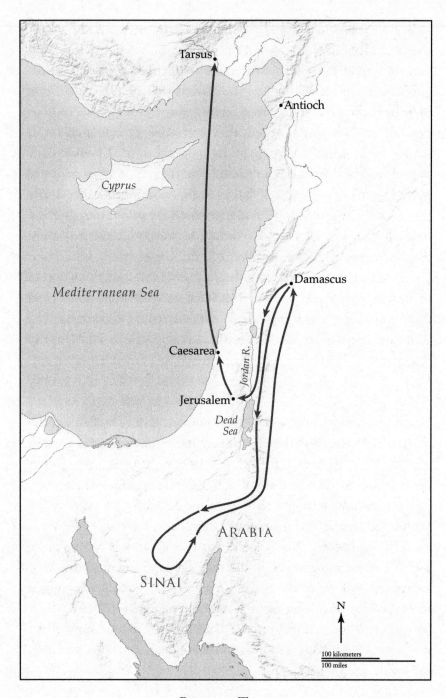

Return to Tarsus

3

Arabia and Tarsus

PAUL'S LETTERS GIVE us a few tantalizing glimpses of his life, and this is one of the strangest:

> When God, who set me apart from my mother's
> womb, and called me by his grace, was pleased
> to unveil his son in me, so that I might announce
> the good news about him among the nations—
> immediately I did not confer with flesh and blood.
> Nor did I go up to Jerusalem to those who were
> apostles before me. No, I went away to Arabia, and
> afterward returned to Damascus.[1]

As we shall see later, Paul is writing this in his own defense. He has apparently been accused of getting his "gospel" secondhand from the Jerusalem apostles. His opponents are therefore going over his head and appealing to Peter, James, and the rest, like someone objecting to the way a band was playing a cover from an old Beatles song and phoning up Paul McCartney himself to check on how it should really be played. Paul is therefore insisting that his message was his own; he had gotten it from Jesus himself, not from other members of the movement. It had come, he says, "through an unveiling of Jesus the Messiah."[2] "The message" in question was not, after all, a theory, a new bit of teaching, or even details of how someone might be "saved." "The message" was the news about Jesus himself: he was raised from the dead, he was therefore Israel's Messiah, he was the Lord of the world. All of that was "given" to Paul on the road to Damascus. Knowing Israel's scriptures as he did, he didn't need anybody else to explain what it all meant. Start with the scriptural story, place the crucified and risen Jesus at the climax of the story, and the meaning, though unexpected and shocking, is not in doubt. That is the point he is making.

So why Arabia? The clunky, obvious, straightforward answer is that Paul was eager to tell people about Jesus and that Arabia was where he went on his first "evangelistic mission." Scholars and preachers have written and spoken about "Paul's missionary activity in Arabia" as though this interpretation was a done deal. But, as often, the obvious answer is almost certainly wrong. And, again as so often, the clue to what Paul means is found in the scriptures he knew so well.

We recall that the young Saul of Tarsus was, in the technical Jewish sense, "extremely zealous for his ancestral traditions"—a line that comes in Galatians immediately before the passage quoted above. We recall, further, that in the Jewish traditions of Saul's day there were two outstanding ancient heroes of "zeal": Phinehas, the young priest who had speared the Israelite man and the Moabite woman, and Elijah, who had tricked and killed the worshippers of the fertility god Baal. Phinehas is important for our understanding of Paul, for reasons to which we will return. Elijah is important for Paul not least because he gives us the clue to the journey to "Arabia."

The word "Arabia" in the first century covered a wide range of territory. It could refer to the ancient Nabataean kingdom, which stretched from a little to the east of Syria—close to Damascus, in fact—southward through what is now Jordan and beyond to include the Sinai Peninsula. But one of the only other references to it in the New Testament—indeed, in the same letter, Paul's letter to the Galatians—gives us a far more specific location: Mt. Sinai, in the peninsula to the south of the Holy Land and to the east of Egypt. Mt. Sinai was where God had come down in fire and had given Moses the Torah; it was the place of revelation, the place of law, the place where the covenant between God and Israel, established earlier with Abraham, Isaac, and Jacob, was solemnly ratified. Sinai, the great mountain in Arabia, was, in that sense, the place of beginnings. It was the place to which subsequent generations looked back as the starting point of the long and checkered relationship, the often shaky marriage, between this strange, rescuing, demanding God and his willful, stiff-necked people. Sinai was where Elijah had gone when it all went horribly wrong. Sinai was where Saul of Tarsus went—for the same reason.

The echoes of the Elijah story are small but significant. After his zealous victory over the prophets of Baal, Elijah is confronted by a messenger from Queen Jezebel, herself an enthusiastic backer of the Baal cult. The royal threat is blunt; Elijah's life is on the line. Zeal turns to panic. He runs away, all the way to Mt. Horeb.³ (Horeb is either another name for Sinai or the name of a mountain close by from which the Israelites set off to Canaan.) There he complains to God that he has been "very zealous for the LORD, the God of hosts" (in other words, he has killed the prophets of Baal), but that it hasn't worked. The people are still rebelling, and he alone is left, the last loyalist. He repeats this complaint a second time after a powerful revelation of wind, earthquake, and fire had been followed by "a sound of sheer silence," one modern translation of a Hebrew phrase that in the King James Version appears as "a still small voice."⁴

When God finally answers, Elijah is told, "Go, return on your way to the wilderness of Damascus," where he is to anoint new kings for Syria and Israel and a new prophet, Elisha, to take his own place.[5] They will do what needs to be done to remove Baal worship from the land. What's more, God declares to the puzzled prophet, "I will leave seven thousand in Israel" who will stay loyal.[6] (Paul quotes that passage in another letter, likening himself to Elijah as the focal point of a "remnant.")[7]

Already those with ears to hear may catch echoes of Paul in Galatians. He has been "exceedingly zealous for the ancestral traditions," leading him to use violence in trying to stamp out heresy. Paul says that he "went away to Arabia"—just as Elijah did—and "afterward returned to Damascus"—again just like Elijah. So what is this all about? Why did Saul go to Arabia?

The parallel with Elijah—the verbal echoes are so close, and the reflection on "zeal" so exact, that Paul must have intended them—indicates that he, like Elijah, made a pilgrimage to Mt. Sinai in order to go back to the place where the covenant was ratified. He wanted to go and present himself before the One God, to explain that he had been "exceedingly zealous," but that his vision, his entire worldview, had been turned on its head. And he received his instructions: "Go back and announce the new king."

The picture in Acts, it turns out, is oversimplified. (The longest histories ever written leave out far more than they put in, and Luke wants his book to fit onto a single scroll.) In Acts 9:20–28, Paul announces Jesus in the synagogue in Damascus until a plot against his life forces him to leave town and go back to Jerusalem. Somewhere in that story there must be room for a desert pilgrimage, after which Paul "returned again to Damascus."

But the point is far more significant for a biographer than simply sorting out a potential conflict between two sources. We discover from the Arabia journey something about Paul's own self-awareness, including at that point a perhaps welcome note of self-doubt in the midst of the zeal—the zeal of the persecutor and then the zeal of the proclaimer. Whether on foot or by donkey, one does not go for several days into a desert just to find a quiet spot to pray. Saul wanted to be clear that the shocking new thing that had been revealed to him really was the fulfillment, the surprising but ultimately satisfying goal, of the ancient purposes of the One God, purposes that had been set out particularly in the law given to Moses on Mt. Sinai. He wanted to stay loyal. Saul was starting to come to terms with the possibility that, if the divine purposes had been completed in Jesus, it might mean that a whole new phase of the divine plan, hitherto barely suspected, had now been launched, a phase in which the Torah itself would be seen in a whole new light. And Saul, like Elijah, was told to go back and get on with the job. Elijah was to anoint a couple of new kings and a prophet as well. Saul of Tarsus was to go back and get on with the prophetic task of announcing that Jesus of Nazareth was the true anointed king, the Messiah, the world's rightful sovereign.

So Saul went back to Damascus, apparently confirmed in his understanding of himself as a prophet fulfilling the ancient role of announcing God's truth and God's anointed king to Israel and the nations. If he has not usually been seen this way, that may be because we have not paid sufficient attention to the scriptural echoes he sets up in many places in his writings, but particularly in the very passage we have been studying. When he speaks of God setting him apart from his mother's womb, he is deliberately echoing the call of Jeremiah.[8] When he speaks of God "unveiling" his son in him, he is using the language of Jewish mystics and seers who spoke of that "unveiling" or "revelation" as constituting a divine commissioning.[9] When he says that the Jerusalem church later "glorified God because of me," he is echoing Isaiah, from one of his all-time favorite chapters, and claiming for himself the prophetic role of the "servant."[10] He continues to echo that chapter in Galatians 2 when he speaks of wondering whether he "might be running, or might have run, to no good effect."[11]

Paul, in other words, is not only making it clear in Galatians 1–2 that his "gospel" was given to him directly, not acquired secondhand through the Jerusalem leaders. He is also making it clear that his call and commissioning have placed him in the ancient prophetic tradition, whether of Isaiah, Jeremiah, or Elijah himself. His opponents are trying to go over his head in their appeal to Jerusalem, but he is going over everybody else's head by appealing to Jesus himself and to the scriptures as foreshadowing not only the gospel, but the prophetic ministry that he, Paul, has now received.

This, then, is why he went to Arabia: to hand in his former commission and to acquire a new one. His loyalty to the One God of Israel was as firm as it had always been. Since many Christians, and many Jews too, have assumed otherwise (suggesting, for instance, that Paul the Apostle was a traitor to the Jewish world or that he had never really understood it in the first place), the point is worth stressing before we even approach the main work of Paul's life.

As we try to figure out what exactly happened next, our sources present us with a confused flurry of incidents, ending with Saul paying a brief visit to Jerusalem before going back home to Tarsus. Saul's time in Damascus, including his trip to Arabia and back, probably took three years, most likely from AD 33 to 36. (Questions of chronology always get complicated, but the main lines are clear.) Thus, though the alarm and anger at his initial proclamation of Jesus may have been real enough, it seems to have taken a little while before this looked like it was turning violent. Only when the threats became severe, with his life in danger not only from the local Jewish population but from a local official as well, did Paul make his famous escape, avoiding the guards on the city gates by being let down the city wall in a basket.

Many years later Paul would use that incident to good rhetorical effect. In his second letter to Corinth, he makes an ironic list of all his "achievements," and the climax of it all is the time when he had to run away![12] It was the shape of things to come. His career, did he but know it, lay before him in outline in this one incident. Announce Jesus as Messiah, and opposition will arise from Jews, offended at the idea of a crucified Messiah, and from pagan authorities, fearing a breach of the peace. Perhaps too from more perceptive pagans, who might glimpse the (scriptural) point that Israel's Messiah was not to be a local or tribal chief only. He would be the master of the entire world.

In any case, to Jerusalem Paul then goes, most likely in AD 36 or 37. Writing to the Galatians over a decade later, he explains that he stayed with Peter (whom he calls by his Aramaic name, Cephas) for two weeks, seeing no other Jesus-followers except James, the Lord's brother, already acknowledged as the central figure in the new movement. The meeting was set up by Barnabas; the Jerusalem leaders were understandably suspicious, but Barnabas assured them that Saul really had seen Jesus on the road, and that in Damascus he really had been boldly announcing Jesus as Messiah. So far, one might think, so good.

But the pattern begins to kick in again. Saul, knowing his scriptures inside out and possessed of a quick mind and a ready tongue, is bound to get into public debate, and public debate is bound to get him into trouble. And trouble, coming just a few years after the stoning of Stephen, is something the Jesus believers can do without. So they escort Paul down to the sea at Caesarea and put him on a boat back home to southern Turkey.

It is hard to know what the Jerusalem community thought would happen next. They were in dangerous, unmapped new territory. Saul of Tarsus, still on fire with having seen the risen Lord, eager to explain from the scriptures what it was all about, apparently careless of the hornets' nests he was stirring up, was one problem too many. "Let him go back to Tarsus," they probably thought. "They like good talkers there. And besides, that's where he came from in the first place . . ."

★ ★ ★

There follows a decade or so of silence: roughly 36 to 46 (like most dates in ancient history, including most of the ones in this book, we are dealing in approximations, with a year or so to be allowed either way). Faced with a silent decade at a formative period of someone's life, a novelist might have a field day; we must be more restrained. But if we send cautious historical and biographical probes into this blank period from either end, we may find at least three themes that need to be explored.

First, and most straightforwardly, we must assume that Saul set to and earned his own living in the family business. As we saw earlier, he was a tentmaker, which involved general skill with leather and fabric of various kinds as well as the specific manufacture of actual tents, awnings, and so on. Jewish teachers did not expect to make a living from their teaching; Saul, as a strange new type of Jewish teacher, would not suppose that going about announcing the crucified Jesus as Israel's Messiah and the world's Lord would earn him a living. His craft was hard physical labor, and his subsequent apostolic letters show that the apostle took a pride in supporting himself by manual work. Saul, by now perhaps in his late twenties or early thirties, would be living and working alongside his family and in close contact with the rich mixture of people who passed through the great city of Tarsus.

Importantly for Saul's later work, tentmaking was a portable trade. As long as he had his working tools, he could set up shop in any town, buying his raw materials locally and offering his regular products for sale. When people in churches today discuss Paul and his letters, they often think only of the man of ideas who dealt with lofty and difficult concepts, implying a world of libraries, seminar rooms, or at least the minister's study for quiet ser-

mon preparation. We easily forget that the author of these letters
spent most of his waking hours with his sleeves rolled up, doing
hard physical work in a hot climate, and that perhaps two-thirds
of the conversations he had with people about Jesus and the gospel
were conducted not in a place of worship or study, not even in
a private home, but in a small, cramped workshop. Saul had his
feet on the ground, and his hands were hardened with labor. But
his head still buzzed with scripture and the news about Jesus. His
heart was still zealous, loyal to the One God.

The second thing we can be sure of is that he prayed, he studied, and he figured out all sorts of things. Faced with his letters (written a decade and more later), dense as they are with
concentrated argument, we cannot imagine that when he wrote
them he was breaking entirely new ground. He could no doubt
improvise on the spot, but in his mature thought he gives every
evidence of long pondering. Saul spent a silent decade deepening
the well of scriptural reflection from which he would thereafter
draw the water he needed.

During this period he had one particular experience from
which, in retrospect, he learned one particular lesson. Writing to
Corinth in AD 56, he seems to be mocking the Corinthians' desire
for spectacular "spiritual" events. "All right," he says, "if I must, I
must. Someone I know in the Messiah . . ."—he won't even say it's
himself, though this becomes clear. "This 'Someone' was snatched
up to the third heaven." (Since heaven was often subdivided into
seven, this itself might have seemed a bit of a letdown.) "I don't
know," he says, "whether this was a bodily experience or one of
those out-of-body things; only God knows that. And this 'Someone' heard . . . but actually I'm not allowed to tell you what was
heard. Oh, and the most important thing about it all was that I was
given 'a thorn in my flesh,' a satanic messenger, to stop me from
getting too exalted with it all." The underlying point in the letter is
clear: *"You shouldn't be asking this kind of question and trying to rank me*

with other people and their 'experiences.' If you do, I will only say that yes, these things have happened, but that the real point was that I had to learn humility, to understand that 'when I'm weak, then I am strong.'"[13]

The underlying point for our understanding of Paul is that he continued the practices of prayer and meditation within which, I have suggested, his Damascus Road vision took place and that sometimes these led to almost equally spectacular results. Perhaps this may have happened to comfort and reassure him at a moment when things were particularly difficult back home in Tarsus. Perhaps the "thorn in the flesh" was the continuing resistance to the gospel on the part of people he loved dearly, though speculation has been rife as to whether it was a bodily ailment, a recurring temptation, or even the recurring nightmare of the stoning of Stephen, in which he himself is standing by giving his grim approval. The point leads to an ironic climax. He prayed three times about this, he says to the Corinthians, asking that it be removed. The Corinthians are no doubt expecting him to log this as a great "answer to prayer" of which they could be proud. Instead, he reveals that the answer was No.

This is the only window we have on the silent years at Tarsus, and Paul seems to have been determined that they would remain more or less silent. "Yes, something happened, but that's not the point." But here too we can see his mind at work: praying, puzzling things out, pondering.

We can infer quite a bit about his pondering. From everything we know of Saul of Tarsus, on the one hand, and Paul the Apostle, on the other, we cannot imagine that in this early period he ever stopped thinking things through, soaking that reflection in Jewish-style prayer, focusing it on Israel's scriptures, and, like many other devout diaspora Jews, engaging with the culture all around him. He searched the ancient scriptures for all he was worth and argued about them in the synagogue and at the workbench with his friends and family. He thought his way backward from the "new fact," as he saw it, of a crucified and risen Messiah, back into the world of Israel's scriptures and traditions, back into the long, dark, and often twisted narrative of Israel that had been groping its way forward to that point without glimpsing its true goal. He reread Genesis. He reread Exodus. He reread the whole Torah, and the prophets, especially Isaiah, and he went on praying the Psalms. With hindsight (and, he would have insisted, with a fresh wisdom that came with the spirit), he saw Jesus all over the place—not arbitrarily, not in fanciful allegory (the only time he says he's using allegory, he is probably teasing those for whom that was a method of first resort), but as the infinite point where the parallel lines of Israel's long narrative would eventually meet.

These parallel lines are central to his mature thinking and foundational for what would later become Christian theology. First, there was *Israel's* own story. According to the prophets, Israel's story (from Abraham all the way through to exile and beyond) would narrow down to a remnant, but would also focus on a coming king, so that the king himself would be Israel personified. But second, there was *God's* story—the story of what the One God had done, was doing, and had promised to do. (The idea of God having a story, making plans, and putting them into operation seems to be part of what Jews and early Christians meant by speaking of this God as being "alive.") And this story too would likewise narrow down to one point. Israel's God would return, visibly and powerfully, to rescue his people from their ultimate enemies and to set up a kingdom that could not be shaken. "All God's promises," Paul would later write, "find their yes in him."[14]

Saul came to see that these two stories, Israel's story and God's story, had, shockingly, merged together. I think this conviction must date to the silent decade in Tarsus, if not earlier. Both narratives were fulfilled in Jesus. Jesus was Israel personified; but he was also Israel's God in person. The great biblical stories of creation and new creation, Exodus and new Exodus, Temple and new Temple all came rushing together at the same point. This was not a new religion. This was a new world—and it was the new world that the One God had always promised, the new world for which Israel had prayed night and day. If you had asked Saul of Tarsus, before the meeting on the road to Damascus, where Israel's story and God's story came together, the two natural answers would have been Temple (the place at the heart of the promised land where God had promised to live) and Torah (the word of God spoken into, and determinative of, Israel's national life). The Temple indicated that Israel's God desired to live in the midst of his people; the Torah, that he would address his people with his life-transforming word. Saul now came to see that both these answers pointed beyond themselves to Jesus and of course to the spirit.

In this new world (this too became axiomatic for Paul's mature thought and thematic for his public career) it mattered that Israel's God was indeed the One God of the whole world. A tight-knit orthodox Jewish community in the midst of a bustling, philosophically minded pagan city must have been a fascinating place to start thinking all this through. At first glance, Israel's scriptures might seem to demand that Israel stay separate from the nations, the *goyim*. The pagans, like the Moabite women sent to seduce the Israelites in the desert, would lead them astray. They should stay separate. But look again, and you will see, not least in the Psalms, not least in the royal predictions of Psalms and prophets alike, that when Israel's true king arrives, he will be the king not only of Israel, but also of the whole world. Saul, in Tarsus, must have reflected on what it would mean for Psalm 2 to come true, where the One God says to the true king:

> *You are my son;*
> *today I have begotten you.*
> *Ask of me, and I will make the nations your heritage,*
> *and the ends of the earth your possession.*

You shall break them with a rod of iron,
And dash them in pieces like a potter's vessel.[15]

This psalm echoes the promises to Abraham, promises about an "inheritance" and a "possession" that would consist of the land of Canaan. But the promises have been globalized. They now extend to the whole world. They say, in effect, that the promises of the "holy land" were a foretaste, a signpost, to a larger reality. The God of Abraham was the Creator, who called Abraham—and then, much later, David—so that through their long story, replete as it was with disasters and false starts, he would bring his restorative purposes to bear on the whole world.

That, indeed, seems to be the message of another psalm:

God is king over the nations;
God sits on his holy throne.
The princes of the peoples gather
as the people of the God of Abraham.
For the shields of the earth belong to God;
he is highly exalted.[16]

Put those psalms together with others such as Psalm 72 ("May he have dominion from sea to sea, and from the River to the ends of the earth"[17]), dip them in the prophetic scriptures like Isaiah 11 (the "shoot from the stump of Jesse," that is, David, will inaugurate the new creation of justice and peace), and you have a composite picture of the hope of Israel: hope for a new world, not just a rescued or renewed people, and hope for a coming king through whose rule it would come about. Put all that into the praying mind of Saul of Tarsus, who is sensing a new energy transforming and redirecting his earlier "zeal," and what do you get? One could not sing those and the other psalms in a Jewish community in a city like Tarsus without wondering what it might mean to say that *the crucified and risen Jesus* was the king of whom Psalm 2 had spoken. How would that work out? What would it look like in practice?

Not far behind that, what did it mean that the promises to Abraham had been universalized? What would a worldwide Abrahamic family consist of? How, so to speak, might it work? These are the questions that underlie much of Paul's mature writing. We cannot imagine that he was not puzzling them out through the long, silent years in Tarsus.

We glimpse, then, Saul at the workbench; Saul praying and thinking; and, third, Saul listening to the ideas all around him, in the philosophical and political as well as religious cultures of cosmopolitan Tarsus. He would be taking it all in, not simply as further evidence of pagan folly (though there would be plenty of that), but as signs that the One God, the creator of all, was at work in the world and in human lives, even if those lives and that wider world were twisted and flawed through the worship of other gods. Tarsus, as we have said, was full of talk, philosophical talk, speculation, logic, wise and not so wise advice about life, death, the gods, virtue, the way to an untroubled existence. Philosophy wasn't just for a small wealthy class, though there were schools where one could study Plato, Aristotle, and the various writers who had developed the great systems that flowed from their writings. The questions that drove philosophical inquiry were everybody's questions. What made a city "just" or a human "wise" or "virtuous"? What constituted a good argument or an effective speech? What was the world made of and how did it happen? What was the purpose of life, and how could you know? These questions and the various standard answers were just as likely to be voiced at the barber's or in the tavern as in a schoolroom with teachers and serious-minded students.

The default mode in Tarsus, and many other parts of the ancient Mediterranean world, would have been some kind of Stoicism, with its all-embracing vision of a united and divine world order in which humans partake through their inner rationality, or *logos*. The famous alternative, Epicureanism, was a minority, elite option that saw the gods, if they existed at all, as themselves a distant, happy elite who took no interest in human affairs and certainly didn't try to intervene in the world. The puzzled uncertainties of the "Academy," the successors to Plato ("We can't be sure whether the gods exist, but we'd better keep the civil religion going just in case") were giving way, in some newer teaching, to a vision of an upstairs/downstairs world such as the picture sketched by the biographer and philosopher Plutarch in the generation after Paul. For Plutarch, the aim of the game was eventually to leave the wicked realm of space, time, and matter and find the way to a "heaven" from which pure souls have been temporarily exiled and to which they would return in everlasting bliss. (If that sounds like much modern Western Christianity, that is our problem. It certainly wasn't what Paul believed.)

And all that was just the rough outline. There were many more themes and variations on themes, an endless round of discussions in the tentmaker's cramped little shop, on the street, over meals with friends, at home. It was, we may suspect, fascinating and frustrating by turns. Like many other Jews of his day, Saul of Tarsus, thinking as a Jew while taking on board the theories of the wider world, would reflect on the similarity and dissimilarity between the wisdom of the world and the wisdom of Israel.

For Saul, with the vision of Genesis, the Psalms, and Isaiah close to his heart, there would be no question of retreat from the world. If the Stoics had a big integrated vision of a united world, so did he. If the Roman Empire was hoping to create a single society in which everyone would give allegiance to a single Lord, so was he. Paul believed that this had already been accomplished through Israel's Messiah. If the Platonists were speaking of possible commerce between "heaven" and "earth," so was he—though his vision was of heaven coming to earth, not of souls escaping earth and going to heaven. As a Jew, he believed that the whole created order was the work of the One

God; as a "Messiah man," he believed that the crucified and risen
Jesus had dealt with the evil that corrupts the world and the human race and that he had begun the long-awaited project of new
creation, of which the communities of baptized and believing
Jesus-followers were the pilot project.

When he writes, later, that he has learned to "take every
thought prisoner and make it obey the Messiah,"[18] it seems highly
likely that this was a conviction to which he had come in the silent decade in Tarsus. So too when he tells the church in Philippi
to consider carefully "whatever is true, whatever is holy, whatever
is upright, whatever is pure, whatever is attractive, whatever has
a good reputation; anything virtuous, anything praiseworthy,"[19]
he is recognizing that human society, even in the radically flawed
non-Jewish world, could and did aspire to live wisely and well.
All this is part of Saul's monotheism, renewed and deepened by
his belief in Jesus. Saul knew that the world needed redeeming.
He also knew that it remained God's world.

Saul then, I propose, spent the silent years in Tarsus laboring,
studying, and praying, putting together in his mind a larger picture of the One God and his truth that would take on the world
and outflank it. If Jesus was the fulfillment of the ancient scriptural stories, that conclusion was inevitable. But all the while he
must have been uncomfortably aware that this still thoroughly
Jewish vision of the One God and his world, reshaped around the
crucified and risen Messiah, was, to put it mildly, not shared by
all his fellow Jews. Saul must already have come up against the social, cultural, exegetical, and theological tension that would stay
with him throughout his career. What sense could it make that
Israel's Messiah would come to his own and that his own would
not receive him?

We have no idea whether there was already a Jesus community in Tarsus, whether Saul was part of such a thing, or whether
he met regularly with a handful of others to break bread in the

name of Jesus. It is hard to imagine Saul as a solitary Jesus believer through all those years, but history offers no clues one way or another. But we certainly cannot imagine him staying silent. And to speak of the crucified and risen Jesus would inevitably be controversial. It wasn't just that a crucified Messiah was bound to be seen by many Jews as blasphemous nonsense. It wasn't simply that the idea of the One God becoming *human* was a shock to the Jewish system (though some strands of Jewish thinking at the time may perhaps have explored such a possibility). It was, just as much, that the implications of all this for the ancestral way of life were either not clear or all too disturbingly clear. Paul's own question, what it would look like if the One God created a new single family of "brothers and sisters" in the Messiah, had potentially revolutionary answers. And traditional societies do not welcome revolution.

For Saul, this question cannot have been merely theoretical. Here we probe, with caution, into one of the most sensitive parts of the silent decade in Tarsus. He had gone back to his family. All we know of Saul indicates that he would have wasted no time in telling them that he had met the risen Jesus, that the scriptures proved him to be God's Messiah, that the One God had unveiled his age-old secret plan in and through him, and that by the power of his spirit this Jesus was at work in human hearts and lives, doing a new thing and creating a new community. How would his family have reacted?

They might conceivably have wanted to cut him some slack. Many young men or women leave home for a while and come back with new and disturbing ideas. Often they settle down eventually, and their elders smile indulgently at their youthful enthusiasm. But it seems more likely, assuming that young Saul learned his traditional "zeal" at home, that there would have been a fierce reaction. Saul would not have held back; he would not have toned down his message. There would have been no stopping him. Either

Jesus was the Messiah, or he wasn't. And, if he was, then there could be no "take it or leave it." One could not shrug one's shoulders and walk away. If Israel's Messiah has come, then Israel must regroup around him, whatever it takes. Every would-be messianic movement in Israel's history carried that challenge. We imagine arguments, misunderstandings, accusations of disloyalty to the ancestral traditions—even though Saul would be at pains to insist that what had happened in Jesus and what was happening through the spirit was what the ancient scriptures had been talking about all along. ("Maybe so," his father might have replied with a weary sigh, "but Moses never said you could be part of Israel without being circumcised . . .")

Among other strong points that emerge again and again in his mature writing and that must have been hammered out on the anvil of these constant arguments, we find Paul's vision of what Jesus had achieved in his death and resurrection. Every time he refers to these earth-shattering events in his later writings, he draws out different drafts from that deep well of earlier reflection. At the heart of it, rooted in the Passover theme, which Saul had known from boyhood and which Jesus himself had made thematic for his own life and death, we find the idea of *victory*. Something had happened in Jesus's death and resurrection as a result of which the world was a different place. It didn't look different outwardly. Saul, returning to the Tarsus of his boyhood, would have seen the same sights, the same idols and temples, the same standard pagan behavior. But what Saul believed about Jesus meant that the underlying center of spiritual gravity had shifted.

The world he had known was full of dark powers. Or, to be more precise, the created order was good, as Genesis had said, but humans had worshipped nongods, pseudogods, "forces" within the natural order, and had thereby handed over to those shadowy beings a power not rightfully theirs. The "forces" had usurped the proper human authority over the world. Evidence was all around.

Tarsus, like every ancient non-Jewish city, was full of shrines, full of strange worship, full of human lives misshapen by dehumanizing practices. *And Paul believed that on the cross Jesus of Nazareth had defeated the ultimate force of evil.* The resurrection proved it. If he had overcome death, it could only be because he had overcome the forces that lead to death, the corrosive power of idolatry and human wickedness.

This is a dark theme to which we shall return. We mention it here partly because Paul must have thought through these questions in this early period and also partly because it is at the root of his understanding of what with hindsight we call his Gentile mission. Here's how it works.

Paul believed that, through Jesus and his death, the One God had overcome the powers that had held the world in their grip. *And that meant that all humans, not just Jews, could be set free to worship the One God.* The Jesus-shaped message of liberation included forgiveness for all past misdeeds, and this message of forgiveness meant that there could be no barriers between Jewish Messiah people and non-Jewish Messiah people. To erect such barriers would mean denying that Jesus had won the messianic victory. Saul the zealot had expected a Messiah to defeat the pagan hordes. Paul the Apostle believed that the Messiah *had* defeated the dark powers that stood behind all evil. This translated directly into one of the great themes of his mature thought and particularly his pastoral efforts: the unity of all Messiah people across ethnic boundary lines. And this is one of the things that Saul's own family must have found impossible to swallow.

Here, I believe, we have the root of the ongoing grief in the heart of the mature Paul as he looks at "his flesh-and-blood relatives."[20] The people over whom he is agonizing (with "great sorrow and endless pain in my heart") are not a generalized mass of "unbelieving Jews." Paul knows their names. He sees their faces and their sorrowful head-shaking. His mother. His father. He hears their voices in his inner ear, praying the *Shema* as they had taught him to pray it, unable to comprehend that their super-bright, utterly devout son—brother—nephew—had turned away to such horrible heresy. And yet they loved him all the same, since Saul always wore his heart on his sleeve, and they knew when he was in distress as well. Love and grief are very close, especially in warm, passionate hearts. Saul shrank from neither. He wrote constantly of love—divine love, human love, "the Messiah's love." And he constantly suffered the grief that went with it.

When we speak of love, and perhaps also grief, there is another silence hidden within the larger silence of the Tarsus years. Everyone who reads Paul asks this question sooner or later. Was there a girl? Had he been betrothed or even married?

We cannot tell and must not rush to fill the silence. Yet when Paul writes about marriage he says that he would be happy "to see everyone be in the same situation as myself."[21] He amplifies this, assuming his audience knows his story and thus leaving it tantalizingly unclear for later readers: "To unmarried people, and to widows, I have this to say: it's perfectly all right for you to remain like me."[22] Why did he put it like this?

He was writing at a time when remaining unmarried—particularly for *women*—was next to scandalous. Who could tell what an unattached person might get into? The dominant cultural assumption was that an unmarried adult, particularly a woman, was a social and moral disaster waiting to happen. But Paul, as we shall see, was challenging the dominant culture with the news of new creation, a new creation with different values. On the one hand, he insists (against any form of dualism that would regard the human body and its pleasures as shameful) that married sexual relations were a good gift from the Creator, to be celebrated. On the other hand, he insists that singleness, celibacy, was also a gift that pointed beyond the present world (with its need to propagate the species) to a new world altogether. And in the middle of it all Paul holds himself up as an example: "the same situation as myself." What was that situation?

Clearly Paul was unmarried during the time covered by his letters. Most of the traveling early Christian teachers were married, and their wives accompanied them on their journeys, but Paul was different (so also, apparently, was Barnabas).[23] That leaves us with four options. Either he had never married at all, despite the fact that most orthodox Jews would have been expected to marry, usually quite young. Or he had been married, presumably during the silent decade in Tarsus, but his wife had died early, as many did, and he had chosen not to marry again. Or maybe his wife had decided to break off the marriage when she realized he really meant all this dangerous new teaching about a crucified Messiah. ("In a case like that," he writes, "a brother or sister is not bound.")[24] Or perhaps—and if I had to guess, this is the one I would choose—he had been betrothed early on, probably to the daughter of family friends. He had come back to Tarsus eager to see her again, but also wondering how it would now work out and praying for her to come to know Jesus as he had. But she or her parents had broken off the engagement when they found out that lively young Saul had returned with his head and heart full of horrible nonsense about the crucified Nazarene. Did Saul "get over her," as we say? Who can tell?

He had plenty of female friends and colleagues later on, as we can see from the greetings in his letters, especially Romans. He seems to have treated them as equals in the work of the gospel, just as he insisted in a famous passage that gender distinctions were irrelevant when it came to membership in the Messiah's family.[25] But he had decided that, for him, marriage was now out of the question, not because he was a super spiritual man who had risen above that kind of shabby second-rate lifestyle (as some later Christians would try to pretend) or because he did not possess normal human desires, but because it was incompatible with his particular vocation. He gives the impression, as we read between the lines of 1 Corinthians, that he had gained mastery over his natural desires, while recognizing that such a discipline required constant vigilance.[26]

Why go into this imponderable question? It is important before we launch into Paul's public career, which we are nearly ready to do, to challenge the perennial idea that Paul was a misogynist. He did not imagine that women and men were identical in all respects. Nobody in the ancient world, and not many in today's world, would think that. But he saw women as fellow members on an equal footing within the people of God, and also, it seems, within the public ministry of that people. He could be friends with women and work alongside them without patronizing them, trying to seduce them, or exploiting them.

For Saul back home in Tarsus, then, the deepest heartbreak was not the loss of an actual or potential spouse, though that may have been there too. What grieved him most was the loss, in a much deeper sense, of many who were very close to him, who had known him from boyhood and still loved him dearly. If he was not a misogynist, neither was he the kind of Jew who (in the odd caricature) hated other Jews because they reminded him of himself. When Paul the Apostle thinks of "unbelieving Jews," they are not, for him, a "theological" category. They are real human beings. One does not suffer ceaseless heartache over a faceless abstraction or a projected fantasy.

The decade or so in Tarsus was clearly formative for Saul. How much he then guessed at his future vocation we cannot begin to imagine. But somewhere in the middle 40s of the first century— still only fifteen years or so after the crucifixion and resurrection of Jesus and when Saul was probably somewhere in his thirties—he received a visit that would take his life in a whole new direction. What motivated him was, at one level, the same as it had always been: utter devotion to the One God and "zeal" to work for his glory in the world. But by the end of the Tarsus decade Saul had worked out in considerable detail what it meant that the One God had revealed himself in and as the crucified and risen Jesus. That meant a new dimension to his devotion, a new shape for his "zeal," a new depth to "loyalty." And that new dimension, shape, and depth would produce a string of hastily written documents whose compact, explosive charge would change the world.

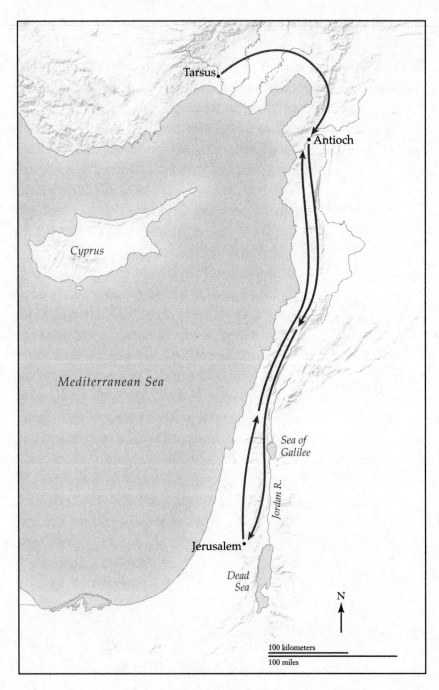

Tarsus to Antioch

4

Antioch

T HE VISITOR WHO came to Tarsus looking for Saul was Barnabas. It was Barnabas, we recall, who had vouched for Saul on his first post-Damascus visit to Jerusalem. One of the minor heroes of the book of Acts, the generous-spirited Barnabas was originally from Cyprus, a Jew from the tribe of Levi. His actual name was Joseph, but Luke explains that the Jesus-followers in Jerusalem gave him the nickname Barnabas, which means "son of encouragement." Some people have the gift of enabling others to flourish. Barnabas was one of those.

So when the Jerusalem leaders received disturbing news about fresh developments in the Jesus community at Antioch and they wanted to send somebody who would understand both the outlook of Greek-speaking communities and the concerns of the Jerusalem church itself, Barnabas was a natural choice. In Antioch a wall had been breached. A crack had appeared in an age-old dam. Should it be mended at once? Or was this a sign that the One God was doing a new thing? To see why all this mattered, and why this question in Antioch shaped the way Saul would see things thereafter—and hence one of the reasons why the movement that came into being through his work became so extraordinarily successful—we need to take another step back. We need to understand the inner dynamic of Jewish life within its wider cultural setting.

The wall in question, the wall that had been breached, was the division between the Jew and the non-Jew. This division, from the Jewish point of view, was greater than any other social or cultural division, more important even than the other two distinctions that ran through the whole ancient world, those between slave and free, on the one hand, and male and female, on the other. As we noted earlier, the question of how high the wall between Jew and non-Jew should be and of what sort of dealings Jews ought to have with those on the other side was controversial then, just as it is today. Different people, and indeed different Jewish community leaders, would draw the line at different places. Business dealings might be fine, business partnerships perhaps not. Friendships might be fine, intermarriage probably not. Lines would be blurred, broken, and then drawn again, sometimes in the same place, sometimes not.

Underneath it all, however, there was always a sense of difference, of "them" and "us." Social and cultural indicators would be the visible markers. What you ate (and what you didn't eat), who you ate it with (and who you didn't eat it with)—those would be the most obvious, but there were others too. Non-Jewish writers of the time sneered at the Jews for their "Sabbath," claiming Jews just wanted a "lazy day" once a week. The fact that Jews didn't eat pork, the meat most ordinarily available, looked like a ploy to appear socially superior. Jewish males were circumcised, so if they participated in athletic training in the gymnasium, which normally meant going naked, they might expect ribald comments.

Beneath these social indicators was the more deep-seated non-Jewish suspicion that the Jews were atheists. After all, they didn't worship the gods. They didn't turn out for the great festivals, they didn't come to the parties at the temples, and they didn't offer animal sacrifices at local shrines. They claimed there was only one true Temple, the one in Jerusalem, but rumors abounded, going back to the time when the Roman general Pompey had marched into the Holy of Holies, that *the Jews had no image, no statue of their god.* Hence the charge of atheism. And the problem with atheism wasn't so much theological beliefs. People believed all kinds of strange things, and the authorities let them get on with it. No, the problem was severely practical. The gods mattered for the life and health of the community. If bad things happened, the obvious reason was that the gods were angry, probably because people hadn't been taking them seriously and offering the required worship. People who didn't believe in the gods were therefore placing the city, the whole culture, or the whole world at risk.

The Jews had their answers for all this, not that many non-Jews even tried to understand them. Saul of Tarsus would have grown up knowing these debates well, and during his time in Tarsus and after his move to Antioch he must have heard them repeated with wearying familiarity. Our God, the Jews would have said, is the One God who made the whole world. He cannot be represented by a human-made image. We will demonstrate who he is by the way we live. If we join the world around in worshipping the local divinities—let alone in worshipping the Roman emperor (as people were starting to do when Saul was growing up)—we will be making the mistake our ancestors made. (Actually, a significant minority of non-Jews admired the Jews for all this, preferring their clear, clean lines of belief and behavior to the dark muddles of paganism. Many attached themselves to the synagogue communities as "God-fearers." Some went all the way to full conversion as "proselytes.") But the Jews were clear about the fact that, if they compromised with the pagan world around them, however "compromise" might have been defined in any particular city or household, they would be giving up their heritage—and their hope.

The heritage mattered, but the hope was all-important—hope for a new world, for the One God to become king at last. On a good day, many Jews would think of the One God bringing peace and justice to the whole world. On a bad day, some might think of the One God finally giving the Gentiles what they deserved, rescuing and vindicating his ancient people Israel in the process. So what would Jewish people, particularly in a diaspora community like Antioch or Tarsus, think of the suggestion that the One God had done what he promised *by sending a crucified Messiah*? What would this mean for Jewish identity? Was this good news simply for Jewish people, or might it be for everyone?

Syrian Antioch, even more than Tarsus, was exactly the kind of place where this question would come quickly to the fore. (We call it Syrian Antioch to distinguish it from other cities with the same name, such as Pisidian Antioch in southern Turkey, where Paul would later preach. They all go back to their founding by Antiochus Epiphanes in the early second century BC, just as the many ancient cities called Alexandria look back to Alexander the Great in the late fourth century.) This Antioch stood on the river Orontes, about 250 miles north of Jerusalem, in the northeastern corner of the Mediterranean. It was a major crossroads and trading center not far from the coast, poised between east and west, north and south, much like Venice in the high Middle Ages.

It boasted a busy, bustling mixture of cultures, ethnic groups, and religious traditions, including a substantial Jewish population. The Roman general Pompey had made Antioch the capital of the new province of Syria, and Julius Caesar had raised it to the level of an autonomous city. With a population of around a quarter of a million, it was widely regarded in antiquity as the third or fourth city of the East, after Alexandria and Seleucia and later Constantinople. It was a classic melting pot. Every kind of social and cultural group was represented. It isn't difficult to imagine the crowded streets, the markets selling exotic fruit as well as local produce, the traders and travelers, foreigners with strange costumes and donkeys needing food and water, the temples on every corner. It wasn't surprising that some of the early Jesus-followers found their way there. Everybody else had, after all.

Nor was it surprising that, once there, the Jesus-followers were eager to share the news of Jesus with non-Jews as well as Jews. They believed that God's Messiah had launched God's kingdom and that the new energy they discovered in announcing this message was the work of God's own spirit, poured out in a new way, ready to embrace the wider world. If the scriptures had seen the coming king as Lord of the whole world, how could membership in this kingdom be for Jews only?

Some of the believers who had come to Antioch from Cyprus and Cyrene saw no reason for any such limitation. They went about telling the non-Jews too about Jesus. A large number of such people believed the message, abandoned their pagan ways, and switched allegiance to Jesus as Lord. One can imagine the reaction to this in the Jewish community; many Jews would naturally have supposed that these Gentiles would then have to go all the way and become full Jews. If they were sharing in the ancient promises, ought they not to share in the ancient culture as well? What sort of a common life ought this new community to develop? These were the questions that buzzed around Paul's head, like large worried bees, for much of his public career.

These were, in fact, massive and fateful questions for the entire new movement. Antioch was where they came to a head. Barnabas and Saul were at the center of them. Their friendship, which went from firm to fluctuating to tragic, helped to shape Saul's mind and teaching.

It all began, then, when the Jerusalem leaders sent Barnabas to Antioch to see what was going on. Good-hearted Barnabas was not the sort to jump instinctively to a negative reaction, to reach for familiar prejudices just because something new was happening. He could see in the transformed lives and transparent faith of the Gentile believers that this was indeed the work of divine grace, reaching out in generous love to people of every background and origin. Barnabas shared Paul's view that with the death and resurrection of Jesus the barriers to Gentile inclusion had gone. Now, the evidence of changed lives, of a new dynamic in worship, and above all of love (remembering that for the early Christians "love" meant a shared family life with obligations of mutual support) told its own story, and Barnabas was not going to deny it. He recognized the work of God when he saw it, and he was glad.

Others from Jerusalem, faced with the same evidence, might have reached a different conclusion. We will meet them soon enough, urging the Jesus believers in Antioch to restrict themselves to their own ethnic groups, at least for mealtimes and perhaps even for the Lord's meal, the "breaking of bread." Many Jews would have assumed that Gentiles still carried a contagious pollution from their culture of idolatry and immorality. But that wasn't how Barnabas saw it. As far as he was concerned, what mattered was the believing allegiance of these Gentiles; they were staying loyal to the Lord from the bottom of their hearts. This new community was not, then, defined by genealogy. It was defined by the Lord himself, and what counted as the sure sign of belonging to this Lord was "loyalty," "faithfulness."

Here we run into the kind of problem that meets all serious readers of Paul. One obvious Greek term for "loyalty" is one of Paul's favorite words, *pistis,* regularly translated "faith," but often carrying the overtones of "faithfulness," "reliability," and, yes, "loyalty." The word *pistis* could mean "faith" in the sense of "belief"—*what was believed* as well as *the fact of believing,* or indeed *the act of believing,* which already seems quite enough meaning for one small word. But *pistis* could also point to the personal commitment that accompanies any genuine belief, in this case that Jesus was now "Lord," the world's rightful sovereign. Hence the term means "loyalty" or "allegiance." This was what Caesar demanded from his subjects.

For Paul, the word meant all of that but also much more. For him, this "believing allegiance" was neither simply a "religious" stance nor a "political" one. It was altogether larger, in a way that our language, like Paul's, has difficulty expressing clearly. For him, this *pistis,* this heartfelt trust in and allegiance to the God revealed in Jesus, was the vital marker, the thing that showed whether someone was really part of this new community or not. That was already the position that Barnabas was taking. He saw a single community living a common life. Saying that he recognized this as the result of divine grace is not simply the kind of pious fantasy some might imagine, since in the ancient Near East the idea of a single community *across the traditional boundaries of culture, gender, and ethnic and social groupings* was unheard of. Unthinkable, in fact. But there it was. A new kind of "family" had come into existence. Its focus of identity was Jesus; its manner of life was shaped by Jesus; its characteristic mark was believing allegiance to Jesus. Barnabas saw it, and he was glad.

To say that this new project, this new community, was going to present a challenge is a gross understatement. The vibrant and excited group of Jesus-followers in Antioch was doing something radically countercultural. Nobody else in the ancient world was trying to live in a house where the old walls were being taken down. Nobody else was experimenting with a whole new way of being human. Barnabas must have realized this and must have seen that, in order even to begin to sustain such a thing, granted the enormous pressures that we might call sociocultural but that resonated also with philosophy, politics, religion, and theology, one would have to help people *to think through what it all really meant.* And that would mean teaching.

It would mean, in fact, the launching of a project (though they couldn't have foreseen this at the time) that with long hindsight we might call "Christian theology." If a community like the one in Antioch was to keep its balance as a group of Jesus-followers in that world of clashing cultures, its members would need to grasp two things. On the one hand, they would have to put down roots firmly into the Jewish traditions, into the scriptures. On the other hand, they would have to think through what precisely it meant that Israel's Messiah, the fulfillment of those same scriptures, had been crucified and raised from the dead. Only by going deeply into the scriptural story of Israel and the events concerning Jesus, reflecting from many different angles on its full significance, could such a community keep its identity, its integrity, and its nerve. Who did Barnabas know who had that kind of knowledge and the eager energy and the way with words that would communicate it? There was one obvious candidate.

It was a decade or so since Saul had gone to Tarsus, after his brief time in Damascus and then Jerusalem. We cannot tell whether anyone in Jerusalem or Antioch had seen or heard of him during that time. But Barnabas hadn't forgotten him. He had a strong sense that Saul was the man for the job. This was the beginning of a partnership that would launch the first recorded official "mission" of the new movement—and that would also, within a few years, reflect the inner tensions within that movement still awaiting resolution. Barnabas and Saul would sing from the same sheet . . . until someone tried to add a new verse to the song.

So Saul came to Antioch. Once again he was leaving home; this time, we assume, with the mixed feelings he would later describe as "great sorrow and endless pain."[1] He worked with Barnabas and the local Antioch leaders for a whole year, teaching and guiding the new and growing community. They did their best to shape the new believers and their common life in accordance with scriptural roots and the "good news" events concerning Jesus. Much as we might like to be a fly on the wall in those early days, all we can be sure of is that the ways of reading scripture and interpreting the Jesus events that we find already fully grown in Paul's mature letters were taking shape, not just in his head and his heart, but in the life of the community. Paul, the greatest theoretician of the new movement, was never *merely* a theoretician. Pretty much every idea he later articulated had been road-tested in the narrow, crowded streets of Antioch.

Luke claims that it was in Antioch, in this period, that the fol-

lowers of Jesus were first called *Christianoi,* "Messiah people."[2]
That claim has been challenged by those who rightly point out
that our word "Christian" implies an organized movement separate from the Jewish world and that there is no evidence of such
a thing for at least a generation or so. The only other places in
the New Testament where the word is used are on the lips of
Herod Agrippa, who teases Paul for "trying to make him a Christian," and in an early letter where Peter refers to people "suffering as Christians."[3] Both of these look as if the word was a
nickname used by outsiders, quite likely in contempt ("Messiah
freaks!"), rather than a word the Jesus-followers used for themselves. But that, anyway, isn't the point. In the Antioch of the
40s you might mistake the word *Christos* for a personal name.
The Jesus-followers, the Messiah people, were, so to say, getting
a name for themselves, and there is no reason why they shouldn't
have acquired a literal name at the same time. The most natural
choice would have been *Christianoi,* Messiah people, a word that,
like the community itself, like Saul of Tarsus himself, had deep
Jewish roots but a strange new reach and power.

That odd sense of a new kind of life, as in all the very early Jesus
communities, was heavily dependent (they would have said) on
the powerful presence and guidance of the holy spirit. Whatever
account we want to give of this phenomenon today, we cannot
begin to understand Saul, Barnabas, and their colleagues without
recognizing that as they prayed, sang, studied scripture, organized
their community life, and (not least) went about talking to both
Jews and non-Jews about Jesus, they were conscious of an energy
and a sense of direction unlike anything they had known before.
They had no hesitation in ascribing that energy and leading to
the divine spirit, which had been promised in the scriptures and
then again, only a few years before, by Jesus's own forerunner,
John the Baptist. These early Jesus-followers were not naive "en-
thusiasts." Already within the first decades it became necessary to
challenge some claims about the work of the spirit and to warn

against the likelihood of deceit, and indeed of self-deceit. But we cannot understand the things that now happened unless we allow that Saul and the others really did believe they were being led and energized by the personal presence of the One God.

It was out of such leading that Barnabas and Saul found themselves being commissioned for their first joint project. One of the spirit-led "prophets" in Antioch, a man named Agabus, warned the community that there was a famine coming over the whole Mediterranean world. (Various pieces of evidence point to the occurrence of this in AD 46.) The reaction to this news tells us a lot about the way the community instinctively thought. We might have imagined that a warning like this would have resulted in knee-jerk inward-looking anxiety. Should they stockpile food? Should they do what Joseph did in Egypt, storing grain in the good years to last through the bad? The Jesus-followers in Antioch resolved at once not to do that. Instead, they would look out for those community members worse off than themselves. And that meant Jerusalem. Jerusalem was where Jesus's first followers had sold their lands and pooled their resources and where now, after a decade or two of hostility from the authorities and probably their own wider communities, they were struggling to stay alive.

The Antioch-based Jesus-followers knew what they had to do. They had never supposed themselves to be independent of the Jerusalem Jesus-followers. Those of us who are used to multinational organizations, including "churches," may need to consider just how unusual the next step was at the time. Just as Antioch was the first place where we see a genuine effort at a new kind of transethnic community life, so in this action Antioch was the first place to demonstrate that the followers of Jesus thought of themselves as a translocal community with mutual responsibilities. The only possible parallels are the network of synagogue communities (but they were not transethnic) and the Roman army and civil service (but they all, though incorporating non-Romans, bore the stamp of Caesar). What might it mean, farther on down the track, to belong to a new kind of worldwide community? That too was to prove a huge question, to which Saul of Tarsus would make a characteristically innovative response. And this, once more, points ahead to the remarkable long-term results of Saul's project.

So Barnabas and Saul were sent from Antioch to Jerusalem with a gift of money for the Jerusalem believers. The date was probably AD 46 or 47. Despite other traditional ways of putting the historical jigsaw together, I assume that this is the same visit that Saul, writing later as Paul, describes in Galatians 2:1–10. It makes sense. He went to Jerusalem, he says, "by revelation," presumably referring to the prophetic warning of Agabus. His own account of the visit ends with the Jerusalem leaders urging him to go on "remembering the poor."[4] That admonition certainly applies more widely. Right from the start, the Jesus-followers believed they had a special obligation toward "the poor" in general. But it was also focused on the Jerusalem community in particular.

When Paul himself describes the visit, however, he takes the financial purpose almost for granted and focuses on what else had happened while he was there. He had now been working in Antioch for a year, in addition to whatever public work he may or may not have done in Tarsus. During that time he had been energetically speaking about Jesus to non-Jews as well as Jews and encouraging the community, Jew and non-Jew alike, to live as a single family. What would the Jerusalem leaders think of this brave new experiment? And if they didn't like the look of it, what would that mean? Had Paul been wasting his time?

This possibility seems to have haunted him at various stages of his work; he worried that he might have been wasting his time, running the race "to no good effect."[5] This is an allusion to Isaiah 49; in v. 4 of that chapter, the "servant," the one tasked with bringing God's light to the nations, wonders if perhaps he has "labored in vain" or "spent his strength for nothing and vanity."

The fact that Paul expresses this particular anxiety in this scriptural language means, of course, that he knows in theory what the answer ought to be. But he says it anyway, here in reference to the trip to Jerusalem, then again in his anxiety over the Thessalonians while waiting in Athens, and again in writing from Ephesus to the Philippians.[6] He keeps on coming back to it, like the tip of the tongue finding its way to a sore tooth. Perhaps it's all been for nothing? But then, following the prophetic train of thought, he might reason that because the "servant" voiced the sentiment, perhaps the feeling was part of the task. But still he couldn't help wondering . . .

This fits as well with the remarkable moment in the first letter to Corinth when Paul reveals one of the sources of his self-discipline. One of the best-known things about Paul's thought is his view that when a person has come to faith in Jesus as the risen Lord, that event is itself a sign of the spirit's work through the gospel, and that, if the spirit has begun that "good work" of which that faith is the first fruit, you can trust that the spirit will finish the job. That is what he says in Philippians 1:6, and it coheres with his larger teaching elsewhere, particularly in Romans 5–8. But Paul knows that this does not occur when disciples sit back, relax, and allow the spirit to do it all, with no human effort involved. On the contrary. Think of athletics, he says; those who go into training have to exercise great self-discipline. This applies to him too:

> I don't run in an aimless fashion! I don't box like someone punching the air! No: I give my body rough treatment, and make it my slave, in case, after announcing the message to others, I myself should end up being disqualified.[7]

Has he, then, been "running in vain"? He lives with the nagging question. At one level, he knows the answer perfectly well.

The truth about Jesus, the power of God at work in the gospel announcement, the presence of the spirit, the witness of scripture—all these point in the same direction. But at another level, Paul has to go on asking the question. And he has to go on making his body a disciplined, obedient slave.

This to-and-fro between natural anxiety and scripturally sourced encouragement is made more complex by the human dynamics of the visit to Jerusalem, raising as they do an issue with which Paul would struggle in the years to come. "Here is the money. Now, by the way, are you happy with our present policy?" Paul would have been the first to say that just because you give generously to others does not mean you are compelling them to agree with your policies or practices. But underneath that question there lies a deeper one. This gift of money, he would be implying, demonstrates that they are part of one family, one partnership, one *koinōnia*. That Greek word is often translated "fellowship," but in Paul's world it also meant, among other things, a business partnership, which would often overlap with family ties. Paul would be asking them, at least by implication, to realize that this *koinōnia* is what it is because in Jesus the One God has done a new thing. He would be asking them to recognize that through Jesus the One God has created a new sort of family, a community that leaps across the walls our traditions have so carefully maintained, as it has now spanned the miles between Antioch and Jerusalem.

This question, posed implicitly when Barnabas and Saul went to Jerusalem, had one particular focal point. They had not gone alone. They had taken with them a young man, a non-Jew who had become an eager and much-loved follower of Jesus, a member of the fellowship in Antioch. His name was Titus. Did Barnabas and Saul realize that Titus was likely to become a test case? Did they realize they might be putting him in a difficult position?

That, anyway, is how it turned out. The main leaders in Jerusalem, according to Paul, were happy with the line Antioch had been taking. Non-Jewish believers were full members of the family. But some other Jesus-followers in Jerusalem were not content. They realized that Titus was a Greek, a non-Jew. He had not been circumcised; he was not therefore a "proselyte," a non-Jew who had fully converted (there were debates at the time as to whether even circumcision made someone a real Jew, but for most it would have been sufficient). They realized that Barnabas and Saul were insisting that Titus be treated on equal terms as a full member of the family, including sharing in the common meals. This group was horrified. "This is precisely the kind of pollution," they said, "that the One God wants us to avoid! Fraternizing with pagans is what landed our ancestors in trouble! If the One God who has raised Jesus is going to fulfill his promises and establish his kingdom on earth as in heaven, setting us free from all enemies and earthly ills, he certainly won't be doing so if we compromise on purity! Either we stay with two tables, one for Jewish Jesus-followers and one for Gentiles, or *Titus will have to be circumcised.* He will have to become a full Jew if you want him to be recognized as a full member of the Jesus family."

Barnabas and Saul stood firm. The problem was not so much the embarrassment and physical pain that circumcision would cause Titus. It was a point of theological principle. It was, so Paul declared later, a matter of "freedom"—a loaded word, a Passover word, the slogan for so much that Jews such as Saul had hoped and prayed for. But now, with the new "Passover" of Jesus's death and resurrection, a new sort of "freedom" had been born. The freedom for all, *Jew and Gentile alike,* to share membership in the new world, the new family, the new messianic and spirit-led life. And if that was the new "freedom," then anything that challenged it was a form of slavery. *These people want to enslave us,* Saul concluded. They want to reverse the Passover moment, to take us back to Egypt. Titus was spared.

The three central Jerusalem leaders, James (the brother of Jesus), Peter, and John, were content. Their view carried weight;

they were known as the "pillars." For us, that might be a dead metaphor. For them, in Jerusalem with the Temple still standing, it was making a polemical claim. The early Jesus-followers, it seems, already understood themselves as an alternative Temple with these three as its "pillars": a new heaven-and-earth society, living and worshipping right alongside the old Temple, making the latter redundant. What Stephen had said was coming true.

That makes it all the more remarkable that James, Peter, and John were able to agree with Barnabas and Saul. Temple meant purity; and purity (for a loyal Jew) would normally have meant extreme care over contact with non-Jews. What Barnabas and Saul had glimpsed, and what (according to Acts) Peter himself had already glimpsed in the house of the non-Jew Cornelius, was a new kind of purity coming to birth. A new freedom. A new Temple. A new *kind* of purity. No wonder confusion abounded, especially among those who were the most eager for God's coming act of deliverance. No wonder some loyal Jews resented Barnabas and Saul for pushing the point so insensitively—and no wonder that the two friends held their ground.

How much Saul had argued his case from scripture at this point we cannot tell. But the "pillars" shook hands with him on it. They struck a deal whose apparently simple terms (as quoted by Paul in Galatians) become more complicated the more we think about them. James, Peter, and John would work with Jewish people, while Saul and his friends would work with non-Jewish people. Put like that, it sounds easy, but it doesn't fit the facts. It may be that the original intention was more geographical than ethnic: the "pillars" would restrict their proclamation of the Messiah to the ancient territory of Israel, while Saul would roam the world. But this hardly fits with Peter's later journeys, whether to Corinth or ultimately to Rome. Equally, an ethnic division, with Saul carefully avoiding any work with Jewish people in the Diaspora, makes no sense either, granted that in Acts he almost always begins in the synagogues, that in 1 Corinthians he speaks of becoming "like a Jew to the Jews, to win Jews,"[8] and that in the decisive opening statement of Romans he says that the gospel is "to the Jew first, and also, equally, to the Greek."[9]

It looks as though the agreement Paul reports in Galatians 2 was a temporary arrangement, a way of mollifying the Jerusalem hard-liners, trying to reassure them that Jewish followers of Jesus, at least, would not have to compromise their own purity, would be able to carry on without straining their consciences. The whole episode, with its swirling theological, personal, and inevitably also political currents, alerts us to the overlapping complexities and challenges that the young movement was facing. Granted Saul's unrivaled knowledge of the scriptures, we may assume that it alerted him too to the need to understand and to articulate powerfully just what it meant that those scriptures had been fulfilled in the crucified Messiah.

Barnabas and Saul returned to Antioch, their mission complete. We assume that Titus went back with them. They had another young colleague in tow as well, John Mark, a youthful relative of Barnabas and also of Peter. If the two friends were pleased with the way things had gone, that was entirely natural. They had worked well as a team. That would stand them in good stead in the surprising new challenge they would now face.

PART TWO

Herald of the King

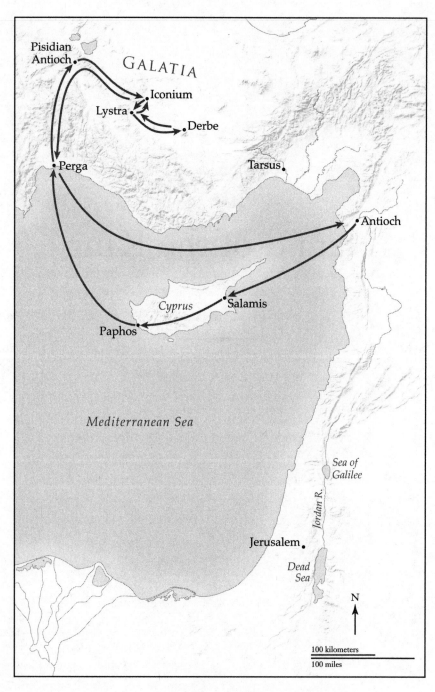

To and from Galatia

5

Cyprus and Galatia

MOST PRINTED BIBLES contain maps, and among the maps there is usually a chart of Paul's journeys. I began to enjoy maps and map reading almost as soon as I could read, and when a schoolteacher gave us an assignment to learn about Paul's various travels, I took to it like a duck to water. It fitted naturally with the classical studies I was already starting to pursue. I had no idea then that some of the lines I so easily traced were controversial, particularly those relating to North and South Galatia. What interested me was the restless, almost relentless way Paul seemed always to be on the move, crossing mountain ranges, fording rivers, staying in exotic places like Ephesus or Corinth, making good use of the remarkable networks of Roman roads and the almost equally remarkable opportunities for sailing across and around the Mediterranean and the Aegean. I had not at that time visited any of the places where Paul had gone. But a good atlas and a few books with photographs of the main cities and other highlights like mountain passes brought it all to life.

It never occurred to me at that stage to ask what exactly Paul thought he was doing, or why. Why did he go in the first place? Why did he go to *those* places rather than anywhere else? Why (according to Acts at least) did he usually begin by speaking in a synagogue? If I had thought about it, I would probably have said simply that he believed God wanted him to tell people about Jesus and that one had to start somewhere. (That is no doubt true enough at one level, but quite unsatisfactory.) A little later on someone pointed out to me that Paul tended to concentrate on major population centers, relying on the movement of people and trade in and out of the great cities to help spread the word. That too is fair enough, but it still leaves some of the fundamental questions unaddressed. Here, as we watch him launch the career of a traveling missionary for which he is famous and that provides the context for his equally famous letters, we arrive once more at our basic questions. What made him tick? And why did it work?

His practice of beginning in synagogues—where he usually met anger and hostility once people realized what he was talking about—poses our other main question in a new form too. The puzzle of what happened on the Damascus Road isn't just a puzzle about one transformative moment in Paul's early experience. It colors, and in turn is colored by, the thorny issue of the relationship between the message Paul announced and the traditions of Israel—and how those traditions were perceived and lived out in the wider non-Jewish world of ancient Turkey and Greece. Was Paul really a loyal member of God's ancient people? Was he rebuilding the house or pulling it down about his own ears? This question would quickly become the source of serious tension not only between Paul and local Jewish groups, but between Paul and some of the other Jesus-followers.

At one level the answers are obvious. Paul went on a mission to tell people about Jesus; he believed that Jesus was Israel's Messiah, the fulfillment of the scriptures, that he had been crucified, raised from the dead, and exalted to God's right hand. Yes, but this fails to address the underlying questions. As I said earlier, I assumed for many years, and many readers will still assume, that the only real point of it all was to get people to "believe" in this Jesus so that they would be "saved" and "go to heaven when they died." But this was not the concern that drove Paul and Barnabas. I have labored this point elsewhere, but it still needs saying as we watch Paul set off on his complex crisscrossing travels.

The early Christians did not focus much attention on the question of what happened to people immediately after they died. If that question came up, their answer might be that they would be "with the Messiah"[1] or, as in Jesus's remark to the dying brigand, that they might be "with him in paradise."[2] But they seldom spoke about it at all. They were much more concerned with the "kingdom of God," which was something that was happening and would ultimately happen completely, "on earth as in heaven." What mattered was the ultimate restoration of the whole of creation, with God's people being raised from the dead to take their place in the running of this new world. Whatever happened to people immediately after death was, by comparison, unimportant, a mere interim. And however much it might seem incredible, the early Jesus-followers really did believe that God's kingdom was not simply a future reality, though obviously it had a strong still-future dimension. God's kingdom had already been launched through the events of Jesus's life. Unless we get this firmly in our heads, we will never understand the inner dynamic of Paul's mission.

This is closely connected with the idea that Jesus was Israel's Messiah. A glance at Jewish history in this period will reveal that if someone were to claim that the Messiah had arrived, this would not be merely what we would call a "religious" claim. It would mean that the One God was acting at last to fulfill his ancient promises, and the mode of that action would be to set up a new regime, a new authoritative rule. When Rabbi Akiba declared in AD 132 that Simeon ben Kosiba was God's Messiah, this meant that Simeon was now the ruler of a small Judaean state in rebellion against Rome. (That "kingdom" lasted for three years before the final disaster, but it shows how the logic works.) If someone went about the communities of diaspora Jews declaring that God had at last sent Israel's Messiah, this would not have seemed at the time to be a message either about "religion" (the Messiah was never supposed to start a new "religion"!) or about "life after death" (devout Jews had long believed that God would take care of them hereafter). Nor would it involve a new philosophy. It would be what we would call "political," though as always for the Jews of the day this would also be profoundly theological. It would be perceived as the announcement of a new state of affairs, a new community owing allegiance to a new Master, the unveiling, at last, of the covenant faithfulness of the One God. That is exactly what Paul intended.

Paul's message was, of course, new in another way as well. It was not simply the replacement of one political power with another (Jesus rather than Caesar). Indeed, Paul's vision of the kingdom both was and wasn't what people often mean today by "political." If by "political" you mean the establishment of a rule of law backed up by police and/or military sanctions—as in an ordinary state today—then clearly what Paul was announcing was not that kind of thing at all. If by "political" you mean a system whereby one person or group imposes its will on others across a geographical area, raising taxes and organizing society at large in a particular way, then obviously nothing in Paul's career points in that direction. But if you use the word "political" to refer to a new state of affairs in which people give their ultimate and wholehearted allegiance to someone other than the ordinary local ruler or someone other than Caesar on the throne in Rome—and if you call "political" the establishment of cells of people loyal to this new ruler, celebrating his rescuing rule and living in new kinds of communities as a result—then what Paul was doing was inescapably "political." It had to do with the foundation of a new *polis,* a new city or community, right at the heart of the existing system. Paul's "missionary" journeys were not simply aimed at telling people about Jesus in order to generate inner personal transformation and a new sense of ultimate hope, though both of

these mattered vitally as well. They were aimed at the establishment of a new kind of kingdom on earth as in heaven. A kingdom
with Jesus as king. The kingdom—Paul was quite emphatic about
this—that Israel's God had always intended to set up.

Humanly speaking, this was of course a fragile project. It was
bound to be, since its character was taken from its starting point,
the Messiah's shameful death. As Paul would later insist, the way
in which the kingdom was put into effect was always going to
be the same: through the suffering of its members, particularly
its leaders. Paul's journeys in Acts are full of troubles, persecu-
tions, beatings, stonings, and the like. But this only highlights
what for Paul lay at the core of the whole thing. Why now? If the
world was so hostile, why not wait for a better opportunity? Why
should this be the moment for the non-Jewish nations to hear the
message? Did Paul not have a sense that he was walking a tightrope across the crater of an active volcano?

Part of the answer has to do with the vocation to which Paul
was obedient. In Acts 26, admittedly in one of Luke's carefully
crafted scenes, we catch an authentic sense of that vocation. This,
according to Luke's report of Paul's speech before Herod Agrippa,
is what Jesus had said to him on the road to Damascus:

> I am going to establish you as a servant, as a witness both
> of the things you have already seen and of the occasions
> I will appear to you in the future. I will rescue you from
> the people, and from the nations to whom I am going to
> send you so that you can open their eyes to enable them
> to turn from darkness to light, and from the power of
> the satan to God—so that they can have forgiveness of
> sins, and an inheritance among those who are made holy
> by their faith in me.[3]

It would be easy, in the midst of that dense summary, to miss a
central point. Like most Jews of his day, Saul of Tarsus had long be-

lieved that the nations of the world had been enslaved by their own idols. They worshipped nongods, and in Jewish thought, rooted in the scriptures, those who worshipped idols became enslaved to them, trapped in a downward spiral of dehumanization. This is what Paul means by "the power of the satan"—the word "satan" is the Hebrew term for "accuser," used popularly and often quite vaguely to refer to the dark power that appears to grip, distort, and ultimately destroy human societies and individuals. *And Paul believed that in his crucifixion Jesus of Nazareth had overcome the power of darkness.* Something happened when Jesus died as a result of which "the satan"—and any dark forces that might be loosely lumped together under such a label—no longer had any actual authority. (Paul explains at various places in his writings how this had been achieved; but what matters for our understanding of his mission is *that* it had happened, that the dark power had been defeated.) Paul's mission was not, then, simply about persuading people to believe in Jesus, as though starting from a blank slate. It was about declaring to the non-Jewish nations that the door to their prison stood open and that they were free to leave. They had to turn around, away from the enslaving idols, to worship and serve the living God.

Being free from the consequences of the past means, of course, being forgiven, as Paul emphasizes in this passage in Acts. Forgiveness is not something the non-Jewish world had thought much about. The ancient pagan gods might decide, for whatever reason, either to punish someone or not, as the case might be; but when a god decided not to punish someone, it wasn't thought of as *forgiveness* as such. That would imply, apart from anything else, a far more intimate relationship between gods and mortals than was normally imagined. One does not say, when the thunderbolt misses you and strikes the person next to you, that this means you have been "forgiven." What is happening, it seems, is that the much more *Jewish* idea of forgiveness, emerging from the idea of Israel's covenant with the One God and particularly from the notion of covenant renewal after catastrophic disobedience, was already being extended, so that the nations of the world were being included, drawn into the embrace of the creator God. The non-Jewish peoples were being invited to discover not just some blind fate to be cheated if possible and endured if not, but personal forgiveness from a living God. They were being summoned to understand themselves, for the first time, as humans who were personally responsible to a wise Creator. It is as though an orphan, brought up by faceless bureaucrats in a threatening institution, were to meet for the first time the parents she never knew she had.

What emerges from this, as the positive side of the point about the dark forces being overthrown, is the idea of a *new humanity*, a different model of the human race. If Jesus had defeated the powers of the world in his death, his resurrection meant the launching of a new creation, a whole new world. Those who found themselves caught up in the "good news" that Paul was announcing were drawn into that new world and were themselves, Paul taught, to become small working models of the same thing. As I think of Paul launching this new venture, the image of the tightrope over the volcano doesn't seem to go far enough. He was inventing, and must have known that he was inventing, a new way of being human. It must have been a bit like the first person to realize that notes sounded in sequence created melody, that notes sounded together created harmony, and that ordering the sequence created rhythm. If we can think of a world without music and then imagine it being invented, offering a hitherto undreamed-of depth and power to space, time, and matter, then we may have a sense of the crazy magnitude of Paul's vocation.

All this will become much clearer as we proceed, following Paul in his initial journey to Cyprus, up into central southern Turkey, and then back again. We can date this trip roughly to AD 47/48. Two more things must be said by way of introduction to Paul's journeys and their purpose.

First, if Paul believed and taught that with Jesus and his death and resurrection something had happened, a one-off event through which the world was now irrevocably different, so he also believed that, when he announced the message about Jesus (the "good news," the "gospel"), a similar one-off event could and would take place in the hearts, minds, and lives of some of his hearers. Paul speaks about this one-off event with the term "power": the power of the gospel, the power of the spirit in and through the gospel, or the power of "the word of God." These seem to be different ways of saying the same thing, namely, that when Paul told the story of Jesus some people found that this Jesus became a living presence, not simply a name from the recent past. A transforming, healing, disturbing, and challenging presence. A presence that at one level was the kind of thing that would be associated with a divine power and at another level seemed personal—*human,* in fact. This then became the focal point of what we said before: people turned away from the idols they had been serving and discovered, in Jesus, a God who was *alive,* who did things, who changed people's lives from the inside out. (The fact that skeptics at the time, like skeptics today, could and did give different explanations of what was taking place does not alter the fact that this is what people said was happening to them, that this is what Paul understood to be going on, and that the consequences, whether they were all deluded or speaking a dangerous truth, were long lasting.)

The change was bound to be dramatic. Worshipping "the gods"—the great pantheon of Greek and Roman gods with plenty of others added on here and there—permeated every aspect of life in Paul's world. To pull back from all of that and to worship "the living God" instead was far more than the equivalent of, say, in the modern West giving up gambling and beginning to attend church once a week. It would mean different actions and patterns of life every hour of every day. Perhaps the only way we can imagine such a thing in today's secular world is to think what it would be like to give up all our usual machines and conveniences: car, cell phone, cooking equipment, central heating, or air-conditioning. You would have to do everything differently, only much more so. The gods were everywhere and involved in everything. In the ancient world, whether you were at home, on the street, or in the public square; attending festivals great and small; or at moments of crisis or joy (weddings, funerals, setting off on a journey)—the gods would be there to be acknowledged, appealed to, pleased, or placated. Once the message of Jesus took hold, all that would have to go. The neighbors would notice. Atheists were socially undesirable.

The most obviously powerful divinity to be given up was Caesar, and this brings us back to the question of geography, of why Paul, with the whole world open before him, went where he did. I have already mentioned the cults of Caesar and Rome. They developed in different ways across the vast Roman Empire, but the point in any case was to solidify the empire itself. People who believe that their ruler is in some sense "son of a god" are less likely to rise in revolt than people who see their rulers merely as ordinary muddled human beings. And when the good news of Jesus called its hearers to turn from "idols," some of those idols, in towns and cities across Paul's world, would have been statues of Caesar or members of his family. It begins to look as though Paul's *geographical* strategy had a quiet but definite *political* undertone. Many of the key places on his journeys—Pisidian Antioch, where we will join him presently, but also such places as Ephesus, Philippi, and Corinth—were key centers of Roman rule and of Roman cult in the eastern Mediterranean. And of course he was then heading for Rome itself, and for Spain, a major center of Roman culture and influence. Connecting the dots of Paul's journeys, actual and planned, is like mapping a royal procession through Caesar's heartlands.

I do not think, then, that Paul's choice of these cities was purely pragmatic, that he was picking good centers from which the message might flow outward. Nor was it simply that Paul, himself a Roman citizen by birth, would find it easier to travel within rather than outside of the vast Roman Empire, though that is true as well. I suspect that Paul was deliberately finding ways to make the point: there is one "Lord," one *Kyrios,* and it isn't Caesar. The communities of those loyal to Jesus (*pistis* again) that grew up as a result of his gospel announcement were marked by a confession of that loyalty that was extremely simple and extremely profound: *Kyrios Iēsous Christos,* "Jesus Messiah is Lord." Paul must have known exactly how this would sound. He was well aware how the imperial rhetoric worked, on coins and inscriptions, in statements of civic loyalty. He was, after all, one of the half dozen most intellectually sophisticated first-century persons for whom we have evidence, up there with Seneca, Plutarch, and a select band of others. He was, after all, heir to the Psalms and prophets, which spoke of a coming king to whom the world's rulers would have to owe allegiance. He and his communities were treading a dangerous line.

But, he would have said, a necessary line. These communities, small at first but growing, were an experiment in a way of being human, of being human *together,* that had never been tried in the world before. It was like a form of Judaism, particularly in its care for the poor, its strict sexual ethic, and its insistence on a monotheism that excluded the pagan divinities. But it was quite unlike the Jewish way of life in its open welcome to all who found themselves grasped by the good news of Jesus. That in itself was confusing enough for most people. Adding the element of apparent political subversion only made it worse.

If all this sounds like a recipe for social and cultural upheaval, we are on the right track. As the stories in Acts will testify—and as Paul's letters will emphasize—anyone propagating this kind of subversive message will be the target of scorn, anger, and violence. It wasn't too long, on his first missionary journey, before Paul would face all three.

★ ★ ★

Luke tells the story of Paul's first journey in Acts 13–14. Like much of Acts, these chapters are page-turners. One thing tumbles out after another, with Paul and Barnabas hurrying from city to city and stirring up excited and/or hostile crowds. Many hear the message; some believe, others are appalled. People are healed, sometimes spectacularly. Local authorities wake up to the fact that something new is going on. These chapters set the scene both for the longer journeys to which this comparatively short trip serves as a prelude and for the fierce controversy into which Paul, Barnabas, and their friends will be plunged not long after they return home.

It seems to have been Barnabas who took the lead as they set off, sailing from Seleucia (Antioch's closest port) to Cyprus. Barnabas himself came originally from Cyprus, and the island may have appeared a natural place to launch the work they had in mind. Barnabas probably still had family connections there. The short sea voyage would have been familiar to him, as it perhaps was not for Saul; the Jews were not a seafaring people, and in their scriptures the sea is often a dark, hostile force. Barnabas's nephew John Mark, accompanying them as an assistant and himself quite possibly a first-time sailor, would have had reason to feel comfortable in Cyprus as well, with relatives and a synagogue culture that would remind him of home.

The synagogue was the natural starting point for Paul's very Jewish message about Israel's long-awaited Messiah. We may assume that the substantial set piece later in Acts 13, where Paul speaks at length in the synagogue at Pisidian Antioch, represents Luke's summary of the kind of thing that Paul (who turns out to be the main speaker in the party) would say in synagogue after synagogue, though as we shall see with varied reactions. We hear nothing, however, of the Jewish reaction on Cyprus, though the fact that Barnabas and John Mark returned to the island later implies that there had been some positive response, producing at least a small community of Jesus-followers. What we do hear about is what happened when the travelers reach Paphos, the capital.

Paphos, in the southwest of the island, had long since upstaged the earlier capital, the northeastern port of Salamis. The city boasted a long and important history, being particularly famous for its huge shrine of the goddess Aphrodite, commemorating her legendary place of birth. (The temple Paul and Barnabas would have seen there was destroyed in an earthquake in AD 76/77; the one you can see there today is a later replacement.) And Paphos, as the capital, was naturally enough the seat of the Roman governor.

Part of the job description of any Roman governor would have been to keep tabs on anything of special interest, particularly anything socially subversive, that might be going on in his territory. Cyprus was quite small. Word would certainly have reached Sergius Paulus about the three itinerant Jewish teachers and their unexpected message. (Luke comments drily that Sergius Paulus was "an intelligent man," perhaps contrasting him with certain other Roman officials who appear elsewhere in the story.)[4] So he summoned the travelers to hear for himself what was going on. But matters quickly became more complicated. There was another strange Jewish teacher already there, a certain Bar-Jesus, who had a local reputation as a magician. Whether this character was trying to represent "a Jewish point of view" to the governor or whether he was trying to use his magic to impress or to earn a living is not clear. The local Jewish communities themselves might well have seen him as a dangerous maverick; we cannot tell. One way or another, he seemed bent upon opposing and denouncing Barnabas and Saul and their message. And this is the point where we sense something new happening, something emerging within the personal standing and self-awareness of Saul of Tarsus himself.

Up to this point Saul has been, it seems, the junior partner, himself a protégé of Barnabas. But now he steps forward, filled, so it seems, with a new kind of energy (the kind of surge that he and other early Christians attributed to the holy spirit), and denounces Bar-Jesus in fierce and uncompromising terms: he's a deceitful villain, a son of the devil, who is taking God's plan and twisting it out of shape. Strong language like that is easy to utter, picking up traditions of invective and hurling them at an opponent. But these words are backed up with action in the form of a curse of temporary blindness. Suddenly the magician finds himself groping around in darkness—the story has an obvious flavor of just retribution, the spellbinder being himself spellbound—and the governor, confronted with a new kind of power, believes what the travelers have been saying. He was, as Luke comments, "astonished at the teaching of the Lord."[5] Why, wonder readers, the "teaching," not the "power"? Presumably because, though many people could perform strange tricks, the power of the travelers seemed to come not from themselves, but from the one about whom they were "teaching," the one whose death, resurrection, and enthronement had revealed him as the true *Kyrios*. With the explanation came the power. And, with this, Saul appears to come of age. He is not now simply a teacher or prophet working within the church as in Antioch. He is out on the front line and finding sudden energy and focus to meet a new kind of challenge.

He emerges not only as the new spokesman, but with a new name. Luke changes gear effortlessly: "Saul, also named Paul."[6] From now on this is how he will be referred to and, in Acts and the letters, how he will refer to himself. Why the change?

"Saul" is obviously a royal name, that of the first king of Israel, from the tribe of Benjamin. Saul of Tarsus, conscious of descent from the same tribe, seems to have reflected on the significance of the name, quoting at one point a passage about God's choice of King Saul and applying it to his own vocation.[7] Some have speculated that he deliberately set aside this name, with its high-born overtones, in order to use a Greek word connected to the adjective *paulos,* "small, little"—a sign, perhaps, of a deliberate humility, "the least of the apostles." Well, perhaps. Others have supposed that he simply chose a name better known in the wider non-Jewish world, shared even by the governor in the present story. Like most Roman citizens, Saul/Paul would have had more than one name, and it is quite possible that he already possessed the name "Paul" and simply switched within available options. It is worth noting as well, however, that in Aristophanes, known to most schoolboys in the Greek world, the word *saulos* was an adjective meaning "mincing," as of a man walking in an exaggeratedly effeminate fashion. One can understand Paul's not wishing to sport that label in the larger Greek-speaking world. One way or another, "Paul" he would be from now on.

★ ★ ★

Our suspicions about John Mark feeling at home in Cyprus are accentuated by what happens next. The travelers sail north from Paphos and arrive on the Pamphylia coastline (south-central Turkey in modern terms). They land at the port of Perga, whereupon John Mark leaves them and returns to Jerusalem. This leaves Paul with a lasting sense of betrayal and suspicion: later on, when Barnabas tries to launch another trip and wants to give Mark a second chance, Paul refuses point-blank to take someone so obviously unreliable. The episode raises other questions too. What precisely did an assistant have to do on such a trip? Look after travel arrangements, accommodations, money? Slip out unnoticed to shop for supplies? Carry extra luggage containing scriptural scrolls? In any case, Paul does not forget, and this will be part of the later rift with Barnabas. The two, though, move on, heading north from Pamphylia on the coast to the inland region of Pisidia, part of the

Roman province of Galatia. They arrive at the city known at that time as "New Rome," Pisidian Antioch.

The reason Pisidian Antioch was thought of as "New Rome" had to do with its recent colonial history. The civil wars that had scarred the Roman world after the death of Julius Caesar in 44 BC had left tens of thousands of military veterans in Greece, Turkey, and elsewhere. Many of them would in any case have been from countries other than Italy in the first place, but all of them, having signed on for active service, would expect to be rewarded. The last thing Rome wanted was such people coming to Italy, let alone to Rome itself; Rome's population was already swollen, causing unemployment and a regular threat of food shortages. Augustus therefore founded colonies for these ex–service personnel well away from Italy. Pisidian Antioch was the most important such colony in the region, retaining its name (Antioch) from its earlier foundation, though now officially renamed Colonia Caesarea ("Caesar's Colony," a telling name in itself) when the province of Galatia, of which it formed the most substantial southern city, was founded in 25 BC.

Pisidian Antioch was the home of a good many first-century senators and other high-ranking Romans, including the Sergius Paulus whom Paul and Barnabas had met in Paphos. As is the way with colonies, the city did its best to imitate Rome in its architecture as well as its style of government, its public holidays, and its entire ethos. By the middle of the first century AD, when Paul and Barnabas arrived, the city center was dominated by a vast complex of buildings focused on the imperial cult. This featured the temple itself along with several other buildings and a massive triumphal arch celebrating the victory of Augustus over the Pisidians. Other typical Roman buildings, including an aqueduct and a theater, are still visible there today. What's more, this was one of the places where one could see, displayed at great length on public buildings, the remarkable autobiographical work *Res Gestae,* "Matters Accomplished," which Augustus had inscribed in Latin and Greek in several locations including the Galatian capital Ancyra, farther north. Rome was not noted for subtle political statements. The entire city of Antioch made the very obvious point about who was in charge and about the "religious" implications of the new imperial reality. Caesar and Rome were the central focus of worship, a worship that would bind together the city and the region and give it security by linking it so obviously to its ultimate patron.

All this is part of the backdrop to the long address that Luke ascribes to Paul in the synagogue at Antioch.[8] Luke, as I have suggested, presumably intended this to be seen as typical of what Paul would have said in one synagogue after another. Earlier scholarship used to cast doubt on whether such speeches were really compatible with what we know of Paul from his letters. This speech in particular, focusing so strongly on Jesus as the true descendant of King David, came under that kind of suspicion when scholars tried to maintain that Paul gave little thought to Jesus's Davidic messiahship. Since, however, there are good reasons for reversing that verdict, we are free to explore the speech not only in its obvious Jewish context but within the larger framework of "New Rome." What did it mean to proclaim the King of the Jews in such a context? What did it mean *for Paul* to be doing that?

Paul must have felt that he'd been preparing for this kind of moment all his life. He was going to tell the story of ancient Israel in a way that everybody would recognize, but with a conclusion nobody had seen coming. He would focus on God's original choice of King David and on the promise that God would eventually send a new David. So he moves rapidly from Abraham to the Exodus, to the settlement of the land, and then to Samuel, Saul, and David himself. He then jumps to the story of Jesus, carefully highlighting the fulfillment of the Davidic promises as witnessed by Jesus's resurrection—for which purpose he quotes key texts from the Psalms and the prophets.[9] He is covering all the bases: the story of the Torah (the first division of the Hebrew Bible) is backed up with the Prophets and the Writings (the second and third). And the climax is that the long hope of Israel has been fulfilled. The law of Moses had ended in a puzzle. Deuteronomy had warned about Israel's long-term covenant unfaithfulness and its results. But now there was a way through. Moses could only take them so far, but now God had broken through that barrier. "Forgiveness of sins" had arrived in space and time, a new reality to open a new world. But, as with Moses, would the present generation listen? Paul's speech ends with another prophetic warning: something new is happening, and they might just be looking the wrong way and miss out on it entirely.

This was, of course, dramatic and revolutionary. Paul had sat through many synagogue addresses in his youth, and he must have known that people simply didn't say this kind of thing. He wasn't giving them a new kind of moral exhortation. He certainly wasn't offering a new "religion" as such. He was not telling them (to forestall the obvious misunderstanding about which I have spoken already) "how to go to heaven." He was announcing *the fulfillment of the long-range divine plan*. The Mosaic covenant could only take them so far. The story that began with Abraham and pointed ahead to the coming Davidic king would, so to speak, break through the Moses barrier and arrive at a new world order entirely. No Jew who had been brought up on the Psalms (not least Psalm 2, which Paul quotes here and which other Jews of his day had studied intensively) could miss the point. If the new David had arrived, he would upstage everything and everyone else— including the New Rome and its great emperor over the sea. This was both exciting and dangerous. Small wonder that many of the synagogue members, both Jews and proselytes, followed Paul and Barnabas after the close of the synagogue meeting. Either this message was a complete hoax, a blasphemous nonsense, or, if it was true, it meant the opening up of a whole new world.

Small wonder too that the next Sabbath a huge crowd gathered to hear what Paul was saying. But this time the local community had had a chance to think through what it all might mean, and the signs were not good. Paul might be clever at expounding scriptures, but nobody had ever heard of a *crucified* Messiah, and nobody had imagined that if Israel's God finally did what he had promised, some of the Jewish people themselves might miss out on it, as Paul (in line with scripture itself) had warned. Underneath this again there is a dark note. If, according to Paul, this new world of forgiveness had opened up to embrace all alike, non-Jew as well as Jew, what would become of the settled but still fragile place of the Jewish communities in the Roman world? Everything was going to change.

The result, as with the young Saul of Tarsus himself, was *zeal*— zeal for Israel's God, zeal for the Torah, zeal against anything that might appear to be overthrowing the ancestral order. Some of the local Jews, we may suppose, glimpsed that what Paul had been saying might just be true. Most could only see the threat to their way of life, the drastic redrawing of the shape their hopes had always taken. They denounced Paul and Barnabas as false teachers leading Israel astray. Paul's response was to quote the prophets once more, this time his regular text, Isaiah 49: "I have set you for a light to the nations, so that you can be salvation-bringers to the end of the earth."[10] The Jewish reaction itself confirmed his scripture-fueled sense that, when Israel's God did for Israel what he had promised, then the nations as a whole would come into the promised blessing.

This naturally delighted the non-Jews who had heard his message: they were free to belong to God's ancient people! But this in turn stiffened the Jewish reaction, and that then produced an altogether more serious turn of events. We have no idea whether Paul had made contact with the leading citizens of Antioch, though if, as some have suggested, he had come with a letter of recommendation from Sergius Paulus in Cyprus, that is altogether possible. But the aristocrats of Antioch would have been alarmed, as

Romans were always alarmed, by any suggestion of strange new subversive teachings that might upset the delicate social and cultural status quo.

Paul's message seemed to point to uncharted territory, to a new kind of "Jewish" community claiming continuity with Abraham, David, and the prophets, but now including any non-Jews who professed allegiance to the newly heralded "Messiah," Jesus, and at the same time threatening (as Paul and Barnabas seem to have threatened) that any Jews who refused to see Jesus as their promised Messiah would themselves be missing out on this new fulfillment. Since Julius Caesar had given the Jewish people the privilege, unique among all groups in the empire, of not being required to worship the Roman gods, it is quite possible that both groups (leading Jews and leading citizens of Antioch) would have seen at once the threat of real civic upheaval. Supposing large numbers of non-Jews started trying to claim the same privilege?

The visit to New Rome thus ends with the start of Paul's new life: that of a suffering apostle, a visible symbol of the crucified Lord he was proclaiming. Opposition turned to violence sufficient to cause Paul and Barnabas to leave town in a hurry, symbolically shaking the dust off their feet as they did so.[11] They left behind them, however, the beginnings of a new community, "filled with joy and with the holy spirit."[12] There was a sense of springtime. Something new had begun, even if the heralds of spring, like migrating birds pausing on their journey, had had to move on quickly.

The next three cities follow in quick succession, and Luke selects one incident in Lystra for particular treatment. If you traveled east from Antioch and followed the main road (the Via Sebaste) across the mountains southeast from Antioch, you would be heading ultimately for Syria via Paul's home city of Tarsus. The first territory you would enter would be Lycaonia, and the first city you would meet there is Iconium, followed closely by Lystra, and then, a little farther, by Derbe.

This area had been part of the Roman province of Asia in the second century BC. It then became part of the new province of Cilicia in roughly 80 BC. Then, following dynastic changes among local client kings, it became part of the new province of Galatia in 25 BC. Both Iconium and Lystra were Roman colonies, used by Augustus to settle veterans in 26 BC. They never had the same importance or vast public buildings as Antioch. But their significance as centers of Roman culture and the Roman cult cannot be underestimated.

We watch, then, as Paul follows the pattern that has already emerged. His message and mission remain firmly anchored in the traditions and hopes of Israel, and he naturally begins with the synagogue, presumably employing some version of the narrative we saw him displaying in Antioch (Abraham, the Exodus, David . . . and Jesus). He receives an enthusiastic reception from some hearers and predictably implacable hostility from others. But there are two other features that emerge in these three cities and also in the letter Paul wrote to these churches not long afterward.

First, Paul's message of a new age dawning, of new creation suddenly leaping into life, is dramatically symbolized by a burst of healing activity. When Paul writes to these churches later on, he refers to the powerful signs that had been performed and it seems were still being performed in their midst.[13] We should be careful, by the way, about the modern word "miracle" in this connection. People often think of "miracles" as the "invasion" of the natural order by a force from outside. That wasn't how the early Christians saw it. For them, dramatic and otherwise inexplicable healings were seen as evidence of *new creation,* of the Creator himself at work in a fresh way. This is especially clear in the incident in Lystra to which we shall return presently.

The second feature of this part of the trip is suffering. The community leaders in Iconium, Jews and Gentiles alike, try to attack Paul and Barnabas and even to stone them.[14] Paul himself is stoned and left for dead in Lystra.[15] As they go back through the region after their initial foray, the message they give is stark: God's kingdom is indeed breaking in, but belonging to that new age, that new divine rule, will mean undergoing suffering. The "present age" and the "age to come" are grinding against one another, like upper and lower millstones, as God's new world is brought to birth. Those who find themselves seized by the message of Jesus will be caught in the middle *and will thereby provide in themselves further evidence of the message,* the news that the crucified Messiah is now the Lord of the whole world.

The paradoxes of Paul's apostleship are thus laid bare right from the start of his traveling career. There is a sense in which all the writing that would later flow from his pen becomes a complicated set of footnotes to the reality he was already discovering and modeling. When Paul writes to the churches in Galatia and refers to his first visit to them, he mentions that it was "through bodily weakness that I announced the gospel to you in the first place."[16] Some have speculated that he was seriously ill at the time. Those who invoked epilepsy or serious migraines as "explanations" for the Damascus Road incident have naturally invoked them here too. As another alternative, some have suggested that when he goes on to say that the Galatians welcomed him so warmly that, had it been possible, they would have torn out their eyes and given them to him, this is an indication that he suffered from some kind of sickness of the eyes.[17] That, I think, is a case (and not the only one) of modern readers failing to spot a well-known first-century metaphor.

I think it far more likely that the poor physical condition to which Paul refers is the result of the violence to which he had been subjected. In the ancient world, just as today, the physical appearance of public figures carries considerable weight in how they are assessed. Someone turning up in a city shortly after being stoned or beaten up would hardly cut an imposing figure. The Galatians, however, had welcomed Paul as if he were an angel from heaven or even the Messiah himself.[18] As Paul would later explain, the bodily marks of identification that mattered to him were not the signs of circumcision, but "the marks of Jesus"—in other words, the signs of the suffering he had undergone. When, later on, he faces suffering at other levels as well—including what looks like a nervous breakdown—he will, through gritted teeth, explain that this too is part of what it means to be an apostle.[19]

Another theme that resonates throughout Paul's public career first emerges here in Lystra. He would have been well aware, from his early days, of the non-Jewish religious culture of ancient Anatolia: many gods, many "lords," many tales of divine goings-on, traceable all the way back in the classical world to Homer, but then diversifying into local legends and folktales. One such, reported by the Roman poet Ovid, tells of the Greek gods Zeus and Hermes wandering unrecognized in the region. Later inscriptions from the area indicate that these two divinities were subsequently celebrated there.[20] So it isn't surprising that, when Paul dramatically heals a man who had been crippled from birth, the locals assume that the old stories have come true: Zeus and Hermes have appeared at last. (Luke, in an interesting bit of local color, tells us that the crowds are shouting out their welcome in the local Lycaonian language.) Since Hermes is the "messenger of the gods," and since Paul seems to be doing all the talking, they assume that Paul is Hermes. That, by process of elimination, means that Barnabas must be Zeus. Before the apostles know what is happening, the local cult swings into action. The priest of Zeus brings out a procession to meet them. He has oxen and garlands, all the paraphernalia for a great sacrifice. There is no doubt music and dancing. They find themselves in the middle of a classic pagan celebration.

At this point all the deep-seated instincts and theology of two lifelong devout Jews come into play. This is exactly the kind of idolatry against which the Jewish world had always re-acted. Early Jewish tales of the call of Abraham himself stress his background in polytheism and how he had given it all up to follow the call of the One God. The law of Moses warns repeat-edly against any kind of compromise with pagan worship. Paul, steeped in the Torah from boyhood, would never forget the threat posed by Balaam when he sent in the Moabite women to tempt the Israelite men to commit idolatry, the moment when Phinehas burned with the "zeal," the moment when Elijah faced the Baal worshippers. Later challenges reinforced the point. The deepest revulsion of the Jewish monotheist was reserved for this kind of thing and all that went with it. Jews from that day to this have accused Paul of compromising with paganism. But this scene makes it abundantly clear that, if Paul ever appears to be sailing close to the wind (he would say that this was a false conclusion, but many have drawn it), this was not because he was becoming some kind of pagan by the back door. He was as fierce and zealous a monotheist as anyone else. He reacts to find-ing himself in the middle of a pagan celebration like a man in a pit of snakes. This is not a good place for him to be.

Nor was this simply a knee-jerk reaction to "other people's religious practices." Throughout his mature work we see evi-dence that Paul had a well-thought-out critique of the world of pagan philosophy and religion, rooted in his belief in the One God as the *creator* of the world. Paganism, he believed, was simply a parody, people worshipping forces within the natural world without realizing that they owed their very existence and such charm and power as they possessed to the creator who had made them in the first place—and that to worship these forces was the quick route to slavery and dehumanization. Completely consistent with his slogan of "turning from idols to serve a liv-ing and true God," Paul insists not only on that challenge but on the underlying narrative: that for a long time this God has allowed the nations to go their own way, but now something new has burst onto the scene.

Paul and Barnabas rush into the crowd and, disrupting the careful liturgical procession and interrupting the music, they do their best to explain that this is precisely what their message is *not* about. They, Paul and Barnabas, are not gods but ordinary humans, and the whole point of their visit is to tell everybody to turn away from such foolishness. The "gods" the local people are invoking are lifeless idols, but they, the apostles, are bringing them news of a God who is alive. He is the Creator; he is the one who supplies humans with all they need. And something has happened to make this message urgent: this living God, having for a long time allowed the nations to go their own way, has now done something to unveil his power and his purpose. That's why it is time to turn away from all this playacting and experience the power and love of the God who puts all the gods to shame.

When we set this incident alongside the opening synagogue sermon in Acts 13, we see clearly how the inner logic of Paul's mission actually works. On the one hand, he is declaring to the Jewish community, and thereafter to all and sundry, that the long-awaited fulfillment of Israel's hope has arrived. The story that began with Abraham—the story, that is, of how the One God was addressing the deep problems of the whole human race and hence of creation itself—had reached its goal. Israel's God had defeated the forces of darkness that had held the nations captive and, in a majestic second Exodus, had brought Jesus through death to resurrection and had thereby declared him to be David's true son, Israel's Messiah, and the world's true Lord.

But, on the other hand, if all this is true, then this does not mean that the Jews are wrong and the pagans are right. On the contrary, the powers that have gripped the pagan world and the fake "gods" that these "powers" have used to deceive the nations have been overthrown. Zeus, Hermes, and the rest have been shown up as shams. They simply do not exist. Any "power" that they have comes not from their own quasi-divinity, but from the fact that humans, worshipping them, have given to the malevolent forces that use their name as a cloak the authority that God always intended humans themselves to exercise. That is why, as we have seen, if these "powers" are overthrown and if the long-awaited new creation has begun under the rule of the Davidic king, then the nations of the world are to be invited to join the people who worship the One God, just as the Jewish people themselves are invited to welcome their Messiah and to discover, as Paul insisted in Antioch, that the puzzling ending to Moses's own words to Israel in Deuteronomy 27–32 has been dealt with. The story that could get no farther because of Israel's ongoing rebellion and hard-heartedness has arrived at its new destination. That which couldn't be dealt with under Moses has now been dealt with once and for all.[21]

The transition is swift. One minute the Lycaonians are ready to worship Paul; the next minute they are ready to stone him. If this seems extreme—but then who are we to judge a totally different culture?—it may be explained more easily than we might imagine, and not only on the principle of the fickleness of crowds (like those who shouted "Hosanna" on Palm Sunday and then "Crucify!" a few days later). Rather, Paul had accomplished an extraordinary feat of healing. That could not be denied. But if he was *not* to be identified with one of the Greek pantheon, then who was he? Some kind of magician?

One person's miracle is another person's magic, and someone performing powerful deeds without proper sanction may be a dangerous deceiver. Jesus himself had been accused of being in league with the devil. Deuteronomy had warned Israel about that kind of thing, and a puzzled pagan crowd would be ready for a similar explanation. Perhaps Paul was bewitching them, dazzling them with magic tricks in order to prey on them. Such a person would be better off out of the way altogether, and the mixture of zealous Jews and angry local pagans leaves Paul for dead under a hail of stones. "Once I was stoned" he says later.[22] Once would have finished off most people, but for whatever reason Paul lives to tell the tale, perhaps by being knocked unconscious early on and so being left for dead.

Equally, one such incident would have convinced many people that they were on a fool's errand and ought to find less risky ways of getting their message across. But Paul's resolve is only stiffened. His friends come around and take him into the city. He explains that this kind of suffering is precisely the sign of two worlds clashing; they are on the cusp of the new world, and if this is what it costs, this is what it costs. So he will go on.

One more visit, this time to Derbe, a little farther down the same road. Had they gone much farther along the Via Sebaste, Paul and Barnabas would have gone up the steep pass through the Cilician Gates in the Taurus Mountains and would then have dropped down to Paul's native city of Tarsus. There may have been reasons for not doing that. Instead, they turn back to revisit the cities where they have launched these little new-creation communities, these surprised groups of people who have found themselves caught up in a movement at once so utterly Jewish and so very unlike (and therefore so threatening to) anything that local Jewish communities had thought of before. As we would expect, they encourage these little groups; they urge them to "remain in the faith," which we could equally well translate as "stay loyal," loyal, in other words, to the Faithful One, to the true King Jesus. They remind them, with Paul's battered body as the obvious evidence, that the ultimate "kingdom of God," the sovereign rule of the One God on earth as in heaven, will come about "through considerable suffering."[23] Suffering, it appears, is not simply something through which the faithful people must pass to get to their destination. It is in itself the way in which the dark powers that have ruled the world will exhaust themselves, the way in which the one-off victory won by the Messiah on the cross will be implemented in the world.

All this Paul and Barnabas now have etched into their conscious and subconscious minds. They have seen the power of God unveiled as they have told the story of Israel reaching its climax in Jesus. They have witnessed "signs and wonders" of various kinds. They have suffered and have discovered that this too is a means of the power by which God's new age is coming to birth. And they have seen, in particular, that many non-Jews, hearing the message, have responded with delight, believed, and stayed loyal to Jesus as the crucified and risen Lord. What they had witnessed earlier in Syrian Antioch—the creation of a new community in which Jews and Gentiles were able to live together because all that had previously separated them had been dealt with on the cross—had come true in city after city.

Every element of this contributes to our initial answer to our first question about Paul's deepest motivations. Every element of it contributes to a deeper understanding of our second question, as to the significance of what happened to Paul on the road to Damascus. There is no suggestion that Paul had embraced a "religion" different from the one he had previously pursued. There is no suggestion that up to that point he had supposed that in order to get to "heaven," one had to please Israel's God by performing good moral works, and that he was now offering an easier way ("You just have to believe!"). Both of these suggestions—widely popular in Western thought over the last few centuries—are simply anachronistic. This is not how Jews or pagans of the time were thinking, and it certainly isn't how Paul's mind worked.

For Paul and Barnabas, what mattered was that Israel's God,

the creator of the world, had done in Jesus the thing he had always promised, fulfilling the ancient narrative that went back to Abraham and David and breaking through "the Moses barrier," the long Jewish sense that Moses himself had warned of covenant failure and its consequences. And if that had now happened, if the Messiah's death had dealt with the "powers" that had held Jew and Gentile alike captive and his resurrection had launched a new world order "on earth as in heaven," then the non-Jewish nations were not only free to turn from their now powerless idols to serve the living and true God, but their "uncleanness"—the idolatry and immorality that were always cited as the reason Jews should not fraternize with them—had itself been dealt with. The radical meaning of the Messiah's cross was the reason, on both counts, that there now had to be a single family consisting of all the Messiah's people. And perhaps this helps, eventually, with the other question that hovers over all study of Paul: Why did this extraordinary movement, launched by this energetic and subversive man, spread in the way it did?

All these questions need as their central point the recognition that this was neither a new "religion" nor a new system of otherworldly salvation. At the heart of Paul's message, teaching, and life was—to use a technical phrase—*radical messianic eschatology*. Eschatology: God's long-awaited new day has arrived. Messianic: Jesus is the true son of David, announced as such in his resurrection, bringing to completion the purposes announced to Abraham and extended in the Psalms to embrace the world. Radical: nothing in Paul's or Barnabas's background had prepared them for this new state of affairs. The fact that they now believed it was what the One God had always planned did not reduce their own sense of awe and astonishment. They knew firsthand that such a program would meet stiff resistance and even violence. What they could not have foreseen, as they traveled back through the southern part of the province of Galatia and then sailed home to (Syrian) Antioch, was that the new reality they had witnessed would become a focus of sharp controversy even among Jesus's followers, let alone that the two of them, Paul and Barnabas, would find themselves on opposite sides as that controversy boiled over.

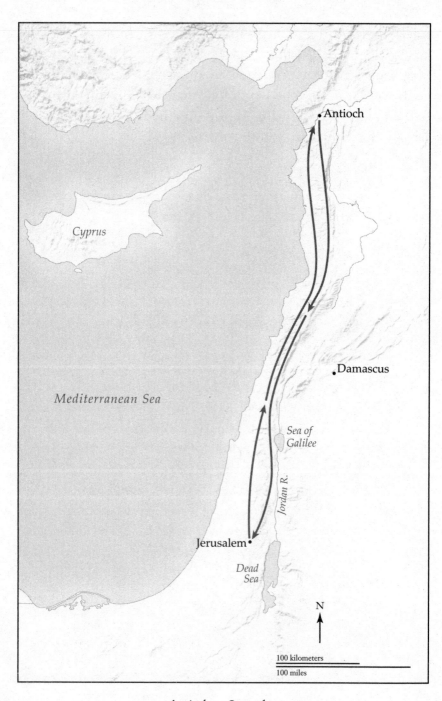

Antioch to Jerusalem

6

Antioch and Jerusalem

BIOGRAPHY, AS WE said before, involves thinking into the
minds of people who did not think the same way we do.
And history often involves trying to think into the minds
of various individuals and groups who, though living at the same
time, thought in very different ways from one another as well as
from ourselves. Trying to keep track of the swirling currents of
thought and action in Paul's world is that kind of exercise.

We have already explored, at least in a preliminary way, the
different points of view that might explain the reaction to Paul's
work in the cities of South Galatia. The Roman authorities
wanted to keep the peace and engender social stability. The leading local citizens, eager to put on a good face before the imperial
world, did their best to work to the same end. The Jewish communities, wanting to live at peace while maintaining their integrity, cherished their special exemption from worshipping "the
gods," including, of course, the imperial divinities. These visions
of stability were inevitably disrupted by Paul's message, backed
up as it was with powerful deeds, announcing the fulfillment of
Israel's scriptures in the messianic events involving Jesus.

The message generated a different vision, a new social reality.

It challenged the regular Jewish taboos against fraternizing with non-Jews, not because Paul had suddenly invented the eighteenth-century ideal of "tolerance," but because he believed a new world order was coming to birth in which all Messiah people were welcome on equal terms, in which all were assured they were the "heirs" of the "kingdom" that was even now being launched. The events of Jesus's death and resurrection and the powerful gift of the divine spirit meant that the "powers" that had held the pagan world captive had been overthrown and that pagans who now came to believe in the Messiah were free from the defilements of idolatry and immorality.

All this formed a tight nexus of One-God beliefs, on the one hand, and a new social and cultural reality, on the other. Later generations have sometimes tried to flatten this out into abstract theology. Some in our own day have tried it the other way, seeing only sociology. But these are oversimplifications. Paul's vision, Jewish to the core but reshaped around the messianic events involving Jesus, was a hundred percent theological and a hundred percent about the formation and maintenance of a new community. And that meant trouble.

Trouble came not only from the context of southern Anatolia or even northwest Syria. A quite different view of reality obtained in Jerusalem, the city Paul knew only too well from his days as a leading young "zealot."

Jerusalem at this time was still very much the center of the Jesus movement. James, the brother of Jesus himself, was the acknowledged and unrivaled leader; he would retain that role until he was murdered by hard-line activists in AD 62. Peter and John, the two remaining members of the three who were closest to Jesus in his last days (John's brother James had been killed by Herod Agrippa in the early 40s), and James seem to have formed a new kind of triumvirate; "James, Peter, and John," as we saw earlier, could be spoken of as "pillars," the sustaining structure of the "new Temple." They believed that Israel's God had come back in person and was now dwelling among and within the followers of Jesus. This belief had now taken root, providing Jesus's followers with a strong, though controversial and dangerous, sense of identity.

It was still, of course, a *Jewish* identity. Like Paul in southern Anatolia, but very unlike him in the conclusions they were drawing, the early community in Jerusalem saw itself as the fulfillment of the ancient promises to Israel. This is not to say that the Jerusalem church was all of one mind. Acts reveals significant divisions. But anyone living in Jerusalem in the middle years of the first century was bound to face the challenge posed by the question: When is the One God going to do at last what he has promised and liberate his ancient people once and for all from the shame and scandal of Roman rule? And since Rome was widely seen as the ultimate form of monstrous pagan rule over the people of God, how and when was the One God going to overthrow the monsters and set up, on earth, his own unshakable kingdom?

That question was far more pressing in Jerusalem than it was for Jews out in the Diaspora. It was one thing for long-term Jewish residents in a city like Pisidian Antioch or indeed Tarsus to reach an accommodation whereby they could keep the Torah themselves while being grateful that Rome had given them dispensation from the otherwise mandatory public observances, festivals, and so on. This is not to say that Jews in that situation did not dream of a different future. The scriptures still spoke of a coming time when the knowledge and glory of the One God would fill the whole world. Some Jews out in the non-Jewish world would see themselves as a secret advance guard, pointing the way to that coming time, that future "kingdom." Most, though, would be content to find a modus vivendi that enabled them to be loyal to Israel's God without coming into direct confrontation with the Roman authorities. But in Jerusalem things were not so easy.

We know about the situation in Jerusalem through the detailed and colorful accounts of Josephus, a younger contemporary of Paul's. He was anything but a neutral observer. He himself was a

wealthy Jewish aristocrat who claimed to have tried out the various Jewish "schools of thought" and who had served as a general
in the army at the start of the war against Rome (AD 66–70) before switching sides and ending his days on an imperial pension
in Rome. To read his descriptions of Jerusalem in the middle of
the first century is to be plunged into a highly complex and confusing world. Different parties, groups, messianic and prophetic
movements, teachers, and preachers all claimed that Israel's God
was acting *here* or *there* or *in this way* and anathematized, often
violently, those who saw things differently or who followed rival leaders. When the Romans closed in on Jerusalem in the last
months of the war, crucifying so many Jews that they ran out of
timber for crosses, Josephus records sorrowfully that more Jews
were in fact killed by other Jews than by the Romans themselves.
And that was not because the Romans were being lenient.

Matters were not helped by the sequence of inept Roman
governors sent to keep the peace during the period. There were
times—not least under the two kings named Herod Agrippa,
both of whom were friendly with the Roman imperial family—
when some must have hoped for a settlement, a live-and-let-live
arrangement. That would never have been enough for the zealous
young Saul of Tarsus, who longed for the ultimate kingdom of
God. The Jerusalem of the 40s, 50s, and 60s was home to an entire generation who took the hard-line view, hating the thought
of compromise with the pagans and looking for something more
like Hezekiah's heaven-sent victory over Sennacherib or the
overthrow of the Egyptians in the Red Sea. What must it have
been like to be a Jesus-follower in a Jerusalem like that?

What mattered, once again, was *loyalty*. Whose side are you
on? Are you an out-and-out zealous supporter of the One God
and his Torah, ready to do whatever is necessary to defend God's
honor and establish his kingdom—or are you a compromiser? Are
you ready to do deals with the pagan world when it suits you?
Are you prepared to go soft on your true allegiance, choosing

to overlook the fact that the pagans worship idols and behave in unmentionable ways as a result? That, after all, was how the wilderness generation had behaved; remember Balaam, remember the Moabite women, remember Phinehas and his "zeal"—and the great covenant promises that Phinehas received as a result ("It was reckoned to him as righteousness"). The scriptures were quite clear that utter loyalty to the One God meant refusing all compromise with the pagan world. The social and cultural pressure to affirm that ancient loyalty and to be seen to abide by it was intense. Now think what it would have been like to be a follower of Jesus in that world. You would face a very different challenge from those faced by Jesus-followers in Syria or Turkey.

If, as we have seen, the Jerusalem church had by this time established a sense of identity as some kind of counter-Temple movement, this did not mean its members were being "anti-Jewish." If anything, they were putting themselves on a par with many other groups who regarded the present Temple hierarchy (the wealthy, aristocratic Sadducees, including the high-priestly family) as a corrupt and compromised bunch, out for their own ends and too eager to do deals with the Romans. The early Jerusalem church seems to have lived in some ways like other groups who believed that God was ushering in "the last days"—whatever they may have meant by that. In the excitement of the early stages, they had shared their property communally; this eager social experiment may well have contributed to their later poverty. They lived a life of prayer, fasting, community, and care for the poor and widows. So far as we can tell they conformed faithfully to Jewish law. From this point of view, they must have seemed to many onlookers like a strange messianic variation on the Pharisees' movement, coupling a fierce loyalty to Israel's One God with their own belief, as yet perhaps comparatively inarticulate, that the One God had revealed himself in *and as* the crucified and risen kingdom-bringer, Jesus himself.

I doubt if anyone, even Paul himself, could have written the book we would all like to read—a careful analysis of exactly which groups in Jerusalem believed what, how their various hopes and expectations lined up, which scriptural texts they used, and so on. But they all believed in the hope of Israel—the hope for a great divine rescue, which for the Jesus-followers had already been launched though obviously had not yet been fully implemented. They all believed in utter loyalty to Israel's One God. Fierce division existed over what precisely that loyalty should mean, but it would have taken a bold maverick to suggest that there might be forms of loyalty in which Israel's ancestral traditions, focused on the Torah, would not play a central role. According to Acts, it was Peter himself who first broke the taboo and went to preach to and to share table fellowship with non-Jews; he received strong divine validation for this radical move and persuaded his suspicious colleagues in Jerusalem that this had been the right thing to do.[1] But this move too seems not to have been thought through with regard to what they believed about Jesus himself. It was a pragmatic decision. This is how the spirit had led; therefore this must be what God wants.

It remained easy, then, for most of the Jerusalem-based Jesus-followers to see their movement as a Jesus-focused variation on the Jewish loyalist agenda. God might, to be sure, bring in some non-Jews. That had always happened in Israel's history, as the book of Ruth and various other passages made clear. But one could hardly imagine that the God whose scriptures warned constantly against covenant disloyalty would suddenly declare the Torah itself redundant.

But that is what many in Jerusalem, including many Jesus-followers, believed that Paul had been teaching. We see this later on, when Paul returns to Jerusalem for the last time in the mid-50s after his extensive travels in Greece and Turkey. Having just written the letter to the Romans, the greatest early Christian treatment of the complex covenant dealings of Israel's One God with his people, Paul finds himself speaking to an angry mob for whom the merest mention of "going to the Gentiles" is clear evidence that he is a careless compromiser.[2] This kind of reaction to garbled rumors, both in Syrian Antioch and in the new churches of southern Anatolia, was, it seems, already alive and well in the mid-40s. After all, Jews, including Jewish Jesus-followers, traveled regularly to and from Jerusalem. Something so strange and dramatic as the message about Jesus and the effects it was having would be an obvious topic of conversation. The word would get out that Paul and Barnabas, not content with belonging to a strange mixed community in Syrian Antioch, had been going around the world telling Jews that they no longer need to obey the law of Moses! If Paul was really saying that God had made a way through the problems that Moses had left behind him—that now they could be "justified" from all the things that were still a problem under Moses[3]—then this was basically saying that the Torah itself could be set aside. Who could tell what appalling results might then follow?

All this focused on the covenant sign of circumcision. Some Jews in Paul's day had tried to "explain" the practice of circumcision by pointing out its moral effects, suggesting that cutting off the foreskin would reduce lust. I know of no evidence that this actually worked, though the strong Jewish taboos against sexual immorality certainly had a restraining effect by contrast with the normal non-Jewish approach. But for centuries before Paul's time circumcision had come to have a strong symbolic value. Going back to Genesis 17 and strongly reinforced at various points in the Pentateuch, the eighth-day circumcision of male babies was the mandatory sign of covenant membership. Some other nations had had similar practices, but by Paul's day the phrases "the circumcision" and "the Jewish people" were virtually synonymous. This meant that if any non-Jewish males wished to become part of the Jewish community they, like the Hivites in Genesis 34, would have had to have been circumcised.[4] It is true that the prophets and Moses himself had spoken of "the circumcision of the heart" as the ultimate reality to which physical circumcision was meant to point. That deep reality was associated with the promise of ultimate covenant renewal. But nobody in the early years of the first century imagined that, if the One God really did renew the covenant, physical circumcision might be dispensed with for the non-Jews who would be included. On the contrary. Circumcision became a touchstone, a telltale symbol, a sign once more of *loyalty*.

When we think of loyalty and of the ways in which a tight-knit community in an overheated political situation actually functions, we realize what was at stake. The Jesus-followers in Jerusalem faced trouble from the start. Many had dispersed following the early persecution, but there was still a tight core, focused particularly on James himself. From at least the time of Stephen's killing they had been regarded as potentially subversive, disloyal to the Temple and its traditions. Now this disloyalty was showing itself in a new way: they were allied with a supposedly Jesus-related movement, out in far-flung lands, teaching Jews that they didn't have to obey the Torah! That was the kind of movement, loyal Jews would naturally think, that would introduce one compromise after another until any Jews still attached to it would find themselves indistinguishable from pagans. Here in Jerusalem all loyal Jews knew that the pagans were the enemy whom God would one day overthrow, just as he overthrew Pharaoh's armies in the Red Sea. But out there in the Diaspora this new movement was, it seemed, treating pagans as equal partners.

The word on the street in Jerusalem, then, would have been that these Jesus-followers were not really loyal Jews. They were letting the side down. That was how the forces of darkness always worked, and there were many in Jerusalem who would be on the lookout for the first signs of it among the local Jesus movement. Already viewed with suspicion, the Jesus-followers might be in danger. They would be hoping against hope that the Jesus movement in the wider world—not least that wild man Paul—would not land them in any deeper trouble, any guilt by association. From all that they had heard, the signs were not encouraging.

These cautious historical proposals about the real-life situation faced by Jesus-followers in Jerusalem and by their colleagues (if they saw them as such) in the Diaspora offer a corrective to the oversimplifications that have all too easily crept into readings of Paul. This has been a particular problem for modern Western readers. Our philosophies have tended to split the world in two: "science" deals only with "hard facts," while the "arts" are imagined to deal in nebulous questions of inner meanings. Equally, in popular culture, inner feelings and motivations ("discovering who you really are" or "going with your heart") are regularly invoked as the true personal reality over against mere outward "identities." Some types of Protestantism have imbibed this deeply, supposing that "the gospel" is all about inner feeling, a disposition of the heart, and not at all about outward reality or actions, whether moral or "religious." Sometimes people have thought that this is the one and only meaning of Paul's teaching about "justification by faith not works." But things were not nearly so simple.

In this climate of thought it has been easy for us to imagine that we have understood why Paul was insisting that circumcision no longer mattered for membership in God's family. Obviously, we think, he was interested in a person's inner reality, over against those fussy legalists who thought you had to obey a string of ritual instructions! He believed, we say, in a message of love rather than law, of inward feeling rather than outward conformity, of faith in the heart rather than rule-book religion or liturgical performance. In particular, we suppose, Paul believed that God didn't require a perfect moral obedience from people, because God in any case always preferred right feelings (including "faith") to right actions (which might make you proud). And so we could go on.

These caricatures are themselves full of contradictions. Anyone who thinks that having right "feelings" doesn't make people proud is singularly blind to the currently fashionable notion that what matters is a correct "attitude" on the questions of the day. But that doesn't make the caricatures any the less powerful. And none of them will help us understand what happened when people in Jerusalem heard what Paul was doing and teaching and reacted with alarm.

★ ★ ★

Four things then happened in quick succession. First, Peter came to Antioch and shared in the life of the church for a while. How long, we do not know, though this and the following incidents— including the writing of Paul's first letter, that to the churches in Galatia—must be dated around AD 48. Second, some others came to Antioch from Jerusalem, claiming to have been sent by James. This precipitated a small earthquake in the Antioch church and a controversy described by Paul himself so sharply that we blush, even at this distance, to overhear such a devastating denunciation. Third, perhaps weeks and months later, Paul received bad news from the little communities of non-Jewish believers in southern Anatolia, so recently founded by himself and Barnabas. All this is interconnected with so many tightly interlocking loops of first-century Jewish and early Christian understanding, misunder-standing, claim and counterclaim, that it makes the fourth event particularly difficult to understand, but particularly important to grapple with. The fourth event was Paul's writing of his famous first letter, Galatians.

He then set off for Jerusalem in the hopes of sorting it all out with those who seemed to be causing the trouble. Of course, they thought *he* was the one causing the trouble. Controversies are always like that. Generations of Christians who have read Gala-tians as part of holy scripture have to remind themselves that, if Galatians is part of the Bible, it is *Galatians as we have it* that is part of the Bible—warts and all, sharp edges and sarcastic remarks in-cluded. Perhaps, indeed, that is what "holy scripture" really is— not a calm, serene list of truths to be learned or commands to be obeyed, but a jagged book that forces you to grow up in your thinking as you grapple with it.

In any case, I do not think that when Paul began to dictate the letter (you can tell he's dictating, because at the end he points out that he is writing the closing greeting in his own hand), he was thinking, "This will be part of 'scripture.'" However, he believed that the One God had called him to be the apostle to the non-Jews, the Gentiles. He believed that Jesus had revealed himself to him and commissioned him with the news of Jesus's victory over death and his installation as Lord. Paul believed that Jesus's own spirit was at work through him to establish and maintain the life-changing communities of people whose lives had themselves been changed by the power of the gospel. And now he believed, as part of that, that he had a responsibility to state clearly what was at stake in the controversy in Antioch, in Jerusalem, in Galatia itself. His own obvious vulnerability throughout this process was part of the point, as he would later stress in another letter. His writing, just like the gospel itself, was part of a radical redefinition of what "authority" might look like within the new world that the One God had launched through Jesus.

Understanding a letter like Galatians—where the author is dictating so fast and assuming so much shared understanding that he skips over a hundred things we wish he had spelled out more fully—is notoriously like listening to one side of a complicated telephone conversation. Speaker and hearer assume a great deal that the listener has to fill in. Misunderstandings are easy, particularly when, in the case of a letter like Galatians, controversies from much later periods have imposed their own grid of expectation and have thus highlighted, and perhaps distorted, some of Paul's key themes. Ideally, the more we understand about the larger worlds within which the whole conversation was taking place, the more we will see why Paul needed to say exactly what he said.

We return, then, to the sequence of events in Antioch. The first occurrence is easy to understand. Peter came to Antioch, perhaps in early 48. His arrival is unexplained, but then all Peter's movements are unrecorded after his surprising escape from prison in Acts 12:17; all we know is that he worked as a traveling missionary. The key point is that he had initially been happy to go along with the practice of the local Jesus-followers, having Jewish believers and Gentile believers living together as "family," sharing the same table. This was, after all, the principle that he, Peter, had himself embraced in Acts 10–11, when he visited Cornelius, justifying his actions to critics in Jerusalem. "What God made clean," he had been told, "you must not regard as common."[5] Peter had acted on that principle, reckoning that the power of the gospel had "cleansed" the Gentiles of the ritual or moral defilement that they possessed in Jewish eyes, defilement that would normally be seen as a barrier to the intimacy of table fellowship.

So far, so good. With the second event, however, everything changes. Some people—we don't know who they are, but Paul says they "came from James" in Jerusalem—arrived in Antioch and insisted that if these Gentiles wanted to be part of the true family, to share in the great rescue operation that the One God had now set in motion, they would have to be circumcised. Paul, describing this moment to the Galatians, says that this made Peter change his mind. Up to this point he had happily sat down to eat with the Jesus-believing Gentiles, but now, seeing that the newcomers were taking a hard line, he drew back. Granted the status that Peter himself had in the movement, it isn't surprising that the other Jewish Jesus believers followed suit. And, says Paul, "Even Barnabas was carried along by their sham."[6]

It was not, then, simply a matter of teaching, of theoretical disagreements. It was about practice, the practice that revealed an underlying belief. The original practice in Antioch had reflected the belief that all Jesus believers, whether circumcised or not, belonged at the same table. The people who came from Judaea to

Antioch were clearly saying that table fellowship with uncircumcised Gentiles was wrong and that Jewish Jesus-followers, as loyal Jews, should withdraw.

The lasting shock of this moment is concentrated in Paul's use of the word "even." There is pain in that word, like someone trying to take a step on a foot with a broken bone in it. *Even Barnabas!* Barnabas had been with him through the joys and the trials of the mission in Galatia. They had shared everything; they had prayed and worked and celebrated and suffered side by side. They had themselves welcomed many non-Jews into the family. And now this. So what had happened?

Paul is careful not to say that James had actually sent the people who came from Jerusalem. However, they seem to have come with some kind of claim to be acting on James's authority. And the focus of their concern, readily explicable in view of the tensions in Jerusalem we explored a moment ago, was the vital importance of maintaining covenant loyalty. Circumcision was nonnegotiable because the purity of God's people was essential. If God was indeed bringing in his kingdom, rescuing Israel and the world from the powers of darkness to which the pagan nations had given their allegiance, then of course a clean break was vital. If pagans were allowed into the covenant people, the people who would inherit God's new creation, they would have to exhibit covenant loyalty too. And that meant circumcision.

From the perspective of a Jerusalem full of eager, zealous kingdom-minded Jews, all this made sense. From the perspective of Paul, who had already thought through what it meant that God was bringing his kingdom *through the crucified Messiah,* it made no sense at all. Paul had come to believe that Jesus couldn't simply be added on to the earlier picture of God's rescuing kingdom. The shocking and unexpected events of the Messiah's death and resurrection, coupled with the dramatic sense of personal renewal for which the only explanation was the outpoured divine spirit, meant that everything had changed. A new world had been launched. And if people were trying to live in that new world while wanting at the same time to put on a good face before people who hadn't realized just how radical this new world was, they were precisely "putting on a face," playing a part, covering up reality with a mask. They were, in short, "playacting." The Greek word for "playacting" is *hypokrisis,* from which we get the English term "hypocrisy."

We can imagine the uproar and confusion, the mutual accusation and recrimination that followed. Paul gives a quick summary of what he himself had said in confronting Peter; how much of this anyone might have been able to hear in the confusion we cannot tell, and as with other summaries we may assume that Paul originally said it at much greater length. The problem was personal as well as theological. As one of the recognized "pillars," Peter had drawn the other Jewish Jesus-followers with him in stepping back from the common table. Once he had made this move as one of the best-known figures in the whole movement, it would have been very hard for the other Jews to hold their nerve. This made it no doubt harder for Paul to confront him, but also all the more necessary. Peter had to be stopped in his tracks. Paul has acquired over time a reputation for being a cantankerous and controversial figure, and no doubt there was that element in his makeup. But if you see a friend about to step out, unawares, into the path of oncoming traffic, leading a group with him, the most loving thing to do is to yell that they must stop at once. That is exactly what Paul did:

> When Cephas came to Antioch, I stood up to him face to face. He was in the wrong. . . . When I saw that they weren't walking straight down the line of gospel truth, I said to Cephas in front of them all: "Look here: you're a Jew, but you've been living like a Gentile. How can you force Gentiles to become Jews?"[7]

Forcing Gentiles to become Jews. That may not have been what Peter thought he had been doing, but Paul looks behind the immediate issue (Peter and the other Jews withdrawing from table fellowship with Gentile Jesus-followers) to the clear implication and effect. Once you create a circle within a circle, you are sending a message to those in the outer ring that they should move into the inner one. But Peter had been already "living like a Gentile"— not in the sense that he had been worshipping idols or indulging in sexual immorality, but in the sense that he had been in the habit of eating with people without regard for the Jew/Gentile distinction. He was therefore "in the wrong." Either his present behavior meant that his previous stance had been wrong, or his previous stance, being right, meant that his present behavior was wrong.

Paul was in no doubt which of these was the correct analysis:

We are Jews by birth, not "Gentile sinners." But we
know that a person is not declared "righteous" by works
of the Jewish law, but through the faithfulness of Jesus
the Messiah.[8]

This is where, traditionally, interpreters have jumped to the wrong conclusion. The question of "righteousness" has dominated Western theological discussion, and most have assumed that Paul here suddenly switches from talking about Peter eating with Gentiles (or not eating, as the case may be) and starts talking about "how someone is justified" in the traditional Western sense, in other words, how someone previously a "sinner" comes to be "righteous" in God's sight.

Now, Paul clearly believes in the importance of sin and of being rescued from it. But that is not what is at stake in Jerusalem, Antioch, or Galatia. What matters is *status within the covenant family.* The word "righteous," like the Greek and Hebrew words that term often translates, refers here to someone "being in a right relationship" with the One God, and the "relationship" in question is the *covenant* that God made with Abraham. As we will see presently, for instance in the decisive conclusion to the central argument in Galatians 3:29, the question Paul has to address is: How can you tell who are the true children of Abraham? And his answer is focused firmly on Jesus. So Paul's point to Peter is simple. What matters is being part of the covenant family, and the covenant family is not defined by Jewish law, but "through the faithfulness of Jesus the Messiah."

Here again we meet the powerful and many-sided word "faithfulness," *pistis* in Greek. As we have seen, that same Greek word can mean "faith" in its various senses and also "faithfulness," "loyalty," or "reliability." Here and elsewhere Paul seems to play on what seem to us multiple meanings; they may not, of course, have looked like that to him. The point is that, in a world where the key thing for a zealous Jew was "loyalty" to God and his law, Paul believed (1) that Jesus the Messiah had been utterly faithful to the divine purpose, "obedient even to the death of the cross" as he says elsewhere;[9] (2) that following Jesus, whatever it took, had to be seen as itself a central expression of loyalty to Israel's God; (3) that the followers of Jesus were themselves marked out by their belief in him, confessing him as "Lord" and believing that he was raised from the dead; and (4) if this Jesus-shaped loyalty was the vital thing, *then nothing that the law could say was to come between one Jesus-follower and another.* In other words (continuing Paul's description of what he said to Peter):

> That is why we too believed in the Messiah, Jesus: so that we might be declared "righteous" on the basis of the Messiah's faithfulness, and not on the basis of works of the Jewish law. On that basis, you see, no creature will be declared "righteous."[10]

This adds another element, which Paul does not here spell out. Once Jewish law is made the standard for membership, that very law will raise sharp questions about anyone at all, Jews included. Read Deuteronomy and see that Israel as a whole will rebel, turn away from the One God, and suffer the consequences. On this basis, Paul urges Peter (and all the others listening to the confrontation or who hear his letter when it is read out loud) to think through the quite new position:

> Well, then: if, in seeking to be declared "righteous" in the Messiah, we ourselves are found to be "sinners," does that make the Messiah an agent of "sin"? Certainly not! If I build up once more the things which I tore down, I demonstrate that I am a lawbreaker.[11]

In other words, if we start with the normal Jewish categories that Paul states above ("We are Jews by birth, not 'Gentile sinners'"), in which Gentiles are automatically "sinners" because they don't have the law, then if someone like Peter finds himself called to live on equal terms with "Gentile sinners" because that is required by his membership of the Messiah's people, does that mean that the Messiah is now condoning or colluding with "sin"? This, we recall, is exactly the kind of thing that people in Jerusalem would be worried about. They might see this as fraternizing with the enemy, just when they, back home, were doing their best to stay loyal to God and the law and so to hasten the coming kingdom! They might see, in Paul's claim to be following the Messiah, a false Messiah who was leading people astray. This, they might say, is just what the law itself had warned might happen.

Paul counters this line of thought at once. If Peter or anyone else starts by pulling down the wall between Jew and Gentile (as Peter had indeed done: "You're a Jew, but you've been living like a Gentile") and then decides to rebuild it, all he is doing is pointing the finger back at himself. He is admitting that he was wrong to "live like a Gentile," and he is invoking the law, which will simply remind him that he is in any case a lawbreaker.

There is only one way forward, and that is to go where the Messiah has led, through death to new life. This journey is the same for all the Messiah's people, Jew and Gentile alike. Here we come to the very heart of Paul's understanding of what had happened in the messianic events involving Jesus. It is the central principle around which his answer to the three very different situations—in Jerusalem, in Syrian Antioch, and in Galatia—had been thought out. Paul describes this in the first-person singular ("I") not because he is holding himself up as a shining example of a particular spiritual experience, but because if even he, as a zealous Jew, had to tread this path, then it would be obvious that it was the only way to go:

> Let me explain it like this. Through the law I died to the law, so that I might live to God. I have been crucified with the Messiah. I am, however, alive—but it isn't me any longer, it's the Messiah who lives in me. And the life I do still live in the flesh, I live within the faithfulness of the son of God, who loved me and gave himself for me.[12]

Through the law I died to the law, so that I might live to God. That is one of the most extraordinary statements ever written by a Jew of the first or perhaps any century. It tells us at the same moment that Paul regards himself as a loyal Jew, loyal to God and the law—and that he had come to see the law itself as pointing forward to a kind of "death," pointing to something beyond itself, something that could only be attained by coming out of the law's own private sphere and emerging into a new world. The law itself had envisaged a moment when it would be upstaged by a new reality, the messianic reality. Though Paul does not mention baptism in this passage—he will come to that a chapter later—the sequence of thought he describes here is exactly what, in his view, baptism is all about (as in Romans 6), which is leaving the old life behind and coming through "death" into a new life entirely.

And insofar as he is still the same flesh-and-blood human being ("the life I do still live in the flesh"), he now finds his identity not in his human genealogy or status, but in the Messiah himself and his (the Messiah's) faithfulness and loyalty. If, in other words, it's loyalty to God and the law that you want, then the Messiah's death and resurrection has defined for all time what that actually looks like. When someone comes to be part of that messianic reality, then this, rather than their previous standing as "Jew" or "Gentile" (along with any outward marks of that standing), is the only thing that matters.

The mention of the Messiah's "love" ("who loved me and gave himself for me") is not merely an appeal to emotion, though it is that as well. The idea of a "love," coming from Israel's God and rescuing people from the fate they would otherwise suffer, goes all the way back to the covenant between God and Israel and the rescuing act of the Exodus. Paul will develop this thought elsewhere. For the moment, as a summary of what he said to Peter in Antioch (and with "certain persons from James" listening in, no doubt shocked at what they were hearing), it leads directly to Paul's conclusion:

> I don't set aside God's grace. If "righteousness" comes
> through the law, then the Messiah died for nothing.[13]

In other words, if Peter and, by implication, those who have come from James try to reestablish a two-tier Jesus movement, with Jews at one table and Gentiles at another, all they are doing is declaring that the movement of God's sovereign love, reaching out to the utterly undeserving ("grace," in other words), was actually irrelevant. God need not have bothered. If the Torah, the Five Books of Moses, was sufficient for all time to define the people of God, then *there is no need for a crucified Messiah.* Or to put it the other way, if God has declared, in the resurrection, that the crucified Jesus really was and is the Messiah, then God is also declaring

that Moses could only take them so far. He pointed to a promised land, an "inheritance," but could not himself take the people
into it. Galatians is all about the ultimate "inheritance" that God
had promised. And, as we shall see presently, Paul insisted that the
"heirs" of this "inheritance" could not be defined by the Torah, but
only by the Messiah himself, the ultimate "heir."

So much, then, for the confrontation between Paul and Peter
at Antioch. It has been commonplace among New Testament interpreters to assume that Paul lost the argument and so had to set
off on his later missionary journeys without the support of the
Antioch church. I see no good reason for this conclusion. The distance from Syrian Antioch to South Galatia is not great, and the
entire situation assumes that people could and did travel quickly
and easily between the two. Had Paul lost the argument, I think
it extremely unlikely that he would have referred to it at all, let
alone in these terms, in writing to Galatia. In any case, he later
returns to Antioch without any hint of trouble.[14] But this brings
us to the point where we have to back up and examine the third
element in the situation at Antioch. What had been going on in
Galatia itself?

★ ★ ★

The situation behind Paul's letter was clearly complex. To recon-
struct it, we will not be relying simply on "mirror reading" from
what Paul actually says, though there is bound to be some of that.
We will also be doing our best to understand the larger situation
in Jerusalem, in Galatia, and in Paul's base at Antioch.

Once again we must avoid oversimplifications, especially
any suggestion (this has been common) that the Galatian Jesus-
followers, having been taught good Reformed theology, were
now embracing Arminianism or Pelagianism and trying to add to
their God-given salvation by doing some "good works" of their
own. We should also, of course, avoid the equal and opposite
suggestion, that Paul was simply trying to manipulate communi-

ties, putting forth a "sociological" agenda and using "theological" arguments as a smokescreen for his real purposes. Neither of these proposals will do. All the signs are that Paul understood the scripturally rooted purposes of the One God to have been fulfilled in the Messiah, Jesus, and that he understood this to involve the creation of a particular type of community. As far as he was concerned, therefore, what we call "theology" and what we call "sociology" belonged firmly together.

But, at around the same time as "certain persons came from James" to Syrian Antioch, it appears that certain persons, also claiming the authority of the Jerusalem church, came to Galatia. Their message was similar to the one the James people seem to have been articulating in Antioch. And that message was that all the fraternizing with Gentiles had to stop. Any Gentiles who wanted to be regarded as members of the true people of Israel, the family of Abraham, would have to be circumcised. God's kingdom would indeed come, rescuing God's people from the world and its wicked ways, but the only people who would inherit that kingdom would be the circumcised.

This sharp message for the little groups of Jesus-followers in Galatia also involved a personal attack on Paul himself. Paul, said the messengers, was only ever a second-order representative of the Jesus message. He had picked up his "gospel" in Jerusalem, but had failed to grasp one of its essential elements or perhaps had simply chosen not to pass it on. If the Galatians appealed to the top of the tree, to Jerusalem itself, they would find a different story from the one Paul told them.

We do not have to look far below the surface to see why all this seemed so urgent to the messengers and so important locally to many people in South Galatia. Jerusalem, as we have seen, was awash with zealous speculation about the coming kingdom, in which "the Gentiles" were usually the wicked villains who would at last receive their punishment. People disagreed on what exactly it meant to keep the Torah, but everyone agreed that keeping the

Torah mattered. People might disagree as to why exactly Gentiles posed a threat to the ancestral beliefs and hopes of Israel, but
everyone agreed that the Gentile threat was real. So any claim
that Israel's Messiah was now welcoming Gentiles on equal terms
into a new community where normal Torah standards (including the covenant badge of circumcision) were set aside must have
seemed a contradiction in terms. It would be like a grand-society
wedding at which the noble-born bridegroom arrives, only to
announce that he is running off with a gypsy girl he'd met down
the street. Any Gentiles who thought they were now sharing the
divine promises of Israel's worldwide inheritance were deceived.
And any Jews who were tempted to treat uncircumcised Gentiles
as "family" were compromising the integrity of God's people.
They were placing the promised inheritance itself in jeopardy.

   We noted a moment ago the pressure on the Jerusalem-based
Jesus-followers themselves. We can see how natural it would be
for them to want to demonstrate to their suspicious friends and
neighbors in Jerusalem just how loyal they really were by trying to put matters right. If only those Gentiles who believed in
Jesus would get circumcised, everybody would be happy! The
charge of disloyalty would collapse. And so, just as Saul of Tarsus had set off a decade earlier to round up those blaspheming
Jesus-followers, someone else—a shadowy, unnamed figure, presumably with a few friends—set off with a different though related agenda. He would bring this new movement into line. Paul
would recognize what this person was doing. It is the sort of
thing he would have done himself. It is quite likely that he knew
the person in question.

   At the same time, pressure would be mounting on the Jewish
communities in South Galatia. As long as everybody in that thoroughly Romanized province knew who the Jews were within a
particular town or city, all would be well. People might sneer at
them for their funny customs, but at least everybody would know
that they had official permission to forgo participation in the lo-

cal cults, particularly the exciting new cults of Rome and Caesar, which were celebrating the new worldwide reality of peace and prosperity provided by the "Lord" and "Savior" in Rome itself.

But one of the first and most important things that happened whenever non-Jews were grasped by the gospel of Jesus was that, once they had heard that there was a true and living God and that he loved them personally, they would turn away from the idols they had previously worshipped. So suddenly a new group would emerge, in a world without privacy, where people knew one another's business, and where social deviance was quickly noted and usually resented. This new group, the Jesus-followers, was not, or not obviously, Jewish; the males were not circumcised, the Sabbath was not being observed, and so on. But on the other hand, like the Jews, the members of this group were staying away from the regular rituals, the weekly, monthly, or annual ceremonies and celebrations. So if the Jesus-followers in Jerusalem were suspected of disloyalty because of their attitude toward Israel's Temple and Torah, the Jesus-followers in the Diaspora would be suspected of disloyalty toward their own communities, and toward Rome itself, because of their attitude toward the local cults.

The Jewish communities in cities like Pisidian Antioch, Iconium, and Lystra—all Roman colonies, we recall—would then find themselves caught in the middle. We can imagine the civic authorities challenging them. "Who are these people," they would ask, "who have suddenly stopped worshipping the gods? Are they Jews or are they not? We need to know! Sort it out or we will have questions to ask." Local synagogue communities might well be divided in their response, but the social pressure would build up. The situation was intolerable. Something would have to be done. So we can easily imagine that local Jewish leaders would want to put pressure on local Jewish Jesus-followers to persuade their surprising new friends, the Gentile Jesus believers, to come into line. "Persuade them to get circumcised," they urged.

"Use any tactics, any pressure you like, but get it done. Otherwise we're all in trouble."

These reconstructions of the likely scenarios in Jerusalem and in Galatia are, of course, guesses. But they fit with what we know of the larger world of the time and with the kinds of challenges that local communities often faced. Above all, they make very good sense of the letter Paul then wrote. Nor should we imagine that these pressures—the grinding of gears between different social and cultural groupings—were seen, either by the people concerned or by Paul himself, as (in our terms) "sociological" *rather than* "religious" or "theological." Such distinctions make no sense in the first century. Everybody knew that divine worship was central to communal life. It kept things together and fostered social stability. For Jesus-followers, worshipping the true and living God, who had acted dramatically in the gospel events and who was now continuing to act powerfully by his spirit, generated and sustained a new kind of communal life, holding it together and fostering its stability—at the necessary cost of disrupting the tidy patterns of all the other communal life of the region.

Paul, therefore, had a complex and challenging task. He would understand only too well the different anxieties, the complex web of social, cultural, religious, and theological pressures and agendas. He would see the communities he had founded caught in the middle—and would be shocked at how easily they, or some of them, had succumbed to the teaching of whoever it was who was "troubling" them. He would be personally hurt (this comes through at various points in the letter) that they would be disloyal to him after all that they had seen him go through on their behalf. But above all he would be shocked that they seemed not to have grasped the very center of it all, the meaning of Jesus himself and his death and resurrection and the fact that through him a new world, a new creation, had already come into being. They were in serious danger of stepping back from that new reality into the old world, as though the cross and resurrection had never taken place, as though the true and living God had not revealed his covenant love once and for all not only *to* Israel but *through* the personification of Israel, the Messiah, to the world.

It would take a whole separate book to work through the letter to the Galatians and explain how Paul, in his rapid-fire writing, hits these nails on the head with all the tools of rhetoric and irony available to him and at the same time with pathos and personal appeal. He has several things to say, and they come tumbling out on top of one another.

He interrupts his own opening greeting to insist that his "apostleship" was a direct gift from God and Jesus, not a secondhand or second-rate thing he got from elsewhere. "Paul, an apostle," he begins—and then interrupts himself by adding, in brackets as it were, "my apostleship doesn't derive from human sources . . ." Then he recovers his balance and states the foundation principle. His apostleship derives from God himself, and from Jesus the Messiah, our *Kyrios,*

> who gave himself for our sins, to rescue us from the
> present evil age, according to the will of God our father,
> to whom be glory to the ages of ages. Amen.[15]

Each element here is vital. The "good news" Paul has announced is what the One God always planned and intended. It is not a sudden afterthought. The message about Jesus may look to Jews in Jerusalem or Galatia as though it's a strange, peculiar eccentricity. But it is in truth the leading edge of the long-awaited new creation. This is central and will remain so throughout Paul's work.

The central point concerns the difference between "the present evil age" and the new day that has dawned. Paul here affirms the well-known and widespread ancient Jewish belief that world history is divided into two "ages," the "present age" of sorrow, shame, exile, and death and the "age to come," when all things will be put right. That belief was common for centuries before Paul, and it remained the norm all the way through the much later rabbinic period. But for Paul something had happened. The living God had acted in person, in the person of Jesus, to rescue people from that "present age" and to launch "the age to come." The two ages were not, as it were, back to back, the first stopping when the second began. The new age had burst upon the scene while the "present age" was still rumbling on. This was the direct effect of the divine plan by which Jesus "gave himself for our sins"; the power of the "present age" was thereby broken, and the new world could begin. There is a sense in which the whole letter, and in a measure all of Paul's work, simply unpacks and explains this opening flourish.

It is always risky to summarize, but part of the point of the present book is to invite readers to so live within Paul's world that they will be able to read the letters in their original contexts and so grasp the full import of what was being said. So, for Galatians, we may simply note five points that come out again and again. Each could be spelled out at length.

First, to repeat, Paul is offering a reminder that what has happened through Jesus is the launching of new creation. The messianic events of Jesus and the spirit are not simply another religious option, a new twist on an old theme. If they mean anything, they mean that the creator God has called time on the old creation and has launched the new one in the middle of it. No wonder this new reality is uncomfortable. "Circumcision . . . is nothing; neither is uncircumcision! What matters is new creation."[16] The messengers from Jerusalem and the local pressure groups are trying to put the hurricane of new creation back into the bottle of the old world. It can't be done. The Messiah's death has defeated the powers of the world. That is why non-Jewish idolaters have been set free from their former slavery. Paul's analysis is sharp: "If you try to reverse this—as you would be doing, were you to get circumcised—you are saying you don't believe in the new creation. You are saying that the Messiah didn't need to die. You are saying you still belong in the old world. You are cutting off the branch you have been sitting on."

Second, what has happened in the gospel events, and what has happened in Paul's own ministry, is in fact the fulfillment of the scripturally sourced divine plan. Paul's long explanation of his own early days in the movement, designed to ward off the charge that he got his gospel secondhand and muddled it up as he did so, echoes again and again the "call" of the prophets and of the "servant" in Isaiah who was to be the light of the nations. "Whatever Jewish messengers may tell you," Paul is saying, "I can show you that what has happened through Jesus *and what has been happening through my own work* is what Israel's scriptures themselves always envisaged." Paul's own commissioning on the Damascus Road and his subsequent visits to Jerusalem make it clear that his gospel was firsthand. The only thing the Jerusalem apostles contributed to it was support. Likewise, Paul's suffering, which the Galatian churches had witnessed up close, was itself a dramatic signpost to the gospel. In particular—and this forms the central theme of the letter—the divine promises to Abraham have been fulfilled in Jesus the Messiah. God promised Abraham a worldwide family. In the Psalms and Isaiah this was focused on the coming king, the son of David who would be the son of God. In Jesus, God has done what he promised, launching the movement through which the new creation is coming about, the kingdom of God on earth as in heaven.

This leads Paul, third, to the vital point. *All this has effectively bypassed the problem posed by Moses.* The third chapter of the letter to the Galatians outflanks the eager Torah loyalty of the Jerusalem zealots and their diaspora cousins. Moses himself leaves Israel, at the end of Deuteronomy, with the warning of a curse, and the curse will culminate in exile, just as it had for Adam and Eve in Genesis 3. Moses's Torah was given by God for a vital purpose, but that purpose was temporary, to cover the period before the

fulfillment of the promise to Abraham. Now that this has happened, the Torah has no more to say on the subject.

All those who belong to the Messiah are the true "seed" of
Abraham, guaranteed to inherit the promise of the kingdom, of
new creation. Abraham believed God, quotes Paul from Genesis, "and it was counted to him for righteousness."[17] There is the
phrase that, we have suggested, had haunted Saul of Tarsus from
his days as a young zealot. Phinehas acted with zeal for God and
the law, "it was counted to him for righteousness," and God established his covenant with him. Mattathias, the father of Judas
Maccabaeus, had quoted this phrase, referring to Abraham and
Phinehas, as he commissioned his sons for their life of holy zeal.[18]
Now Paul is reinterpreting both covenant and zeal. God has fulfilled his promises to Abraham, but this does not drive a wedge
between holy Jews and wicked Gentiles; instead, it is establishing
a Jew-plus-Gentile family of faith—as God always intended.

Fourth, this has been accomplished through the long-awaited
"new Exodus." Every Jew knew the story: slavery in Egypt; divine victory over Pharaoh; Israel (as "God's firstborn son") redeemed and brought through the Red Sea; the gift of the Torah
on Sinai; the glorious divine presence coming to dwell in the
Tabernacle; Abraham's children heading home to the "inheritance" of the promised land. Paul retells that story in Galatians
4:1–7 with Jesus and the spirit at the heart of it. The whole world
is enslaved; God sent his son to redeem and his spirit to indwell;
Abraham's children are assured of their "inheritance." There is
a sting in the tail, however.[19] Paul warns the Galatians that they
are now in danger of behaving like those Israelites in the wilderness who wanted to go back to Egypt. If they get circumcised,
they will be saying that they prefer the old slavery to the new
freedom.

So, finally and decisively, the living God has created *the single family* he always envisaged, and it is marked *by faith, pistis*.
God had not promised Abraham two families, a Jewish one and

a non-Jewish one—which is what would have been implied by Peter's behavior at Antioch, where Jewish and non-Jewish Jesus-followers were to eat at separate tables. Nor would it do to create that single family artificially, as it were, simply by circumcising male Gentile converts. If covenant membership were available through the Torah, the Messiah wouldn't have needed to die.

How can you tell, then, where this single family is? The only sure indication is *pistis*—faith, faithfulness, loyalty. All of those and more besides. Not, of course, a generalized "religious faith," but "Messiah faith," the faithfulness of the Messiah himself, whose death overcame the power of sin and thus delivered people from the present evil age; the faith evoked by the gospel message, the kind that echoed the Messiah's own faithfulness by confessing that Jesus is *Kyrios* and believing that God raised him from the dead; the loyalty that now clings to that message and refuses to be blown off course. Paul has taken one of the central themes that had motivated both the Torah loyalists in Jerusalem and the Caesar loyalists in Galatia and replaced it with a word, elevated almost to a technical term, that denoted loyalty to the One God, the true and living one now made known in and as Jesus and now active through the spirit. It was a new, contested loyalty. Without leaving this home base of meanings, however, the word *pistis* encompassed so much more, especially the personal knowledge and trust that sprang up in hearts and minds at the news of Jesus, the sense of God's intimate presence and love.

This, then, is Paul's famous doctrine of "justification by faith." It is not that "faith" in the sense of a "religious awareness" is somehow a kind of human experience that is superior to others, but that those who believed the gospel and who were loyal to the One God it unveiled were to be known, and were to know themselves, as the single worldwide family promised to Abraham. And that meant a new community sharing a common table despite all differences: neither Jew nor Greek, neither slave nor free, no "male and female," since "all are one in the Messiah, Jesus."[20]

A new kind of community, then, as the advance guard of the new creation. A dramatic new vision, claiming the deepest of roots in Israel's scriptures and the most personal of relationships with Israel's God. Paul tells the Galatians that because they are new-Exodus people, the true "children" of God, "God has sent the spirit of his son" into their hearts, "calling out 'Abba, Father!'"[21] The spirit thus anticipates and points to the ultimate inheritance, the promised land of new creation itself. And anyone who tries to disrupt this new reality, anyone who, for whatever mixture of motives, tries to drag them back into the old world—such a person is to be shunned. Anyone who suggests that Jerusalem is still the center of everything, so that its leaders must have the last word, is to be reminded that what counts is the heavenly Jerusalem.[22] There cannot be "another gospel," whether the "gospel" of Caesar or a supposed "gospel" of Torah-plus-Jesus. "What matters is new creation."[23]

How much of all this the churches in Galatia would have understood at first hearing we may doubt. But the letter would be read aloud to them over and over again. It would have been discussed, argued over. Whoever had delivered the letter would almost certainly be called upon to explain what Paul meant. The teachers in the churches—teaching being a vital part of early church life—would do their best to help converts understand the dense web of scriptural references and allusions. We do not know how effective it was at the time, whether some non-Jewish Jesus-followers in Galatia did go ahead and get circumcised or whether they all decided to go with Paul rather than with the eager zealots who had been urging them to become full Jews. (The next time Paul is in the area Luke tells us little about the state of the churches in question.) Since we do not know who it was that had come to Galatia as an anti-Pauline missionary, we have no idea what happened to this person and his colleagues afterward.

Not that Paul had time to worry about that. He and Barnabas were already packing their bags for the trip to Jerusalem. It was time to discuss, face-to-face, the issues that had threatened the unity of the new movement and with it, from Paul's point of view at least, the integrity of the gospel itself.

★ ★ ★

Paul never mentions the "Jerusalem Conference" described in Acts 15, so we cannot be sure what he thought of it all. Clearly things could not go on as they were, with different groups sending frantic and contradictory messages this way and that. At least, if things *did* go on as they were, they would precipitate a major and lasting rift among the Jesus-followers.

Why would this matter? It is interesting that, from the first and despite great pressures to split, all the early leaders of the movement seem to have valued unity, even if they had very different suggestions as to how to achieve it. Partly this may have been pragmatic. They were under multiple pressures from the outside, and they needed to hold together. But for Paul himself, right across his letters, and it seems for the Jerusalem leadership as well, it mattered that the followers of Jesus should find a way of living together as a single family despite the inevitable tensions that a new but suddenly far-flung movement would experience. This reminds us again—and it will be a feature of much of Paul's life—that there really was no analogy in the ancient world for a movement of this kind. As we saw, the Roman army and civil service, on the one hand, and the network of Jewish synagogues, on the other hand, provide partial parallels, but Paul is trying something different from either. The challenge facing Paul and the others was how to live as an extended family without ties of kinship or ancestral symbols, without the geographical focus of Jerusalem and the Temple, and without a central authority like that of Caesar.

To Jerusalem, then, they went; not for reasons of sacred geography (Paul was now skeptical of that, as he hints in Galatians when he says that "the present Jerusalem" is "in slavery with her

children"[24]), but because that was the center of the protest movement that was objecting to what Paul and Barnabas had been doing. The meeting took place, fairly certainly, in either late 48 or
early 49.

We can imagine the conversations on the way. Paul would
now be somewhat uneasy after Barnabas's (I assume temporary)
change of stance in Antioch. Paul the thinker, the scholar, the
teacher would be eager to go into full sail, to expound the scriptures at length, to explain in great detail how the message about
Jesus's crucifixion and resurrection not only made sense of all
the old prophecies, but pointed directly to a new day in which
all humans, Gentiles as well as Jews, would be welcomed into a
single family.

Barnabas, we may suspect, would be urging restraint. He would
have picked up the signals from the Jerusalem visitors in Antioch:
they had always been suspicious of Paul, and the longer he went
on, the more they would stop listening to the scriptural detail
and start feeling that he was bullying them into a corner. The
Jerusalem Jesus-followers might not have been able to refute his
scriptural arguments, but they would still take it all with a pinch
of salt and conclude that there must be a flaw somewhere, since
they knew ahead of time that Paul was a dangerous and subversive character. In addition, Paul was an upstart former persecutor,
presuming to tell them about the meaning of Jesus's work just
because he knew his Bible rather well, whereas they had known
Jesus personally! Much better, Barnabas would suggest, for them
to tell the stories of what had happened in Galatia, and indeed
of what had been happening in Antioch itself, of how non-Jews
had found the spirit powerfully at work in their lives and communities. Much wiser, then, to put Peter and James on the spot,
to get them to recall Peter's visit to Cornelius, to challenge them
to expound the relevant scriptures. Let them do the theological
heavy lifting.

The journey itself was encouraging. As the two traveled south through Phoenicia and Galilee and into Samaria, approaching Jerusalem, they told the little groups of believers they encountered on the way what had happened in the Galatian churches. The response was encouraging. This would not only have strengthened their resolve; it would have given them practice in telling their stories to good effect. That was what they then did in Jerusalem, setting out in one story after another the extraordinary things that God had done through their work. They would have explained too the violent opposition they had received, but the important thing was the way that Gentiles had been grasped by the gospel and transformed by the spirit. We can imagine Paul biting his lip, restraining his desire to expound Genesis, Deuteronomy, Isaiah, and the rest, and Barnabas shooting him warning looks and hoping and praying that the plan would work. It did.

The hard-line party made its position clear: Gentile converts must be circumcised and keep the Torah. There was general discussion, in which Paul and Barnabas played a restrained part but held themselves back, we suspect, from any larger theological discourse. There were plenty of people who wished to contribute, and their testimony carried its own power. Finally Peter and James stood up to speak.

Peter went back again to what had happened when he visited Cornelius and God visibly gave his spirit to the Gentiles without their needing to be circumcised. Something had happened to these Gentiles as a result of which the normal Jewish taboos preventing contact with impure people were no longer relevant. What's more, Peter drew attention to something we have already noted—a recognition, precisely among devout Jews, that Mosaic law in its entirety, as it stood, left its adherents in a bad place. It simply warned that Israel was hard-hearted and that this would result in the covenantal curse. Why, then, should Jewish Jesus-followers place a restriction on Gentile converts that the Jewish people themselves, according to their own scriptures, find to be a burden? Peter left the assembly in no doubt that the sheer grace of God, through the message of Jesus, had transformed the hearts and lives of non-Jews without those non-Jews having to come under Mosaic law, without their being circumcised.

We sense the sigh of relief from Paul and Barnabas. They exchange quick glances. This was what they needed Peter to do. He has reinforced the impact of their own missionary stories, and they now add some more. The meeting, they think, has turned the corner.

The final word is then left to James, who we know from various sources was held in enormous respect not simply because he was Jesus's own brother, but because he devoted himself so assiduously to prayer. James sets all the strange stories they have heard in the context of scripture. What has happened, he says, is the clear fulfillment of ancient biblical hopes, that when God finally sends the Messiah, the true son of David, then his inheritance will consist of the whole world. God will "rebuild the Tabernacle of David which had collapsed," and the result will be that "the rest of the human race may seek the Lord, and all the nations upon whom [God's] name has been called."[25] The point could have been made from other prophets or indeed from a good many psalms, but the message is clear as it stands. Ancient Israel's messianic expectation had included the promise that David's son would be Lord of the whole world. This does not explicitly indicate that such a new community would leave behind the restrictions of the Mosaic code. But everybody knew that Moses's Torah was for the nation of Israel. If the other nations were now coming in, then a new dispensation had been inaugurated for which the Mosaic restrictions were no longer relevant.

Barnabas and Paul allow themselves a quiet smile of gratitude. This is what they have been hoping for. The crisis has been averted.

The main point at issue had thus been dealt with—though we should not imagine that everyone meekly acquiesced. Things do not work like that in real communities. Just because an official pronouncement has been made, that does not mean that all churches will at once fall into line. However, there was an important pragmatic consequence. Just because they did not need to be circumcised, that didn't mean that Gentile Jesus-followers were free to behave as they liked. They were to be careful to avoid giving offense to their Jewish neighbors, including their Jesus-believing Jewish neighbors. For that reason, there were certain areas where their freedom would need to be curtailed. There was to be no sexual immorality (one of the major differences between Jewish and pagan lifestyles) and no contact with what has been "polluted by idols" or "sacrificed to idols" or with meat that has been slaughtered in a nonkosher way, so that one would be eating blood, the God-given sign and bearer of life. There were, then, some typically Jewish taboos that were still to be observed, at least when in close contact with Jewish communities; the Jesus-followers were to take care when surrounded with Jewish sensibilities.

But the main point at issue—circumcision—was conceded. A letter was agreed upon, from the whole church to "our Gentile brothers and sisters." That already made the point that the uncircumcised believers were indeed *part of the family.* The letter was sent to Antioch, Syria, and Cilicia (Cilicia, the broad swath of southern Turkey, had by this time been divided between the Roman provinces of Galatia and Syria, but the name was still in common use for the area as a whole). In addition to its main points, the document also made it clear that, although the people who had arrived in Antioch and in Galatia had come from Jerusalem, they had not been authorized by James and the others. A delicate diplomatic solution all around.

Like many diplomatic solutions, it was designed to keep things together at least for a while, though it left many questions unaddressed. Paul and the others would have to go on grappling with them, as we shall see. But the hard-liners in Jerusalem, though no doubt bitterly disappointed at losing their demand that

Gentile converts be circumcised, would at least have been molli-
fied by the thought that the main causes of Gentile pollution, the
idolatry and sexual immorality that were the norm in non-Jewish
societies, would be avoided.

Supposing Paul's story had ended at this point, in AD 49 in Jerusalem, what would we say about him? What motivated him, and
how had he come to this point? If Galatians was the only thing he
had ever written, we would already know that he was a man of
enormous intellectual reach and energy. The letter still feels hot
off the press, covering huge areas in swift strokes, leaving much
to be filled in but focusing intently on what really mattered, what
had already come to define Paul. "I have been crucified with the
Messiah. I am, however, alive—but it isn't me any longer; it's the
Messiah who lives in me. And the life I do still live in the flesh,
I live within the faithfulness of the son of God, who loved me
and gave himself for me."[26] It doesn't get any clearer or any more
intimate than that. Paul's own answer to the question of what
motivated him to do what he did was Jesus—Jesus crucified and
risen, Jesus as the living embodiment of the love of the One God.

Paul's own answer to the question of what happened on the
road to Damascus and what it meant is equally clear. "God set me
apart from my mother's womb, and called me by his grace . . .
so that I might announce the good news about him among the
nations."[27] This was not a "conversion" in the sense of leaving
behind the Jewish world and starting or propagating a new "religion." But it was a "conversion" in the sense that Israel's Messiah
himself, going down into death, had taken with him the whole
world, including the whole Jewish world and its traditions, in
order then to emerge from death in a new form; and in the sense
that all those who now belonged to the Messiah shared that death,
that resurrection, and the new identity that followed. There had
never been a moment when Paul had not been out-and-out loyal
to the One God. But the One God had unveiled his age-old

purpose in the shocking form of the crucified Messiah, and that changed everything. A contested loyalty.

If we find all this puzzling or paradoxical, we can be sure that many of Paul's friends and associates, not to mention his opponents, would have said the same thing. The letter we know as 2 Peter puts it like this, speaking of Paul's letters (the only New Testament reference, outside Paul himself, to Paul as a letter writer):

> There are some things in them [i.e., in Paul's letters] which are difficult to understand. Untaught and unstable people twist his words to their own destruction, as they do with the other scriptures.[28]

It is not particularly remarkable that some found Paul's letters hard to understand and open to misinterpretation. What is remarkable is that Paul's writings were already being referred to as "scriptures." That points us to the larger question his work raises to this day. What was he doing that caused these little communities, with all their problems, contested loyalties, and external threats, not only to survive, but to thrive? This question is sharpened to a point by what happened next.

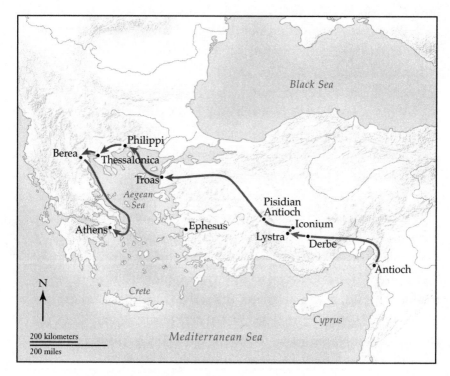

Antioch to Athens

7

Into Europe

L UKE DOES NOT spare Paul's blushes. The apostle to the Gentiles may be the main subject of Acts, at least in its second half, but there is a tale now to be told from which nobody comes out well. Paul will later characterize his vocation as "the ministry of reconciliation." His whole theme in Galatians and in all the activity that surrounded it had been the reconciliation of Jews and Gentiles in the single messianic family. But when it came to reconciliation, Paul must always have had a sense of shame and failure. He and Barnabas had a falling-out.

Perhaps it was the long-term result of that shocking moment in Antioch when Peter had separated himself from the non-Jewish believers and "even Barnabas" had been led astray by their "hypocrisy." They had made up then, it seems. They had gone together to Jerusalem and, side by side, had argued the case for Gentile inclusion. But Paul's trust in his friend and colleague had received a heavy blow. If things went wrong on another trip, would Barnabas prove utterly reliable? His ability to encourage and help people had been vital in Paul's own early work. But the real strength of his character—his desire to get alongside people and support them—

had led him in the wrong direction in Antioch. Might the same thing happen once more?

The specific flash point concerned Barnabas's nephew, John Mark (normally reckoned to be the Mark of the Gospel that bears his name). It was natural that Paul would suggest revisiting the churches of southern Anatolia. He felt a close bond with them, and, having written the letter, he was eager to see how things had turned out, to visit them again (as he had said) and be able to use a different tone of voice.[1] It was equally natural that Barnabas would want to take Mark, to give him a second chance. And it was utterly predictable that Paul would refuse.

Ostensibly, this was about reliability. Mark had abandoned them on the earlier journey as soon as they landed on the south Turkish mainland. If they were going to have assistance on another trip, it would make sense to have someone they knew would not let them down that way again. But there may be other factors at work. Mark was related not only to Barnabas, but also to Peter. Peter had of course supported Paul's mission at the Jerusalem Conference; but Mark, a young man with a question mark already over his character, might be inclined to take the same line that Peter had taken in Antioch. Supposing there were still some in Galatia who were claiming the authority of Peter or James in support of a two-table mealtime policy—in support, in other words, of some version of the circumcision agenda? What might Mark do then?

For his part, Barnabas would have found it intolerable that Paul would question his judgment. He had himself stood up for Paul ten years before when others were doubtful. Now he wanted to do the same for Mark. He had most likely spoken privately with the young man and believed that he had learned his lesson.

With the ease of hindsight we can think of many ways in which this could have been resolved amicably. Indeed, the solution that emerged—Barnabas and John Mark going back to Cyprus, Paul and someone else going to Galatia and beyond—was staring them in the face and could have been agreed on with prayer and mutual encouragement. But no. There was what Luke calls a *paroxysmos:* a blazing, horrible, bitter row. Nobody came out of it well. Goodness knows what the young church in Antioch made of it. We must assume that some of what Paul would later write about avoiding angry and bitter speech had already been part of his regular ethical teaching. But on this occasion all of that went out of the window, leaving not only a bad taste in everyone's mouth, but also a sorrowful memory.

So Barnabas and Mark sail away, not only to Cyprus, but right out of the narrative of Acts. Mark reappears as one of Paul's coworkers during his Ephesian imprisonment, and a later mention indicates that he had become a valued colleague at last.[2] Paul knows of Barnabas's continuing work, but they never team up again.[3] Paul now chooses a different companion, Silas (or Silvanus), like Paul a Roman citizen, a member of the Jerusalem church, indeed, one of those entrusted with the letter that the Jerusalem leaders had sent to the wider churches. It made good sense. The Antioch church sends them on their way, commending them to God's grace. They were going to need it.

The biblical writers of "histories" only seldom draw explicit moral lessons from the stories they tell. The classic example is Absalom's rebellion, which follows soon after David's adultery and the murder of Uriah. The connection is not made explicit, but there is an obvious link between David's casual attitude toward sexual liaison and human life, on the one hand, and the sexual malpractice and murder that precipitated the rebellion, on the other. And in the book of Ruth, to take a happier example, the narrator does not say, "And this was what God did next." We are simply told that Ruth and Naomi arrived at Bethlehem at the time of the barley harvest, and we are left to discover that this was the time and the means by which, against all expectation, Ruth would find a husband. One may also recall, in this connection, that wonderful plot-changing line in the middle of the book of Esther: "That night the king could not sleep."[4]

Something similar may be going on in Luke's narration of the journey that Paul and Silas now take, a journey from Antioch all the way to Corinth, probably to be dated from late 49 to early 51. After Timothy joins the party in Lystra, the three then move on, but without a real sense of direction. They try one thing, then another. The only divine guidance they get is negative: not this way, not that way. They go north, it seems, through Phrygia and Galatia, with the spirit forbidding them to go west into the province of Asia (the southwest coastal areas focused on Ephesus). Then they try to go through Mysia into Bithynia, the area up by the Black Sea, but again they are not permitted to go there. Like the children of Israel in the wilderness looking for the pillar of cloud and fire, they are relying on the spirit of Jesus, and the spirit appears to be allowing them to wander this way and that without a clear sense of guidance. It looks as though Paul had been expecting to work his way around some of the main parts of Anatolia, planting more churches as he had done in Galatia. But it wasn't to be.

It takes two verses for Luke to tell us all this, but the areas the travelers were covering were not small. Granted the roads they seem to have been taking, they journeyed at least three hundred miles after leaving Antioch to the point where they arrived, puzzled and weary, on the far northwestern shore of Mysia. It probably took them several weeks. Early on in the trip, they had visited the churches in South Galatia and had been encouraged by what they found. After that, there seems to be no more activity, either evangelistic or pastoral.

One could say that this was a good time for Paul and Silas to get to know one another better and for them both to act as mentors and guides for Timothy, who had been invited to join them as they passed through Lystra. But one could also say, and perhaps Luke is saying this, that this is what happens when someone makes hasty decisions in a hot temper. If so, this will not be the only cooling-off period of Paul's ministry. He seems to have learned from these times, but the learning was usually painful.

The bright spot in this otherwise puzzling period was Timothy himself. Timothy was from Lystra, where Paul had healed the crippled man and been mistaken for a Greek god. Paul was by this time in his late thirties or early forties (assuming he was born by AD 10 at the latest). Timothy, most likely in his late teens or early twenties, must have seemed like the son that Paul never had. Certainly a bond of understanding and mutual trust developed between them of the sort that happened with few others.

Timothy was the son of a believing Jewish woman and a Greek father. So, says Luke, Paul circumcised him "because of the Jews in those regions, since they all knew that his father was Greek."[5] Paul's action here has perplexed many readers. We cast our minds back to the time when Paul and Barnabas, going to Jerusalem with famine relief, took Titus with them. Despite intense pressure from the hard-line Jerusalem activists who wanted to have Titus circumcised, Paul stood firm. Paul stressed this point when writing to the Galatians.[6] In his mission in Galatia and then back in Antioch, Paul had stoutly resisted any suggestion that Gentile converts should be circumcised. He had gone to Jerusalem to argue for this principle and had won the day. But now he circumcises Timothy. Why? Is this not inconsistent? What is Paul's justification?

Here we see the start of the tricky policy that Paul spells out in 1 Corinthians 9. Everything depends on motivation. If someone says that Titus has to be circumcised *because otherwise he won't be able to join the family at the table,* Paul will object, saying Titus is a believer and he belongs there. But he wants to take Timothy with him on the next phase of his work, and that will involve going again and again into synagogues. It seems unlikely that synagogue officials would go to the lengths of making a physical check on whether newcomers had been circumcised, but Paul wants to be able to assure any doubters that all the members of the party are in fact officially Jewish.

This is what he means when he says, "I became like a Jew to the Jews, to win Jews. I became like someone under the law to the people who are under the law, even though I'm not myself under the law, so that I could win those under the law."[7] That is in itself an extraordinary statement. How could Paul become "like a Jew"? He *was* a Jew. The answer must be that, when seeking to work with Jewish communities or individuals, he would behave Jewishly, taking care to observe taboos for the sake of his work, not because he believed God required it of him for his standing as part of the messianic family.

He was treading a fine line, risking the charge of inconsistency at every turn. But, as with the foundational question of belonging to the Messiah's people, what counted for Paul was the gospel itself. He wanted to be able to continue his practice of worshipping in the synagogue and taking every opportunity to expound Israel's story (Abraham, Exodus, David, then the unresolved "exile") with its new and shocking messianic conclusion. And for that purpose Timothy, along with the rest of the party, would have to be a bona fide Jew.

There is one more addition to the party, and again Luke asks us to read between the lines. (There are many different theories to explain this, but the simplest is likely to be the best.) Paul and the others have arrived at Troas, the port on the edge of a mountainous area in the far northwest of modern Turkey. Troas, near the site of ancient Troy, stood on the edge of the Hellespont, the narrow waterway, four miles wide, famous in ancient history for separating the Greeks and the Persians and in modern literary history for Lord Byron's successful attempt to swim across it on May 3, 1810. Troas had been a strategic city in the time of Alexander, but it had suffered considerably during the Roman civil wars, and its importance had diminished—except insofar as it was the obvious port for anyone wanting to cross over into mainland Greece.

It may be, of course, that Paul and the others had come there because, having been forbidden to go elsewhere, they had already decided that they should probably move into quite different territories. It may even be that Paul had had some thoughts of heading straight for Rome following the Via Egnatia, which they could pick up at Philippi in northern Greece, and then making for the crossing between western Greece and the heel of Italy. But as I read Luke's description of this whole sequence of events, I think something else was going on. I think Luke knew that when Paul, Silas, and Timothy reached Troas, they were weary, disheartened, and puzzled. And I think that the reason Luke knew this was because this was the point at which he joined the party himself.

This is far and away the simplest explanation for the fact that his narrative suddenly says "we" instead of "they." Paul had a vision in the night (as so often, one receives guidance when it's needed rather than when it's wanted). A man from Macedonia was standing there, pleading, "Come across to Macedonia and help us!" (This itself strengthens my view that Paul had not previously thought of doing this, but had hoped to this point to plant more churches throughout what we now call Turkey.) So, says Luke:

> When he saw the vision, at once we set about finding
> a way to get across to Macedonia, concluding that God
> had called us to preach the good news to them.[8]

There are other theories, of course. There always are. But Occam's razor is still helpful: always go for the hypothesis requiring the fewest extra assumptions. So, although it is perfectly possible that the "we" passages in Acts are, say, part of a source available to a much later author, it is equally possible, and in my judgment more plausible, that "we" here is the author's signature. Luke turns up among those sending greetings in three Pauline letters

(Colossians, Philemon, and 2 Timothy). We cannot be certain, but the signs suggest that the person who joined the party at Troas was the same person who later on wrote the story down.

★★★

Philippi offered a different sort of challenge from the ones Paul and Barnabas had met on the earlier journey. It had been founded, or strictly speaking enlarged and refounded, out of an earlier settlement, by Philip II, king of Macedon from 382 to 336 BC, the father of Alexander the Great. The area was important in antiquity because of good-quality gold mines, of which Philip made considerable use. But the most significant event in Philippi's history came in the early stage of the Roman civil wars, when in the Battle of Philippi in 42 BC Mark Antony and the young Octavian Caesar defeated Brutus and Cassius, who had killed Octavian's adoptive father Julius Caesar two years before. Antony and Octavian then enlarged the city once more, establishing it as a Roman colony to settle veteran soldiers. (As with Pisidian Antioch and the other South Galatian colonies, Rome was anxious not to have old soldiers coming to Italy claiming or simply seizing land as a reward for loyal service.) Philippi is one of the better preserved of Paul's cities, and one can still see the layout of streets, a fine theater, and the Via Egnatia going by on its way from Rome in the West to Byzantium in the East. It is, in other words, right on one of the major routes for civic and trading purposes. Paul and his companions reached Philippi after a straightforward crossing via the island of Samothrace and the port of Neapolis.

One of the big differences between Philippi and the earlier cities of Paul's mission was that there was no synagogue. That became significant when the locals identified Paul as a Jew; it looks as though the city knew just enough about Jews to be prejudiced against them. (How often must Paul have been stung by this. He had grown up familiar with the normal Gentile sneers against his people, and now he heard them again.) There was, however, a *proseuchē,* a "place of prayer" where a small number of Jews and "God-fearers" (non-Jews who wanted to join in synagogue worship) would meet regularly. This is where, after a few days settling in, Paul and the others made a start.

Their first convert was a businesswoman from Thyatira, Lydia by name, described as "a seller of purple." Her occupation, and actually her name as well, fit with her place of origin, Thyatira, a city in Asia Minor, in the district of Lydia. There a technique had been developed to procure the prestigious purple dye from the root of the madder plant, a much cheaper way of producing the dye than extracting it from shellfish, as was done elsewhere. The implication is that Lydia was a woman of independent means: she was the head of a household, perhaps indicating that she had been widowed or divorced. Her story of response to the gospel appears the most straightforward of any in Acts: "The Lord opened her heart to pay attention to what Paul was saying."[9] She was baptized with all her household and insisted on inviting the whole party, Paul, Silas, Timothy, and Luke, to come and stay at her home.

The announcement of Jesus as Israel's Messiah and the world's Lord seems to have caused no difficulty in the small Jewish meeting place. But trouble of a different sort was not far away, taking a form that Paul would meet at least once more. On the way to and from the *proseuchē,* the group encountered a girl who had what we might describe as "second sight," but what Luke refers to as "a spirit of divination." She was a slave girl who by telling oracles ("fortunes," we might call them) made a good living for her owners. Unfortunately both for the owners and for Paul, something about his party and its message attracted her attention. As in some of the scenes in the Gospels in which spirit-possessed people shouted out Jesus's secret identity, so this girl announced to all and sundry in a loud voice: "These men are servants of God Most High! They are declaring to you the way of salvation!"[10]

The phrase "God Most High" would ring bells with people. Many in the ancient world, fed up with the complex muddle of pagan gods and goddesses, came to believe in a single ultimate power, a "most high" divinity. The phrase "the way of salvation," though, is a bit of a tease. "Salvation" was something the Roman Empire claimed to offer its citizens (rescue from civil war, social unrest, and so on), but the phrase could also refer, in some philosophies, to the "rescue" of souls from the wicked world of space, time, and matter. The early Christians, of course, had a robust view of "salvation" that was neither of the above. There is a sense here, as in some other passages, of someone saying more than she knew.

One might think that there was little harm in this poor girl shouting after the group day after day, but it was not the kind of attention Paul and his friends wanted. Eventually, as with the magician in Cyprus, Paul turned to the girl and, in the name of Jesus, commanded the spirit to leave her, which it did then and there. One can imagine the looks passing between Silas, Timothy, and Luke. Was this another case of Paul blowing his short fuse and getting himself and everyone else into trouble? So it seemed.

It didn't take the girl's owners long to realize that their line of business was finished. She wasn't going to be giving any more oracles or telling any more fortunes; they wouldn't be making any more money from her special ability. (This is one of many occasions in Acts where we wish we knew what happened next. One would like to think that perhaps Lydia rescued the girl and adopted her, because her other options would not have been good, but we have no information.) But instead of complaining that Paul had taken away their livelihood, the girl's owners jumped straight to a charge that was, in our terms, both "civil" and "religious," though with the emphasis on the first. They grabbed hold of Paul and Silas (why them; did Timothy and Luke melt into the crowd at that point?), dragged them into the public square, and presented them to the magistrates. "These men," they said, "are throwing our city into an uproar! They are Jews, and they are teaching customs which it's illegal for us Romans to accept or practice!"[11]

We may hope that Paul, despite his plight, was alive to the irony. The anger and violence he had faced in Galatia and the opposition to his missionary strategy in Jerusalem and Antioch had been instigated by Jewish groups, furious that he seemed to be disloyal to the ancestral traditions. Now he was accused of being a Jew teaching people to be disloyal to Rome!—a charge that might resonate uncomfortably in a world where it was known that the Jewish people had rebelled against Rome before and might well do so again.

Of course, the motive for the charge was clear, even though the underlying sequence of thought was bewildering. Paul's exorcism of the girl (an initially "religious" problem) quickly translated into loss of income (an economic problem), and this was turned, vengefully, into the accusation that Paul and Silas were Jews (an ethnic problem) who were teaching customs that it would be illegal for Romans to practice (a political problem). The last of these is a genuine puzzle, since it isn't clear that any Roman law prohibited Romans from adopting Jewish practices; many did so with impunity. The only sense that can be made of it—always supposing that Luke himself thought it made sense, which perhaps he didn't—might be that the gospel message about Jesus, which demanded that people stop worshipping "idols" and turn to the living God, could be seen as a Jewish message urging people to abandon the imperial or state cults.

With that, the accusers might just have had a point. It is clear from the charge, however distorted, that some kind of gossip about the group had already been going around Philippi, as one would expect. These strangers really were teaching a Jewish message, a message about Israel's God doing something dramatic, installing Israel's Messiah as the world's true Lord. So, though the accusers' argument and conclusions were flawed at every turn, there was more than a grain of truth in what they ended up saying.

Without waiting for any formal process—an omission that would come back to haunt them—the magistrates had Paul and

Silas stripped, beaten with rods, and thrown into prison. (Again, we wonder why only Paul and Silas were picked out. Timothy and Luke must have appeared to be of lesser importance or have managed to hide in Lydia's house or elsewhere.) So far as we know, this was Paul's first taste of prison. It would not be his last.

In Paul's world, unlike ours, prison was not a "sentence" in itself. It was where magistrates put people while they decided what to do with them. No provision was made for the prisoners' welfare. They had to rely on friends or family to bring them food and other necessities. Sanitation would be minimal; rodents and other vermin would be normal. The company would not be one's first choice of friends. A few days in such a hole might well make one hope for almost any punishment, a heavy fine, or banishment at least, if only one could get out of the horrid place.

Paul and Silas did not have long to wait. What follows reads like a sequence from a movie or a somewhat overwritten thriller. The two men were praying and singing hymns at midnight. After their ordeal and with their feet in the stocks, there was not much chance of sleep, though one wonders what the other prisoners thought of being kept awake in this strange manner. That, however, was the least of their worries, since they suddenly felt the whole building shaking. Northern Greece is an earthquake zone, and suddenly the whole prison shook. This was bad news for the jailer. He was responsible for keeping the prisoners under lock and key; with doors bursting open and chains being loosened, the poor man feared the worst. He did what many a junior Roman official would think of doing in the circumstances: he drew his sword and was about to take his own life rather than face the torture and possible death he might expect for failing his duty.

Paul had other ideas. "Don't harm yourself!" he yelled. "We're all still here!"[12] The jailor called for lights and rushed into the prison. It seems that his panic was not only because of the penalty he might face for letting prisoners escape, but because he knew, as the whole town would, that Paul and Silas were there on some kind of a religious charge, and he would have been aware of traditions in which angry gods used earthquakes to make their displeasure known. That explains not only his panic but also his trembling question: "Gentlemen," he said, "will you please tell me how I can get out of this mess?"[13]

The traditional translation of his question, "What must I do to be saved?" makes it sound more like a plea from a seventeenth-century Puritan anxious about how to go to heaven. But the language of "salvation" worked at several levels in the ancient world. The slave girl whom Paul had exorcised had been shouting out that the travelers were announcing "the way of salvation." The Roman Empire offered "salvation" to its subjects, meaning rescue from war, social upheaval, and destitution. Later in Acts, when Luke is describing the shipwreck, he speaks of the whole company being "saved" in the very concrete sense of being rescued from drowning. So it is natural to take the jailer's panic-stricken question at the most obvious level: he wants the nightmare to end and to avoid any trouble. But then there is the deeper level, at which believing in Jesus would at once give the jailer and his household membership in the family that was already celebrating Jesus's victory over sin and death. And there is the ultimate level: Luke and Paul both believed that one day God would rescue the whole creation from its "slavery to decay," bringing it and all Jesus's people into the full and final new creation.

How much any of this flashed across Paul's mind at such a bizarre moment it is hard to say, though with his quick wit and his overall sense of an integrated cosmic divine plan he would in principle have been able to glimpse it. What he says works at all these levels: "Believe in the Lord Jesus, and you will be rescued— you and your household."[14] The jailer is only too glad to bring Paul and Silas into his house and let them explain what this actually means. He fetches water and washes their wounds; they reciprocate by baptizing him and his household, perhaps with the same water. The near tragedy turns into a celebration as the whole family shares a meal. What happened to the other prisoners we have no idea.

There follows another of those moments when Paul's companions must have thought he was pushing his luck. At first light, the magistrates sent word to the prison that Paul and Silas were to be released and should leave town. Paul objected, producing a trump card that must have sent shock waves through the locality. "We are Roman citizens!" he says. "They didn't put us on trial, they beat us in public, they threw us into prison, and now they are sending us away secretly? No way! Let them come themselves and take us out."[15] He is on safe ground. Roman citizens were entitled to full legal rights. Public beating and imprisonment without trial was normal practice for noncitizens, but in the case of citizens this would have been enough to turn the tables and get the magistrates themselves into serious trouble, should Paul have chosen to follow it up. (Roman officials would know this well, ever since Cicero's prosecution of Verres in 70 BC; Verres's crowning fault was the crucifixion of a Roman citizen.)

Another irony: the original charge was that he was teaching customs it wasn't lawful for Romans to adopt, but by the end Paul is accusing the magistrates themselves of illegal behavior against Romans. It is, of course, a wonderfully confusing situation, but that is the kind of thing to expect when a new world is breaking in on the old one. It ends with a public apology and with the magistrates, clearly at a loss to know what to do next, imploring Paul and Silas to go away. They take their time about complying, first visiting Lydia's house and conversing with the group of believers there.

When they go, it is not clear whether Timothy and Luke go too (though Timothy has at least caught up with Paul by the time the apostle is in Beroea). But Luke, in the next scene, no longer writes "we."

★ ★ ★

Philippi was an important city in its own right, but Thessalonica, Paul's next port of call, was even more so. It was on a main crossroads, and its role as a port at the head of the Thermaic Gulf to the west of the Chalcidice Peninsula guaranteed it prosperity. It was the capital of the Roman province of Macedonia, and the Roman general Pompey had used it as his base in the civil war. It was not, in Paul's day, an official Roman colony. That would come two centuries later. But it was clearly a major center of Roman influence.

Thessalonica, unlike Philippi, had a Jewish population of sufficient numbers to sustain a synagogue. Luke's summary of what Paul said on the three Sabbaths he spoke there conforms both to the earlier summaries, particularly Paul's address in Pisidian Antioch (Abraham, Exodus, David, exile, hope), and to Paul's own repeated statements in his letters. The message can be summed up in two basic points: first, the scriptures point to the suffering, death, and resurrection of Israel's Messiah; second, Jesus was and is that Messiah. The message was accepted by some of the Jews, several of the God-fearing Greeks, and quite a number of the leading women. It also appears from Paul's first letter to Thessalonica, written not long after this initial visit, that many in the young church there had been polytheistic pagans and had "turned to God from idols, to serve a living and true God."[16] Clearly this was a significant group of both Jews and Gentiles.

One member in particular, Jason, gave hospitality to Paul and Silas and then faced the brunt of the anger that was aroused when, as in Galatia, some of the synagogue community decided that enough was enough. A mob was stirred up, bent on violence, but the traveling missionaries could not be found. What

matters here, though, is the political nature of the charges that
were thrown around as all this was going on:

> "These are the people who are turning the world upside
> down!" they yelled. "Now they've come here! Jason
> has had them in his house! They are all acting against
> the decrees of Caesar—and they're saying that there is
> another king, Jesus!"[17]

Once again the charges are complicated. A Jewish objection to
the apostles' message (we Jews are not convinced that Jesus really
is Israel's Messiah) is easily translated into a charge of sedition
against Rome (if there really is a Jewish Messiah, then according
to scripture such a person will rule the whole world). Another
king, indeed! Mixed in with that there may be a hint of the problem we identified as one key element in the Galatian situation: if
non-Jews were abandoning idols and coming to worship the God
of Israel, but without formally becoming Jews in the process, then
they were indeed disobeying Caesar's decrees. Only genuine Jews
had that permission.

Does this mean, then, that Paul and the others really were
"turning the world upside down"? Broadly speaking, yes it does.
Exactly in line with Jesus's own announcement of God's kingdom, which took normal political values and power structures
and stood them on their heads, Paul and his friends were announcing and modeling in their own lives a different way of being human, a different kind of community, and all because there
was a very different kind of "king." Of course, one would not
expect a mob to understand the finer points of the early Christian
message. But Luke, summarizing the accusation, seems content to
allow the muddled pagan crowd to say more than they know. In
any case, Jason and his friends are bound over to keep the peace,
while Paul and Silas are smuggled out of town by night and sent
on to Beroea, fifty miles or so to the west, but off the main route.

They leave in a hurry, with a sense that the little body of believers is under threat.

The first letter Paul wrote back to this community, most likely in late 50 or early 51, makes it clear that in the relatively short time he had been with them they had established a close and loving bond. "We were gentle among you," he writes,

> like a nurse taking care of her own children. We were so devoted to you that we gladly intended to share with you not only the gospel of God but our own lives, because you became so dear to us.[18]

He was snatched away from them, he says, "in person though not in heart," because he "longed eagerly, with a great desire," to see them "face to face."[19] So strong was this feeling that when Paul reached Athens soon afterward, he sent Timothy back to Thessalonica to see how things were going, and he returned with good news, which Paul reports to the Thessalonians: "You always have good memories of us, and . . . are longing to see us, just as we are to see you."[20]

These short references, an intimate exchange very soon after Paul's initial visit, tell us a great deal about Paul's way of life, his style of teaching and pastoral engagement—and also perhaps about his own personal needs. The split with Barnabas, the long and apparently aimless journey through central Anatolia with all its nagging uncertainties, the sense of arriving in a new culture, the shock of public beating and imprisonment—all this would have left him vulnerable at quite a deep level. In that context, to sense the genuine, unaffected love and support of people he had only just met, to discover through the work of the gospel a deep bond for which the language of "family" was the only appropriate description—all this must have given him comfort and strength.

As he had worried in early days about working in vain, so he wonders, by himself in Athens, whether all he had done in Thes-

salonica was wasted effort.[21] Once more, the fact that he expresses
this anxiety in terms of Isaiah's "servant" theme doesn't mean that
the anxiety was any the less real. Paul looks back on his time in
northern Greece with, no doubt, some shocking memories, but
with an overarching sense that he now belongs with those communities and they with him. This, however, needs reinforcing
with news. Antioch, his original base, is far away. What he is discovering is not exactly a new home—he would never spend very
long in northern Greece—but a place where he has left part of his
heart. A place from which he might derive either real encouragement or devastating disappointment.

So Paul, Silas, and Timothy head south rather than west. I
rather think that this meant a change of plan. I suggested earlier
that Paul had not originally intended to cross over the Aegean Sea
into Greece. But once he was there, sensing a positive response
to the gospel of *Kyrios Iēsous* in these very Roman cities and finding himself on the Via Egnatia, it must have been tempting to
continue all the way to the port of Dyrrhachium on the Adriatic
coast, to cross over to Italy, and to make straight for Rome. But
the violence of the opposition in Thessalonica and the fact that he
had to leave town in hurried secrecy would have made it difficult
to proceed openly along the great east–west highway. Instead, the
party set a different course, slightly south of west, and soon arrived in Beroea.

The stay in Beroea is short, perhaps shorter than the few weeks
in Thessalonica. The city is at this time a major center of the imperial cult as well as the headquarters of the Macedonian "confed-
eration." As in Thessalonica, there is a synagogue, but the Jewish
community here takes a quite different approach. They are prepared to listen carefully and in a generous spirit to what Paul is
saying and to work through the scriptures he was expounding to
see if what he said fitted the texts. We imagine them sitting down
with him, sharing hospitality, and looking carefully at the story of
Abraham, at the drama of the Exodus, at the anointing of David,

at the Psalms and the prophets who pointed forward through the darkness of exile to the possibility of a new dawn. That shared study sounds like a promising start. Many of the Jews become believers, as do some of the Gentiles, notably some of the well-born women. They are, perhaps, among those who would find the synagogue culture to be a welcome change from the surrounding pagan world. The clear, strong ethic and the simple, almost stark, belief in the One God contrasted sharply with the ordinary life of the Roman world. Paul insists, writing later to Corinth, that among the believers "not many were nobly born."[22] But "not many" does not mean "not any." The small groups of Jesus-followers were mixed socially as well as in gender and ethnic origin.

The good beginning in Beroea did not last. Word got back to Thessalonica that the troublemakers had moved down the road, and those Jews who had opposed Paul in Thessalonica came after him and whipped up a crowd to make trouble once more. So Paul had to move on again, though this time it seems he was the sole target of the crowd's anger, while Silas and Timothy were able to stay behind. It would have been possible to travel south to Athens by public roads. But the group from Beroea accompanying Paul seems to have chosen to take him by sea. He arrived at Athens and, saying farewell to his escorts, urged them to tell Silas and Timothy to join him as soon as they can.

We have followed Luke's account of Paul's arrival in Europe and the short stays in Philippi, Thessalonica, and Beroea. These are confirmed from Paul's own letters. Yet Luke's version can easily give us a false impression. By highlighting the swift events of arrival, gospel announcement, opposition and persecution, and departure, Luke has written a page-turner, but as we read it we have to remind ourselves that these things did not, in fact, happen in quick bursts of twenty-four hours. The hints are that Paul was in Philippi for several weeks at least. His letter to the church there, written a few years later, is so full of love that we cannot imagine his stay to have been as short as a quick reading of Acts might suggest. By the same token, we discover from that letter that when Paul was in prison (in Ephesus, as I shall later explain) the Philippian church sent him money—and Paul comments that they had done that as soon as he had left them, supporting his work in Thessalonica as well. Paul was clear that he was not preaching the gospel in order to earn money. But those whose lives had been changed by his preaching and teaching seem spontaneously to have wanted to support him, and the Philippians were preeminent in this. Such a desire is hardly raised by a visit of a few days.

It is worth laboring this point, because when people in our own day wonder what made Paul the man he was and ultimately why his project succeeded, it has been fashionable to suggest that he was a difficult, awkward, cross-grained customer who always disagreed with everyone about everything. There is no doubt that he could come across like that, especially when he could see straight through the fudge and muddle of what someone else was saying, whether a senior apostle like Peter or a local magistrate like those in Philippi. But—and it is perhaps important to stress this before we see him move on to southern Greece, where relations were not always so easy—all the signs are that in the northern Greek churches Paul quickly established a deep and lasting bond of mutual love and trust.

He would say, of course, that this came about because of the gospel. The power of the spirit, through the message and the strange personal presence of Jesus, transformed not only the individual hearts, minds, and lives of those who received it, but also the relationships between speakers and hearers. "Sharing not only the gospel of God but our own lives"[23]—that line tells its own story.

Yes, it is of course Paul himself who is saying this. But it is hard to believe that Paul could write that to a group he had been with only a few weeks earlier unless *he* knew that *they* would know it was true. When we wonder what most strongly motivated Paul, we must put near the center the fact that at a deeply human level he was sustained and nourished by what he came to call *koinōnia*.

As we saw earlier, the normal translation of *koinōnia* is "fellow-ship," but that coin has worn smooth with long use. It can mean "business partnership" too; that is part of it, but again it doesn't get to the heart. And the heart is what matters. When our words run out, we need images: the look of delight when a dear friend pays an unexpected visit, the glance of understanding between musicians as together they say something utterly beautiful, the long squeeze of a hand by a hospital bed, the contentment and gratitude that accompany shared worship and prayer—all this and more. The other Greek word for which Paul would reach is of course *agapē*, "love," but once again our English term is so over-used that we can easily fail to recognize it as it walks nearby, like a short-sighted lover failing to recognize the beloved; what we so often miss is that it means the world, and more than the world. "The son of God loved me," Paul had written to the Galatians, "and gave himself for me." What we see as Paul makes his way around the cities of northern Greece is what that love looks like when it translates into the personal and pastoral ministry of the suffering and celebrating apostle.

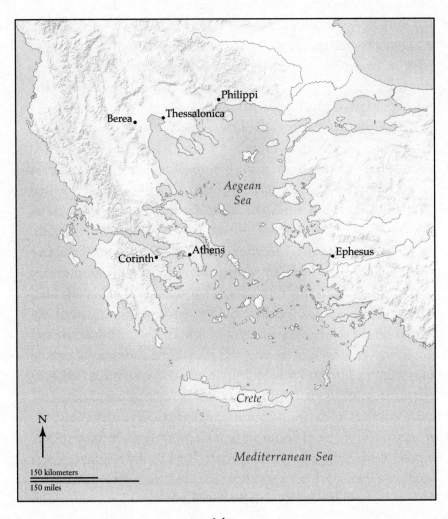

150 kilometers

150 miles

Athens

8

Athens

T HE PARTHENON IS probably the only building of its period to be instantly recognizable today. A glance at a photograph is enough. Everyone knows what it is, or at least *where* it is: Athens, the center of the classical world. Built to celebrate the goddess Athene after the victory over the Persians in the fifth century BC, the brilliantly designed marble structure, perfect in its proportions and dazzling in its location on the Acropolis, functioned for centuries as the main focal point for worship in Athens. There were of course many other temples, including the smaller but still dramatic Temple of Nike ("Victory"), built close to the Parthenon around 410 BC, and others scattered elsewhere in the city. The Temple of Jupiter, just down the hill, was vast. But the Parthenon was, and remains, in a category of its own.

You can see the Acropolis to excellent effect, displaying the Parthenon, the Temple of Nike, and all the rest, from another steep hill a few hundred yards to the northwest. This is the Areopagus, the "Hill of Mars"—Mars was the god of war—where from early times the senior council of Athens used to meet. Athens was in that period ruled by "archons" (the word simply means "the ruling ones"), nine of whom were elected each year. When their term of office was over, they automatically became members of the Areopagus, the hill giving its name to the body that met there. Though the status and role of the body changed as political reforms came and went, it continued to be a powerful influence in Athenian public life, and it also functioned as a court to try serious offenses, including homicide, arson, and some religious cases.

So when Paul was brought to the Areopagus, probably in late 50 or early 51, and when he began by declaring that temples to the gods were a category mistake, we should not suppose that he was engaging a philosophers' debating society. Generations of readers, studying what has been called Paul's "Areopagus address" in Acts 17:22–31, have supposed that he was trying to argue his way, on philosophical grounds, up to a statement of Christian belief. Many in the modern period who have wanted to construct what is sometimes called "natural theology"—arguing for the existence of God and perhaps the truth of Christianity by observation of the natural world alone, without appeal to special divine revelation—have hailed this speech as a forerunner of their efforts. And many who have wanted, for various reasons, to resist such "natural theology," have looked at Acts 17 and declared that, whatever Luke may have thought, the Paul we know from the letters would never have gone in for that kind of discourse. That just wasn't his kind of thing.

But all this is a misunderstanding. The Areopagus was a *court*. Paul was on trial. It was a dangerous moment. It could have gone badly wrong. He was all alone, or so it seems, still waiting for Silas and Timothy to join him. It appears that Timothy had come to him in Athens,[1] but that Paul, anxious about the little church in Thessalonica, had sent Timothy back at once to see how they were getting on. He has important things on his mind; as he says on another occasion, there are battles outside and fears inside. He has no leisure, physical or mental, to play the detached philosopher. It is, however, utterly characteristic of the man that he would seize the opportunity not merely to defend himself—though that is what he is doing throughout the speech—but to do so in such a way as to challenge, with considerable rhetorical skill, the basic assumptions of the Greek worldview.

I say "with rhetorical skill," but of course we have only a bare summary of what Paul said. If you read the Greek text of Paul's speech as Luke reports it at the speed you might expect him to speak to a large gathering in the open air, it will take two minutes, or perhaps a little longer if you allow for a few well-judged rhetorical pauses. It is just possible that the court was busy that day, that Paul's case was scheduled in between several others, and that the court officials told him (as I was once told in the House of Lords when we were debating "assisted dying" and far too many people wanted to contribute) that he could speak for only two minutes. But I find that highly unlikely. There is no evidence that the Areopagus rushed through business. And Paul, of all people, would not want to pass up a chance like this to address the highest court in the proud capital of ancient culture, the home of philosophy, the cradle of democracy. I suspect that he spoke for two hours rather than two minutes. His speech would form a book in itself, but Luke has no space for such a thing within his own work. He has boiled it down to the bones.

So what might have caused them to take Paul before the highest court in the land? People often say that the ancient pagan world was tolerant of religious diversity, and there is a sense in which that is true. Many "gods," many "lords," and many miscellaneous cults thrived in the countries that bordered the Mediterranean. It was easy for new divinities to make their way into a city, with a temple here and a small shrine there. A cult like that of Mithras was soon to become popular with the Roman army. The new cults of Rome and of Caesar himself were able to find a place alongside, sometimes upstaging but not normally displacing, the existing shrines of the pantheon.

However, tolerance was limited and controlled. There is evidence that philosophers were banished from cities because of their teaching. In particular, Athens itself had staged the trial of Socrates (399 BC), seen from that day to this as one of the most important events in the history of philosophy. What was Socrates's crime? Corrupting the young and *introducing foreign divinities*. Since there were political motives as well behind Socrates's trial, we cannot be entirely sure what this meant, but the memory lived on. In Athens of all places, conscious of its long and distinguished history and of the association of that history with the goddess Athene and the victory over the Persians by which her preeminent status had been assured, to have an outsider like Paul bringing strange new teachings would have been much more than a mere philosophical curiosity. He would have been a potential threat to society, to stability, to the worship of the divinities by whose beneficence the city lived, moved, and had its being. He had to be investigated.

Luke mocks the Athenian mixture of civic pride, on the one hand, and mere love of novelty, on the other. "All the Athenians, and the foreigners who live there," he says with a sniff of disdain, "spend their time simply and solely in telling and hearing the latest novelty."[2] He is doing his best to play down the seriousness of the charge against Paul; the mention of "the foreigners who live there" implies "so Paul isn't the only outsider, and they can hardly object to yet one more new idea." Even before Paul gets to the Areopagus to face a charge of introducing novel theological ideas, Luke is insinuating that the whole city was eager for that kind of thing anyway. But you do not take someone to the highest court in the land unless there are serious questions to be addressed, with the undertones of a potential capital charge. The Areopagus, to repeat, was not a philosophers' debating society.

The philosophers were more likely to debate in the marketplace, and that, as well as the synagogue, is where Paul had begun. We hear nothing of the local Jewish reaction; our attention is drawn to the debates with the Epicureans and the Stoics. Here Paul must have been in his element—or rather, one of his elements, since he was obviously at home in the synagogue as well, handling the scriptures with a lifetime's easy fluency. But he was from Tarsus, one of the main centers of philosophy in the ancient world, and now here he was in Athens, the ultimate home of learned discourse, the city of Socrates, of Plato, of Aristotle . . .

The Epicureans and the Stoics were two of the main philosophical schools of the time. There was also the "Academy," the ancient school of Plato, which was making a comeback after years of cautious agnosticism. But the Epicureans, the most famous of whom at the time was the Roman poet Lucretius, and the Stoics, among whom were Paul's near contemporaries Seneca and Epictetus, were the main contenders. Of the two, Stoicism was the more popular. The overlaps and differences between these two great systems can be seen on many fronts, but for Paul's purposes what mattered was their view about "God" or "the gods." What he was saying about the One God fitted with neither. Yet he could see that both schools were hinting at things that pointed beyond their own proposals.

The key question concerned the relationship between "God" or "the gods" and the world, particularly the lives of humans. The Epicureans held that, though the gods might well exist, they live in a world of their own entirely separate from the human world. The world inhabited by humans carries on under its own impetus. Its atoms (this view goes back to the fifth-century BC Democritus) move to and fro, "swerving" this way and that and thereby colliding with one another and producing different effects, different evolving life-forms. Everything in the world and human life thus has "natural" causes, and at death the constituent atoms are dispersed beyond recall and the entire human person ceases to exist. This worldview remained the opinion of a small minority right up until the eighteenth century. Since then, it has become the dominant one in modern Western culture. Many imagine it to be a modern "discovery."

The Stoics, by contrast, were basically pantheists. "God" and the world are more or less the same thing, and the divine spark of life, the *logos,* exists within everything. This life consists of a fire or spirit that animates the whole universe and that will eventually blaze out in a great moment of conflagration. After that, like the phoenix, the whole world will begin all over again, and events will take exactly the same course as before. Wise and virtuous human life then consists in thinking and acting in accordance with the inner *logos* of the world. Many Stoics, however, of whom Epictetus was a good example, enjoyed a flexible sort of pantheism in which, though they were themselves technically as much a part of "the divinity" as anything else, they could address the divine being in respectful and grateful worship.

The philosophers were not, of course, the only people who thought about such questions. Many of the ancient poets wrote movingly about the strange commerce between the gods and the world, and some pointed to the possibility of a beneficent force behind the messy world of the pagan pantheon. Some of these poets were playwrights. One famous play by the fifth-century BC tragedian Aeschylus describes the foundation of the court of the Areopagus itself, at which the god Apollo presided—and declared, among other things and as part of the logic of trials for murder, that when people die and their blood is spilled on the ground, *there is no resurrection.*[3] That denial formed part of the foundation charter of the court before which Paul found himself.

To the philosophers in the marketplace, Paul seemed a mere oddity. His essentially Jewish view of the One God and a created universe and his specifically Christian variation on this simply didn't fit. They were scornful: What can this man be on about, they wondered, scattering words around like someone sowing seeds in every direction? The one thing they picked up on was that he was talking about someone called Jesus and someone or something called "Anastasis"—the Greek word for "resurrection." They assumed "Jesus and Anastasis" were a new pair of divinities, and

"Anastasis," a feminine noun in Greek, was Jesus's consort; the two were a divine couple, rather like Isis and Osiris (though there the female is always mentioned first). The result, though, was clear. To the philosophers, Paul seemed to be proclaiming foreign divinities. The echoes of Socrates's trial were obvious. That is why they took him to the Areopagus.

That too is why the opening question was hardly an innocent invitation to deliver a seminar paper. We have to imagine the opening remarks said in a voice of icy calm, with just the hint of a sneer, by a presiding magistrate who knows he has the power to have the person before him beaten, banished, or possibly even killed. "Are we able to know"—in other words, is this some top-secret mystery, or are we mere mortals capable of getting the point—"what this new teaching really is that you are talking about? You are putting very strange ideas into our minds. We'd like to find out what it all means."[4]

Paul is thus on the spot. Few people who have studied the apostle would start with Acts 17 to explain who this remarkable man really was or what made him tick. But a strong case can be made for doing just that. Once we set aside the notion that he was trying out some arguments in "natural theology" and realize that he was speaking in self-defense, but also using the opportunity to score several points of his own within a framework cleverly designed to offset the wrong sort of reaction, we see the whole man at work. He comes across, of course, as a Jewish thinker, not just in his denunciation of idolatry and pagan temples, not just in his final punch line about the world's Creator having a time line at the end of which he will call the whole world to account, and not even in the utterly Jewish (and, to Greeks, utterly ridiculous) notion of resurrection. The entire speech is Jewish in the way that the book of Proverbs is Jewish or the Wisdom of Solomon is Jewish, taking (as Paul says elsewhere) "every thought prisoner" to "make it obey the Messiah."[5] It is Jewish thought, with its strong view of the One

God as the creator of all, claiming the intellectual high ground, able to see why this or that philosophy has a point to make but hasn't yet grasped the whole picture.

It is, above all, Jewish thought that speaks of the utter transcendence and yet the intimate personal presence of the One God. Paul does not quote the Psalms or Isaiah, but we can see the influence of their double vision of the One God all the way through: the sovereign God, high above and beyond the earth so that its inhabitants are like grasshoppers, yet gently at hand, gathering the lambs in his arms and leading the mother sheep. Paul has absorbed the ancient wisdom of Israel deep into his heart. Thus equipped, he can look out on local inscriptions, monumental temples, philosophical debates, and poetic fancies with equanimity. This is Paul the Jew at the top of his game.

Equally, this is Paul the Roman citizen. His experience in Philippi must have helped him to realize that, however paradoxical it might be for a Jesus-follower to be an official citizen of Caesar's empire, that is who he is and it can be turned to his advantage. Athens had no great love for Rome—the Romans had sacked the city a little over a century earlier—but Paul knew that if things turned rough, it would do him no harm to point out that he came with the judicial backing of the current great empire. Nor was this merely pragmatic. Once again his Jewish roots helped. Paul believed (as even Jesus had acknowledged at the most unlikely moment[6]) that the ruling powers of the world exercised their rule at the good pleasure of the One God, who would hold them to account. Paul must already have realized that the remarkable network of communications, particularly the roads and the local judicial systems, had created conditions never before imagined in which a wandering preacher like himself could make his way from country to country. He knew, of course, that things could still go horribly wrong. His experiences in Galatia and northern Greece would be fresh in his mind. But part of his belief in divine providence included the belief that the One God had strangely but surely established the Roman world, with all its pagan wickedness, for which it would be called to account, as a means by which, however paradoxically, he and others could proclaim Jesus as Lord. We would be right to suppose that he took courage in this knowledge.

Jew and Roman meet in Paul the Greek thinker and traveler. Again we must stress that this has nothing to do (as many generations have supposed, particularly when modern European thinkers have wanted to reject something called "Jewish thought") with Paul leaving behind his Jewishness and taking on a different kind of thought altogether. No: for reasons already stated, Paul the loyal Jew can see all truth as God's truth and therefore all observation and debate as observation of God's world and debate about what it all means. He is thoroughly familiar with the language and ideas of Greek thought. (I suspect he relished the fact that when he said *pneuma,* he knew that what he meant by "spirit" both was and wasn't the same as what a Stoic would have meant by it, or that when he spoke of Jesus as the *eikōn theou,* this idea of "the image of God" would mean different things to different people. Yes, misunderstandings would occur, and he would endlessly correct them.) He would speak not from the defensive position that unless one retreats into "pure" Jewish culture, everything will fall apart, but from the positive high ground that idolatry and the false thinking it engenders are perversions, distortions of the truth, and that when one pulls hard on the truth, the knots and tangles farther down the rope will eventually come loose.

This complex man, then, carries in his own person the deeply biblical and Jewish worldview, which has been brought into startling new focus by Jesus and the spirit, but not abandoned or marginalized. From that point of view he can travel the world of Rome and think the thoughts of Greece without fear or shame. In particular, his message of Jesus's resurrection, without which his whole life and work would mean nothing, contains within itself the news that Jesus's crucifixion was a victory, not a defeat. His

denunciation of idols and temples in his Areopagus speech is not
simply Jewish-style polemic, though it is that as well. It is the position of someone who believes that all the would-be divine powers
in the world have been dethroned, shamed, led in someone else's
triumphal procession as a defeated rabble. The victory of Jesus on
the cross, as we have seen, has a deeply intimate meaning for Paul:
"The son of God loved me and gave himself for me." But this is
bound up tightly with its cosmic meaning: "He stripped the rulers and authorities of their armor," he writes to the Colossians,
"and displayed them contemptuously to public view, celebrating
his triumph over them in him."[7] He is the Messiah's man, and that
includes all the other elements we have just listed.

All this is on display, then, as he addresses the graybeards in the
senior court of Athens. His main point ought now to be clear:
*"What I am saying to you may sound 'new,' but it is in fact hidden
within your own culture.* It is well hidden; in fact, you have covered
it up with foolish and unnecessary superstructures. But though
the specific news about Jesus and the resurrection may be a shock
to your system"—it was, and they laughed at him for it—"the
underlying truth that it unveils is a truth about the world and its
One Creator God to which, at its best, your culture dimly and
distantly bears witness." Paul is not trying to begin with Athenian
cultural symbols and build up a philosophical argument that will
arrive at Christian truth. He is managing at one and the same
time to rebut the charge of "proclaiming foreign divinities" *and*
to sketch a worldview, a metaphysic, in which it might just make
sense to say that the One God has unveiled his purpose for the
world by raising Jesus from the dead. He is a Sherlock Holmes
figure, explaining to the puzzled police chiefs that their different
theories about the crime all have some sense to them, but that
there is a different overall framework, under their noses all the time
but never observed, that will solve the whole thing.

So he begins with the famous altar inscription "To an Unknown God." Much ink has been spilled by scholars on what

exactly such an inscription might originally have meant, but Paul is not concerned so much with its past history as with the excellent opportunity it presents him. It isn't just that he is grasping at a kind of theological straw ("Here you are yourselves, admitting that there might be one god you don't know yet, so let's see if we can build on that"). He is picking up the idea of "ignorance" itself and using it as a lever to critique the entire world of normal pagan religion.

"That was just *ignorance*," he says, in the tone of voice the Athenians themselves might use to dismiss the muddled thinking of less sophisticated peoples, referring to the idols of gold, silver, or stone, made by skillful human beings, that were ubiquitous in Athens itself as well as everywhere else. Paul is echoing, of course, the normal critique of idolatry, again as found in the Psalms or Isaiah and closer to Paul's day in a book like the Wisdom of Solomon; it echoes too what he had said at Lystra. Some of his philosophically inclined hearers would have agreed. "If you set aside this ignorance," he continues, "you will discover not only that idols are a shabby and misleading representation of the true God, but also that this God doesn't live in temples made by human hands." So much, then, for the majestic Parthenon, there in plain sight across the valley. "Our wonderful temple," the Athenians realize he is saying, "is a category mistake!" "So too," insists Paul, "is the kind of worship offered at temples. People are *trying to feed the divinity,* when all along *he* is the one who gives everything to *us*" (again, just as Paul had said at Lystra). "If I was hungry," Israel's God had said in the Psalms, "do you really suppose that I would tell you about it?"[8]

So who is the true God, what is he like, and what relation does he have to the world? Here Paul steers a thoroughly Jewish course, acknowledging the half-truths of the ruling philosophies, but seeing them all within the larger whole he is advocating. The One God is the creator of all. As Moses had said (Paul does not refer to him, but this idea is deeply rooted in Israel's scriptures), this One

God made all peoples and allotted them their times and places. Above all, he wanted them to *know* him—ignorance was never his plan. He wanted them, after all, to be image-bearing humans, not unreflective puppets. The Stoics, though, are wrong: the true God is the creator of all, not the divine depth within everybody and everything. He is set apart from the world, but he is not (this time against the Epicureans) detached from the world. "He is actually not far from each one of us, for in him we live and move and exist."[9] One poet, the third-century BC Stoic Aratus, whose work *Phaenomena* was the most widely read poem in Paul's world after Homer himself, put it like this: "For we are his offspring." Quoting this is as close as Paul comes to something that, taken out of context, might easily be mistaken for Stoicism. What follows makes it clear that this would be a serious error.

First, the Stoics had never suggested that human-made idols were a bad idea. If, as they believed, there was divinity in everything, then it would follow that (though of course popular ideas would need to be critiqued) there was no harm in having an idol as a focus of worship. Paul waves this aside: more ignorance, he says.

Second, although, as I noted, some Stoics like Epictetus could speak warmly of a personal relationship with "the divine," Paul's Jewish and now Jesus-focused vision of a personal relationship with the world's Creator moves beyond that into a different sphere. God intended for people to search for him! Perhaps even reach out for him and find him! This is not simply a matter of humans getting in touch with their inner divine self. Nor is it about a self-propelled and potentially arrogant "quest for God" in which humans take the initiative and God remains passive. God gives everything to everyone; what he is looking for is not initiative, whether theological or epistemological, but response. Nothing like that is found in Stoicism. Still less in Epicureanism.

Third, the Stoics' view of history was cyclic. Their vast whirligigs of time, with periodic conflagrations and restarts, were the inevitable result of pantheism; if *to pan,* "the all," is all that there is, then it must be what it is forever, going around in a great circle and repeating itself endlessly and exactly. No, says Paul, history is linear. The "ignorance" admitted by the inscription "To an Unknown God" is a temporary phenomenon. The Creator has allowed it for a while and is now prepared to draw a veil over it. History—time itself!—is moving forward toward a goal very different from either the Stoic "conflagration" or the Epicurean idea of everything simply dissolving into its component atoms. The goal is now a day of ultimate, world-righting justice.

All this of course provides a further irony. Again we find ourselves wondering whether an onlooker would have winced and thought, "Is Paul going too far? Is he now going to tease the judges with the news that their oh-so-superior court is at best a secondary forum? Is that the best way to win friends and influence people in Athens?" But Paul is in full stride. God has established a day "on which he intends to call the world to account with full and proper justice by a man whom he has appointed."[10] *Full and proper justice.* I slightly overtranslate here, but it makes the point I think Paul was making, which is that this will be true justice, not the second-rate variety provided by the highest court in Athens! As he says in 1 Corinthians, he regards it as a matter of minimal concern to be judged by any human court, since what matters is God's ultimate judgment, which will be based on the secrets and intentions of the heart.[11]

Here, then, comes Paul's thoroughly Jewish and messianic view of God's future. Like some other Jewish writers of the time and in tune with a good deal of other early Christian evidence, Paul is echoing Psalm 2. The nations of the earth can rage, plot, and strut their stuff, vaunting themselves against the true God; but God will laugh at them and announce that he has established his true king, his "son," who will call the nations to account. "Now therefore," says the psalm, "be wise; be warned, O rulers of the earth."[12] Again we sense Paul's subtext. Athens, with its symbol of the owl, prided itself as the home of wisdom. No, Paul implies, true wisdom would consist in recognizing that the One Creator God has now unveiled his purpose for the world before all the nations. That purpose is focused on the Jesus who was crucified and raised and marked out thereby as God's son, the one through whom God would fulfill his ancient promises and put the whole world at last to rights.

Paul has thus worked his way around at last to explaining "Jesus and Anastasis": it is Jesus and resurrection! These are new ideas, of course, and "foreign" in the sense of coming from the Jewish world, not being homegrown in Athens, and indeed flying in the face of the old slogan from Aeschylus. But at a deeper level, Paul is implying that this is not foreign at all; it is, rather, the reality to which so many signposts had been pointing. Paul is not suggesting for a moment that one could start from those signposts and work one's way up to Jesus and the resurrection. But he is certainly suggesting that the puzzles and inconsistencies—the ignorances, in fact—within the world of Athenian and other pagan cultures functioned like signposts pointing into the dark, and that when the true God revealed his ultimate purposes for the world in Jesus's resurrection, one would then be able to see that this might be where the signposts had been pointing all along. Yes, this is new. The final punch line explicitly contradicts what Apollo himself had said at the foundation of this very court. But it makes sense.

People have sometimes sneered at Paul for a failed bit of philosophical theology. Hardly anyone was converted—though one member of the court, Dionysius, came to faith along with a woman named Damaris and others. But that wasn't the point. What mattered is that *Paul went out from their presence.*[13] He got off. If this was a trial, he was acquitted. Jesus and Anastasis might be new, strange, and even ridiculous to these senior Athenians. But Paul had convinced them that the heart of his message was something to which their own traditions, read admittedly from a certain angle, might all along have been pointing.

His polemic against temples and idols must have seemed unrealistic. One might as well stand in the middle of Wall Street and declare that the entire banking system is a category mistake. But he had a coherent point of view that justified his claim that he was not merely "introducing foreign divinities." When some of the court said, "We will give you another hearing about this," this didn't imply a second *legal* hearing. It seems that some at least thought that what Paul was saying had more to it than met the eye. They would welcome another chance to ponder it all. But Paul, perhaps wisely, was not going to stay long in Athens. He saw no point in pandering to the local desire for novelty. He may also have realized that to get off with a speech quite different from what the court might have anticipated could only be a temporary expedient. He moved on once more, still traveling alone. From the lofty heights of Athenian culture to the bustling, thrusting world of Corinth.

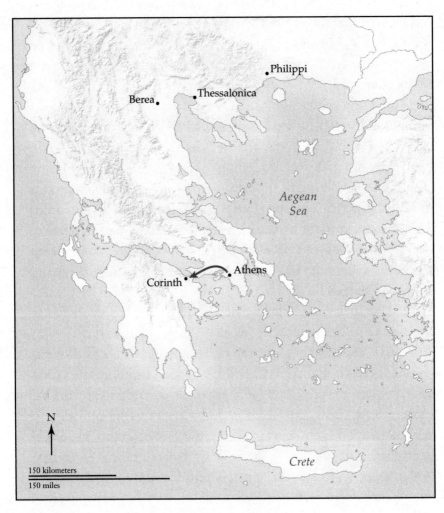

Athens to Corinth

9

Corinth I

THANKS TO PAUL, we know more about life in Corinth than we do about life in any other first-century city in Greece. Poets like Martial and Juvenal give us a (no doubt jaundiced) vision of Rome in the first two centuries. Josephus, in a very different register, lets us look on as mid-century Jerusalem descends into chaos. But Paul, as a by-product of his urgent pastoral and theological concerns, shows us Corinth as a lively and lascivious city, with its class distinctions and its law courts; its temples, markets, and brothels; its dinner parties, weddings, and festivals. We watch, in a way we cannot do with any of Paul's other churches, as a community comes to terms with what it meant to be Messiah people in a world full of challenges and questions. And—in keeping with our purpose in this book in particular—we watch as Paul himself faces new challenges, new opportunities, and not least new heartache. Corinth was famous in any case, but Paul gives it an assured place in any account of ancient city life.

Corinth occupied an enviable civic position. Greece divides geographically in two; its most famous cities were Athens in the northern part and Sparta in the southern. The narrow neck of land that joins the two, carrying traffic and trade between them to this day, is the Isthmus of Corinth, and the city itself sits right there, on the southwest corner of the isthmus and the southeast corner of the western gulf. Attempts were made in antiquity to dig a canal across the four miles of the isthmus to enable ships to avoid the long trip around the Peloponnese by passing directly from the Adriatic to the Aegean (or vice versa) through the Gulf of Corinth on the west side and the Saronic Gulf on the east. Nero himself took a pickax and tried to start such a project in AD 67 (using Jewish prisoners from the early years of the Roman-Jewish war), but like all the other ancient attempts his was unsuccessful. Alternative arrangements were made using a stone carriageway to drag ships overland, though that was laborious and costly. The present canal was finally dug and opened for sea traffic in the late nineteenth century. Even then, and to this day, the canal is too shallow, narrow, and susceptible to rockfalls to accomplish what was really wanted. Most larger ships cannot use it. What you are likely to see there now are smaller tourist boats.

Even without a canal, however, Corinth was bound to thrive. It has several freshwater springs that made the site attractive for dwellings and commerce. In addition to being located right by the main shipping and land routes, it commands a coastal plain that was proverbial in antiquity for its fertility. Corinth was also proverbial for its morals, or rather the lack thereof. It was a classic port city—though actually the ports proper were Lechaeum, two miles to the west, and Cenchreae, six miles to the east—where every type of human behavior might flourish unchecked. (A large temple to Aphrodite, on the summit of the Corinthian acropolis, made its own statement, even though the climb to the top was and is far more demanding than the trek up the much smaller Athenian acropolis.) After a century in which the city lay in ruins, having been sacked by the Romans in 146 BC, it was refounded in 44 BC as a Roman colony by Julius Caesar not long before his assassination. (He was another who tried to have a canal dug.

Indeed, people spoke of a curse on the project; Caesar, Nero, and Caligula all died violently after trying to get the scheme going.) Corinth was the capital of the province of Achaea, administered by a proconsul.

Like other colonies, if anything more so, Corinth was excessively proud of its *Romanitas*, its "Romanness." The new temple for the imperial cult is still prominent in the Corinthian Forum, deliberately raised just a little higher than the other local temples, of which, of course, there were many, including those to Aphrodite, Poseidon (god of earthquakes as well as of the sea), Apollo, and the healing god Asclepius. The symbolism of raising the imperial shrine higher than the others was, and is, obvious. Even though by the standards of the day Corinth was a large city, to our eyes everything seems close together. When you walk around the city center today, you are reminded again how easy it was for everyone to know everyone else's business. Except for the very rich, life happened in public. And Paul was not rich.

The original members of the colony were Roman freedmen, ex-slaves on the way up the social scale. They were joined by Roman businessmen with their eye on the profits to be made in such an ideal trading and transport post. Like every other city in the ancient world, Corinth had a huge social imbalance, with few rich, many poor, and at least half the population in any case enslaved. Still, it was a city full of possibility, including the chance of social mobility—in either direction—and hence there was a high probability that people would pay close attention to markers of social standing.

Paul has few such markers. As he trudges into town—we normally assume he traveled on foot, and it would have taken perhaps three or four days from Athens—he does not cut a fine figure. It is now early 51. It is a matter of weeks, perhaps at most a couple of months, since he was badly beaten in Philippi; but since then he has had to leave three cities in a hurry, he is anxious about the Thessalonians after the riots and the threats against Jason, and he may well be short of funds. Having sent Timothy back to Thessalonica, he is alone. "I came to you in weakness," he would later write to the Corinthian church, "in great fear and trembling."[1] But at this point he makes some new friends who will be among his most important supporters in the days to come.

Aquila and Priscilla (in Paul's letters he abbreviates her name as Prisca) were a Jewish couple who came from Pontus, on the Black Sea shore of ancient Turkey. They had, however, been living in Rome until Claudius banished the Jews for rioting. It is hard to pin down exactly what had gone on, or indeed when. The Roman historian Suetonius says that the riots had been instigated by "Chrestus," which could reflect a garbled account of trouble in the Jewish community in Rome when the gospel of Messiah Jesus ("Christus," with the middle vowel pronounced long) arrived in town. Suetonius gives no date for the incident, but the convergence of other evidence makes it likely that it happened around AD 49, and that Aquila and Priscilla arrived in Corinth—adding to the many Roman businesspeople already there—not long before Paul did himself. Like him, they were tentmakers. They seem not only to have struck up an instant friendship, but to have become sufficiently close for Paul to lodge in their house, share in their business, and also travel with them to Ephesus. By the time Paul wrote Romans, they were back in Rome again. The way Luke tells the story of their first meeting and going into business together makes the moment seem full of hope and fresh possibility.

As usual, Paul starts his apostolic work (as opposed to his tentmaking work) in the synagogue. We must assume that he rehearses yet again the familiar narrative: Abraham, Exodus, David, exile, hope. The focus is likewise the same: scripture speaks of a Messiah who dies and rises again, and this Messiah is Jesus. It is to his Corinthian listeners, in the first of the two letters, that he later writes to remind them of the very simple terms of his initial gospel announcement:

The Messiah died for our sins in accordance with the
Bible; he was buried; he was raised on the third day in
accordance with the Bible; he was seen . . .[2]

He summarizes this even more sharply: "When I came to
you . . . ," he says, "I decided to know nothing in my dealings
with you except Jesus the Messiah, especially his crucifixion."[3]
That, however, would take a great deal of explaining, and Sabbath by Sabbath Paul gives it all he's got, arguing and expounding, winning over a good many of the Jews in the synagogue and
also several of the God-fearing Greeks. This is how Timothy and
Silas find him when they finally catch up with him, Timothy
having made the double journey from Thessalonica to Athens and
back and now on to Corinth itself.

When Paul later described his initial preaching in Corinth, he
reflected on his wider experience of announcing the gospel:

Jews look for signs, you see, and Greeks search for wisdom; but we announce the crucified Messiah, a scandal
to Jews and folly to Gentiles, but to those who are called,
Jews and Greeks alike, the Messiah—God's power and
God's wisdom. God's folly is wiser than humans, you
see, and God's weakness is stronger than humans.[4]

In other words, every time Paul came into a new town or city
and opened his mouth, he knew perfectly well that what he was
saying would make no sense. As with Jesus himself, the kind of
"signs" that were on offer were not the sort of thing that the Jewish world was wanting or expecting. A crucified Messiah was a
contradiction in terms.

As for the non-Jewish world—well, the suggestion that a *Jew*
might be the new "Lord" over all other Lords was bad enough,
but a *crucified* man? Everybody knew that was the most shameful
and horrible death imaginable. How could such a person then be

hailed as *Kyrios*? And if the answer was (as it would be for Paul) that God had raised this man from the dead, that would merely convince his hearers that he was indeed out of his mind. (A Roman governor would accuse him of that later on, but Paul must have been quite used to people saying it.) Everybody knew resurrection didn't happen. A nice dream, perhaps—though many would have said they'd prefer to leave the body behind for good, thank you very much. Anyway, there's no point living in fantasy land.

Paul seems to have accepted this role—saying things that made people think he was mad or blaspheming, but that then appeared to carry a life-changing power of their own. He must have known that some, on the edge of the crowd as it were, might even see him as a magician, someone saying incomprehensible things, with a magic name thrown into the mix, as a result of which—poof!—something dramatic would happen. Someone would be healed. Some well-known local character would be transformed and become a new person. Paul clearly had to resist the temptation to suppose that this power was somehow in his possession or under his control. He was simply a steward, dispensing God's power and wisdom in the most unlikely fashion. But it tells us a lot about Paul that, in the first Corinthian letter at least, he can speak of this paradoxical vocation in a deliberately sharp-edged and teasing way. The passage is, of course, rhetorically crafted—in order to say that clever rhetoric isn't where it's at. Paul must have enjoyed that, not least because he would know that several of the Corinthians would see what he was doing and enjoy it too. But the fact remains that Paul had, to this point, made a career out of telling people things he knew they would find either mad or blasphemous or both. He had grown used to it. This was what he did.

★ ★ ★

Timothy's arrival brought news from Thessalonica, and this resulted at once in the outpouring of relief and affection that we know as 1 Thessalonians. The letter is famous for many reasons, and those who date Galatians much later than I do see it as the first of Paul's letters, or at least the first to survive. In any case, the tone is completely different from the frantic alarm of Galatians. Nothing has gone wrong in the Thessalonian church; they are holding fast in the face of persecution; and Paul is proud of them, pleased with them, mightily relieved that they have not given in to the pressure of violent opposition. He reminds them of how it all began, with his visit, the sheer power of the gospel itself, which transformed their lives, and the strange combination of suffering and joy that they saw in him and then experienced for themselves. Timothy and Silas (or Silvanus, as he calls him in the letters) have reported that news of the Thessalonians' newfound faith in the One God and loyalty to *Kyrios Iēsous* has radiated out into the whole of Greece, into both Macedonia in the north and Achaea in the south.

Paul's summary of the rumors that had gone around the country are telling. They include the way the Thessalonians had welcomed him personally and received his message and the way they readily "turned"—Paul uses the word we would think of as "convert," "turn around"—from idols "to serve a living and true God."[5] Clearly the heart of it was the Jewish message over against the practices of the pagan world. The results would be visible on the street. People would notice ("You know that family three doors down? They haven't been to a single festival all month!"). But the reason this ancient Jewish message now had power to change pagan hearts and lives is because of what had happened through Jesus: the power of the idols had been broken. If we ask Paul the question historians always want to ask, taking the long view, as to why this unlikely message achieved such remarkable success, his own answer would undoubtedly include this point.

Through this victory, Jesus had established the new world order, *and he would return to complete the work.* Paul reminded his hearers that, as part of his message, he had explained that the One

God would do what scripture had long promised and indeed what Paul had said to the surprised judges on the Areopagus: this God would sort the whole world out once and for all. On that day, when all human corruption and wickedness would face "anger and fury" and "trouble and distress,"[6] those who had turned away from idols would be rescued by Jesus himself.

Paul then ruminates on the deep relationship that had begun in those early days and that continued in the all-too-short time he was with them. It had been time enough, though, for him to be both a pastor and a teacher, a model of the new way of life both in his manual labor to provide for his own needs and in his own personal life:

> You are witnesses, and so is God, of our holy, upright and blameless behavior toward you believers. You know how, like a father to his own children, we encouraged each of you, and strengthened you, and made it clear to you that you should behave in a manner worthy of the God who calls you into his own kingdom and glory.[7]

This reminds us, as Paul is writing from Corinth, just what a challenge he faced in city after city. It is hard for any Christian worker today in all but the newest mission fields to imagine this. After two thousand years, most people in most cultures have at least a sketchy idea of what a Christian way of life might be, at least in theory and allowing for cynicism about actual Christian practice. But when Paul arrived in a new town, there was no expectation. Nobody had the slightest idea that there was a new way of life suddenly available, let alone what it might look like. Paul had to model it from scratch. He had done so, and he was naturally overjoyed that it had worked; they were copying him, not least in facing up to suffering. He was overflowing with joy and clearly regarded the Thessalonian church as a pinnacle of his life's work so far:

When our Lord Jesus is present once more, what is our
hope, our joy, the crown of our boasting before him? It's
you! Yes: you are our glory and our joy.[8]

One wonders what the people in the Corinthian church, among
whom Paul was writing this, might have thought of it. Were they
coming a poor second in his favors? But perhaps—and this may be
an important insight into Paul's understanding of his own work—
the Thessalonian church was particularly special to him precisely
because he had been there so briefly. He had not had time to
settle down and manage its growth in faith. It had all happened so
fast that he really couldn't claim any credit for it all, even had he
wanted to; the gospel did its own powerful work, since it was after
all God's own word at work in people's hearts.[9] So when he looks
back, he sees the church in Thessalonica, thriving now in the midst
of suffering, as the great sign that the true and living God is indeed
at work through the word of the gospel. It is one thing to believe
that this happens, as Paul obviously had already believed for a long
time by this time. It is another thing, out in strange territory, to
discover it so obviously happening despite adverse circumstances.
This letter, written in the early days in Corinth, resonates with
faith reaffirmed and hope strengthened.

There are three matters about which Paul is eager to say more.
Each of these will be important—and more than important—in
Corinth, and here we get an early taste of them. It looks as though
these are issues that were bound to come up precisely because the
early Christian worldview was so radically different from anything people had imagined before.

If we make a list of three topics beginning with "sex" and
"money," we might expect the third to be "power," but in this case
it is the *parousia,* the "appearing" of Jesus. The first two are obvious,
but need to be stressed. Sexual holiness is mandatory, not optional,
for followers of Jesus.[10] What that means in practice Paul will later
spell out in his first letter to Corinth. But already the reason for this

rule is made clear. Unbridled, crazy, and inflamed lust is a sign *that one does not know God.* Sexual holiness isn't just a "rule," an arbitrary commandment. It is part of what it means to turn from idols and serve the true and living God. It is part of being a genuine, image-bearing human being. Paul will emphasize the same point again in the later letters Ephesians and Colossians, but it is already crystal clear in this passage, however briefly stated. Clearly Paul often had his work cut out to give pastoral help to people who heard what he said, but found themselves still stuck in long-lasting habits of life. But at the end of the day a clean break had to be made.

Money was part of Christian discipleship from the start. Paul had agreed with the "pillars" in Jerusalem that he would go on "remembering the poor"; that was one of the signs of the new community that would carry forward as an identifying mark for centuries to come. For Paul this was simply the outworking of "love," *agapē*. That was never simply about feelings, but about mutual support, first of all within the family of Jesus-followers[11] and then, as far as ability allowed, to the larger world (note the repeated emphasis on "good works" in the wider community in the letter to Titus). It is noticeable that here and then particularly in the second letter to Thessalonica, Paul is already dealing with the second-order problems that arise in any community known to make generosity a way of life: there must be no freeloading, no sponging. Jesus-followers must "behave in a way which outsiders will respect, and so that none . . . may be in financial difficulties."[12] Sex and money are important, but they are not to be worshipped. Sexual purity and financial generosity were to be built into the Christian DNA from the start.

An altogether more complicated issue concerns the *parousia,* or "royal presence" or "manifestation," of Jesus. Clearly it was always part of Paul's message that the kingdom, on earth as in heaven, had already been launched through the events of Jesus's death and resurrection, but it needed to be completed, and that would happen at Jesus's return. But what language could he use to get this point across to people in different cultures, with different worldviews and metaphysical assumptions? Paul was heir to the long Jewish tradition of richly metaphorical language to speak of the ways in which the life and power of God's realm ("heaven") would impinge on the life and reality of the human sphere ("earth"). His hearers may not have been so familiar with it, just as many people today find this language alien or incomprehensible (or, perhaps worse, assume they *do* understand it when clearly they do not). And Paul was not just writing about a theoretical question. There was a pressing pastoral need.

The presenting problem in Thessalonica was Paul's teaching that Jesus, who had already defeated death, would return to complete the job. At least some of his hearers had gained the impression that none of them, having come to faith, would die before that time. So now that some of them had indeed died, they wondered if the whole thing was a mistake.

This draws out of Paul something he obviously hadn't said when he was with them, though it builds on things that he had believed long before. His ways of expressing things develops over time, no doubt partly as he discovers which lines of exposition his hearers can grasp easily and which ones they tend to misunderstand. But at the heart of it he is teaching non-Jews to *think Jewishly* and teaching both non-Jews and Jews to think in the Jewish way *as radically modified by Jesus*. This is a difficult double task. It involves nothing short of that hardest conversion of all, the conversion of the imagination. But that is what is required if people are to understand where they are and who they are as the family of God.

As I said when discussing the Epicureans and Stoics, the ancient non-Jewish world did not have much of an "eschatology," a sense of time going somewhere, a sense of history having an ultimate purpose that would eventually be realized. The Stoic idea of a once-in-a-millennium conflagration is not the same thing, since that is part of a cycle. The only other serious "eschatology" in Paul's world was, tellingly, the one offered by the new imperial ideology, which had revived a much older idea about a sequence of "ages," starting with gold and working down to base metals. (A variation on this is found in the sequence of four metals in the statue dreamed of by Nebuchadnezzar in Daniel 2.) Now at last, sang the Augustan court poets, the golden age has returned! The imperial propaganda machine, featuring some of the greatest poets and architects of the day, relentlessly put out the word that with Augustus Caesar history had reached a surprising but joyful new day.

That was, no doubt, an exciting message for those who could glimpse, as many could not, the possibility that they might benefit from the rule of Rome. It was certainly a new idea for many who had lived in a world largely without hope except on the lowest personal levels. But for Paul all this was simply a parody of the truth. The real "golden age"—not that he called it that—had begun when the Messiah had defeated death and been raised from the dead. So—back to the Thessalonians' question—what should one think about believers who had died before the Lord's return?

It is significant that Paul is writing about this while in Corinth, because it is in the two letters to Corinth later on that he gives the fullest account of these important matters. But here in 1 Thessalonians he makes a start. Speaking pastorally, Paul distinguishes between two different types of grief.[13] He tells the Thessalonians that they do not have the hope*less* kind of grief, the bleak, dark horror of loss with no mitigating circumstances or beliefs, but rather a hope*ful* grief, which, although there is still the tearing, wrenching sense of loss, has within it the strong and clear hope of reunion. Paul doesn't say exactly when the reunion will occur, because that's not where he wants the focus to be. The point is that all will in the end be together "with the Lord."

To make this point he uses three quite different images. First, he recalls Moses coming down the mountain accompanied by the sound of a trumpet, suggesting that Jesus will appear in like manner coming down from heaven. We should not make the mistake of supposing that Paul thought "heaven" was literally "up there," a place within our space-time continuum. Ancient Jews were quite capable of using the language of a "three-decker universe" without supposing it was to be taken literally. Heaven (we might say) is a different *dimension of* reality, not a location within *our* dimension. Second, he recalls the image from Daniel 7 of "one like a son of man coming with the clouds" from earth to heaven, vindicated at last after suffering, exalted to the place of sovereign rule and kingdom. Even so, he says, those who belong to the Lord will be exalted like that, vindicated, sharing the Lord's throne. Third, he recalls what happens when an emperor or grand official pays a state visit to a city or province. The leading citizens, seeing him coming, go out to meet him in the open country in order then to escort him royally into the city. Like that, those "who are alive," he says, will "meet the Lord in the air." How else can he describe the coming together of heaven and earth? The point is not that people will be snatched away from earth and end up in "heaven." As we see frequently in his letters, that is never Paul's view. The point is that heaven and earth will come together[14] and those who belong to the Messiah will be part of it.

The one "literal" statement in this text is the central and important one—the Messiah's people who have already died will rise first.[15] Those who have died while believing in Jesus are safe in his presence, and they will be raised when he appears. Then all these other things will happen too. Each time Paul returns to this topic, he says it a little differently. But once we grasp how the imagery works, the underlying sense is always the same.

A different image, though, challenges the Thessalonians with another echo of imperial propaganda. The Lord will come like a midnight robber, just when people are saying "peace and security."[16] Who in that world was claiming to offer "peace and security"? The Roman Empire, of course; it proclaimed, on coins and other symbols, that with the rise of the empire the whole world was now "safe." It was a lie, of course, a classic piece of political propaganda, comparable to the lies exposed by the prophet Jeremiah.[17] The sequence of awful emperors—Tiberius, Caligula, Claudius, Nero—was bad enough, but then there came "the year of the four emperors" (AD 69), when the whole Roman world seemed to go into prolonged convulsions once more. No "peace and security" there. Paul's answer to the Roman boast is once more to teach the converts to think Christianly about time itself:

> You are not in darkness. That day won't surprise you like
> a robber. You are all children of light, children of the
> day! We don't belong to the night, or to darkness. . . .
> We daytime people should be self-controlled. . . . The
> Messiah . . . died for us, so that whether we stay awake
> or go to sleep we should live together with him.[18]

Followers of Jesus, then, must get used to living with a form of theological jet lag. The world all around is still in darkness, but they have set their clocks for a different time zone. It is already daytime on their worldview clock, and they must live as daytime people. This is one of the greatest challenges Paul faced: how to teach people who had never thought eschatologically that time is going somewhere and they must learn how to reset their watches; how to teach Jews who had thought the ultimate kingdom was going to come all at once that the kingdom had *already* broken in to world history with Jesus, but that it was *not yet* consummated and wouldn't be until his return and the renewal of all things.

This is a more familiar challenge to us in the modern West, though it isn't always thought of in this way. From time to time politicians and philosophers proclaim that the world entered a great new day with the eighteenth-century Enlightenment. This, they say, is a new *saeculum,* a different "age" of world history, and the world must learn to live in the light of it. But, they often complain, things aren't working out as well as they should. Not everyone has woken up to the brave new world we thought was

arriving. This is a particular problem for those who saw the French
and American Revolutions of the 1770s and 1780s or the Russian
Revolution of 1917 as ushering in some kind of new time. What
happens then? How do you live between the supposed arrival
of the new day and its actual implementation? That is a good
question, and it only arises, we may suppose, because the ideals of
revolutionary Europe, not least those associated with Karl Marx,
were themselves echoes or even parodies of Jewish and Christian
eschatology.

That is a story for another time. But we note that Paul, writing
to Thessalonica while living in Corinth, would have been very
much aware that one of his prime tasks was to teach his churches
to think of God's coming kingdom in this two-stage way. Knowing what time it was would be crucial for how they would then
live. In fact, though the question of the Lord's "royal appearing"
(*parousia*) might seem to be quite unrelated to the earlier questions of sex and money, they are all of a piece. If you are already
living in the new world, there are new ways of behaving.

The question of when Jesus would return and what that event
would look like is the main focus of the second letter to Thessalonica, probably written from Corinth not long after the first
one. Since Paul in effect includes Silas (Silvanus) and Timothy as
coauthors, the probability is that it dates from later on in this first
visit to Corinth, perhaps sometime in 51. Suffering and judgment
dominate, the present suffering of the church and the coming
judgment in which God will sort everything out at last.

It has been fashionable in modern times to imagine that the
early Christians saw the coming judgment as the literal "end of
the world," the collapse and destruction of the planet and perhaps
the entire cosmos as we know it. This letter, though full of lurid
imagery, makes it clear that that cannot be right. Paul warns the
Thessalonians not to be unsettled by anyone saying or writing in
a letter that purports to be by Paul "that the day of the Lord has
already arrived." The "day of the Lord," in other words—the

new, Jesus-focused version of the ancient Israelite hope for "the day of the Lord"—will not mean the end of the present space-time order. One would not expect to be informed of such a thing through the Roman postal system. As so often in Jewish writing of roughly this period, what sounds to us like "end-of-the-world" language is used to denote and refer to things that we might call major world events, the sudden rise and fall of ruling powers and the like, and to *invest* those events with their inner, God-related significance.

Classic examples are found in books like Isaiah, where the *language* of the sun and the moon being darkened and the stars falling from heaven is deployed to *denote* the fall of Babylon and to *invest* that event with its "cosmic" significance, which is that the powers of the heavens are shaken![19] Or take the case of Jeremiah, who in his early days had prophesied that the world would return to chaos. Since the Temple in Jerusalem was regarded as the focal point of creation, of heaven and earth coming together, this was the appropriate language to use when speaking prophetically of a time when the Temple would be destroyed.[20] Jeremiah spent many years worrying about whether he was after all a false prophet, not because the world had not come to an end, but because the Temple had not fallen.

This is how such language was used across many centuries in the Israelite and Jewish culture, which had always believed in the close link of "heaven" and "earth" and found it natural to use the language of "natural disasters" to bring out the significance of what we might call major sociopolitical upheavals. Actually, we do the very same thing, speaking of a political "earthquake" or of an election producing a "landslide." Our own metaphors seem so natural that we forget they are metaphors. Other people's metaphors, alien to our way of speaking, are often misinterpreted as though they are not metaphors at all. No doubt Paul faced the same kind of problem, moving as he did within a complex and confusing range of cultures.

So what was he really saying to the Thessalonians when warning them about the coming "day"? The best way of taking his strange, allusive language is to see it as the natural extension of what he says back in 1 Thessalonians 5. There, we recall, he had warned about those who say "peace and security," but who would face sudden ruin. This can only be a coded reference to the imperial propaganda put out by Rome, which, claiming to have gained control over the whole world, offered its citizens an assurance of safety far beyond its power to deliver. Paul already knew—the whole Jewish world already knew—what that might look like in reality. Paul was writing this letter while Claudius was emperor, but everybody knew what his predecessor, Gaius Caligula, had tried to do.

He had nearly achieved it. Becoming emperor in his middle twenties, Caligula had become increasingly erratic and megalomaniacal, insisting on divine honors in Rome itself, something his predecessors Augustus and Tiberius had been careful never to do. One thing stood in his way: the permission given to the Jews to worship their own God in their own way. He planned to do to Jerusalem what Antiochus Epiphanes had done two centuries earlier, only more so; he would convert the Jerusalem Temple into a great shrine focused on a giant statue of himself. He would be the divine image in the holy place.

Like his grand plans for the Corinthian canal, this didn't happen. Caligula was assassinated in January AD 41. His name was removed from public records, and his statues were destroyed. But for many Jews who knew their scriptures, not least the prophecies of Daniel, there was a sense that the great evil, the vast, chaotic, and horrible "mystery of lawlessness," had been thwarted once, but would return. Something was holding it back, "restraining" it, for a time.[21] What did that mean? Some have thought Paul meant that Claudius, a very different kind of emperor, was following a different kind of policy, but that when he departed another Caligula might arise. Others have supposed Paul was referring to the power of the gospel itself, that the work of announcing Jesus as Lord was establishing a bridgehead into the power structures of the world, so that when the great evil returned it could be properly defeated. Paul's purpose, in any case, was not to encourage the Thessalonians' tendency toward lurid apocalyptic speculation, but to assure them that, despite fears and rumors, God was in charge. Jesus was indeed the coming world ruler, and they, as his people, were secure.[22]

He had one more message for them, again reminding us that the church was from the first a community of mutual support. Here, within twenty years of Jesus's crucifixion and resurrection, was a "family" already running into the problem of people taking advantage of generosity, of *agapē*! Paul's instruction here is brisk: those who won't work shouldn't eat.[23] This no doubt made the point at the time, but for us the important thing is perhaps what Paul and the Thessalonians were all taking for granted: that the followers of Jesus were to live as "family," with all that this entailed in mutual support. Paul stressed the responsibilities of the individual: "Do your own work in peace" (as Paul himself had done, deliberately setting the example), "and eat your own bread."[24] The modern Western church has taken individualism to an extreme, and there are great strengths in focusing on the challenge to every single church member, both to believe and to work. But for Paul this did not undermine, but rather gave appropriate balance to, the more foundational reality, that those who belonged to the Messiah were "brothers and sisters."

★ ★ ★

As we think back to the experience of the Galatian cities and then of Thessalonica and Beroea, we might imagine that Paul's work in the Corinthian synagogue would result in riots, in the stirring up of local hostility from whatever quarter, and in his being run out of town. For whatever reason this didn't happen, and indeed things took a much more hopeful turn all around. He did meet the predictable opposition, but by that time Crispus, the ruler of the synagogue, had himself become a believer, which must have caused quite a stir both in the Jewish community itself and more widely in Corinth as a whole. When eventually it was no longer possible for Paul to work in the synagogue, one of the converts from among the God-fearers offered an alternative meeting place—his own house, right across the street. Once more, if Paul had been a shrinking violet he might have sought a less confrontational position. But that was never his style.

Around this time too Paul had a vision of Jesus himself encouraging him. "Don't be afraid," he said. "Speak on, and don't be silent, because I am with you, and nobody will be able to lay a finger on you to harm you. There are many of my people in this city."[25] Visions like this, in the modern world as well as the ancient, are not normally luxuries. Paul needed assurance that he was in for a longer haul than in most of his previous cities.

Paul may, then, have been asking for trouble by holding meetings across the street from the synagogue. But, once more, he not only got away with it, but, as with his public apology in Philippi, he came out even better. After over a year of his teaching and pastoring in Corinth, the remaining synagogue members—the Jews who had not, like Crispus, decided to follow Jesus—made a concerted attack on the apostle. We recall the ironies of the two earlier charges, which must have resonated with Paul's own sense of a new and paradoxical identity. In Philippi, he had been accused of *teaching Jewish customs* that would be illegal for Romans; in Thessalonica, he was accused *by the Jewish community* of teachings contrary to Caesar's decrees. Here things were less specific but still, in a proud Roman colony, potentially threatening. He was accused of "teaching people to worship God in illegal ways."[26]

The tribunal to which he was taken was that of Gallio, the brother of the famous philosopher Seneca. Gallio had been appointed by Claudius to be proconsul of the province of Achaea; an inscription from Delphi dates this fairly exactly, indicating that Gallio finished his term of office in AD 52. The normal term of office was a single year, though some stayed longer; the probability is that Gallio had arrived in late 51. Paul's eighteen months in Corinth probably lasted from sometime early in 51 to sometime late in 52.

What might his Jewish opponents have meant by "worshipping God in illegal ways"? We cannot be sure, but an interesting and revealing answer suggests itself. The Jewish communities had official permission to worship their own God. From what we know of Paul's prayers, he regularly used Jewish-style formulations *but included Jesus in them.* The best-known example, which I think was very important to Paul, is the prayer he quotes in the first letter to Corinth incorporating Jesus into the central monotheistic prayer, the *Shema:* "For us there is one God, the father, . . . and one Lord, Jesus the Messiah."[27] This was bound to be offensive to Jews who did not see Jesus either as Israel's Messiah or as the embodiment of Israel's God. It ought, therefore, so the accusers suggested, to be regarded by the Roman authorities as "illegal," going beyond what had been authorized. Rome had, so to speak, given permission for a lodger to bring a piano into an apartment; Paul was bringing in a small orchestra.

It is possible, though less likely, that they might also have hinted that to call Jesus *Kyrios* or "son of God" and to regard him as the true king of Israel was potentially seditious against Rome itself; that is, Paul's small orchestra included a trumpet summoning the troops for battle. And the accusers would have had a point. If Paul was adapting the permitted liturgies in a new form, claiming that this was the fulfillment of the Jewish way of life and the hope of Israel, this might well be going beyond what Rome thought it had sanctioned in permitting Jewish worship. And calling Jesus by titles that Caesar had made his own was throwing caution to the winds.

This proposal is confirmed, I think, by Gallio's response. Gallio was not interested in the Jewish charges. He stopped the case before Paul could say anything; perhaps he had heard about his loquacity and was not prepared to sit through a lengthy exposition of Jewish and Christian teaching. There was to be no repeat of the Areopagus discourse. Gallio declared that the charges had nothing to do with actual illegal or vicious conduct. They were matters internal to the Jewish community, "a dispute," he says, "about words, names, and laws within your own customs."[28] As far as Gallio was concerned, if Paul wanted to adapt Jewish styles of prayer by adding this or that name or title, that was up to him. Gallio refused to be a judge of such things. They would have to sort it out themselves.

This was a momentous event in the history of the church, and one wonders if even Paul had seen it coming. What it meant was that, unlike the authorities in the other territories he had visited, the official Roman governor of southern Greece ("Achaea") had declared *that being a Jesus-follower was to be seen as a variation of the Jewish way of life.* At a stroke, this drew the sting that had been part of the pain in Galatia. It meant (among other things) that when non-Jewish Jesus-followers absented themselves from the civic cult—which, we note once more, could hardly remain hidden in a proud Roman city—they would be able to claim the same exemption as their Jewish neighbors.

The other major difference between what happened in Corinth and what had happened in Paul's earlier legal and quasi-legal conflicts is that the mob—always a volatile element in a crowded city—saw which way the wind was blowing and took out its frustrations not on Paul and his friends, but on Sosthenes, the new synagogue ruler. Gallio, who could easily have sent in officers to stop the beating, did nothing.[29]

★ ★ ★

Shortly after that, Paul left Corinth, though we have no idea why. He seems to have wanted to get to Jerusalem, perhaps for a particular festival. Perhaps for that reason he had taken a vow, preparing himself in a traditional way for a special act of worship. Acts states, with a suddenness that has taken some interpreters by surprise and made them wonder whether the real Paul would ever have behaved like this, that while Paul was at the eastern port of Cenchreae awaiting his departure by sea, he had his hair cut off because of this vow. The odd thing about this, at one level anyway, is that one might expect the haircut to be scheduled for the *end* of a special time (during which the hair had grown freely) rather than at the start; unless, of course, the vow was going to take some time, in which case (and remembering that in 1 Cor. 11 Paul disapproved of men with long hair) it might make sense to have it cut at the start of the period of purification, so that even with a long subsequent period of growth it would not get *too* long.

The other odd thing, at a deeper level, is that interpreters of Paul for many years have come to him with the assumptions of modern European Protestantism, in which the idea of doing something so "Catholic"—or so Jewish!—as taking a purificatory vow that might require a special haircut was unthinkable. But these are simply modern prejudices. Paul's doctrine of justification by faith has nothing to say about the rightness or wrongness of particular devotional practices. Since Paul obviously still saw himself as a loyal Jew, worshipping the God of his ancestors albeit in the new dispensation launched by Israel's Messiah, there was no earthly (or heavenly!) reason why he should not engage in particular practices. The truly odd thing, however, is that Luke, after mentioning this out of the blue, says nothing more about it, though it connects at long range with the other purificatory rituals that Paul undergoes on his final arrival in Jerusalem in Acts 21:22–26.

So Paul sails away, with Priscilla and Aquila accompanying him (nothing is said about Silas or Timothy), and crosses the Aegean to Ephesus, where Priscilla and Aquila stay on. Paul makes a brief visit to the synagogue there (we know the script by now:

Abraham, Exodus, David, exile, hope, Messiah), but he is eager to get on his way. He sails to Caesarea, from there travels up to Jerusalem, and then returns to Syrian Antioch. The trip is probably to be dated in late 52, and the final leg of it, traveling north from Jerusalem to Antioch, in early 53.

While he was traveling—on the sea, on the roads—he prayed. We know this. When he tells people that they should "never stop praying," this can hardly be something that applies to everybody else but not to himself.[30] But how do you go on praying all the time? Is it simply ceaseless chatter, a stream-of-consciousness monologue (or indeed dialogue) with the God who through the spirit was as present as breath itself? This may have been part of it, but reading back from the letters Paul wrote over the next three or four years I think we can be much more precise and focused. At several points in his letters he seems to be adapting Jewish prayers and liturgies to include Jesus in recognition of the new life that had erupted into the ancient tradition. We know from many passages in the letters that he prayed the Psalms, focusing them on Jesus; Jesus was the promised king, the ultimate sufferer, the truly human one who would now be crowned with glory and honor. We can guess, from the easy way he weaves it into his argument, that the astonishing adaptation of the *Shema* prayer had already been Paul's daily, perhaps thrice-daily, way of invoking Jesus, of expressing his loyalty to him and his kingdom: *For us there is one God . . . and one Lord . . .*[31]

So too the "benedictions" in Jewish liturgy ("Blessed be the God who . . . ") had become part of his celebration of the way in which the One God had fulfilled his purposes in Jesus. They were Exodus prayers, kingdom prayers, messianic prayers, Jesus prayers. Paul's experience of articulating the crazy, nonsensical message about Jesus and watching as it grasped and gripped and changed people's lives had given him concrete reasons to pray like this, to invoke the name and power of Jesus, to seek his protection, his guidance, his encouragement, his hope, to know his presence as the focus of what in Paul's earlier life he had experienced as the covenant love of the One God.

It is easy as we follow the outward course of Paul's life to forget that the inward course was just as important. But unless we step to one side from his relentless journeyings and imagine him praying like this, praying as he and his friends break bread in Jesus's name; praying as he waits for the next ship, for the turn of the tide, for the right weather to sail; praying for sick friends and for newly founded little churches; praying as he makes his way toward what may be a wonderful reunion with old friends or an awkward confrontation with old enemies—unless we build this into the very heart of our picture of this extraordinary, energetic, bold, and yet vulnerable man, we will not understand him at all. In particular, we will not understand what happened next.

At every stage of this journey, from his extraordinarily successful missionary venture around the Aegean back to Jerusalem and Antioch, we would like to know what happened. Where did he stay? Who did he meet? What was said, how was he received, what scriptures did they study together, was there fresh agreement or new tension? Did he get back together with Barnabas? Did he meet John Mark, and if so, what did they say to one another? Did he report back to James and the others in Jerusalem about the practical difficulties of organizing and maintaining communities of faith across cultural boundaries—and, in particular, about the ways in which the letter written by the Jerusalem church at the conference a few years before both was and wasn't helpful in real-life situations? Had James written his own letter ("the Letter of James") by this time, and did they discuss justification, faith, works, and the significance of Abraham? Was it on this visit that, realizing both the hardship faced by the Jerusalem church and the sense that the Jesus-followers there had only the sketchiest idea of who their far-flung brothers and sisters actually were, Paul conceived the plan for a large-scale collection to bring real relief to

Jerusalem and to function as a sign of unity across the miles and the cultures?

We are not told. Paul himself never mentions this trip. Luke describes it in a single verse: "Then he went up to Jerusalem, greeted the church, and went back to Antioch."[32] Our sources give us the sense of a lull before the storm.

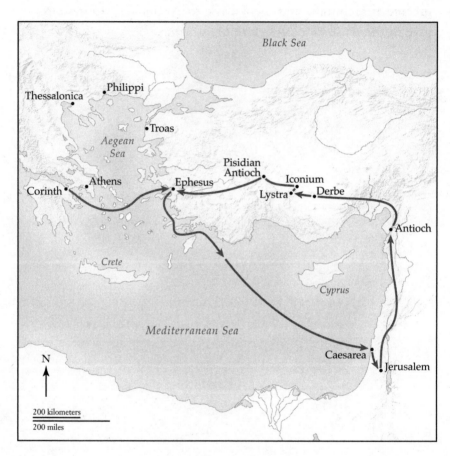

Journeys Through Asia Minor

10

Ephesus I

"W E DON'T WANT to keep you in the dark," Paul wrote to Corinth, probably in AD 56, "about the suffering we went through in Asia."[1] Our problem is that though Paul wanted the Corinthians to know about what a bad time he had had, he doesn't say what exactly had happened. We, at least, are still in the dark. Apart from what Paul says in this letter we have only hints and guesses. Luke, wanting no doubt to tone down any serious trouble that his principal subject had faced, gives graphic descriptions of various things that Paul did in Ephesus, the main city in the province of Asia, and of the famous riot in the theater with a vast crowd shouting "Great is Ephesian Artemis!" (as well they might; the Temple of Artemis, on the northeast side of the city, was one of the seven wonders of the ancient world).[2] But nothing in his account of Paul's time in Ephesus suggests anything out of line with what we have come to expect, which is that Paul preaches the Messiah in the synagogue, opposition mounts, there are threats and disturbances involving local magistrates, and Paul finally has to leave town.

But 2 Corinthians tells a different story. With this, we probe into a dark place in Paul's life, and perhaps a dark place in his heart and mind. Some have even suggested that his theological position changed radically as a result of these experiences. I do not think that is the case, but we are now approaching a quite new stage in our investigation about what drove him on and how what he had seen of Jesus on the Damascus Road had left its transforming mark on his life, his heart of hearts, and his outward vocation. We may also be pointing ahead, from this darkness, to the extra question of why on earth Paul's work turned out to be, in historical and human terms, so ultimately successful.

These questions are already raised by what he says at the start of 2 Corinthians:

> The load we had to carry was far too heavy for us; it got
> to the point where we gave up on life itself. Yes: deep
> inside ourselves we received the death sentence.[3]

If somebody came to see me and said something like this, I would recognize the signs of serious depression. This was not just an outward death sentence—the Paul we have come to know could have coped with that reasonably well—but one "deep inside ourselves." (The "we" in this letter is clearly a way of referring to himself. Though he mentions Timothy as being with him in writing the letter in 1:1, what he says is so personal and intimate that we must take it as a roundabout way of talking about himself while perhaps shrinking from the shocking immediacy of the first-person singular.)

He goes on at once to describe his eventual reaction to this inner death sentence: "This was to stop us relying on ourselves, and to make us rely on the God who raises the dead."[4] He can look back on the darkness now and see it within a larger rhythm of God's mercy, but at the time he was completely overwhelmed by it. He returns to the theme more than once in the letter, and in chapter 4 what he says is especially revealing:

We are under all kinds of pressure, but we are not
crushed completely; we are at a loss, but not at our wits'
end; we are persecuted, but not abandoned; we are cast
down, but not destroyed.[5]

Yes, but the point of what he said in the first chapter was that
at the time he *had* felt that he was crushed completely; he *did* find
himself at his wits' end; he *did* feel abandoned; he *did* feel destroyed. It is only with hindsight that he looks back and says, "But
I wasn't, after all." In his first letter to Corinth Paul uses the image
of the boxer; if we were to develop that, the present case looks as
though he had received what he thought was a knock-out blow
and expected to wake up, if at all, in a hospital; but here he is, still
on his feet. How did that happen? Paul being Paul, he interprets
this entire sequence of events as part of the meaning of being the
Messiah's man: "We always carry the deadness of Jesus about in
the body, so that the life of Jesus may be revealed in our body."[6]

It isn't only these very revealing passages. When we read
1 Corinthians and 2 Corinthians in quick succession—especially
in Greek, though I think the point still comes through in translation—we are aware at once that something has happened. The
style is different. People have run all kinds of tests on Paul's writing style, including using computer technology to analyze the
way the sentences work and so on. That tells its own story—the
variation across the complete collection of letters is not that great,
despite what some have suggested. But these two letters, written
to the same church and within two or three years of one another
at most, are strikingly different to the naked eye. The first, dealing with all kinds of problems in the Corinthian church, is cheerful, upbeat, expository, sometimes teasing, and challenging, but
always with a flow of thought, a confidence of expression. The
second, though it too can tease by the end, feels as if it is being
dragged out of Paul through a filter of darkness and pain.

In the second letter, he repeats himself like an old-fashioned gramophone record clicking on the same phrase:

> The God of all comfort . . . comforts us in all our trouble, so that we can then comfort people in every kind of trouble, through the comfort with which God comforts us. . . . If we are troubled, it's for the sake of your comfort and salvation; if we are comforted, it's because of your comfort. . . . Just as you've shared in our sufferings, so you will also share in our comfort.[7]

He doubles back on himself, modifying and correcting what he's just said:

> We are not writing anything to you, after all, except what you can read and understand. And I hope you will go on understanding right through to the end, just as you have understood us already—well, partly, at least![8]

He adds phrase to phrase like someone picking up heavy bricks one by one and placing them laboriously in a wall:

> Who is sufficient for these things? For we are not, like the many, peddlers of the word of God, but as from sincerity, but as from God, in the presence of God, in the Messiah, we speak.[9]

Nothing in 1 Corinthians—or in Galatians or the Thessalonian letters, for that matter—sounds and feels like this. We are listening to a man dictating from a heart that, though now lightened in various ways, has been heavier than it knew possible. He sounds exhausted.

By the end of 2 Corinthians, though, he has cheered up. There are signs that the letter is actually being written while he was on the road around northern Greece, on his way from Ephesus to Corinth by the land route, and that he has had good news on the way. But at the start and at several points in the letter, we are made aware that something has happened that has marked his heart, his mind, and his language in the same sort of way that the stoning and the beatings had earlier marked his face and his body. As a translator, I sensed all this when, within a couple of months in the spring of 2002, I moved from the first letter to the second. The second one is much harder Greek, perhaps the hardest in the New Testament and certainly in Paul. It ties itself in knots.

So what had happened? Some have looked back to a hint in the first Corinthian letter where Paul describes himself facing danger every hour and even "dying" every day: "If, in human terms," he says, "I fought with wild animals at Ephesus, what use is that to me?"[10] He is speaking about the future resurrection and stressing that without that hope there would be no point going through what he is going through. But it all still feels quite upbeat, and the "wild animals" are likely, here at least, to be a metaphor for the hostile reception he was, by now, well used to. He is positive about his present work in Ephesus; there are splendid opportunities, he says, as well as serious opposition.[11] But it looks as though what he describes as his "boast" of suffering was about to come true in ways, and in depths, he had not expected.

The best guess—it remains a guess, but it's the best one—is that Paul was imprisoned in Ephesus and put on trial for his life. And that made a "perfect storm," because it followed hard on the heels of a nasty shock from Corinth. The church there had turned against him.

The evidence for an Ephesian imprisonment, not mentioned by Luke, is strong. In the little letter to Philemon, Paul asks Philemon to "get a guest room ready" for him. Philemon lived in Colossae, about 125 miles inland from Ephesus on the river Lycus. Though Paul was still in prison, by the time he wrote this letter he was hoping that, through the prayers of his friends, he would be released. When that happened, he was planning to pay Philemon a visit, not least, we may suppose, to find out what had become of the former runaway slave Onesimus. We will return to that question, but for now that mention of a guest room is vital.

Other than Ephesus, the only places where we know Paul was in prison are Caesarea[12] and Rome. When he was in Caesarea, he had already said farewell to the churches around the Aegean shoreline. When he was in Rome, he was intent on going farther west, to Spain.[13] Even if he had changed his plans and decided in Caesarea to revisit Ephesus or had decided in Rome to return to the East one more time, it is not likely that his primary destination would have been a small town up the Lycus valley. So the guest room in Colossae provides the telltale hint that Paul was in prison in Ephesus.

The fact that Luke doesn't mention this then becomes significant in itself, like Sherlock Holmes's dog that failed to bark in the night. Luke is content to report Paul's stoning, beatings, and other attacks and legal charges. He tells us about the imprisonment in Caesarea and the house arrest in Rome. Ephesus must have been a darker moment. It was, perhaps, less clear-cut. Elsewhere, one could tell the story of Paul as a loyal apostle and evangelist who was falsely accused and then, when the authorities saw sense, released. This was murkier. And that fits with the mood that Paul reports at the start of 2 Corinthians. It is noticeable as well that 2 Corinthians has several thematic links with Colossians. This would fit with Colossians being written not long before Paul's release from prison and 2 Corinthians not long afterward.

This also makes sense of Paul's avoiding Ephesus on his final journey back to the East. Luke explains at that point that he didn't want to spend much time in the area, since he was eager to be in Jerusalem for Pentecost, and that may well also be true.[14] But to sail right by the city where he had spent two or three years appears more than simply a scheduling problem. Paul was never one to shirk a battle, but by this time he may have realized that one had to pick which battles to fight and which ones simply to avoid.

What, after all, do we know about Ephesus? As well as being the home of the magnificent temple of "Ephesian Artemis," it was in this period the proud host of the imperial cult. Local officials in various towns and cities would vie with one another for the privilege of sporting a new temple to Rome and/or Caesar (and of course for the economic perks that would go with that status). Ephesus was given that honor twice in the first century and once more two centuries later. In addition, Ephesus was famous as the home of all kinds of magic, the dark and powerful arts that were always popular on the edge of mainstream paganism. When Acts describes converted magicians burning their secret books as evidence of the impact of Paul's teaching,[15] this makes sense precisely in Ephesus. But it would also make sense to imagine a backlash. And when the dark forces strike back, they do not play fair.

I therefore agree with the several scholars who have insisted that Paul was imprisoned in Ephesus, and I suggest that this makes best sense of all the evidence—as well as providing a location from which he wrote not only his letter to Philemon but also the other Prison Letters, including Ephesians itself. That letter, as I shall suggest presently, is a circular written to churches in the area and is therefore couched in more general terms than normal. But it was also in Ephesus that Paul experienced what we might call the "Corinthian crisis." This had several elements, and though it may now be impossible to ascertain all the details of what had happened, the key points stand out. For our purposes, what really matters is the effect all this had on Paul himself and the way he responded to it. Because these two things are going on at the same time—trouble in Ephesus itself and trouble in relation to Corinth—we will have to move backward and forward between the two in order to understand why Paul felt as if he had received the death sentence.

★ ★ ★

When Paul wrote 1 Corinthians, probably around AD 53, he had to deal with many problems in the church, and two of these in particular may have been part of the larger crisis that then ensued. He had already written a shorter preliminary letter, which has not survived, urging the believers not to associate with people who flouted the strict Jewish and Christian code of ethics, particularly relating to sex, money, idolatry, and other spheres where inappropriate behavior was rife.[16] He followed this up with more specific instructions about the need to expel one particular church member who had been living with his father's wife. Some in the church, perhaps friends of the person in question, may have thought all this too harsh by far. At the same time, there were divisions in the church; several members declared that they didn't regard Paul as their real leader. They preferred Peter (Cephas) or Apollos instead. These two problems may have overlapped; if people were cross with the strict line Paul was taking, it might be natural for them to favor an alternative teacher. A second-order problem thus emerges.

We know about Peter (well, a bit). What about Apollos? Apollos was a powerful scripture teacher, originally from Alexandria, who had been in Ephesus just after Paul's initial visit and had then gone on to Corinth. While Apollos was in Ephesus, it had become clear to the small group of believers that though he knew the basic facts about Jesus, he was thinking of Jesus as the extension and application of John the Baptist, rather than of Jesus as the Messiah whose death and resurrection had accomplished what John could only foresee. At that point, Paul's friends Priscilla and Aquila had taken Apollos to one side and explained things in more detail, providing one of the moments at which we would love to have been flies on the wall. (There was a strange little sequel: in Ephesus Paul met a small group of followers of John the Baptist, and he explained to them that John's words had come true in Jesus.)[17] For our purposes the point is that Apollos had gone to Corinth after Paul had left and had made a great impression on the church, causing some members to decide that he, rather than Paul, was the kind of teacher they really wanted.

Meanwhile, Cephas himself—Peter, Jesus's own right-hand man—had also been in Corinth. Some had decided that *he* was their man. People have often suggested that this may have involved a rerun of the clash in Antioch, as in Galatians 2, and that Peter might have again been trying to insist on a two-tier fellowship and a separation at mealtimes of Jewish and Gentile Jesus-followers. There is no evidence for this, but that doesn't mean that Paul would have been entirely happy to think of Peter coming in to teach, in his absence, a church Paul had planted and looked after through the first eighteen months of its life.

Paul addresses all this in 1 Corinthians in the general terms of what we call "personality cults." But underneath that there must have been a deeper sense of personal hurt. He was the one who had told them about Jesus in the first place. He had rejoiced as the spirit worked powerfully among the new believers. He had loved them, prayed with them, worked among them, wept with them. He must have wished that Priscilla and Aquila had still been in Corinth rather than coming with him across to Ephesus; surely they would have put people straight . . .

Anyway, Paul wrote 1 Corinthians, perhaps late in 53, and then made what turned out to be a bad mistake. He crossed the Aegean for a quick visit to Corinth.[18] Though he tried to exert a measure of authority over the situation, this was rebuffed. He was made to feel decidedly unwelcome. He found it best to leave in a hurry. It was suggested to him—and unless you have been a pastor yourself, you will not know just how deeply hurtful this would be—that if he ever wanted to come back, he would have to obtain letters of recommendation from someone the Corinthians trusted.

We already know enough about Paul to know how this would have affected him. He had had the rich experience of loving and trusting those with whom he had shared the Messiah faith and of being loved and trusted by them. That was how it had been in northern Greece, as we can tell from the letters he had already written to Thessalonica and from the letter he would later write to Philippi. But southern Greece—the place where the Roman authorities had given the green light for the gospel!—was turning against him. And if this happened at the same time that he was suddenly meeting a darker level of opposition in Ephesus itself, we can begin to understand why, as he later emerged into a battered and chastened new day, he spoke as he did in 2 Corinthians of reaching the point where he was giving up on life itself.

★ ★ ★

It had all started so well. At least, it had started in much the same way as in the cities of his earlier journeys. He had traveled, quite quickly it seems, from Antioch through Cilicia and Galatia and so into Asia. (Did he stop in Tarsus as he went by? Did he visit family? Had he once again been hoping for a change of heart, only to be disappointed? Was that part of the background to his breakdown?) Anyway, he arrived in Ephesus and began as always in the synagogue, this time for three months. A dozen Sabbaths, each ringing with Paul's scriptural arguments and evidences: Abraham, Exodus, David, exile, hope, Messiah. Twelve Sabbaths, plenty of time to get into the details of Genesis, Deuteronomy, the Psalms, Isaiah, Jeremiah, and Ezekiel. Plenty of time to speak of a Messiah who, Paul says, "loved me and gave himself for me."

Opposition, however, grew as the disturbing implications of Paul's way of reading the familiar story dawned upon the puzzled hearers. Resistance hardened. This may have been one of the occasions when, submitting to synagogue discipline, Paul received the official Jewish beating of forty lashes. (Deuteronomy 25:3 specifies forty as the maximum; by Paul's day, Jewish teachers had reduced this by one in case somebody miscounted, appearing more anxious about technical infringement than about the suffering caused.) He says he had received this five times; this itself indicates his steady commitment to working with the synagogue communities as long as he could, since he could easily have avoided the punishment by merely not turning up.[19]

Some of the Jewish community in Ephesus had begun to spread rumors about what this "Messiah cult" was doing. From later writings we can guess at the kind of innuendo that went around, sneering comments about what these Jesus-followers were up to behind closed doors, with men and women meeting together and talking a lot about a new kind of "love," not to mention the disturbing gossip about eating someone's body and drinking their blood. So Paul realized, as he had done in Corinth, that he could no longer treat the synagogue as his base. It was time to move elsewhere. Perhaps this was the time he refers to in the first letter to Corinth with the metaphor of the arena, suggesting that he had "fought with wild animals at Ephesus."[20] This letter was written while things were going well, with no shadow of the trouble that haunts the second letter. It is very unlikely that he had literally been thrown to wild beasts. He seems to be referring to some great tussle with opponents, though we cannot now tell who they were or what the issue was.

Anyway, he rented a local lecture hall belonging to one Tyrannus, and for two years he divided his time between his tentmaking business and the public exposition and discussion of the faith. Ephesus being Ephesus, another center both of trade routes and culture, this was an excellent way to disseminate the message. People came from far and wide, spent time in the city, and then went on their way. In a culture without print or social media, people simply chatted about anything strange or new that they had come across in their travels. "Yes, I've just come from Ephesus; and you'd never believe it, but there's a strange group there apparently saying . . ."

We can see how this worked in one close-up example. At the start of Colossians Paul thanks God that in Colossae, a small town inland from Ephesus, there is now a community of people who love one another across the deep divisions of ethnic, social, and cultural divisions. "Epaphras," he says, "gave us the news about your love in the spirit."[21] Epaphras was one of Paul's fellow workers in Ephesus, and he had been into the inland regions to spread the good news there, returning to Paul to declare that the power of the good news was evident all over the place; the gospel was "producing fruit and growing in all the world."[22] Philemon himself, now one of the leaders in the Colossian church, owed Paul his very life; this presumably means that Philemon had heard and believed Paul's gospel on a business trip to the metropolis. If the gospel was at work like this in Colossae, there is every reason to suppose that it was also at work in other towns and cities in the region, nearby places like Laodicea and Hierapolis and many others of which we know less.

In Ephesus itself, Paul's work appeared to be going from strength to strength. In his letters Paul and his hearers seemed to be able to take for granted the fact that sometimes the living God did remarkable things not only in their hearts and minds, but also in their bodies. Remarkable healings, signs of a new creation breaking in to the old world in ways not normally expected, were never the real center of attention and in any case were always mysterious (people still got sick and died, and prayers for healing were not always answered positively). But in Ephesus it seems that Paul's launching of the church was accompanied by healing powers that went beyond what might have been expected or experienced elsewhere. Luke reports, as a seemingly strange temporary phenomenon, that handkerchiefs and towels that had touched Paul's skin possessed healing properties.[23] Paul's very name was being spoken of with awe, and some were indeed using it to powerful effect. Some local Jewish exorcists, sons of a high priest, were coupling the names of Jesus and Paul in their efforts to expel demons, until one particular demon-possessed man answered them with the famous line, "I know Jesus, and I am well acquainted with Paul; but who are you?"[24] Tales like this, says Luke, spread around the area. Luke himself comments that the name of Jesus was held in great honor, but we cannot imagine that the name of Paul was not also being venerated.

Paul must have loved those days. He was busy in the shop and busy teaching. People crowded into his lectures, brought sick people for healing, and turned to look as he went by. Jesus was Lord, and he was his apostle.

The community at large, it seemed, was being transformed. In a city famous for its different levels of power, a natural magnet for people who knew how to manipulate unseen forces to their advantage, the power of the gospel, of the announcement of Jesus as the true Lord, was having a remarkable effect. In one scene that must have shaken that world to its core, a substantial group of magicians made public confession of what they had been up to and brought their valuable magic books to be burned.[25] The dark arts were being smoked out of hiding, almost literally. All those prayers that Paul had prayed, invoking the name and the power of the crucified and risen Lord, were having their effect. Ephesus, even more than Corinth or the cities of northern Greece, was turning into a living example of what the gospel could do, not just in a few individuals here and there, but in an entire community.

But the dark powers do not give up so easily. Something terrible happened that resulted not only in imprisonment, but in crushing despair. Since Luke has foreshortened his account here as elsewhere, we cannot be sure exactly when this took place. The positive, early phase of Paul's time in Ephesus ends with the burning of the magic books. That is when Paul decides to revisit

Greece, going overland through Macedonia and then down to
Corinth;[26] so he sends Timothy and Erastus on ahead.[27] All Luke
says then is that Paul "spent a little more time in Asia," and that
may be when everything suddenly went horribly wrong.

On balance, though, I think it more likely that the catastrophe
happened after the riot that Luke so graphically describes in Acts
19:23–41. Luke says that Paul was able to leave town "after the
hue and cry had died down,"[28] but that hue and cry might well
have included not only the riot he describes, one of his splendid
set pieces, but also the time that he does not describe, the disaster
that struck, perhaps in the aftermath of the riot, just when Paul
thought he had once again escaped real trouble. If you take on the
shadowy powers that stand behind the corruption and wickedness
of the world, you can expect the struggle to take unexpected and
very nasty turns.

★ ★ ★

Before we plunge into the darkness of what happened to Paul
in Ephesus, we must return to Corinth. I strongly suspect that
the sudden deterioration of relations with that church was one
of the factors that sapped Paul's confidence and laid him open
to attack.

He had not been away that long, but things had clearly developed in his absence. He had had various visitors from Corinth.
"Chloe's people" had brought him news. That phrase, "Chloe's
people," could mean Chloe herself and her actual family. But the
implication is that Chloe, like Lydia in Philippi and (later on)
Phoebe in Cenchreae, was an independent and probably wealthy
businesswoman whose associates or slaves, also we presume Jesus-
followers, would have been coming to Ephesus anyway and would
then have made contact with Paul. Anyway, "Chloe's people"
brought news of a quarrelsome church in which different groups
were siding with different preachers (Paul, Apollos, Cephas) and a

final group (or is this Paul's sarcastic response?) said, "I'm with the Messiah!" What was going on?

Some nineteenth-century scholars, eager to project the cultural "either/or" of modern European philosophy back onto the early church, tried to glimpse in this a major ideological cleavage between a supposed "Jewish Christianity" focused on the law (with analogies therefore to the Galatian "agitators") and a supposedly Pauline "Gentile Christianity," which had broken with Jewish law. Some think Peter himself was the leader of the first party. This is not only simplistic, unsubstantiated, and counterintuitive (Paul himself insists in various places that he is a "Jewish Christian"!); it is anachronistic.

The issue seems to be quite different. It has to do with *style*. Paul's rebuttal of the party spirit in Corinth has very little to do with Jewish law and everything to do with "the wisdom of the world." Hence his emphatic statement about the foolishness of God. The Corinthians, it seems, were wanting leaders whose speaking abilities would command social respect. They found Paul disappointing. But, as he explains, there are different kinds of wisdom: the wisdom of the world, on the one hand, and, on the other, the true, hidden wisdom that comes from God.

Here and throughout the letter Paul is teaching the Corinthians, as he had surely been teaching them in person earlier, to *think eschatologically,* that is, to imagine a world quite unlike the world of ordinary Greco-Roman paganism, a world in which the One God was living and active and had started up something quite new, something that would be complete on the coming day. That something involved the creation of the new Temple; the church, which the Corinthians were pulling apart in their search for the ideal clever teacher, was the new Temple, the place where the living God had come to dwell by the spirit.[29] No first-century Jew could use imagery like that as a mere "illustration" of a different kind of truth. Paul's vision of the church picked up the ancient Jewish hope of an ultimate Temple and put forth a new creation for which the Jerusalem Temple and the wilderness Tabernacle were advance signposts. This is it, says Paul. And if they belonged to it—if they belonged to the Messiah—then they should be above these petty squabbles:

> Everything belongs to you, whether it's Paul or Apol-
> los or Cephas, whether it's the world or life or death,
> whether it's the present or the future—everything
> belongs to you! And you belong to the Messiah; and the
> Messiah belongs to God.[30]

And if they all belong to the Messiah—the *crucified* Messiah, as Paul never lets them forget—then they should expect the world's standards to be stood on their heads. In particular (a point Paul will develop in the second letter) apostles are precisely not supposed to be people of great standing in the wider community. They are like bedraggled prisoners at the end of a triumphal procession, on their way to a shameful death. That is part of the point, but it is also the source of the power.[31] This whole opening section of the letter is about power, a theme that obviously concerned Paul both as he was thinking about Corinth and as he was dealing with various sorts of power in Ephesus. The foolish gospel of the crucified Messiah is God's power; God's weakness is stronger than human strength; their faith, as evoked by Paul's preaching, did not rest on human wisdom but on God's power; and now, dramatically and with a somewhat shocking threat, "the kingdom of God isn't about talk—it's about power," the "power" in question being the power Paul thinks he may have to use in confronting those who are "puffed up" with their own sense of worth and importance.[32] (The charge that the Corinthians are "puffed up" is a major theme of the whole letter. This has nothing to do with Jewish law and everything to do with ordinary human pride and folly.)

So Paul comes to specific issues. Here is the man guilty of

incest—and many in the church are supporting him because it shows how "free" they are as Messiah people! Paul reminds them of the earlier letter (the one that has not survived). Church discipline is vital. They are Passover people, and no moral "leaven" must be allowed in the house.[33] So too with lawsuits in the church. They are the Messiah's people, and as such they are destined to assist in the final cosmic judgment, so they ought to be able to settle local in-house disputes without using the secular courts. And, as he wrote to the Galatians, this is all about the ultimate inheritance. God's kingdom, already established in the Messiah, will be complete at last, with the glorious worldwide inheritance promised to the Messiah and his people.[34] But the whole point of the kingdom is that God is putting all things right, restoring the human race to its proper role and dignity, and those who persist in styles of life that corrupt and destroy that genuine humanity cannot inherit it. This isn't an arbitrary bit of legalism. It is analytical truth.

With some fundamental issues about sexual morality briefly laid out, Paul turns to marriage itself in chapter 7. Here too the requirement is to think eschatologically. God is remaking the world from top to bottom, and everything looks different as a result.

His next topic is a very different, and very difficult, issue: meat that had been offered in sacrifice in pagan temples. In a city like Corinth, that meant almost all meat available for purchase, since temples functioned effectively as a combination of butcher's shop and restaurant. A sacrificial animal was brought in and offered in worship to this or that deity, and then the family enjoyed the meal. What was left would be sold on the open market. Some large Jewish communities in towns like Corinth would have their own kosher butchers, but in many cases Jews simply avoided meat altogether, not simply because of the rules about blood, but because they avoided pagan worship and everything that went with it.

This is where the letter from the Jerusalem leaders in Acts 15 might have come into its own. Paul has reemphasized what that letter said about sexual morality. There is no leeway there, no principle of "tolerance" for different opinions. But what we see in 1 Corinthians 8–10, discussing idol temples and meat that had been sacrificed there, is a sophisticated and delicate discussion of the pastoral challenges involved in dealing with two different opinions, which he calls the "strong" and the "weak." These are Paul's technical terms. Those with "strong" consciences are those who, like him, know that idols don't exist, so that meat offered to them is merely meat. The "weak" are those who, after a lifetime of actually worshipping idols and imagining themselves to be participating in the life of the god by eating sacrificial meat, cannot now touch the meat without feeling themselves being dragged back into the murky world of idolatry and all that went with it.

This question draws out of Paul a fundamental theological principle and a remarkable statement of how he understood his own vocation. Both need to be at the heart of any ultimate assessment of who he thought he was, of what made him the man he was.

The theological principle is a robust *creational monotheism*. Idols have no real existence, and as the great prayer the *Shema* declares, God is one. Paul knows perfectly well that in Corinth and everywhere else there are "many gods, many lords," but his new version of the *Shema* upstages them all. This, as we saw, might be the prayer to which the Jewish community in Corinth had objected in their petition to Gallio; if not, it may well have been another one like it. This prayer dwells in his heart and on his lips day by day, and now as at some other times when he wants to talk *about* the One God, he prefers to do so by invoking and praying *to* this God, declaring his loyalty to his kingdom:

> For us there is one God, the father,
> From whom are all things, and we live to him and for him;
> And one Lord, Jesus the Messiah,
> Through whom are all things, and we live through him.[35]

This translation is a bit wooden, but longer paraphrases do not bring out the remarkable way in which Paul has adapted the *Shema* ("Hear, O Israel: the LORD our God, the LORD is one") by making "Lord" refer to Jesus and "God" refer to "the father." This prayer contains, in compressed form, a wealth of theology, but Paul's point in quoting it here is to emphasize the practical outworking of creational monotheism. The One God made all things, so nothing is to be rejected if received with gratitude. He returns to the same point at the end of the long discussion where this time he quotes Psalm 24:1: "The earth and its fullness belong to the LORD."[36] This is not mere pragmatics ("It will be difficult to get people to stop eating idol meat"). It is rooted in the most basic Jewish theological assertion: there is one God, creator of all.

Of course, emphasizing that point does rather undermine the normal Jewish codes in which several varieties of meat are off limits even if they have never seen the inside of a pagan temple. That is part of the paradox of Paul's position, a paradox that, we may suppose, the Jerusalem church never fully understood (and that certainly did not square with the letter they had sent out after the Jerusalem Conference). The central section of his argument here, in chapter 9, focuses on the fact that as an apostle he enjoys "freedom"—freedom to be married, to be paid for his work, and so on—but stresses that he has chosen, for the sake of the gospel, not to make use of these freedoms. In particular, and quite shocking to some in its implications:

> I am indeed free from everyone; but I have enslaved
> myself to everyone, so that I can win all the more. I be-
> came like a Jew to the Jews, to win Jews. I became like
> someone under the law to the people who are under the
> law, even though I'm not myself under the law, so that I
> could win those under the law. To the lawless I became
> like someone lawless (even though I'm not lawless be-
> fore God, but under the Messiah's law), so that I could

win the lawless. I became weak to the weak, to win the
weak. I have become all things to all people, so that in
all ways I might save some. I do it all because of the gospel, so that I can be a partner in its benefits.[37]

Paul was not as fixated on the idea of "identity" as we are in
our contemporary culture. But, if the question had been asked,
this passage offers a sharp answer. "I became *like a Jew.*" "Why,
Paul," we want to say, "you *are* a Jew." "Not in that sense," he
replies. "I am not 'under the law.'" If he were, he could never
have quoted Psalm 24:1 as meaning that all foods are now acceptable. He has a different identity, the *messianic* identity. He is
"under the Messiah's law"; he is "in the Messiah." The Messiah's
people, as he says in a climactic passage in Galatians, have *died;*
they have left behind the old identities and have come into a new
identity, the messianic identity.[38] That is part of why the gospel is
"a scandal to Jews," but of course it nonetheless makes sense only
within a deeply Jewish, and now messianic, view of the world.
And, charged with his specific responsibility, Paul is able, without
compromising *that* messianic identity, to live alongside people of
all sorts, sharing their customs while he is with them.

This must mean—this can only mean—that when Paul goes to
a dinner with Jewish friends (or when he invites them to share his
own meal), they will eat kosher food, and he will do the same. But
it must mean—it can only mean—that when Paul goes to dinner
with non-Jewish friends, he will eat whatever they put in front of
him.[39] What would then make the difference is "conscience"—
not Paul's, but that of anyone else who might be offended, who
might be led back into idolatry.

This must have been a much harder path to tread than that
sketched in the apostolic letter issued after the Jerusalem Conference. There, simple abstinence from all relevant foods was enjoined.
But Paul has seen that this is not only unnecessary; it violates the
foundational principles of Jewish belief itself. His own pragmatic

solution must have seemed not just paradoxical, but perverse to some. Think, for instance, of a Jewish family in Corinth who had shared a meal with Paul and watched him keep all the Jewish customs, only to find out that the same week he had dined with a Gentile family and eaten what they were eating. One might imagine a certain surprise in the other direction too, though the Gentile family would most likely just shrug their shoulders and see no harm in it. But, once again, what Paul is doing in writing this letter is *teaching the Corinthians to think as Messiah people;* he is building on the foundation of Israel's scriptures, interpreting them afresh in the light of the crucified and risen Messiah himself.

So the letter moves toward its powerful conclusion. Chapter 11 deals with problems at the family meal, the Lord's Supper or Eucharist. Chapter 12 addresses the question of unity in the fellowship and the way in which the spirit gives to each member of "the Messiah's body" different gifts to be used for the benefit of all. Chapter 14 applies this to the corporate worship of the church. And chapter 13, nested in between 12 and 14 like the soft middle movement of a powerful symphony, is Paul's exquisite poem about love, *agapē*. Here too he is not just teaching them "ethics"; he is teaching them to *think eschatologically:*

> *We know, you see, in part;*
> *We prophesy in part; but, with perfection,*
> *The partial is abolished. As a child*
> *I spoke, and thought, and reasoned like a child;*
> *When I grew up, I threw off childish ways.*
> *For at the moment all that we can see*
> *Are puzzling reflections in a mirror;*
> *Then, face to face. I know in part, for now;*
> *But then I'll know completely, through and through,*
> *Even as I'm completely known. So, now,*
> *Faith, hope and love remain, these three; and, of them*
> *Love is the greatest.*[40]

Love is not just a duty. Paul's point is that love is the believer's *destiny*. It is the reality that belongs to God's future, glimpsed in the present like a puzzling reflection, but waiting there in full reality for the face-to-face future. And the point is that this future *has come forward into the present time* in the events involving Jesus and in the power of the spirit. That is why love matters for Paul—more even than "faith," which many have seen as his central theme. Love is the present virtue in which believers anticipate, and practice, the life of the ultimate age to come.

That is why the final theological chapter in the letter, chapter 15, dealing with the resurrection of the body, comes where it does. It is not a detached discussion tacked onto the end of the letter dealing with a distinct topic unrelated to what has gone before. It is the center of everything. "If the Messiah wasn't raised," he declares, "your faith is pointless, and you are still in your sins."[41] Unless this is at the heart of who they are, he says (here is his own regular anxiety, now framed as a challenge to the Corinthians), their faith is in vain, "for nothing." But it isn't: the resurrection of Jesus means that a new world has opened up, so that, "in the Lord . . . the work you're doing will not be worthless."[42] The resurrection is the ultimate answer to the nagging question of whether one's life and work have been "in vain."

With this, we uncover the roots of Paul's entire public career. The chapter on resurrection is not simply the underlying reasoning behind the whole letter. It is basic to everything Paul believed. It is the reason he became an apostle in the first place. The Messiah's resurrection has constituted him as the world's true Lord, as already the world's rightful ruler, and "He has to go on ruling, you see, until 'he has put all his enemies under his feet.'"[43] Victory *has already* been won over the dark powers of sin and death that have crippled the world and, with it, the humans who were supposed to be God's image-bearers in the world. This victory *will at last* be completed when death itself is destroyed. For Paul, learning to be a Messiah person—learning to live within the great biblical story now culminating in Jesus and the spirit—was all about having the mind and heart, the imagination and understanding transformed, so that it made sense to live in this already/not-yet world.

This was not the easiest place to live, but it was certainly one of the most exhilarating. The Messiah *has already* been raised; all the Messiah's people *will* be raised at his "royal arrival."[44] Christian living, loving, praying, celebrating, suffering, and not least the apostolic ministries that have nothing to do with social prestige or clever rhetoric—all this makes the sense it makes within this eschatological framework. That is the main thing Paul wants to tell the Corinthians. Sitting there in Ephesus, watching the gospel go to work in homes and shops, confronting the powers of the world and seeing magicians burn their books, Paul can sound confident. This is the future, and it works. What they do in the present, within God's new world, is not in vain.

The closing greetings give notice of a new project (though Paul indicates that he has already broached the subject to the churches in Galatia, presumably on the journey described briefly in Acts 18:23). He had realized just how poor the Jerusalem church had become, and he had imagined to himself what an impact it would have if the churches of which Jerusalem had been so suspicious— those communities that were allowing Gentiles into full membership without circumcision—were to band together and send real and lasting financial help. This would take some organizing. But Paul clearly saw it as a sign and means of the unity of the Messiah's people, which, with every passing day, had become more important to him. So he made his plans. He intended to travel through northern Greece and then to spend a good period of time with the Corinthians. It all made sense.

Until it all fell apart.

We do not know exactly when it was that Paul made the extra

visit described in 2 Corinthians 2:1 ("I settled it in my mind," he says there, "that I wouldn't make you another sad visit"). He stayed in Ephesus for around two and a half years, probably from 53 to 56, and this visit would have been early on in that time, after the writing of 1 Corinthians itself. Nor do we know what precisely happened on that occasion. He had in any case changed his mind, at some point, from the plans he had sketched in 1 Corinthians 16:5–7, where he had been intending to go from Ephesus to northern Greece and then down to Corinth before moving on once more. Then, later, he had had a different idea; he would sail across to Corinth from Ephesus and then go north to Macedonia, before returning from Macedonia to Corinth again and having them send him on his way to Jerusalem.[45] But when he got to Corinth something happened. We do not know what.

Some have speculated that one or more members or leaders in the church opposed Paul to his face, perhaps with insults and mockery. Others have suggested that there were financial irregularities in connection with the early stages of the projected collection, and that when Paul confronted the offenders, they denied it all. There may well have been other problems as well, perhaps moral failures or lapses in the church that Paul tried to put right and was rebuffed. (The references to an offender who has "caused sadness" in 2 Corinthians 2:7–8 might refer to the incestuous man of 1 Corinthians 5, but the two pictures do not quite fit, and there is every reason to suppose that this was not the only case of immorality or other inappropriate behavior in the church.) Some in Corinth seem to have declared that he was unreliable, making different plans every other day like a fool who can't make his mind up.[46]

Paul, finding that his normal exercise of power seemed to have deserted him, was shocked and dismayed. Why could he not simply confront the problem and the problem people, as he had done with the magician in Paphos or the slave girl in Philippi? What had happened to the power, the power of which he had boasted in 1 Corinthians 4? He abandoned his plan to go on to Macedonia. He went back to Ephesus with his tail between his legs. We imagine him on the return voyage across the Aegean, pacing the deck, staring at the islands, asking himself, asking God, asking the Lord whom he loved, where it had all gone wrong. What had happened to the power? What was the point of having his name up in lights in Ephesus if his own people in Corinth were turning against him?

Returning to Ephesus was not going to be easy either. Paul was now in a very different frame of mind, dazed and upset by the way his beloved Corinthians had treated him. He wrote them a "painful letter," which, like the first letter referred to in 1 Corinthians 5, we do not possess. He gave it to Titus, sent him off, and awaited developments.

This is not a good place for a pastor to be. I was once lecturing in the United States—on 2 Corinthians, as it happens—when I received word that members of the community for which I was responsible were in deep disarray over a moral issue that had arisen in my absence. Even in a world with telephones (this was before the days of e-mail), one cannot even begin to put things right. You simply have to pray and agonize, and pray some more, and be patient in the hope that the spirit will be at work. Anyone who ever supposed that Paul sailed through his apostolic work carrying all before him in a blaze of glory can never have studied 2 Corinthians.

★ ★ ★

It was at this point that the enemy struck, and struck hard. I explained earlier why I am convinced that Paul was imprisoned in Ephesus. Some suggest that this occurred at least twice. We know enough about the sort of things that happened to Paul from one place to another to guess what may have landed him in jail. In

Philippi it was an exorcism that ruined a business whose owners said that Paul was teaching Jewish customs illegal for Romans, in other words, a spiritual battle with economic consequences framed as a religious problem with political implications. In Thessalonica he was accused of turning the world upside down by saying that there was "another king." In one place after another, Jewish horror at the message of a crucified Messiah—and, we may suppose, at the teaching that this Messiah was now welcoming non-Jews without circumcision—led to opposition, which was sometimes augmented by local hostility from non-Jews who may have had no special sympathy for the Jewish people, but who saw Paul as a social and cultural threat. Sometimes, in other words, opposition was aroused because pagans saw him as a dangerous kind of Jew; sometimes it was because Jews saw him as flirting dangerously with paganism. The irony, surely not wasted on Paul, did not make it any easier for him when facing violence.

Now, in Ephesus, matters came to a head. The pattern would seem familiar. Though, as we saw, the city boasted fine new premises for the imperial cult, the long-standing local devotion to the goddess Artemis was famous throughout the known world, focused not least on a splendid statue of the goddess that, some claimed, had been sent from heaven, a gift from Zeus himself. This statue was on display in the massive Temple of Artemis, where the all-female cult of the goddess wielded considerable power in the city and beyond. Artemis was a fertility goddess whose many-breasted silver statues were themselves famous. (They still are; the last time I was in Ephesus the local tourist shops were full of them.)

But what the modern tourist sees as a souvenir, the ancient citizen saw as an object of worship. When people placed one of these silver statues in their home, in its own little shrine, they were assured that the goddess was there with them, blessing their family and their fields, their business and their livestock. They prayed to her, greeted her when they went in and out, placed fresh flowers in front of her, and perhaps lit a candle or two. She looked after them. So the local silversmiths' guild had the same problem with Paul as the slave-owners did in Philippi, only much more so. There, Paul had simply exorcised one slave girl. Here, he was denouncing the great goddess herself, telling people "that gods made with hands are not gods after all."[47] If even the magicians were burning their books, then it wasn't surprising that the local trade in silver Artemis shrines was in a slump as well.

Here, just as in Thessalonica or Athens, the primary impact of Paul's message was not "how to be saved," though that was part of it, nor even "the Messiah died for your sins," though that remained central. The announcement of a Messiah itself only made sense within the larger picture of the One God; it was an essentially Jewish message confronting a world full of fake gods with the news of a living one.

The silversmiths, led by one Demetrius, stirred up civic pride: "Who does this fellow think he is, coming here to tell us that our great goddess doesn't exist?" A theological proclamation had produced economic challenges, which were then interpreted as civic insults. The silversmiths started to chant their slogan and soon the whole city took it up: "Great is Ephesian Artemis! Great is Ephesian Artemis!"[48] A riot had begun. The crowd rushed into the vast amphitheater, whose magnificent acoustics would amplify the chant. Imagine a huge football crowd, angry at a wrongly awarded penalty, setting up a rhythmic shout that became louder and louder. This is one of Luke's great set-piece scenes; it would go well in a movie, though we still await the director who will do justice to Paul. It might have been fun if you were one of the crowd, shouting in unison with fifty thousand others, with gestures to match. It wouldn't have been much fun if you were the person it was all aimed at.

The person it was all aimed at, Paul himself, was eager to go in and speak to the people (of course!). A surge of adrenaline, after the sad and worrying visit to Corinth, might do him a

powerful lot of good. But some of the local magistrates, friendly
to Paul, sent word that he shouldn't risk going to the theater,
and in any case his friends refused to let him. (Did they tie
him up, as the sailors did with Odysseus? Did they lock him in
his own shop? How did he cope with his frustration—he, the
speaker, the one who had lectured the graybeards in Athens, the
one who had told the magistrates in Philippi what they could do
with their get-out-of-jail-free card?) The crowd did manage to
grab hold of two of Paul's friends, the Macedonians Gaius and
Aristarchus. They must have thought their last hour had come.
Trampling by the mob would perhaps be the kindest fate they
might expect.

Then comes the revealing moment that brings the whole problem into sharp focus. The theological challenge, the economic
problem, and the wounded civic pride rush together and show, in
a flash, the ugly face of ethnic prejudice: "It's the Jews!" A Jewish
group pushes forward a representative, one Alexander; perhaps
he is hoping to explain to the crowd that the local Jewish community has nothing to do with this heretic Paul and his friends. If
that is the intention, it backfires. The mob realizes that he is a Jew.
The whisper goes around. Then the volume of the chant increases
once more, going on for two straight hours: "Great is Ephesian
Artemis!" It isn't difficult to imagine that being chanted, even in
English, but when we put it back into Greek we can envisage a
rhythm being set up: *Megalē hē Artemis Ephesiōn! Megalē hē Artemis
Ephesiōn!* Emphasize every other syllable, starting on the first, and
imagine tens of thousands chanting it together, punching the air
in time.

We imagine Paul, restrained by his friends, listening to the
chant. He would be praying, of course. If you are the sort of
person who sings hymns in prison at midnight, you are certainly
the sort of person who goes on praying when there's a deafening
riot happening down the road, especially when it's all your fault.

As his surge of excitement ebbs away, he is more drained than before. *Has it all been for nothing?* Is the message of the One God and his son going to remain forever a small, specialized option for a subgroup of the Jewish people, the followers of Messiah Jesus? Suppose he had managed to give his friends the slip and get into the theater after all to address the huge crowd. Would he have been able to pull it off? Would he have found words? Would the spirit have given him power? Would he have been able to speak freshly and clearly about Jesus, the true Lord? It hadn't happened during his recent visit to Corinth. Suppose it didn't happen here? Suppose it never happened again? And always the nagging question: *Has it all been in vain?*

Luke does his best to play the whole thing down. Most of the crowd, he says, had no idea why they had all come together in the first place. In any case, the local magistrate, perhaps surprisingly, managed to calm things down. Perhaps after two hours the crowds were ready for a break. As with the other magistrates and local officials who feature in Luke's account, this one basically says what the writer wants his readers to know, that despite the noisy riot, Paul and his companions had not in fact broken any laws. If they had, people could bring charges against them in the normal way. Luke must have known that it wasn't as easy as that. The perfect storm of economic disruption, religious challenge, civic pride, and ethnic prejudice could hardly be contained by Roman provincial legislation.

I suspect that Luke highlights the riot, which he can interpret as a lot of fuss about nothing, partly because it would be well known and people might ask about it ("Didn't I hear that he caused a riot in Ephesus, of all places?") and partly because it would distract attention from what happened next. This is where the biographer enters a dark tunnel, the tunnel between the cheerful Paul of 1 Corinthians and the crushed, battered Paul of 2 Corinthians; the tunnel between the Paul who believes that

Jesus will come back during his lifetime and the Paul who now expects to die in advance of that glorious moment; the black night when, ahead of any actual judicial decision, Paul heard, deep within himself, the sentence of death. We have no idea what precisely occurred. But he got to the point where he despaired of life itself.

So what happened? There were some parallels with the problem in Philippi. But there it had been easy enough; after a night in the cells, he pointed out that he was a Roman citizen and had been beaten and imprisoned without a charge or a trial. Things may have been more complicated this time, and perhaps he decided that to play the "citizen" card again might be unwise. Depending on the charge, it might not have been enough to get him off. So he allowed the tide of hostility to do its worst.

It looks, in short, as though someone managed to succeed where Demetrius the silversmith had failed. Or perhaps Demetrius and his colleagues took the hint from the town clerk and manufactured a charge against Paul, suggesting that he was in fact guilty of blasphemy against Artemis or her great shrine. (Perhaps Paul, hearing tales of a statue falling from heaven, had poured scorn on such ideas.) Paul's robust monotheism had led him to sail close to the wind in Athens. Maybe this time he had taken his hand off the tiller at the crucial moment as the wind shifted.

And perhaps some people to whom he looked for support let him down. The hints in the letter to Philippi (written most likely toward the end of this imprisonment) suggest that it wasn't just pagan hostility that landed Paul where he was. Local people he had considered friends turned out in reality to be enemies, or at least rivals. One way or another, Paul found himself in prison, on a charge that might very easily have meant death. Like Samson shorn of his hair, he was suddenly powerless. The riot was just the noisy prelude. The dark powers had other ways of striking back at someone who dared to encroach on their territory with the essentially Jewish message of the One God redefined around the shocking message of the crucified and risen Messiah.

As we have seen, prisons in the Roman world were not normally used as a place of punishment, but only as a remand center to keep people who were coming up to trial—though, since that might well take some time, it would have had the effect of punishment in advance of sentence. No effort was made to look after prisoners. If they wanted food, friends would have to bring it. Later, by the time we find him writing letters, Paul clearly had some friends attending to his needs—and at least one friend who was thrown into prison with him—but it is quite possible that for some time after his arrest his friends may not even have known where he was or may have been too frightened, granted what had happened, to be associated with him.

It doesn't take too long with little food and water for the spirits to sink. Paul and Silas had sung hymns in the jail at Philippi, precipitating the earthquake and their sudden change of fortune. I presume that Paul prayed and perhaps sang in the jail in Ephesus. Some of the ancient psalms fit his situation exactly. Some of the early Christian poems, not least those celebrating Jesus as Lord, would have been in his head and his heart as well. But when, after a few days and then a few weeks, nothing much seemed to have happened, it would have been easy for him to get to the point we noticed in 2 Corinthians 4, where in retrospect it *seemed* as though he was crushed, abandoned, destroyed, and at his wits' end. No earthquake came to his rescue. He may well have been subject to regular beatings. He may have been cold, perhaps ill. All this is of course speculation, but we have to give some sort of account for what he says as he looks back to this dark moment as well as the other evidence that locates at least some of the Prison Letters in just this period.

When he mentions, in greeting Prisca and Aquila, who have now moved back to Rome, that they "put their lives on the line" for him, we have no means of knowing what the emergency was or how they risked their lives on his behalf.[49] The chances are that it was something to do with the terrible plight into which Paul had now fallen. Perhaps they were the ones who eventually plucked up courage, said their prayers, and went to the magistrates to testify that their star prisoner was being held on a fraudulent charge. That might have been enough to get them arrested as accomplices, but perhaps they did it anyway.

How long this shocking period lasted we do not know. As we saw, Paul was in Ephesus most likely from middle to late 53 till early or middle 56, apart from the short and highly unsatisfactory visit to Corinth. At some point after that visit he had sent Titus to Corinth with the "painful letter," but we cannot be sure when that was done and hence how long there might have been between that moment and his eventual release and subsequent travels. There is easily enough time in that schedule to fit in all the activities described in Acts, including the riot plus at least one significant spell in jail. In any case, as we try to assess Paul's mental and emotional state, we might reflect that it would have taken only a few weeks of prison, where he was subjected to various kinds of mental and physical torture, including having no idea how long he would be there, to get him into the condition he describes in 2 Corinthians 1.

For reasons that will become clear, I think Paul interpreted his imprisonment as the revenge of the powers into whose world he had been making inroads. He was used to confronting synagogue authorities; he knew how to deal with Roman magistrates. He knew Jewish law and Roman law just as well as they did. He was easily able to turn a phrase and win a rhetorical point and perhaps a legal one too. But in this case he had sensed that something else was going on. The forces ranged against him were not simply human. He had stirred up a hornets' nest with his powerful ministry in Ephesus. Think of all those magic books going up in smoke. Just as Jesus warned his followers not to fear those who could merely kill the body, but rather to fear the dark power that could wreak a more terrible destruction,[50] so Paul was learning that human authorities, though important in themselves, might sometimes be acting merely as a front for other powers that would attack through them. And, though he had taught, preached, and celebrated the fact that in his death Jesus had defeated all the dark powers and that in his resurrection he had launched God's new creation, that dogged belief, seen from the cold and smelly depths of a prison, with no light at night, flies and vermin for company, and little food in his stomach, must have been tested to the uttermost and beyond. Hence the despair.

Looking back with hindsight after his release, he explained to the Corinthians that this was to make him trust in the God who raises the dead.[51] Not, of course, that he had not believed and trusted this God before, but now it was put on the line in a whole new way. So how did he get back to that point of trust? Did he just go on gritting his teeth and saying, "I must trust the God who raises the dead" until it happened? I doubt it. That kind of so-called positive thinking was not Paul's style. I think something more specific was at work.

We noticed, as Paul was on his way back to Jerusalem and then Antioch after his early time in Corinth, that his praying was rooted in the Jewish traditions of prayer but now focused on Jesus. We saw this as he breathtakingly adapted one of the main Jewish daily prayers, the *Shema,* so that it now expressed loyalty to the "father" and the "Lord" together.[52] So if Paul had these prayers forming and taking shape in his mind and if, as we know, he had an enviable gift for vivid and fluent language, we might not be surprised if his prayers from the depths of despair began to develop from biblical roots into Jesus-shaped expressions, and from Jesus-shaped expressions into more formal and shaped invocations and celebrations that, recalling the ancient biblical celebrations of

God's sovereignty and victory, now placed the sovereign lordship of Jesus himself at the center.

I think that, like a plant in harsh winter, Paul in prison was forced to put his roots down even deeper than he had yet gone into the biblical tradition, and deeper again, still within that tradition, into the meaning of Jesus and his death. The roots slowly found moisture. From the depth of that dark soil, way below previous consciousness, he drew hope and new possibilities. The fruit of that labor remains to this day near the heart of Christian belief.

I think, in other words, not only that the four Prison Letters were all written from Ephesus, but that the writing of them grew directly out of the struggle Paul had experienced. Their vision of Jesus the Messiah, sovereign over all the powers of the world, was Paul's hard-won affirmation of the truth he had believed all along but had never before had to explore in such unpromising circumstances. And I think that as he pondered, prayed, and heard in his mind's ear phrases and biblical echoes turning into poetry, he began to long once more to share this vision with those around him. And with that longing and that prayer he found he was, at an even deeper level than he had known before, trusting in the God who raises the dead. The poems of Philippians 2 and Colossians 1 and the sustained liturgical drama of the first three chapters of Ephesians all bear witness to this celebration—not of Paul's faith or stamina, but of the victory of God and the lordship of Jesus. As he says in 2 Corinthians 4, right after a passage that belongs very closely with the poem in Colossians 1, "We have this treasure in earthenware pots, so that the extraordinary quality of the power may belong to God, not to us."[53] That, I think, was what was going on while Paul was in prison.

Some have suggested that this whole experience was in effect a "second conversion," in which Paul finally learned the humility that had previously eluded him. I do not subscribe to this view. Things are more complicated, and indeed more interesting, than that. But I do think that his long-held practice of Jesus-focused prayer, taking the ancient scriptural poems and patterns and finding Jesus at their heart, was crucial in helping him to find his way out of despair and back into hope. Christology and therapy go well together, even if, like Jacob, an apostle may limp, in style and perhaps also in body, after the dark night spent wrestling with the angel.

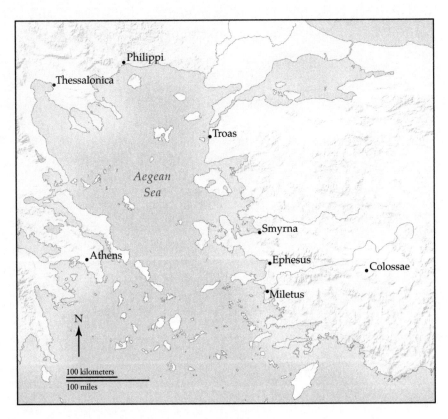

Ephesus

11

Ephesus II

I THINK PHILIPPIANS was the first of the Prison Letters to be written (perhaps in 55?), and this is why. In the first chapter Paul is still quite uncertain how his trial is going to go. The Messiah is going to be honored one way or another, he says. He "is going to gain a great reputation through my body, whether in life or in death."[1] Paul has thus turned the tables on his accusers and judges. He declares that his imprisonment is itself serving the purposes of the gospel, since people are talking about him and his message. Even those who are trying to make extra trouble for him (who are they? It isn't clear) are simply drawing attention to the message of the crucified and risen Lord Jesus. He writes as if it is now up to him to choose whether he will live or die, and he has learned how to face both options with equanimity—though he believes he will in fact be released, since there is still so much work for him to do, even though he "would really love to leave all this and be with the king, because that would be far better."[2]

The occasion for the letter is that Paul wants to thank the church in Philippi for a gift of money. The distance from Philippi to Ephesus is about three hundred miles as the crow flies; Epaphroditus, the Philippian messenger who had brought it, would have come a somewhat longer distance, whether by sea or by land. But then there was a problem. Epaphroditus got sick, seriously ill. The Philippians must have wondered what had happened. When you entrust a significant sum of money to someone and the person never reappears, you start to ask questions. Paul is answering those implicit questions, and more. He explains that Epaphroditus, who is now going to take the return message back to Philippi, has been a faithful fellow worker who has risked his life in the royal service.[3]

But the heart of this short letter is Jesus himself. Paul urges the Philippians to let their public behavior match up to the gospel, which will mean sharing the Messiah's suffering—as Paul himself has done and is doing. In particular, he urges them to cherish and guard their unity and their holiness. He knows only too well (if he had not already, the recent experience with Corinth would have taught him) that a community composed of people from very different social, ethnic, and cultural backgrounds will find all sorts of interesting reasons for divisions, perhaps over seemingly unrelated issues. Every such impulse must be resisted. And he knows too well, again with all too many Corinthian examples, that the behavior of Jesus's followers can pick up inappropriate coloring from the pagan world around them. That too must be resisted.

But how? The central appeal of the first half of the letter explains. Unity and holiness will come, and will only come, as the mind of the community and of the individuals within it are transformed to reflect the mind of the Messiah himself.[4]

The "mind of the Messiah" is then the subject of one of the greatest Jesus-focused poems of all time. Echoing Genesis, the Psalms, and Isaiah in particular, it tells the story of Jesus going down to the lowest depths and then being exalted as Lord of the whole world. The poem works at several levels. It expresses many things Paul believed about Jesus himself—the truly human one, the ultimate Israelite, the Servant of the Lord, the embodiment of Israel's God in person, the reality of which Caesar was a shallow parody:

> *Who, though in God's form, did not*
> *Regard his equality with God*
> *As something he ought to exploit.*

> *Instead, he emptied himself,*
> *And received the form of a slave,*
> *Being born in the likeness of humans.*

> *And then, having human appearance,*
> *He humbled himself, and became*
> *Obedient even to death,*

> *Yes, even the death of the cross.*

> *And so God has greatly exalted him,*
> *And to him in his favor has given*
> *The name which is over all names:*

> *That now at the name of Jesus*
> *Every knee within heaven shall bow—*
> *On earth, too, and under the earth;*

> *And every tongue shall confess*
> *That Jesus, Messiah, is Lord,*
> *To the glory of God, the father.*[5]

This is the story of Adam (everyone), of Israel, of the One God—all in the form of a perfectly balanced poem about Jesus. The poem is cast in the idiom of a Hellenistic paean of praise for a great man, but the content is of course deeply Jewish and scriptural. It is, in fact, a poem that sums up a great deal of what Paul believed: that Jesus is the messianic fulfillment of Israel's story, the embodiment of Israel's One God, and hence the appointed Lord of the whole world. Its careful structure, giving full weight to the cross in the very center, encapsulates exactly what Paul most deeply believed about the gospel. It is *because* of the cross—the defeat of the powers—that Jesus has been exalted as Lord and that every knee shall bow at his name.

This poem, I suggest, grows directly out of Paul's much earlier belief (already in Galatians and presumably before that as well) about who Jesus was. But, shaped by his own sustained scriptural reflection and teaching, it now draws many different elements of that biblical material into a tight structure. By celebrating the ultimate victory and power of Jesus over all other powers in the universe, Paul has meditated deeply on the fact that even at his own lowest moment "the God who raises the dead" had come down to that same point. The poem may thus have functioned as one of the ladders out of Paul's own pit of despair long before it then functioned as the model to teach the Philippians, and the church ever since, how to think.

The poem suggests, above all, a radical redefinition of *power*. This was the very theme that had concerned Paul so much in Ephesus and in his first letter to Corinth. It was the subject he found himself rethinking from the ground up as he discovered that the power of the gospel belonged utterly to God and not at all to himself. Learning how to think as the Messiah had thought, Paul insisted, was the only way to radical unity in the church, and it was also the secret of how to live as "pure and spotless children of God in the middle of a twisted and depraved generation."[6]

Once again, Paul is using letters to teach his churches not just what to think, but how to think. He cannot tell them everything he would like to tell them. He would run out of papyrus scrolls long before he got to the end. But that wasn't his job. His job was to inculcate in them the mind of the Messiah. If that happened, then it would show that he had not after all been wasting his time[7] (that old worry again; Paul never seems to have shaken it off). And Paul, I suggest, came to this extraordinary expression of the Messiah's mind not least through the combination of his Jesus-focused scriptural meditation, on the one hand, and his own in-voluntary imitation of the Jesus pattern, on the other. He too had been humbled under the weight of suffering. He had pondered the fact that this was the means by which Jesus had attained his exaltation as Lord.

There is an awkward break at the end of the second chapter of Philippians. This is perhaps a sign that Paul, writing from prison, had intended to stop there, but that then, deciding to carry on after all, he had not had the opportunity to smooth out the tran-sition.

The second half, though, is modeled closely on the first, particu-larly the poem in chapter 2. The exhortation reaches a climax at the end of chapter 3, where Paul declares that "the savior, the Lord, King Jesus" will come from heaven to transform our present body to be "like his glorious body," since, as Psalm 8 declares, he has the power "to bring everything into line under his authority."[8] As in the similar passage in 1 Corinthians 15:20–28, this is part of Paul's belief in Jesus as the truly human one. We who live on the other side of centuries of puzzlement about "humanity" and "divinity" may sometimes be startled at how easily someone like Paul, believ-ing that humans were made to reflect the divine image, could see the true human as the one who shared the glory that the One God had said he would not share with another.[9] For Paul, this was a truth he could explore from several different angles, as we see again in Colossians. And it was, of course, a truth not simply to be gazed at in wonder, but to be used as the motivating power for a different kind of life—a life the Jewish traditions had claimed to be able to produce, but for which they turned out to be ineffective.

That is the key to the sharp polemic at the start of chapter 3. Paul is anxious about the backlash against his message from people who shared the agenda of the "agitators" or "troublemakers" in Galatia. Such people have not yet, it seems, arrived in Philippi, but it may only be a matter of time. This is probably a sign that they are already at work in Ephesus; perhaps their opposition to his mission there had itself contributed to the crisis he had suffered. (That may be the meaning too of the curious passage in 1:15–18, about people who are announcing the messianic message with the sole object of making life harder for him in prison.)

All this might explain the tone of voice in his opening warning:

> Watch out for the dogs! Watch out for the "bad works"
> people! Watch out for the "incision" party, that is, the
> mutilators! We are the "circumcision," you see—we who
> worship God by the spirit, and boast in King Jesus, and
> refuse to trust in the flesh.[10]

The point is clear. "Dogs" was what Jews often called Gentiles. "Bad works" is a parody for the "good works" advocated by zealous Torah teachers. "The incision" or "the mutilation" is a translator's attempt to bring out the force of Paul's pun: instead of *peritomē*, "circumcision," he writes *katatomē*, the act of making a cut in something, perhaps as a matter of pagan religious ritual. That is what it has come to, he says; people who go around insisting that converts should get circumcised are no better than pagan cult members who want to make knife marks in people's flesh.

"We are the 'circumcision'" is a breathtaking claim, but utterly consistent with Paul's whole stance, ever since the road to Damascus. Once again, this is not about comparative religion. He is not saying, "We Jesus-followers have found a better sort of religion than the old Jewish one." It is about *messianic eschatology*. This was the ultimate fulfillment of Israel's hope: Messiah and resurrection! He is not saying, "I've decided to move from my old house to a nicer one down the road." He is saying that his own home has been taken over by the architect who built it in the first place and that it is now being rebuilt around him. He intends to stay and see the business through. If others are saying they prefer the old house the way it was, they are missing the point: if Israel's Messiah

has come and has been raised from the dead, then those who follow him are the true people of God. This is blunt, but consistent. The followers of other first-century Jewish leaders would have said the same. This is not disloyalty to Israel's God. It is the contested messianic loyalty that has characterized Paul throughout.

Paul was himself in an excellent position to push this point home. He knew the Jewish world from the inside. His credentials there were impeccable, up to and including the "zeal" because of which he persecuted the church. But this is where his meeting with the Messiah fulfilled everything, and thereby changed everything. If we want to know what drove Paul on and what the Damascus Road event had done to him, this is perhaps the clearest statement we have:

> Whatever I had written in on the profit side, I calculated it instead as a loss—because of the Messiah. Yes, I know that's weird, but there's more: I calculate everything as a loss, because knowing King Jesus as my Lord is worth far more than everything else put together! In fact, because of the Messiah I've suffered the loss of everything, and I now calculate it as trash, so that my profit may be the Messiah, and that I may be discovered in him, not having my own covenant status defined by the Torah, but the status which comes through the Messiah's faithfulness: the covenant status from God which is given to faith. This means knowing him, knowing the power of his resurrection, and knowing the partnership of his sufferings. It means sharing the form and pattern of his death, so that somehow I may arrive at the final resurrection from the dead.[11]

Out of the many things one could say about this passage, there are three important points for our present purposes. First, Paul is following the messianic pattern set out in the poem of 2:6–11. The Messiah regarded his status ("equality with God") not as something to exploit, but as committing him instead to the life and the shameful death of the "slave." That is why he is now exalted as Lord over all. Paul knows that he must therefore regard his own privileged status as a fully fledged member of God's people as something he must not exploit. Instead, he will discover the true status of covenant membership and the resurrection hope that goes with it not through the Torah, but through the Messiah's faithfulness.

Second, this passage is focused not just on a belief or theory *about* the Messiah, but on personal knowledge. He speaks of "knowing King Jesus as my Lord," of "knowing him, knowing the power of his resurrection, and knowing the partnership of his sufferings."[12] Paul knows the theory through and through. He can expound it all day and, if need be, all night. But it means nothing without the awareness of the person and presence of Jesus himself.

Third, he has learned—perhaps he has learned this in new ways in the weeks and months before writing this letter—that this personal "knowledge" of the Messiah finds intimate expression in suffering. He speaks of this as a "partnership," "the partnership of his sufferings." The word is *koinōnia,* "fellowship" or "sharing." But, as we saw, for Paul this expressed a mutual belonging for which modern English does not provide exact words. Perhaps this, seen in the light of Paul's terrible experience, on the one hand, and, on the other, the poem of 2:6–11, gets us as close as we can come to the way in which he was now learning to "rely on the God who raises the dead."[13] Paul had come to the point where he was content to share the Messiah's death in order that he might arrive with him at the ultimate hope of Israel, "the resurrection from the dead." The ancient story of Israel had been fulfilled—in the Messiah. All Paul's previous zeal for God and the Torah had had to be counted as "trash" by contrast. This is an expanded version of what he had said in Galatians 2:19–20:

Through the law I died to the law, so that I might live
to God. I have been crucified with the Messiah. I am,
however, alive—but it isn't me any longer; it's the Messiah who lives in me.

That is why he now forgets his past and, like an athlete with his
eye on the finishing line, aims "to strain every nerve to go after
what's ahead."[14]

Then comes the point of all this: the Philippians must learn to
imitate him, as he is imitating the Messiah.[15] But how can they
imitate him? They have not been zealous Jews, eager for the Torah. No, but they all have their own status, their own personal
or civic pride. And even if they don't have any (because they are
poor, or slaves, or women—though some women, like Lydia,
were independent and free), they all have the standing temptation to lapse back into pagan lifestyles. So whether they are
Romans reverting to proud colonial ways or simply people who
find themselves lured back into sensual indulgence,[16] all must resist and find instead the way of holiness and unity that is shaped
by the Messiah himself, by his choice of the way of the cross, by
his status as the truly human one, the true embodiment of the
One God.

Writing all this, celebrating the victory of the Messiah, Paul
has arrived at a very different place from the one he describes in
2 Corinthians 1. In one of many allusions in this letter to the great
philosophies of his time, Paul declares that being the Messiah's
man has produced the "contentment" for which both Stoics and
Epicureans aim:

I'm not talking about lacking anything. I've learned to
be content with what I have. I know how to do without,
and I know how to cope with plenty. In every possible
situation I've learned the hidden secret of being full and
hungry, of having plenty and going without, and it's this:

I have strength for everything in the one who gives me
power.[17]

There it is again: *power*. But "the extraordinary quality of the
power belongs to God, not to us."[18] Paul has learned this now. His
meditation on the victory of Jesus, growing out of the scripturally
rooted prayers of many years, with those roots going down into
the dark of suffering and despair, have brought him to a new place.
All power is vested by God in Jesus. Any power Jesus's followers
may have comes only through his work. He thanks the Philippians
once more for the gift. He sends Epaphroditus on his way.

★ ★ ★

As the weeks turned into months during the dark prison days
sometime in 55 or early 56, some of Paul's friends were able to
come and help take care of him, and he had a visitor, a frightened young man named Onesimus. Onesimus was a slave. He
belonged to Philemon, a wealthy householder in the small city
of Colossae, some 150 miles inland from Ephesus. He had run
away, as slaves sometimes did, probably grabbing some money as
he went. He knew the risk he was taking. Runaways were regularly punished with death; crucifixion ("to discourage the others," of course) was common in such cases. Harboring or helping
a runaway was also a serious crime. But Onesimus had come to
Paul. Paul, having himself recently faced despair and death and
having seen Onesimus's master Philemon come to faith on a visit
to Ephesus, found himself in a complex little situation that would
have made a fascinating seminar in moral philosophy, had not so
much immediate danger been riding on it. What to do?

The first thing was to share the gospel with Onesimus. The
frightened slave, hearing the news of one who died the slave's death
out of sheer love—the same love that had made the world—was
captivated by it. No doubt some converts, then as now, professed a
quick faith in the hope of a quick reward, but Paul could see that

the young man's heart had truly been changed. He became like a son to Paul, eager to learn, eager to help (his name meant "useful," and he was keen to live up to it). But the situation couldn't last forever.

Paul could simply have helped the young man move away from trouble. He could have instructed one of his friends to take him to Greece or even farther afield. But what would Paul then say to Philemon the next time they met? And how would it be if word got out that this subversive jailbird, in addition to his other notorious antisocial behavior, had taken to sheltering runaway slaves? Moreover, when Paul reflected on the vocation he had been given, one of the best descriptions he could find was the word "reconciliation," *katallagē*. The gospel was about the One God reconciling the world to himself, and also—as he had written to the Galatians less than a decade earlier—about Jew and Greek, slave and free, male and female coming to be "all one in the Messiah, Jesus." If this was real—if it wasn't just a grandiose idea in his head—it had to work on the ground. Real Jews, real Greeks. Real men and women. Real slaves, real masters.

Slavery is of course revolting. We know this. We know only too well the terrible ways in which slavery was developed in the eighteenth and nineteenth centuries, until brave campaigners abolished it, often in the teeth of principled opposition that claimed, among other things, to be grounded in the Bible. In particular, we associate slavery with racism. And we know that, despite abolition, the practice has made its way back into the modern world. We wish Paul had said, "Free them all! It's a wicked practice!"

That would have been a futile gesture. Slavery in the ancient world did, more or less, everything that is done in our world by oil, gas, or electricity, everything that we accomplish through our technology. Denouncing slavery would have been like denouncing electricity and the internal combustion engine. What's more, we must remind ourselves that slavery in Paul's world had nothing to do with ethnic origin. All you had to do to become a slave was to be on the losing side in battle or even to fail in business. Slaves were, of course, often exploited, abused, treated like trash, but they could also become respected, cherished, and valued members of a family. Cicero's slave Tiro was his right-hand man. He even invented shorthand. Slavery was complex but omnipresent.

Paul knew that the God of Israel had defined himself in action as the slave-freeing God. That is what the story of the Exodus was all about. Paul believed (and he believed that God believed) in ultimate freedom, a freedom of creation itself from the "slavery to decay," a freedom that would mean resurrection life for all God's children.[19] As always, Paul's challenge was to bring this cosmic vision into the real world of compromised and perplexed humans. And he hit upon a plan to make Philemon and Onesimus a small working model of what Messiah-based freedom might look like.

He couldn't just write to Philemon and say, "By the way, Onesimus has come to me. Please give him his freedom and let him stay here." That was, we may suppose, what he wanted, but it wouldn't address the real issue. It would merely encourage other slaves to come and try the same thing. Nor could he say, as the Roman letter writer Pliny had said when writing to a friend in similar circumstances, "I've given him a good talking-to, and I want you to let him off this time."[20]

Paul's aim is higher and deeper. He has been meditating in prison, as he worked through the shock and horror of his own plight, on the way in which God himself was present in the Messiah, reconciling the world to himself. Now, perhaps, God would be present in him, Paul, reconciling these two dear people through a high-risk pastoral strategy. Onesimus will go back to Philemon (accompanied, so it seems from Col. 4:7–9, by Paul's friend Tychicus) with a letter from Paul. It is asking a lot of them both. It is dangerous for Onesimus and extremely awkward for Philemon.

But perhaps the letter will not only explain what ought to happen, but actually help to bring it about.

It is a small masterpiece. Paul explains to Philemon that he is praying that their *koinōnia* will have its full, powerful effect, bringing them all together "into the king," into the Messiah. From Paul's other uses of this idea we see what he means: "the Messiah" is not only Jesus, but all those who are "in the Messiah." It is an *incorporative* term, as it was in Galatians ("You are all one *in the Messiah, Jesus*") and 1 Corinthians ("as the body is one, and has many members, . . . *so also is the Messiah*").[21] "We must," he says in Ephesians, "speak the truth in love, and so grow up in everything *into him*"—that is, *into the Messiah*.[22] This rich unity is one of Paul's constant imperatives; the other is holiness. But how is it to be achieved?

"God was reconciling the world to himself in the Messiah," Paul wrote later, "not counting their transgressions against them, *and entrusting us with the message of reconciliation*."[23] The message of reconciliation is then, at that point, reembodying God's action. Paul stands between Philemon and Onesimus, joining them together in his own person and appeal. "Here," he says (stretching out one arm), "is Onesimus, my son, my own heart, who has been looking after me here in prison, on your behalf as it were!" And (stretching out the other arm) to Philemon, he says, "Your love gives me so much comfort. You are my partner in the gospel. You owe me, after all, your own very self. You have the chance now to refresh me, even here in prison." Paul stands metaphorically between the two men, reaching out in the shape of the cross. "Oh, and by the way," he says ("not counting their transgressions against them"), "if he's wronged you, put it down on my account. I'll make it good." And then he adds, "One more thing. Get a guest room ready for me. Keep praying, and I will be out of here soon. Then I'll be coming to visit."

This would demand humility and trust on both sides. Onesimus was not going to set off to Colossae with a spring in his step, imagining everything was going to be easy. There had been reasons why he ran away, and those reasons, whatever they were, would have to be confronted. Philemon would be astonished and quite possibly angry to see him return; he would also realize the delicate balance both of what Paul had said and of what he was being asked to do. As a policy statement about slavery, the letter falls short of what we would want. As an experiment in a one-off, down-to-earth pastoral strategy, it is brilliant. And it seems to have worked. Fifty years later the bishop of Ephesus is a man called Onesimus. The young slave, now an elderly Christian leader? Or a name already respected within the early community?

★ ★ ★

If Paul is going to send Onesimus and Tychicus all the way to Colossae, there are other things he wants to say to the church there as a whole. In any case, he has had in mind the possibility of writing a circular, a letter to all the churches in the area. He has it mapped out already in his head, and he will write the two, as it were, side by side, the general letter to all the churches and the particular one to Colossae. Both of them, probably written therefore in 55 or early 56, explain, in slightly different but convergent ways, why he is in prison and why the churches, hearing about this, ought not to worry as though it might mean that the gospel itself were at risk. Both of them address this by embodying his deep meditation on the power of Jesus over all the powers of the world, the theme that (I am suggesting) has helped Paul back into a position of trust after despair. Both of them, true to his whole worldview, are rooted in the world of ancient Jewish and biblical thought refashioned around Jesus and addressing the world of pagan power with the new and subversive message of the gospel.

Before we plunge into these two letters, Colossians and Ephesians, we need to say a word about Paul's authorship. The present book is not the place to go into technical arguments, but a short explanation may be in order.

Most modern Western critics still express doubts about Paul's authorship of one or both of these letters. These doubts are based partly on style, though in fact most of Paul's letters exhibit different styles, and I have already explained that perhaps the sharpest stylistic difference among the Pauline letters is that between the first and second Corinthian letters, both of which are normally accepted as authentic. The questions of style mostly concern Ephesians rather than Colossians, but I have been impressed by the proposals of some scholars that in these letters, written from and to the heart of the province of Asia, Paul may well have been deliberately adopting the "Asiatic" style of writing, with its word-play, florid sentences, and rhythm. This was well known (though controversial) at the time, not least among Roman orators, some of whom were imitating "Asiatic" Greek models and others of whom regarded this as degenerate.

In any case, three things have to be said about Pauline style. First, those who have done computer analysis of these things have tended to say that most of the letters come from him. Second, Paul's surviving letters are in fact so short, by comparison with most literary products from the ancient world, that it is hard to be sure we have enough to make a valid comparison. Third, it is easy for critics to be too wooden in their view of how this or that person ought to write. It is perfectly possible for the same person to write, in the same week, a learned article for a journal, a speech for a political meeting, a children's talk, and perhaps some scraps of poetry. Small variations in style—and that is all that they are in the case of the Pauline letters—are to be expected when the same person faces different situations. And, in the case of Ephesians, Paul is writing a general letter without a specific situation or audience in mind.

The real problem, of course, is that from the nineteenth century onward the leading edge of Pauline scholarship was located within German liberal Protestantism. In that world, the remarkably "high" view of the church in these letters was thought to contrast with the more "protestant" view of Romans, Galatians, and the Corinthian letters. This is in fact a straightforward mistake. Paul's view of the church, though variously expressed, is consistent across the whole corpus, and it is only by shrinking what Paul says in Romans and Galatians that one can imagine Ephesians and Colossians as radically different. There are other related points, for instance, about the view of Jesus. But these too are based on a shrunken view of what Paul was saying in Romans and the other obviously authentic letters.

In any case, though this is something that has only become clear with more recent work on the Jewish world of the day, Ephesians and Colossians are both deeply Jewish in their orientation—rethought around Jesus, of course, but making the sense they make within that worldview. Nineteenth-century Protestantism didn't favor Jewish thought either, and it certainly didn't want Paul to be too Jewish. Much more recently, some people have taken exception to the "household codes" in Ephesians and Colossians, supposing them to be anathema to the liberal agenda they find in Galatians and elsewhere. This too is a mistake. As historians, we must not set up the artificial standards of contemporary moralizing and then construct a "Paul" to fit. Fashions come and go in the scholarly world. The fashion for rejecting Ephesians and Colossians—or perhaps we should say for helping the Protestant Paul to keep his distance from Judaism, on the one hand, and from Catholicism, on the other—has had a long run for its money. Because it appears "critical," many are frightened to challenge it for fear of appearing "uncritical." Once we place the letters in Ephesus, where I think they belong, these problems begin to look as though they are generated by ideology rather than historical study.

★ ★ ★

Colossians is written, it appears, to a young church. Paul has been informed of its existence by Epaphras, himself from Colossae, who seems to have been converted under Paul in Ephesus and to have returned home to spread the word. Paul is praying for the church to grow in faith, wisdom, and understanding and to be able— here is that theme again—to draw on the "power" of Jesus in living and working to his glory.[24] In particular, Paul longs that they would develop and enrich the practice of *giving thanks.* To that end he supplies them with a poem that, like the poem in Philippians 2, celebrates the universal lordship of Jesus over all the powers of the world.

This, as I have suggested, was part of the tonic Paul himself had needed as he battled with the powers. Indeed, part of the meaning of this poem is precisely that it is written by someone in prison. It is, in other words, inviting those who read it or pray it to imagine a different world from the one they see all around them—a world with a different Lord, a world in which the One God rules and rescues, a world in which a new sort of wisdom has been unveiled, a world in which there is a different way to be human.

"Wisdom" is in fact the subtext of much of Colossians. As always, Paul wants people to learn to *think*—not simply to imbibe rules and principles to learn by heart, but to be able to grow up as genuine humans, experiencing "all the wealth of definite understanding" and coming to "the knowledge of God's mystery."[25] All this will happen as they realize that it is Jesus himself who reveals that "mystery." The Messiah himself is "the place" where they are to find "all the hidden treasures of wisdom and knowledge."[26]

Paul is here drawing deeply upon two important strands of Jewish thinking. On the one hand, as we have seen, he knows very well the traditions of prayerful meditation through which devout Jews hoped for a vision of the heavenly realm, and perhaps even of the One God himself. These traditions seem to have been developed at a time when, with pagans still ruling even after the Babylonian exile itself had ended, there was a sense that the greatest prophetic promises, particularly those concerning the visible and powerful return of Israel's God to the Temple in Zion, had not been realized. Perhaps this was a time of testing and patience, in which some might glimpse, in advance as it were, the reality that would one day fill the Temple and flood the whole creation . . .

That whole creation, second, was made by the One God *through his wisdom*. That was what Proverbs 8 had said, starting a line of thought that would be developed by Jewish thinkers down to Paul's own day. It began, to be sure, as a metaphor; to speak of "Lady Wisdom" as God's handmaid in creation was a poetic way of saying that when God made the world, his work was neither random nor muddled, but *wise*—coherent and well ordered; it made sense. And, of course—this is the point of the book of Proverbs as a whole and the later literature that echoes and develops it—if you want to be a genuine human being, reflecting God's image, then *you need to be wise as well.* You need to get to know Lady Wisdom.

The "mystery" tradition and the "wisdom" tradition were both focused by some writers in the period on the Temple. That was where the One God had promised to dwell. If there was to be a display of the ultimate mystery, you might expect either that it would be in the Temple or that it would be *as if* you were in the Temple. The book known as Ecclesiasticus, or the Wisdom of Jesus ben Sirach, written around 200 BC, imagines Lady Wisdom wanting to come and live among humans and wondering where to establish her dwelling. There is no contest: the Temple, of course, is the answer.[27] All this gets bound together in yet another strand of Jewish thinking: David's son Solomon, the ultimate "wise man" in the Bible, is also the king who builds the Temple. When Solomon consecrates the newly built shrine, the divine glory comes to fill the house in such blazing brilliance that the priests cannot stand there to do their work.[28]

For us, living in a different culture entirely, all this feels like an odd combination of disparate ideas. In Paul's world, and especially for a well-educated Jew, all these apparently separate notions belonged together like a single well-oiled machine—or, perhaps better, like a single human being, in this case Jesus. What does it mean to say that *he* is the place where you'll find all the treasures of wisdom and knowledge?

This is what it means, Paul declares, as he lays out another astonishing poem in which all that I have just said comes not only to expression, but to beautiful expression. Here is the secret of creation, of wisdom, of mystery, of the Temple. Here is how it fits together.

The book of Genesis begins with "In the beginning," which in Hebrew is a single word, *bereshith*. The particle *be* can mean "in" or "through" or "for"; the noun *reshith* can mean "beginning," "head," "sum total," or "first fruits." Proverbs 8 had Lady Wisdom declare that God created her "as the beginning of his work," *bereshith darkō*. And the account of creation in Genesis 1 reaches its climax with the creation of the humans in the *image* of God. Creation as a whole is a Temple, the heaven-and-earth reality in which God wants to dwell, and the mode of his presence in that Temple (as anyone in the ancient world would have known perfectly well) was the "image," the cult object that would represent the creator to the world and that wider world before the creator. Complicated? Yes, but it only seems that way to us, because our culture has done its best to unlearn this kind of thought. Complex but coherent, a bit like creation itself, in fact, or indeed like a human being.

Now imagine all that complex but coherent Jewish thought pondered and prayed by Paul as he travels, as he works in his hot little shop, as he stays in a wayside inn, as he teaches young Timothy the vast world of scripture, which is his natural habitat. Imagine him praying all that in the Temple itself as he visits Jerusalem after watching the gospel at work in Turkey and Greece. Imagine, particularly, Paul finding here fresh insight into the way in which, as the focal point of creation, of wisdom and mystery, and of the deep meaning of humanness itself, Jesus is now enthroned as Lord over all possible powers. And now imagine Paul in his moment of crisis, of despair, feeling that the "powers" had overcome him after all, reaching down into the depths of this fathomless well of truth to find, in a fresh way, what it might mean to trust in the God who raises the dead. This is what he comes up with:

> *He is the image of God, the invisible one,*
> *The firstborn of all creation.*
> *For in him all things were created,*
> *In the heavens and here on the earth.*
> *Things we can see and things we cannot—*
> *Thrones and lordships and rulers and powers—*
> *All things were created both through him and for him.*
>
> *And he is ahead, prior to all else*
> *And in him all things hold together;*
> *And he himself is supreme, the head*
> *Over the body, the church.*
>
> *He is the start of it all,*
> *Firstborn from realms of the dead;*
> *So in all things he might be the chief.*
> *For in him all the Fullness was glad to dwell*
> *And through him to reconcile all to himself,*
> *Making peace through the blood of his cross,*
> *Through him—yes, things on the earth,*
> *And also the things in the heavens.*[29]

If this poem were less elegant, one might say that Paul was shaking his fist at the powers, the powers on earth and the powers in the dark realms beyond the earth, the powers that had put him in prison and crushed his spirit to the breaking point. But he is not. The theological effect is the same; he is invoking and celebrating a world in which Jesus, the one through whom all things were made, is now the one through whom, by means of his crucifixion, all things are reconciled. This is not, of course, the world that he and his friends can see with the naked eye. They see local officials giving allegiance to Caesar. They see bullying magistrates, threatening officers. They see prisons and torture. But they are now invited to see the world with the eye of faith, the eye that has learned to look through the lens of scripture and see Jesus.

Like an apocalyptic vision, this mystery-revealing poem offers a glimpse of another world, a truer world than the violent and brutish world of paganism then and now. It was a Jewish world, but with a difference—a Jewish world made sense of at last by the coming of the Messiah, the true son of David, the truly human one (the "image"), for whose reality and meaning even the Jerusalem Temple was the advance signpost. "All the Fullness"—the full divinity of the One God—"was glad to dwell" in him. This is Temple language. It offers the highest view of Jesus one could have, up there along with John's simple but profound statement: "The Word became flesh, and lived among us."[30] And Jesus is the Image, the truly human one at the heart of the world temple, the one who straddles heaven and earth, holding them together at last, the one whose shameful death has reconciled all things to the Creator.

With this brief but breathtaking vision of Jesus, Paul puts the Colossians and himself into the picture. They have come to be part of it all, and Paul's own sufferings too are part of the way in which Jesus's lordship is implemented in the world. The Messiah, indeed, is living within them, just as Paul had said to the Galatians. The ancient Jewish hope that the glory of the One God would return and fill the world is thus starting to come true. It may not look like it in Colossae, as ten or twenty oddly assorted people crowd into Philemon's house to pray, to invoke Jesus as they worship the One God, to break bread together, and to intercede for one another and the world; but actually the Messiah, there in their midst, is "the hope of glory."[31] One day the whole creation will be

flooded with his presence. Then they will look back and realize
that they, like the Temple itself, had been a small working model,
an advance blueprint, of that renewed creation.

This leads to a warning that functions rather as Philippians
3:2–11 had. It is not so clear in this passage that Paul is warning
the Colossians against a repeat of what had happened in Galatia,
but when we read the whole passage, we get the point. "You
are already," he says, "the true monotheists, focused on the true
Temple.[32] You have already been 'circumcised,' not in the ordinary physical way, but through dying and rising with the Messiah.[33] And the Torah, which might have stood in your way, has
been set aside.[34] Therefore, recognize that you are under no obligation to obey regulations regarding diet, festivals or Sabbaths,
no matter what visions and revelations people may claim as they
instruct you."[35] What does all this add up to? Monotheism, Temple, circumcision, Torah, food laws, Sabbaths, visions, and revelations . . . this sounds exactly like the Jewish world that Paul
knows so well. The warnings are indeed similar to those in Philippians 3. We do not need to imagine, as many have done, that a
strange syncretistic "philosophy" had invaded Colossae. This is a
coded warning against being lured into the Jewish fold.

Why, then, does he speak of "philosophy and hollow trickery"
that people might use to "take them captive"?[36] As in Galatians 4,
he is clear that, when a synagogue community rejects the message
about the crucified Messiah, what is left is simply one philosophy among many. "Philosophy" in Paul's world was a way of
life; some Jewish writers referred to their own worldview that
way. The key word, though, is "take you captive," a single and
very rare Greek word: *sylagōgōn*. Change one letter—a single pen
stroke in the Greek—and it would become *synagōgōn*, "lead you
into the synagogue." We remember how, in Philippians 3, Paul
warned against the *katatomē*, "mutilation," as a contemptuous pun
on *peritomē*, "circumcision." In the same way, he is here sweeping aside any possibility that Jewish (or Jewish Christian) teachers

might come and persuade the Colossian Jesus-followers to get circumcised. That's already happened, he says. They have already died and been raised with the Messiah.

That then forms the framework for his brief instructions that run from the end of chapter 2 to near the end of the letter. This is a longer application of Galatians 2:19–20: "Through the law I died to the law . . . I am, however, alive." "Realize," he says, "who you really are. The Messiah died and was raised; you are in him; therefore, you have died and been raised—and you must learn to live accordingly. The day is coming when the new creation, at present hidden, will be unveiled, and the king, the Messiah, will be revealed in glory. When that happens, the person you already are in him will be revealed as well. Believe it, and live accordingly."[37] The instructions that follow—emphasizing sexual purity; wise, kind, and truthful speech; and unity across traditional boundaries—are crisp and basic. All comes back to thanksgiving.[38] That is the context for the brief "household code" of instructions for wives, husbands, and—strikingly—children and slaves, who are treated as real human beings with responsibilities.

Prayers and greetings conclude matters. As with Romans (the only other letter written to a church Paul hadn't visited himself), these greetings are fuller than usual. The list of Paul's companions corresponds closely to the list at the end of the letter to Philemon, but with more description: Aristarchus appears to be imprisoned alongside Paul; Mark (Barnabas's nephew) is assisting Paul as well, having apparently gotten over whatever problems he had had seven or eight years earlier. In addition to the rise in Paul's spirits, caused (I have suggested) by his prolonged meditation on the sovereignty of Jesus over all powers of whatever sort, these companions have clearly been a great encouragement to him, not least the three who are themselves Jewish (Aristarchus, Mark, and Jesus Justus, the only one not mentioned in Philemon). This is significant for a number of reasons. Paul was constantly aware of the danger that, well known as he was for insisting that the Gentiles should be full members of the church without circumcision, Jews, including Jewish Jesus-followers, would shun him. The fact that Mark in particular is working with him may well indicate that any rift between Paul and the family that included Peter as well as Barnabas has been properly patched up.

Paul tells the Colossians, intriguingly, that when they have had the letter read to them, they should pass it on to the church in Laodicea, and also that they should be sure to read the letter that will come on to them *from* Laodicea. There is clearly a circular coming around. Tychicus and Onesimus, it seems, will bring them both. It will, however, be an interesting and challenging trip for the two messengers. Tychicus will have his work cut out to keep Onesimus cheerful during the week that it will take them to walk to Colossae.

★ ★ ★

From where I sit I can see dozens of photographs, mixed in between piles of books and papers, coffee cups and candlesticks. Most of them are small, particular shots: family members, holiday scenery, a white pony by the seashore, a distant cityscape. There is even a picture of my wife taking a picture of the pope (don't ask). But in the next room, just out of sight but clear in memory, there is a frame that contains fourteen photographs, cut and joined to make a complete panorama. It was taken on vacation in Switzerland, on the mountain ridge called Schynige Platte in the Bernese Oberland. The camera has swung through a full circle, so that the left end of the panorama actually joins up with the right end. In the center are the great peaks: the Eiger, the Mönch, and the glorious Jungfrau. All around are lesser but still dramatic mountains, snowy and tremendous, bathed in summer sunlight. It is a different kind of picture altogether from the ones in front of me, though it includes elements familiar from the smaller photos: a family member, holiday scenery, grazing animals (in this case cows), and even, in the far distance, a small town. They are all now in the one frame, and they mean all the more as a result. In a single glance, you can take in an entire world.

Ephesians is like that. It seems to be a circular; there are no personal greetings or mention of a specific church. The words "in Ephesus" in the first verse ("to the holy ones *in Ephesus* who are also loyal believers in King Jesus") are not found in the earliest and best manuscripts, and it looks as though a scribe, perhaps sometime in the fourth or fifth century, puzzled by the absence of an address, added one. There might be a good reason for this. If the letter was indeed a circular, but if it was written from prison in Ephesus, it is very likely that a copy would have been kept by the church in Ephesus itself, or even that someone from Laodicea or Colossae made a copy that found its way back to where it started. So the scribe, finding no address but knowing that the letter was located in Ephesus itself, would seem to be doing the sensible thing by adding the words.

It isn't only the absence of an address and greeting that make many people think the letter was a circular. Like the panoramic photograph, it covers a huge sweep of territory, with many different elements held together in a single view. There are stunning peaks and distant glimpses, but the point is that its author has stood back and tried to express it all at once. That is why some, even among those who are unsure whether Paul wrote it, have referred to it as "the crown of Paulinism," the place where Paul's ideas are put together in a single frame. A different kind of picture, indeed, but recognizable, I believe, as the work of the same man.

Ephesians has much in common with Colossians, so much so that some have thought that one letter was the model for the other. Equally likely in my view is that they were both composed at much the same time to serve slightly different purposes; Colossians has a specific focus for that particular community while Ephesians stands a bit farther back and lets the view speak for itself. Ephesians is where we can, I think, see Paul's own situation and understand why this was what he wanted to say from his prison cell to the churches in the province of Asia. The letter combines two apparently quite different things, but when we think of Paul and his Ephesian crisis it makes sense.

First, there is the cosmic and global vision of the divine purpose and of the church as the agent and representative of that plan. This occupies the first three chapters, and they make a continuous flow of exalted prose (perhaps, indeed, "Asiatic" in their long sentences and florid expressions), a single stream of praise, worship, and prayer. It is all very Jewish. It offers a vision of Creator and cosmos, of heaven and earth joined together, of the powers of the world as subject to the creator God and to his exalted Messiah, the truly human being under whose feet the Creator has placed "all things."[39] As a result of his death and resurrection the new Exodus has occurred, the "inheritance" is assured by the down payment of the spirit, and "all rule and authority and power and lordship" is now subject to him, including—and everyone in Asia would know who was being referred to—"every name that is invoked, both in the present age and also in the age to come."[40]

The second chapter speaks of the act of grace and rich mercy whereby God has rescued Jew and Gentile alike from sin and from the "powers" that feed off human idolatry. It speaks of the Messiah's people as a new creation, God's *poiēma,* the word from which we get "poem," rescued in order to model and take forward God's good purposes in the world. It speaks of the new Temple, long awaited by Jews of Paul's day (especially those who knew perfectly well that Herod's reconstruction of the Jerusalem Temple was an expensive sham); only now the Temple consists of the community of Jesus-followers, the place where the living God dwells by his spirit. Paul then explains in the third chapter where his own work and his present suffering belong on the map of God's age-old purposes. The powers of the world are now, as always intended, being confronted by the power of God. On that basis, Paul prays that all those to whom he is writing would come to grasp "the breadth and length and height and depth"—this really is a panorama he is spreading out—and to know, in particular, the love of the Messiah himself, so that they may be filled with all the divine fullness.[41]

The first half of the letter is therefore all about *power* and *unity*— the power of God in the gospel and the unity of heaven and earth, of Jew and Gentile in the church.[42] This will then give rise to the remarkable exhortations about the unity of the church through its many different gifts and not least the unity of man and woman in marriage.[43] There are mysteries here, as Paul readily acknowledges. But the sense of the Creator's plan for the whole creation coming to fruition and of the advance signs of that in Jew and Gentile and male and female is so clear—and for that matter so obviously Pauline, resonating with Galatians in particular—that the big picture, the panorama, ought not to be in doubt.

The second half of the letter is strongly and explicitly practical. The different gifts that God gives to the church are designed to bring it into a rich, variegated unity in which its members will be "growing up into the Messiah" as Paul had said to Philemon. And this gives rise to a sustained exhortation to live by the moral standards that diaspora Jews would recognize, particularly in matters of sexual ethics. That naturally leads to the delicate balance of relationship within marriage itself and so to another version of the "household codes." But then there comes the surprise—though, in retrospect, we ought not to be so surprised.

One might have thought, reading the first three chapters of the letter, that everything in the garden was, if not already lovely, then heading that way. The grand vision of God's redeeming purposes already accomplished in the Messiah; the church as the community that will now, by its life and unity, declare to the world that the One God is God, that Jesus is Lord, and that all other powers are in subjection to him—this might seem, and indeed has seemed to many in our own day, an impossibly grandiose, naive fantasy. But with the end of chapter 6 comes the reminder of the continuing reality. Believers are locked in a power struggle, and it is dangerous and unpleasant, calling for vigilance and for all the defensive equipment the gospel can provide.

This is exactly, we may suppose, the place Paul has come to after the terrible experience to which he refers in 2 Corinthians 1. His sustained meditation on the sovereignty of Jesus, rooted in his earlier prayer life, which, growing out of its deep Jewish roots, celebrated Jesus as the humble Servant, as the truly human Image, as the exalted Lord, as the place where "the full measure of divinity has taken up bodily residence"[44]—all this has helped him finally to climb out of the dark interior prison before he is released from the exterior one. But he has not forgotten the way in which the principalities and powers, so openly challenged in the early days of his work in Ephesus, were able to strike back. He sensed it, he smelled it, the whiff of sulfur surrounding the hard faces of the magistrates, the diabolical glee of the guards entrusted with whipping or beating their new prisoner, perhaps even the smug faces of people he had thought might be friends but turned out to be enemies. He knows, he has learned, that when you celebrate all the truths that he rehearses in chapters 1–3, particularly the truth that "God's wisdom, in all its rich variety, was to be made known to the rulers and authorities in the heavenly places—through the church!"[45] then the rulers and authorities are unlikely to take this kindly. As he explains in that same passage, his own suffering itself is making the point. The victory that was won by the cross must be implemented through the cross.

I think, in fact, that Ephesians 6:10–20, the passage on spiritual warfare, functions in relation to the whole of the rest of the letter much like 1 Corinthians 15, the long argument about the resurrection of the body, functions in relation to the earlier material in that letter. You might not have seen it coming, but when you get there it turns out not to be an appendix on an unrelated topic, but rather the deeper reality that makes sense of all that has gone before. In particular, everything Paul says in chapters 4–6 constitutes a rolling back of the frontiers in the world's moral power struggles. To make widely differing gifts work for unity, not division, as in chapter 4, is hard enough. To retrain the imagination and the natural impulses to resist the murky short-term delights of the pagan world is harder still. To make and sustain marriages of genuine mutual submission is perhaps hardest of all. Compromises and second-best solutions are easy. To go for the full version of discipleship is to sign on for spiritual warfare.

So too with the first half of the letter. Paul knew, much better than many modern theoreticians, that there is no incompatibility, but rather an inevitable link between, on the one hand, the celebration of the One God and his work of creation and new creation, Exodus and new Exodus, and, on the other, the challenge to the powers of the world. It will not do to accuse Ephesians 1–3 of having too much of the "now" and not enough of the "not yet." The "not yet" is there in chapters 4 and 5, and particularly 6, and it is there for a very good reason. Paul had come to Ephesus and had lived and taught the powerful victory of God. He had then discovered, first in Corinth and then back in Ephesus again, that as with the gospel itself the divine power could only be made known through human weakness. And so he offers this realistic warning and urgent appeal to the churches of Asia, not least the little communities in the Lycus valley, not to detract from what he has said earlier in the letter, but to give it its necessarily humble frame:

> Be strong in the Lord, and in the strength of his power.
> Put on God's complete armor. Then you'll be able to
> stand firm against the devil's trickery. The warfare we're
> engaged in, you see, isn't against flesh and blood. It's
> against the leaders, against the authorities, against the
> powers that rule the world in this dark age, against the
> wicked spiritual elements in the heavenly places.

For this reason, you must take up God's complete
armor. Then, when wickedness grabs its moment, you'll
be able to withstand, to do what needs to be done, and
still to be on your feet when it's all over. So stand firm!
Put the belt of truth around your waist; put on justice as
your breastplate; for shoes on your feet, ready for battle,
take the good news of peace. With it all, take the shield
of faith; if you've got that, you'll be able to quench all
the flaming arrows of the evil one. Take the helmet of
salvation, and the sword of the spirit, which is God's
word.

Pray on every occasion in the spirit, with every type
of prayer and intercession. You'll need to keep awake
and alert for this, with all perseverance and intercession
for all God's holy ones—and also for me! Please pray
that God will give me his words to speak when I open
my mouth, so that I can make known, loud and clear,
the secret truth of the gospel. That, after all, is why I'm
a chained-up ambassador! Pray that I may announce it
boldly; that's what I'm duty-bound to do.[46]

Paul has learned the hard way that the powers will strike back.
Every line of this warning says, "This is what I've had to do."
And, though he has now come, through sustained meditation on
the sovereignty of Jesus, to a fresh sense of trust in "the God who
raises the dead," he knows very well that there are at least two
major challenges still ahead. Ultimately, he wants to go to Rome.
Later, he will even think of Rome itself as a stopover on the way
to Spain. But the two challenges mean that he can hardly be planning those journeys just yet.

First, he has to go to Corinth, without any idea of what sort
of a reception will await him there. (Titus has still not returned;
surely, Paul thinks, that is a bad sign right there . . .) Then he

hopes and intends to go to Jerusalem, and though he will be taking with him the collection that, he hopes, the largely Gentile churches have raised, that may simply make matters worse. What will the Jewish traditionalists think of this battered wreck of an apostle, coming with his pagan friends and his tainted money to taunt the traditionalists in the Holy City?

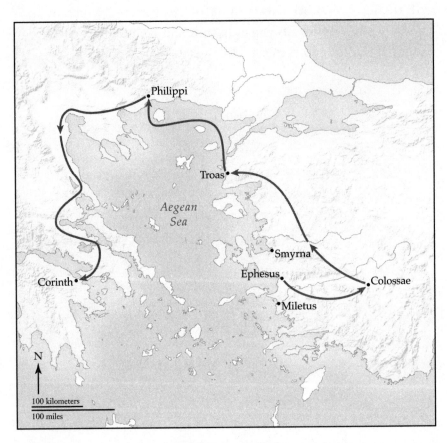

Ephesus to Corinth

12

Corinth II

THE TANGLED DIFFICULTIES into which Paul and the Corinthian church had tumbled are matched by the convoluted investigations of those researchers who have tried to figure out exactly what happened next. The second letter to Corinth is not only, as we saw earlier, quite different in style (at least for several chapters) from Paul's other letters. It is also jerkier in its overall structure, with what appear to be false starts, extra paragraphs injected into the argument, sudden resumptions of earlier themes, and not least a sudden change of mood toward the end, as it goes from the agonized and halting early chapters to a sudden combative, teasing, and upbeat conclusion. As with Galatians, we wish again and again that we could hear the other end of the telephone conversation. Since we cannot, the letter has been a magpie's nest into which all kinds of bright little theories about Paul, his opponents, his motives, and his theology have been stuffed. Every so often the extraneous collection of oddments needs to be shaken out of the nest, so that the bird can perch there again. Since this book is not the place to engage in the relevant scholarly debates, I propose to take a fresh run at the whole thing and try to maximize the sense the letter makes within the story of Paul as we have been following it.

The starting point must be the mingled sense of shock and relief when Paul was released from prison. (I date this to sometime in middle or late 56.) Imprisonment leaves a lasting scar; we today are sadly familiar with the techniques used to break the spirit of "detainees," and we should not imagine that they were all invented in the last hundred years. Paul was used by now to bodily suffering, but in Ephesus he had experienced torture at a deeper level. His emotions, his imagination, his innermost heart had been unbearably crushed. The fact that someone comes along one day, flings open the prison door, and tells you to be on your way doesn't mean you can take a deep breath, give yourself a shake, and emerge smiling into the sunlight. The memories are ever present; the voices, both outside and inside; the nightmares, ready to pounce the minute you close your eyes. The mental scars remain after the physical ones have healed.

He took those scars first, we can be sure, to Colossae. Philemon's guest room was waiting for him. Perhaps he spent some weeks there, slowly allowing the nightmares to subside. But, to be sure, his main purpose was to head for Corinth, and he was not going to risk doing what he'd done before, taking a ship straight across the Aegean. He did not want to appear suddenly at Cenchreae, the eastern port, and have the church in Corinth startled at his unheralded approach. He wanted to know, well in advance, what sort of reception he might get. Would they, after all, be loyal to him?

This involved meeting up with Titus. After the debacle of the "sorrowful visit," Paul had written the "painful letter," no doubt rebuking the church members for the way they had treated him (Was it one or two people in particular? We don't know.) and urging them toward reconciliation. Had they really suggested—he could hardly believe it, but it still rang in his ears—that if he wanted to come back, he'd better get some new references? Had they really told him that his personal presence and public speaking style were out of line with what they now wanted in a leader in an up-market city like Corinth? And had they really been so annoyed by his switching of his travel plans that they were now saying they couldn't believe a word he said?

Yes, they had said all those things—or so we infer from the letter. But the letter we call 2 Corinthians seems itself to have been dragged out of Paul in bits and pieces. It stops and starts and changes gears abruptly, and it's not hard to see why. It isn't just that Paul is writing it in bits, on the move around northern Greece in late 56 or early 57. It isn't just that any early exhilaration following his release from prison and his recovery of freedom has worn off or that the painful memories still haunt him every night. It is also that he is genuinely anxious; he still doesn't know if the "painful letter" has simply caused more trouble, or if the Corinthians have abandoned their hostility toward him and now want to be reconciled. Titus had taken the letter, but where was he?

So Paul traveled north to Troas, nearly two hundred miles, hoping against hope that he would find Titus there. The little group of disciples in the city was eager for him to stay and preach the gospel; he calls it "an open door waiting for me in the Lord."[1] But he couldn't rest. His spirit was troubled. If the nightmare from Ephesus was fading, the older one from Corinth was still there. He played it through in his head again and again, the scenes he never expected to see from the people to whom he had sent that wonderful poem about love: angry faces, raised voices, people he considered friends now looking the other way, people with whom he had once prayed and wept now either absenting themselves or telling him to his face that he was out of line, no longer required. He was desperate to know how things now stood. What would he find when he got there? And—even more troubling—what would now become of his great project, the collection for Jerusalem? The northern Greek cities would contribute, he was sure of that; but they were poor. Without a contribution from Corinth, it might look meager, a small gesture that would be scorned because of its size as well as suspect because of its source.

So he pressed on to Macedonia, to Philippi and Thessalonica. "Don't worry about anything," he had written to the Philippians not that long before.[2] That, he knows, is easier said than done; it was always a goal to be striven for, not a permanent condition of smug spirituality. Now, arriving in Philippi, he was "troubled in every way," with "battles outside and fears inside."[3]

We have a sense in these clipped, tortured remarks that we are privy to a man's inmost feelings in a way paralleled in few ancient texts. There are occasional flashes in the letters of Cicero or Seneca, perhaps, though they are written with a conscious polish and display. The urbane Marcus Aurelius projects his cool, studied Stoicism. The nearest we come might be Augustine, four hundred years later. The normal modern perception of Paul as a strident, overconfident moralist will not do. Not only is he physically and emotionally battered; *he doesn't mind if the Corinthians know it.* That, in a world where leaders were supposed to be socially respectable, exemplary characters, is exactly the point.

So once more he goes around the tracks. Moving on from Troas to Macedonia, retracing the journey he had made with such excitement just a few years before, he still cannot relax or rest. And always the nagging question: Has it, after all, been all in vain?

Then, suddenly, the clouds roll away and the sun comes out again. His beloved churches in Philippi and Thessalonica hadn't been able to comfort him. Only one thing would do that. At last, it happened:

> The God who comforts the downcast comforted us by the arrival of Titus, and not only by his arrival but in the comfort he had received from you, as he told us about your longing for us, your lamenting, and your enthusiasm for me personally.[4]

The news was good. The Corinthians were appalled to think how badly they had treated him, and they were falling over themselves to apologize. They were doing everything they could to put things right. The underlying problem had involved some actual wrongdoing (what this was, as we saw, it's impossible now to tell), and they were keen to sort it all out. Their loyalty has been contested, but it has held firm. So Paul, having been downcast beyond measure as he waited for news, is now over the top in his celebration:

> As a result, I was more inclined to celebrate; because, if
> I did make you sad by my letter, I don't regret it; and, if
> I did regret it, it was because I saw that I made you sad
> for a while by what I had written. Anyway, I'm celebrat-
> ing now, not because you were saddened, but because
> your sadness brought you to repentance. It was a sadness
> from God, you see, and it did you no harm at all on our
> account. . . .
>
> The real celebration, though, on top of all our com-
> fort, came because Titus was so overjoyed. You really
> did cheer him up and set his mind at rest. . . . I am
> celebrating the fact that I have confidence in you in
> everything.[5]

With that, he can get down to business in a very different frame of mind. The next two chapters are about the Jerusalem collection. The Macedonian churches have already sorted out their contribution, and it is remarkably substantial, considering their own suffering and poverty. Now it is Corinth's turn. Paul is sending Titus back again, with two other companions (tantaliz-ingly for us, he doesn't say who they are). They are to instruct the Corinthians to have their contributions ready, so that there will be no embarrassment when Paul arrives.

Having mentioned the varieties of writing style in 2 Corinthians, we should note—as a measure of something about Paul's personality—that chapters 8 and 9, the fund-raising section so to speak, are written in very labored and tortured Greek. I have myself done a small amount of church fund-raising, and I find it comforting that the awkwardness I have always felt in asking people for money, even for causes in which I passionately believed, appears similar to what Paul obviously felt in writing these chapters. A measure of this awkwardness is that at no point in thirty-nine verses does he mention the word "money" or anything close to it. He talks of "the grace" and "the deed," "the service," "your service in this ministry," and of course "partnership," *koinōnia*.

All of this sets the scene for us to look at the letter as a whole. As we have noticed, it moves jerkily between one theme and another. But the underlying topic is Paul's own apostolic ministry. Whatever specific problems there had been, they stemmed from the Corinthians' failure to understand what apostolic ministry really ought to be like. That failure, in turn, grew out of a shallow or inadequate view of the gospel itself. Having had his own ministry challenged at the deepest level, he addresses head on the question of what an apostle is and does. His answer focuses on the strange way in which the death of Jesus plays out in the work of the apostle. That is how the "ministry of reconciliation" will go forward, with the apostle as it were embodying the divine faithfulness, thereby demonstrating once more the way in which Paul is modeled upon the "servant" of Isaiah 49.[6]

In particular, Paul challenges any suggestion that he might need "official references" if he wanted to return to Corinth. "Look in the mirror," he says. "*You* are our official reference!" The Corinthian church, as it stands, indwelt by the spirit, is "a letter from the Messiah, with us as the messengers."[7] This shows that they are indeed people of the renewed covenant promised in scripture, and this in turn shows that Paul's apostleship was and is the real thing. Paul argues this point in chapter 3 by means of an extended comparison between Moses's hearers and Paul's own. Moses couldn't speak plainly because his hearers' hearts were hard, but Paul can and does speak plainly and boldly (to the Corinthians' obvious discomfort), because their hearts have been transformed by the spirit.

This itself is clear enough. But Paul goes on to insist that the ministry he exercises is simply the extended ministry of the crucified and exalted Lord himself:

> The god of this world has blinded the minds of unbelievers, so that they won't see the light of the gospel of the glory of the Messiah, who is God's image. We don't proclaim ourselves, you see, but Jesus the Messiah as Lord, and ourselves as your servants because of Jesus; because the God who said, "Let light shine out of darkness," has shone in our hearts, to produce the light of the knowledge of the glory of God in the face of Jesus the Messiah.[8]

We are here very close to Paul's words about Jesus in Colossians, and with the same effect: Jesus is the true Image of God, the genuine human who embodies in himself the loving purposes of God, purposes that involve the creator God himself launching his new creation, through the gospel of Jesus and the power of the spirit, in the hearts and lives of his people.

This brings Paul back to the truth that had been burned into him, painfully, over the previous months:

> We have this treasure in earthenware pots, so that the extraordinary quality of the power may belong to God, not to us. We are under all kinds of pressure, but we are not crushed completely; we are at a loss, but not at our wits' end; we are persecuted, but not abandoned; we are cast down, but not destroyed. We always carry the deadness of Jesus about in the body, so that the life of Jesus may be revealed in our body.[9]

This leads in turn to further reflections on death and life, developing things Paul had said about the resurrection in the previous letter.

One point stands out of particular interest as we continue our quest to find out what drove him on. He still expects the return of Jesus, and with it the resurrection of the dead. But whereas in 1 Corinthians he had assumed he would be among those still alive at the time,[10] *he is now facing the prospect that he may well die before it all happens.* This has been anticipated in Philippians[11] and is now built into his thinking, no doubt as part of his having "received the death sentence" in Ephesus.[12] His view of God's future has not changed. What has shifted is his view of where he might fit into that future. But, however all that will work out, the coming resurrection with all that it entails is the platform on which Paul places one of his most characteristic and central statements of what his lifelong vocation really meant. This, in his own words, is what made him the person he was:

> We must all appear before the judgment seat of the
> Messiah, so that each may receive what has been done
> through the body, whether good or bad.
>
> So we know the fear of the Lord; and that's why we
> are persuading people—but we are open to God, and
> open as well, I hope, to your consciences. We aren't trying to recommend ourselves again! We are giving you
> a chance to be proud of us, to have something to say
> to those who take pride in appearances rather than in
> people's hearts.
>
> If we are beside ourselves, you see, it's for God; and if
> we are in our right mind, it's for you. For the Messiah's
> love makes us press on. We have come to the conviction
> that one died for all, and therefore all died. And he died
> for all in order that those who live should live no longer

for themselves, but for him who died and was raised on their behalf.[13]

"The fear of the Lord" is a reverent fear; but there is also, and above all, love. A day of judgment is coming when all work will be assessed, but behind that, and motivating Paul far more deeply than anything else, was that sense of a personal love, love for him, love *through* him. The love of which he spoke in his first letter ("the son of God, who loved me and gave himself for me"). The love that he saw at work now in Corinth and Ephesus, in Philippi and Thessalonica; the love that then became a rich bond with friends and fellow workers despite all disagreements and disappointments. The love that would, after all, hold strong despite everything. In and through it all, the new covenant in Messiah and spirit means new creation:

> Thus, if anyone is in the Messiah, there is a new cre-
> ation! Old things have gone, and look—everything has
> become new! It all comes from God. He reconciled us to
> himself through the Messiah, and he gave us the minis-
> try of reconciliation.[14]

If the Corinthians had never understood what Paul was about before, they surely do now. He is not playing at being an apostle. He is not conforming his message or his methods to the social and cultural standards of any city or civilization. If people don't like what they see, that is their problem; Jews demand signs, Greeks seek wisdom, and all they get is a crucified Messiah.

Yes, *and a suffering apostle*. This is the whole point, the theme that ties together everything else in 2 Corinthians, the theme that had been etched into Paul's heart as well as his body by the last year or two even more than it had been already. Having stressed to the Corinthians that he doesn't use rhetoric and simply tells it like it is, as he was warming to his theme he must have smiled darkly at the prospect of giving them a couple of volleys of verbal pyrotechnics. Here is the first:

> We recommend ourselves as God's servants: with much patience, with sufferings, difficulties, hardships, beatings, imprisonments, riots, hard work, sleepless nights, going without food, with purity, knowledge, great-heartedness, kindness, the holy spirit, genuine love, by speaking the truth, by God's power, with weapons for God's faithful work in left and right hand alike, through glory and shame, through slander and praise; as deceivers, and yet true; as unknown, yet very well known; as dying, and look—we are alive; as punished, yet not killed; as sad, yet always celebrating; as poor, yet bringing riches to many; as having nothing, yet possessing everything.[15]

And yet there is more. Now that Titus has met him and has assured him that the Corinthians are in a penitent and eager frame of mind, he relaxes. And this enables him, in the last chapters of the letter, to address a deeper problem that seems to have lain under some of the surface noise. There are some people, whether still in Corinth or still having an influence over the Corinthians, who have been lauding themselves, claiming some kind of superiority over Paul himself. They are Jews, that much is clear. But whether they are the kind of Jews who would insist on circumcision for Gentile converts we may doubt, since Paul nowhere here deploys any of the arguments he uses in Galatians and elsewhere against that position.

From what he says it appears that they have been "boasting" of their status, their achievements, their methods, and maybe other things as well. *And they are angry because Paul refuses to dance to their tunes.* He will not play their games. He had seen that problem coming a long time before, which is why, though he has accepted financial support from the churches of Macedonia in northern Greece, he has always refused such help from Corinth itself. He said this already in 1 Corinthians 9, and now he reemphasizes it in 2 Corinthians 11.[16] This was, and is, his "boast": that he has made the gospel what it really is, "free of charge."[17] And now he is himself accused of being standoffish, of not really loving them.[18] Nobody will be able to "buy" him, to pay the piper and then call the tunes. Anyone who has had to deal with the complexities of church finances, especially in a community with wide differences of wealth, knows that the mixture of money and ministry can easily cause tension, especially where, underneath it all, there is a question of social status.

All this precipitates one of the finest and indeed funniest flights of rhetoric anywhere in the New Testament. After all the heartache earlier in the letter, in 2 Corinthians 11:16–12:10 Paul finally draws himself up to his full height.

To understand how this passage works and to get a new and sharp insight into how Paul's mind and imagination themselves seem to have worked, we have to put ourselves into the world of a Roman colony like Corinth. Roman officials, in both Rome itself and the provinces, were expected to celebrate their achievements. As they looked forward to the end of their time in office, they would hope to carve, in stone or even marble, their list of achievements, their public works projects. That is what Augustus had done, spectacularly carving his list of achievements in huge letters on monuments all around the empire. The Roman equivalent of a curriculum vitae (remember that the Corinthians wanted fresh letters of recommendation for Paul) was called the *cursus honorum,* the "course of honors." You would list your time as quaestor, your elevation to praetor. You would note the time when you had been in charge of the city waterworks or other important civic roles. Then, if you were fortunate, you would note the year when you served as consul. That remained, for most, the pinnacle of a political career, even under the empire, when everyone knew the consuls took second place to the emperor himself. Then you would note your service as proconsul, running a province. In addition, there was your army career: a list of campaigns fought, wounds, decorations received.

For a soldier there was a special honor. In the siege of a city, ladders were put up to get over the city wall. Since that was one of the most dangerous, indeed crazy, things to attempt, the first person over the wall in an attack (always supposing he survived) could claim as his prize the coveted *Corona Muralis,* the "Wall Crown." But with several ladders going up simultaneously, it was hard to be sure who made it first. You might therefore have to claim this award on oath. It was the equivalent of the British Victoria Cross, the highest honor a soldier could achieve.

That is the kind of person the Corinthians were prepared to look up to. They would have been delighted with the "celebrity culture" in some parts of today's Western church. That is what they were hoping Paul would be like, which is why they were so ashamed of his shabby presence, his awkward speaking manner, his blunt and direct teaching style. It speaks volumes for Paul as a person, for what 2 Corinthians is all about, and for what (he would have said) *the gospel* is all about, that the climax of the letter is a glorious parody of this whole world of imperial boasting, achievements, going over the wall, and everything else. *He boasts of all the wrong things.* Having warned them that he is going to be speaking like a complete fool, he launches in:

> Are they servants of the Messiah?—I'm talking like a
> raving madman—I'm a better one. I've worked harder,
> been in prison more often, been beaten more times than
> I can count, and I've often been close to death. Five
> times I've had the Jewish beating, forty lashes less one.
> Three times I was beaten with rods; once I was stoned;
> three times I was shipwrecked; I was adrift in the sea for
> a night and a day. I've been constantly traveling, facing

dangers from rivers, dangers from brigands, dangers from my own people, dangers from foreigners, dangers in the town, dangers in the countryside, dangers at sea, dangers from false believers. I've toiled and labored, I've burned the candle at both ends, I've been hungry and thirsty, I've often gone without food altogether, I've been cold and naked.

Quite apart from all that, I have this daily pressure on me, my care for all the churches. Who is weak and I'm not weak? Who is offended without me burning with shame?

If I must boast, I will boast of my weaknesses. The God and father of the Lord Jesus, who is blessed forever, knows that I'm not lying: in Damascus, King Aretas, the local ruler, was guarding the city of Damascus so that he could capture me, but I was let down in a basket through a window and over the wall, and I escaped his clutches.[19]

"So there you have it. Here is my list of achievements," he says. "Here is my curriculum vitae, my job application as an apostle! And, as the climax of it all, I declare on oath that when the going got tough, I was the first one over the wall running away." We have to hope that by this point the great majority of those listening to the letter in Corinth were at least smiling broadly. Here is a majestic piece of rhetoric in order to explain that rhetoric doesn't matter ("I am no orator as Brutus is"). Here is an upside-down boasting list, a *cursus pudorum,* if you like, a "course of shame."

Paul then continues in chapter 12 with his spiritual experiences, but he seems strangely reticent: "Someone . . . fourteen years ago . . . was snatched up to the third heaven . . . and heard . . . words . . . humans are not allowed to repeat."[20] It's the same point. Yes, obviously Paul has had extraordinary experiences, but that isn't the basis on which he stands before them as an apostle of the crucified Messiah. The main thing is that Paul, at the end of it all, received "a thorn in the flesh." Speculation has been rife. Was it an illness? A particular physical weakness? A special nagging temptation that kept coming back to bite him? A sorrowful conscience about his former violent life or his bitter public row with Barnabas? He doesn't say.

What he does say, and it's worth more than all the actual information we could have, is what he had learned through that experience and particularly, we may suppose, through the entire horrible process of the confrontation in Corinth and the breakdown in Ephesus. "My grace is enough for you," said the Lord. "My power comes to perfection in weakness."[21] Exactly what Paul needed to hear; exactly what the Corinthians did not want to hear. But hear it they must, because it comes at the end of the most powerful and personal letter Paul has written to date:

> So I will be all the more pleased to boast of my weaknesses, so that the Messiah's power may rest upon me. So I'm delighted when I'm weak, insulted, in difficulties, persecuted. and facing disasters, for the Messiah's sake. When I'm weak, you see, then I am strong.[22]

So Paul returns to Corinth at last. The Lord has given him authority, he says, not to pull down, but to build up.[23] If there is still pulling down to do, he will do it; but he has learned, as he had said to the Philippians, to be content with whatever comes. The final resolution of Paul's long and complex relationship with Corinth reveals him as a man into whom the gospel of the crucified and risen Lord has burned like a brand. He is recognizable. Corinth and Ephesus themselves have done it to him. He is marked out, beyond any question, as the representative of the crucified Messiah.

★ ★ ★

Throughout these turbulent years, something had been stirring in Paul's mind and heart. He knew his vocation, the thing for which

Jesus had called him on the Damascus Road. He had sometimes been tempted to wonder whether he had been wasting his time, but each time that thought returned, he played it through the mental loop of Isaiah 49 (the servant's question whether it was all in vain and the divine vocation that always answered that question). He carried on through heartache and collapse, but also through moments of great encouragement and celebration. He had taught, and argued, and preached, and discussed, in brief conversations and lengthy dialogues, with strangers and friends, with eager colleagues and suspicious onlookers. He had been around the tracks. He knew what he believed, how the great scriptural narratives of Abraham, Exodus, David, exile, and Messiah worked. He had expounded it a thousand times and discussed its implications and outworkings in every conceivable variation and against every possible objection. So now, as he settled down to plan and then to dictate his great letter to Rome, he was not, to put it mildly, thinking things through for the first time. Romans itself was new, but every idea it expounded had been tried, tested, and worked out in detail.

There were specific reasons for writing Romans at that moment (probably in the spring or summer of 57). We will come to those presently. But why write it *like this?* Romans is in a different category from Paul's other letters for many reasons, but particularly because of its careful and powerful structure. It comes in four sections, each of which has its own integrity, underlying argument, and inner movement. Together these four sections form a single line of thought, rising and falling but always on the way to the particular points that he wants to make. It remains an open question (at least for me) whether Paul was aware of literary models or precedents for this kind of thing. What cannot be doubted is that he had thought it through very carefully and knew exactly what he was doing. Scholars and preachers sometimes speak and write as though Paul just made things up on the fly. There may be passages like that—one thinks of some of the sharp phrases in

Galatians, for instance, which a cooler editorial eye might have struck out—but not in Romans. He has thought, prayed, and taught this material again and again. He has now decided to pour this distilled essence of his biblical and Jesus-focused teaching into these four jars and place them in a row where together they will say more than the sum of their parts.

This does not happen by accident. Romans is not like, say, 1 Corinthians (the next longest letter), where, though there is a flow of thought, one thing follows another in something more like a list. Romans has a quality of literary artistry attempted nowhere else by Paul, or, one might add, by any of his contemporaries. It should be listened to in the way one might listen to a symphony—not simply for the next big tune, but for the larger whole to which all the tunes contribute.

Some have suggested, naturally enough, that Romans was a deliberate "systematic theology," summing up the beliefs that Paul had hammered out over the previous decade of work. There is more than a grain of truth in that. But not only are there significant omissions (no mention, for instance, of the Eucharist, which we know from 1 Corinthians was a vital focus of early Christian worship), but, despite the "divisions" and "headings" in some translations, the flow of thought in the letter is not a matter of moving from one "topic" to another. It is, to say it again, a sustained and integrated argument, in which Paul comes back again and again to similar topics, but each time (to continue the musical analogy) in a different key or with different orchestration.

The letter is not simply a summary of everything Paul had been teaching. It is designed to make vital points to the church in Rome. Paul had not visited Rome, but from the greetings at the end of the letter he obviously had several friends there, and he knew quite a bit about what was going on in both the church and the wider society. All this is relevant to what he says and why.

The most obvious reason is that he now intended to round off his work in the eastern end of the Mediterranean world and to move on to the West. As I suggested earlier, I think this is a more focused ambition than simply finding more people to preach to, more "souls" to "save" (not that Paul would have put it like that). He wanted to plant the flag of the messianic gospel in key points where another "gospel" was being flaunted, namely, the "gospel" of the Roman Empire, of Caesar and all his works. Rome itself was therefore the obvious target; but out beyond that, Spain, the western edge of the world so far as Paul's contemporaries were aware, was a major center of Roman culture and influence. Paul's great contemporary Seneca had come from there. Galba, soon to enjoy a few months as emperor, had been governor there, based in the port of Tarragona, which would presumably be Paul's initial target. Tarragona boasted a large temple to Caesar. As in Ephesus or Corinth, Paul would have longed to announce that Jesus was the true *Kyrios* right under Caesar's nose. No matter what it cost.

But for this he needed a base, both, we may assume, as a source of financial and practical support and also as a community that would enter into *koinōnia* with him in prayer. And for that there had to be deep mutual understanding. They had to know who he was and what his work was all about. They might have heard all sorts of rumors about him. Some might distrust him, either because he was too Jewish or because he treated elements of Jewish practice too loosely (both accusations had been made, after all). Some kind of outline of his teaching was a basic necessity.

But that is only a start. There was a more pressing need. Something had happened in the recent past that had put the Roman Jesus-followers in a new and complex position. We recall that Claudius, who became emperor in AD 41, had banished the Jews from Rome after riots in their community. We have less information about this than we would like, but such evidence as we have suggests the late 40s as the probable time. (We should also assume that not all Jews would actually have left, only that the community would have been decimated and that any remaining Jews might have had to go to ground to hide their identity.)

Paul's friends Priscilla and Aquila were among those who had left, which was why they were there in Corinth when Paul first arrived, probably in 49. But with Claudius's death in 54 and Nero's accession to the throne, Claudius's edict was revoked. Jews could once again be, if not exactly welcome, at least permitted back in town.

I say "if not exactly welcome" because in this period, as in many other times and cultures, there was a streak, and sometimes more than a streak, of anti-Jewish sentiment in Rome. (We use the term "anti-Jewish" not "anti-Semitic," because the latter implies some kind of racial theory unknown until the nineteenth century.) Think of the charge in Philippi that Paul and Silas were Jews, teaching things it would be illegal for Romans to practice. Think of the angry whispers when Alexander, a Jew, stood up to speak in the amphitheater at Ephesus. The same thing can be sensed on the edge of remarks in poets like Juvenal or sneering historians like Tacitus.

Underneath the ethnic prejudice there was always the theological suspicion, which would then be transferred in subsequent centuries to the Christians, that Jews didn't worship the gods, so if bad things happened, people knew who to blame. Even in Corinth, Gallio's refusal to make a judgment about Paul causes the mob to beat up the synagogue president, and they get away with it. Going after the Jews was a default mode for many, right across the Roman Empire. The Romans had allowed the Jewish people to worship their own God, to raise taxes for the Temple in Jerusalem, and to be exempt from religious observances that would compromise their beliefs, including the worship of Rome and the emperor. But that didn't mean that the Romans liked them. And Paul could see, only too clearly, what that might lead to.

A century later, he was proved dramatically right. A leader called Marcion, originally from Sinope on the Black Sea shore of Asia Minor, arrived in Rome teaching a version of Christianity in which the God of Jesus was sharply distinguished from the

God of the Jews. He produced a heavily truncated edition of the New Testament, with the Jewish and scriptural bits omitted or amended. The Christian faith as he taught it—and he became very popular—left no room for Jews and their traditions. It had become a completely Gentile phenomenon.

It didn't take much imagination to see this danger coming. It had been less likely in the churches Paul had founded in Asia Minor and Greece, since he always started in the synagogue and made it clear that the message was "to the Jew first, and also, equally, to the Greek."[24] Paul had given no opportunity for any idea of a Gentile-only Jesus community. In most of the cities where he had preached, with the possible exception of a large metropolis like Ephesus, the probability is that the community of Jesus-followers was never very large, perhaps only ever a few dozen, or in Corinth conceivably a hundred or two. It would have been harder, though still not impossible, for significantly different theological positions to develop in such communities, at least to begin with. But in Rome things were different. The message of Jesus had evidently arrived there sometime in the 40s (tradition says that Peter brought it, but there is no first-century evidence for that), and Rome was in any case a city where, as in some large cities today, different cultural and ethnic groups from all over the empire would cluster in their own parts of town. It is highly likely, and this is borne out by the greetings to the different house-churches in Romans 16, that there were many different groups in Rome all worshipping Jesus *but not really in contact with one another* and almost certainly with different local customs that would owe more than a little to the culture from which they had come.

This was a new situation, and it called for a new kind of exposition. That is why, by the way, it makes no sense to see Paul's letters as successive drafts of a "systematic theology," so that, for instance, Galatians might be a first draft and Romans a final draft of essentially the same script. Galatians and Romans of course

cover similar topics up to a point. But whereas Galatians is written in haste and heat to say, *Under no circumstances must you get
circumcised and take on the Torah,* Romans is written at more leisure
and with more compositional care to say, *You must work out the
gospel-shaped balance of Jew and Greek.*

It isn't that he is "anti-law" in Galatians and "pro-law" in Romans. That kind of shallow analysis has long had its day. It is,
rather, that he can see one kind of danger in Galatia and realizes
that it must be headed off immediately. He can see another, more
long-term danger in Rome, and he decides to draw on his entire lifetime of biblical and pastoral reflection to construct a work
that ought to ward off what to him would be the utter nonsense
of a Jesus movement that was now eager to leave its Jewish and
scriptural roots behind. He knew only too well from personal
experience that Jews would regard him as a traitor, no better than
a pagan, and that pagans might regard him as one of those an-
noying Jews, with some extra irritating bits of his own. The new
wine of the gospel would be too sweet for some and too dry for
others. But he had no choice. "The Messiah's love," he had written to Corinth, "makes us press on.[25]

Paul saw, then, the danger that a new generation of Roman
Jesus-followers would have grown up, in the absence of Jews
between 49 and 54, to be proud of the fact that this new cult,
though "accidentally" having begun in the Jewish world, had
now become a completely Gentile phenomenon. The temptation
would then be for such a new generation to look at the powerful
synagogue communities in Rome, up and running again after
five years in abeyance, and to assume that the God of Jesus had
finished with the Jews once and for all. The proud and vital word
"Messiah" would just become a proper name. Worshipping Jesus
would no longer be invested with the echoes of the Psalms and
prophets, according to whom Israel's Messiah would be the Lord
of the whole world. The Jesus movement would turn itself into a
kind of private spirituality, less concerned with the kingdom of

God on earth as in heaven and more concerned with cultivating one's own spiritual interiority. It would no longer be a movement based on messianic eschatology. It would become a "religion" that saw itself as different from "the Jewish religion," a private religion that would no longer pose much of a threat to the principalities and powers, the rulers and authorities.

This is exactly what happened in the second half of the second century with the rise of so-called Gnosticism, a religion of inner self-discovery rather than of rescue, of private devotion rather than public witness. Though Marcion regarded Paul as a hero (because he misunderstood him to be saying that God had finished with the Jews and their law), Paul himself, and especially Romans, stands firmly in the way of his entire scheme.

If the Roman church was going to be tempted to think that God had now cut off the Jewish people for good—and it might not only be Gentile Christians who thought that; perhaps some Jewish Christians, fed up with their recalcitrant unbelieving fellow Jews, might go that route as well—then there would be an equal problem among the different house-churches in Rome itself. The high probability is that Romans 14 and 15, where Paul addresses the question of different practices within different Christian circles, was addressed specifically to small groups that had become settled in their ways, whether it had to do with dietary laws (or the decision not to observe them) or Sabbaths and other holy days (and the question of whether they mattered anymore).

This question is obviously cognate with the question Paul faced in 1 Corinthians 8–10, but it is not exactly the same. There is no suggestion in 1 Corinthians that Paul was there dealing with separate groups worshipping in different locations, in different house-churches. He was addressing Jesus-followers holding different opinions, but all belonging to the one church in Corinth; in this situation differences of practice might have an immediate impact on the unity and fellowship of that church. In Rome it was different. The groups were already separate. They had already developed different codes of practice. They would now regard one another with suspicion. They would not be able to worship together. They probably used different songs; they might well speak Greek with very different accents, reflecting their countries of origin. (Latin was the elite language; a good many inhabitants of Rome at this time were basically Greek-speaking.)

Paul, coming to Rome for the first time but hoping to use it as a base for mission farther west, could not build on a foundation like that. He could not simply align himself with one or two of the Roman house-churches and ignore the rest. The unity he so passionately advocated was not just a pleasant ideal. It was vital for the coherence of his own mission. It was also, as he had said in Ephesians, the way in which God's wisdom in all its rich variety would be made known to the rulers and authorities in the heavenly places. If Caesar and the dark powers that stood behind him were to be confronted with the "good news" that there was "another king, Jesus," the community that was living by that message had to be united. This would of course be a differentiated unity ("God's wisdom in all its rich variety"; and we may compare the vivid lists of ministries in 1 Cor. 12 and Eph. 4). But if it was all differentiation and no unity, Caesar need take no notice; they were just a few more peculiar eastern cults come to town.

The underlying message of Romans, with these sharp-edged issues as key notes to be struck at some of the letter's climactic points, is of course the lordship of Jesus as Israel's Messiah and hence the world's rightful sovereign. The grand formal introduction to the letter makes it clear: the resurrection of the crucified Jesus had demonstrated him to be Messiah, "son of God," and the messianic psalms, particularly Psalm 2, challenged the kings of the world to come humbly before him and learn wisdom. From the time of Augustus onward, the Caesars had let it be known that events of their rule, including their accession, their birthday, and so on, were matters of "good news," *euangelia* in Greek, since with Caesar as *Kyrios*

("Lord") and *Sōtēr* ("Savior") a new golden age had arrived in the world, an age particularly characterized by *dikaiosynē* ("justice"), *sōtēria* ("salvation"), and *eirēnē* ("peace"). Caesar's all-conquering power (*dynamis*) had achieved these and would maintain them. The appropriate response from his subjects was "loyalty" or "faithfulness" (*pistis*), "believing obedience," you might say.

Paul's *euangelion* used the same terms, but meant something quite different. The differences were marked not least in poems like Philippians 2:6–11 and in Paul's own embracing of the *cursus pudorum,* the "course of shame," over against the Roman *cursus honorum,* "course of honor." It was never a simple matter of a single scale with Caesar at the wrong end and Jesus at the right end. That would pull Jesus down to Caesar's level, which could itself be a disastrous mistake if the church, in Rome or elsewhere, thought that allegiance to Jesus meant disobeying, on principle, the divinely appointed civil ruler. That would itself be a paganization of the essentially Jewish monotheistic vision of earthly rulers articulated by Jesus, Paul, and Peter.[26] This didn't mean, of course, that earthly rulers could do no wrong. Far from it. Paul, as usual, is resisting shallow and simplistic reductions. Instead, the main theological argument of the letter is framed by an introduction and conclusion that look Caesar in the face and declare that Jesus is not only the true Lord, but also a different *kind* of Lord:

> Paul, a slave of King Jesus, called to be an apostle, set apart for God's good news, which he promised beforehand through his prophets in the sacred writings—the good news about his son, who was descended from David's seed in terms of flesh, and who was marked out powerfully as God's son in terms of the spirit of holiness by the resurrection of the dead: Jesus, the king, our Lord!

Through him we have received grace and apostleship
to bring about believing obedience among all the nations
for the sake of his name. That includes you too who are
called by Jesus the king. . . .

I'm not ashamed of the good news; it's God's power,
bringing salvation to everyone who believes—to the
Jew first, and also, equally, to the Greek. This is because
God's covenant justice is unveiled in it, from faithfulness
to faithfulness.[27]

Here we have it all—David's true son, marked out as such by the
resurrection and hence exalted as Lord over all human authorities, inaugurating a reign of true justice and salvation for all who
would be loyal.

So too at the close of the great argument:

The Messiah became a servant of the circumcised people
in order to demonstrate the truthfulness of God—that is,
to confirm the promises to the patriarchs, and to bring
the nations to praise God for his mercy. As the Bible
says:

That is why I will praise you among the nations,
and will sing to your name.

And again it says,

Rejoice, you nations, with his people.

And again,

Praise the Lord, all nations,
And let all the peoples sing his praise.

And Isaiah says once more:

There shall be the root of Jesse,
The one who rises up to rule the nations;
The nations shall hope in him.[28]

It is noticeable that this final peroration is introduced with the clear imperative to the Roman house-churches: "Welcome one another, therefore, as the Messiah has welcomed you, to God's glory."[29] The unity of the Messiah's people across traditional divisions is part of the vital way in which the followers of Jesus will be a sign of his worldwide rule, already inaugurated. The "root of Jesse" (David's true heir, in other words) is the one *who rises to rule the nations.* The resurrection of Jesus is the foundation of a genuinely Pauline political and social theology—as well as of everything else that Paul believed about him.

Romans, then, is a many-sided letter, but with a single line of thought. It would be silly to try to give an adequate summary of it in a book like the present one. Those who want to do business with Paul the man, Paul the thinker, Paul the pastor and preacher will sooner or later want to sit down and try to figure it all out for themselves. Reading it straight through at a sitting, perhaps often, is something few modern readers attempt, though it is of course how it would first have been heard, when Phoebe from Cenchreae, having been entrusted with it by Paul, read it out loud in the congregations in Rome. She probably expounded it too, answering the questions that would naturally arise. It would then have been copied and read again and again, normally straight through. We may then assume that it was studied in shorter sections by some at least, particularly the teachers, in the Roman congregations, and indeed in the other churches to which copies would have been sent (we have early evidence of a copy in Ephesus from which the long list of greetings to Rome was omitted).

That discipline, of reading straight through and then studying section by section, all bathed in the praying and worshipping life of the community, remains essential to this day.

But something at least must be said as a start. *God has done what he always said he would,* Paul is saying, *and this is what that means today.* The gospel events—the crucifixion and resurrection of Jesus and the gift of the spirit—have burst upon an unready world, and also upon a Jewish world that was looking the other way. But God has thereby unveiled his faithfulness to the covenant, the covenant with Abraham and Israel through which he always purposed to put the whole creation right at last. God's creation has been spoiled by human idolatry and sin, and even his chosen people have appeared unable to do anything about it. But now (that's one of Paul's favorite phrases, for example, in Romans 3:21) God has revealed that what his covenant purposes had always involved was the "putting forth" of Jesus the Messiah as the means of establishing a new reality, a single family whose sins are forgiven, a Jew-plus-Gentile covenant family, as he always promised to Abraham. That is the thrust of the first part, chapters 1–4.

Here at last Paul pulls out that saying that he knew from the traditions of "zeal" studied in his boyhood. Phinehas killed the idolatrous man, *and it was reckoned to him as righteousness;* in other words, God established a covenant with him. Maybe so, Paul now thinks, but according to Genesis 15:6 Abraham believed God—believed, that is, the promise that he would be the father of an uncountable family that would inherit the whole world—*and it was reckoned to him as righteousness.* This faith, this trust, this loyalty was Abraham's covenant badge. A covenant, Paul saw, to which the One God had been faithful in the events of Jesus's crucifixion and resurrection. A covenant in which all who believed in "the one who raised from the dead Jesus our Lord" were now full members.

Now, therefore, the loyal faith by which a Jew or Gentile reaches out to grasp the promise, believing "in the God who raises the dead," would be the one and only badge of membership in Abraham's family. The family could not be created either by circumcision (which was added later than Gen. 15) or by following the law (which was added hundreds of years afterward). It could only be by a fresh act of God's grace, received by faith. The use of Romans 1–4 in popular teaching today to declare universal human sinfulness and "justification" by grace alone and through faith alone is fine as far as it goes. Sadly, it routinely shrinks what Paul is actually saying in these chapters and fails to see that they are only one part of a larger argument and do not make full sense without the material that then follows. Romans is not written to explain how people may be saved. It describes that, to be sure, vividly and compellingly, but it does so in order to highlight the faithfulness of God and, with that, the challenges facing the covenant people. Those were the themes the Roman church urgently needed to understand.

What was the point, after all, of being part of Abraham's family? Simply this (as Paul had expounded it in one synagogue after another across Turkey and Greece): according to Genesis itself and to many subsequent Jewish traditions, the call of Abraham was the divine answer to the sin of Adam. What we have in Abraham is therefore the promise that God will deal once and for all with sin and with the death that it brings in its wake. That is how the first four chapters of Romans work. And with that Paul has a natural transition to the second main section of the letter, chapters 5–8.

This time he tells more explicitly the story of the human race from Adam to the Messiah and on to the final promise of renewed creation. These chapters offer an astonishingly rich and multilayered account of the new Exodus, which was such a strong theme in early Christianity. The whole section is carefully structured in paragraphs almost all of which lead back to Jesus the Messiah. After the basic statement of "from Adam to the Messiah" in 5:12–21, Paul retells the Exodus narrative. Coming through the waters of baptism (chapter 6) is like going through the Red

Sea, leaving behind slavery and discovering freedom. But then Israel arrives at Mt. Sinai and is given the Torah—which promptly declares that Israel has already transgressed. Indeed, as Deuteronomy made clear, the Torah simply brought Israel to the place of exile, of a new kind of slavery. The lament at the close of chapter 7 is the lament, seen with gospel hindsight, of "the Jew" who rightly celebrates the Torah and longs to be loyal to it, but finds that loyalty thwarted by the dark Adamic strain that runs through all humans, Jews included.

This is the complex problem—Adam's problem, if you like, magnified enormously in the rebellion of God's own people—to which Romans 8 is the matchless answer. The death of the Messiah and the gift of the spirit together do "what the law was incapable of doing,"[30] that is, giving the life the law promised but could not bring about because of human (and Israelite) sin. Throughout chapter 8, Paul hints at a key theme from Exodus and from early Christianity as a whole: as the glorious divine presence guided the children of Israel through the wilderness, coming to dwell in the Tabernacle,[31] so the spirit leads the Messiah's people to their inheritance, which turns out to be not a single "promised land," but the entire renewed creation.[32]

Because the whole renewed creation is the "inheritance" of the Messiah and his people, as in Psalm 2, this means that human beings are at last, as in Psalm 8, "crowned with glory and honor" and given the authority over creation that had been promised originally. As throughout Paul's thought, and especially in 2 Corinthians, written so recently before Romans, the highly paradoxical mode of this "glory" is in fact suffering and the prayer that is wrenched from that suffering in "groanings too deep for words."[33] But in all these things, he concludes triumphantly, "we are completely victorious through the one who loved us."[34] That is the point to which he always returns when speaking from his deepest heart and mind: "the son of God, who loved me and gave himself for me"; "the Messiah's love makes us press on." Now nothing in all creation "will be able to separate us from the love of God in King Jesus our Lord."[35] God's covenant was always the bond of love and the promise of that love having its full effect. Now, in the Messiah and by the spirit, that covenant love is seen to be victorious. Romans 8 is the richest, deepest, and most powerfully sustained climax anywhere in the literature of the early Christian movement, and perhaps anywhere else as well.

Romans 5–8 (and indeed Romans 1–8) have often been allowed to stand by themselves as though they constituted "the gospel" and the rest of the letter was a mere succession of appendixes or "practical applications." It is true that one can take these first two sections, perhaps especially 5–8, and let them have their own impact. Perhaps it is even good to do that from time to time to be sure that their full flavor has been realized. But if we are to understand Paul at this moment in his career, at an exciting but fateful transition, we are bound to conclude that, though these two opening sections have their own integrity, they are in fact designed as the foundations for a building of a very different sort. Romans 9–11 and 12–16 are part of Paul's direct appeal to his Roman audience, or, as we should presumably say, audiences. Knowing that this was where he was going has colored and shaped chapters 1–4 and 5–8 as well. Unless we see the ultimate goal, we will not fully appreciate those sections for what they truly are.

Romans 9–11, the third and in many ways decisive section of the letter, is one of the most careful and sustained arguments anywhere in Paul's letters. People sometimes talk as if, in this passage, Paul is just winging it, blundering ahead in the dark and trying out ideas, only then to modify or reject them and propose something else instead. Nothing could be farther from the truth. For a start, the section is carefully framed, in classic Jewish fashion, in prayer. Like many psalms, it opens with lament and closes with ringing praise. The long opening section (9:6–29) is matched by the long closing section (11:1–32); in between, the heart of the argument is found in 9:30–10:21, which itself focuses on a text that was vital throughout the Second Temple period, namely, the closing chapters of Deuteronomy, coming at the point where Paul has just finished the story of Israel as set out in the Torah. The Five Books of Moses, in fact, telling Israel's story from Abraham to the warning of exile and the promise of restoration, remain the gold standard. Paul retells that story, just as many Jewish writers of his time had done and were to do again. At the vital point he insists, as he had done in synagogues from Antioch to Corinth, that the goal of the Torah, the aim and ultimate purpose of the whole great narrative, was the Messiah. *Telos gar nomou Christos*, "The Messiah is the goal of the law,"[36] so that covenant membership may be available for all who believe.

This, then, is Israel's story, the story of God's covenant faithfulness to Israel, with Israel's Messiah as its climax. *It is not, and never can be, a story cut loose from the story of Israel*, as Marcion would argue later on and as perhaps some in Rome were already supposing. Paul wants them to know of his "great sorrow and endless pain,"[37] not now the anguish he suffered in Ephesus, but a more long-lasting torture of the heart, which started with the looks of rejection when he returned home to Tarsus for those ten silent years, continued as interest turned to anger in one synagogue after another, and climaxed in plots and violence from the very people who, he might have thought, ought to welcome their Messiah now that Paul had explained so clearly the scriptural basis for understanding the events concerning Jesus. (Paul was not alone in this sad reflection: "He came to what was his own," John wrote of Jesus, "and his own people did not accept him.")[38] That is the substance of Paul's lament, as also of the prayer "for their salvation."[39] And the way to that is stated in the clearest terms at the very center of this section: "If you profess with your mouth that Jesus is Lord, and believe in your heart that God raised him from the dead, you will be saved."[40]

Jesus, then, had not started a "new religion," and Paul was not offering one. Either Jesus was Israel's Messiah—which means, as any first-century Jew would know, that God was reconstituting "Israel" around him—or he was an imposter and his followers were blaspheming. There was no middle ground. And it was because of this Jewish, scripturally based vision of covenant fulfilled, of messianic reality come to birth, that there was such a thing as apostleship; in other words, Paul is saying to the church in Rome, "This is why I do what I do, and why I want you to back me as I do it all the way to Spain." How are the nations to call on the Messiah without believing in him? How are they to believe if they don't hear? "And how will they hear without someone announcing it to them? And how will people make that announcement unless they are sent?"[41] Paul once again links his vocation to the "servant" passages in Isaiah and then pans back to show from the Psalms, Isaiah, and Deuteronomy (Writings, Prophets, and Torah) that *God has done what he always said he would,* however shocking and unexpected it now appears. And this brings us, he implies, to where we are today.

Romans 11 then forms a sustained argument of its own, thinking forward into this new and unprecedented moment in the story of God and Israel. Paul here, we remember, is writing to head off any suggestion in the Roman church that it's now time for the followers of Jesus to cut loose from their Jewish context and see themselves as simply a Gentile community. We who know the equivalent diabolical forces in Europe in the nineteenth and twentieth centuries can readily imagine how easily this might fit in with the social and cultural pressures in Rome. Paul will have none of it. He himself is a Jew; there is a remnant, marked out by grace and faith, and he is a representative of this group. But if that remnant is what it is by grace and faith rather than national privilege then, instead of shrinking to nothing, such a remnant can and will grow. "If they do not remain in unbelief, they will be grafted back in."[42] (We should note that "unbelief" here is more or less a technical term for "not recognizing Jesus as Israel's Messiah"; Paul is well aware that the Jews of whom he speaks have a strong faith in and zeal for the One God, as he himself had had.)[43]

People have probed Romans 11 for specific promises about what it would mean for Jews to abandon this "unbelief," in other words, when and how they might come to see Jesus as Messiah. Popular myths abound, some even suggesting that Romans 11 predicts the return of Jewish people to their ancestral homeland (which at the time of his writing they had not left). That is not the point. Paul is not trying to second-guess what God has in mind. He is saying, as strongly as he can, to a church in danger of Marcionism, of rejecting its Jewish heritage: "Don't boast over the branches,"[44] the branches that have been broken off from the original olive tree because of unbelief. God can graft them back again. What is more, the present fate of unbelieving Israel is itself the long outworking, as though in a shadow, of the messianic vocation itself:

> By their trespass, salvation has come to the nations, in
> order to make them jealous. If their trespass means riches
> for the world, and their impoverishment means riches for
> the nations, how much more will their fullness mean?
>   Now I am speaking to you Gentiles. Insofar as I am
> the apostle of the Gentiles, I celebrate my particular
> ministry, so that, if possible, I can make my "flesh" jeal-
> ous, and save some of them. If their casting away, you
> see, means reconciliation for the world, what will their
> acceptance mean but life from the dead?[45]

I do not think that Paul is here attempting, as it were, to tie God's hands. He is not saying what exactly will happen or when. He is not even saying, "You in Rome must evangelize your lo-cal synagogue members"—though his opening statement in the letter, that the gospel is "for the Jew first, and also, equally, for the Greek," presumably means that when he arrives in Rome, he intends to follow his usual pattern and that, assuming there are Jewish communities in Spain, he will do so there as well. He is saying that Jews are always to be part of God's faithful family and that God can and will bring "some of them" to that faith.[46] But the point, as throughout Romans, is the faithfulness of God. God has been loyal to what he had promised. The messianic pattern now etched into history shows that "God has shut up all people in disobedience, so that he may have mercy upon all."[47] If the Roman church can hold on to that, they will be able to live with the true messianic mystery.

The final section of Romans, chapters 12–16, opens with broad general instructions about communal and individual life for the church, starting with a theme we know to be dear to Paul's heart: Paul wants them to learn to worship the true God with their whole selves and to that end learn to *think* as people who live in the new world. "Be transformed by the renewing of your minds, so that you can work out what God's will is, what is good, acceptable, and complete."[48] As so often in Paul, the general exhortations home in finally on love, balanced by the bracing ethic, consistent across all Paul's writings, of living *now* in the light of the day that *has* already dawned and *will* one day dawn completely.[49] Framed within that is the short but important reminder of the normal Jewish view of civic authorities.[50] A robust monotheism knows that the Creator wants there to be such authorities, and they are themselves responsible, whether they know it or not, to God himself. The gospel does not sanction the apolitical spirituality of *gnosis,* nor does it sanction the one-dimensional revolution for which many of Paul's countrymen were even then preparing. He does not want the Jesus movement to be confused with the zealotry of Jerusalem. That shallow "loyalty," to say it again, was "not based on knowledge."[51] The Christians in Rome had to grow up in their thinking beyond those disastrous reductionisms.

This paves the way for the central point of the final section, which is Paul's appeal for unity within the scattered and quite possibly mutually suspicious churches in Rome. It is noticeable that right up to the end of this section (14:1–15:13) he does not mention the underlying problem: that some of the house-churches are Jewish and some are Gentile. (Of course, things may well have been more complicated than that. Some of the Gentile Christians may, like some in Galatia, have been eager to take on the Jewish Torah; some of the Jewish Christians may, like Paul himself, have embraced what he calls the "strong" position.) But Paul will not address the questions in those terms. "Some of us prefer to do this . . . some of us prefer to do that," he says.

He wants the members of the Roman churches to respect one another across these differences. (We note, to ward off a very different problem in today's contemporary Western churches, that this supposed "tolerance" does not extend to all areas of behavior, as the closing lines of chapter 13 and the equivalent sections of other letters make abundantly clear.) And, once again, he reminds them they are living out the pattern of the Messiah. The death and resurrection of Jesus is, for Paul, not simply a historical reality that has created a new situation, but a pattern that must be woven into every aspect of church life. For Paul, what matters is the life of praise and worship that now, in the spirit, couples Jesus with God the father himself. This is the worship that, when united across traditional barriers, will shake Caesar's ideology to its foundations:

> Whatever was written ahead of time, you see, was written for us to learn from, so that through patience, and through the encouragement of the Bible, we might have hope. May the God of patience and encouragement grant you to come to a common mind among yourselves, in accordance with the Messiah, Jesus, so that, with one

mind and one mouth, you may glorify the God and father of our Lord Jesus the Messiah.[52]

The letter closes with travel plans, reflecting on Paul's mission across the eastern Mediterranean lands. "From Jerusalem around as far as Illyricum," he says;[53] Illyricum, northwest of Thessalonica, is not mentioned in Acts or even hinted at elsewhere in his letters, though Acts says more generally "he went through those regions,"[54] which might easily include northwest Greece. Central to those travel plans is the journey he is about to take to Jerusalem, bringing the collection. He asks the Roman Jesus-followers to pray for safety and that his "service for Jerusalem may be welcomed gladly by God's people."[55] A hint, in other words, of new anxieties just around the corner.

Phoebe, then, will travel west with the letter, while he will travel east with the money. He greets around thirty people in Rome—covering the bases, we may suppose, of all the different house-churches—and sends greetings from eight friends, including "Erastus the city treasurer" and "I, Tertius, the scribe for this letter."[56] We may detect a sigh of relief from Tertius, for whom the previous hours would have been demanding in more ways than one.

There is a final warning against people who cause division and problems and then a closing benediction,[57] which goes on and on a bit like the end of a Beethoven symphony. At last the letter is done. It is one of the most ecstatic and exhilarating, dense and difficult, intellectually and spiritually challenging, and rewarding writings from any period of church history and, some might argue, from anybody else's history as well.

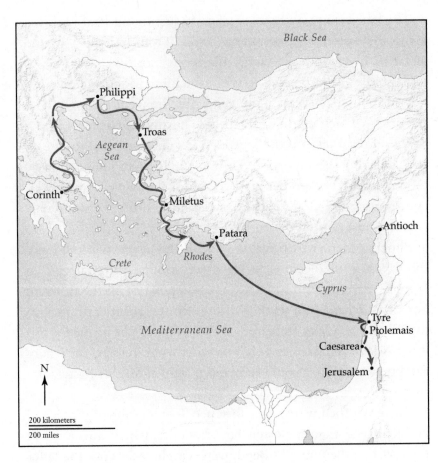

Corinth to Jerusalem

13

Jerusalem Again

NOW AT LAST it was time for Paul to set off to Jerusalem with the money. This great collection project, so long in the planning, drew together two of his guiding passions, two strands of hope and ambition that had been central since at least the late 40s. First, "Remember the poor"! Second, "There is no longer Jew or Greek . . . in the Messiah, Jesus."[1] Paul had set out the rationale for this project, complex and dangerous as it must have been, in 2 Corinthians 8–9 and Romans 15. Generosity was itself one of the hallmarks of following Jesus, not least because the entire drama of the gospel involved the ultimate generosity of Jesus himself:

> You know the grace of our Lord, King Jesus: he was
> rich, but because of you he became poor, so that by his
> poverty you might become rich.[2]

One single sentence gives us Paul's entire vision of Jesus, as in Philippians 2 and Colossians 1, shaped as an exhortation to act with "enthusiasm and love" and serving the vital purpose of unity across the greatest of traditional divides:

> If the nations have shared in the Jews' spiritual blessings,
> it is right and proper that they should minister to their
> earthly needs.[3]

In other words, the collection was designed to remind the (largely) Gentile churches of their deep and lasting obligation to the Jewish people in general and the Jerusalem church in particular. And it was designed to communicate to the Jerusalem church, and perhaps to a wider Jewish audience, the fact that the Gentile churches did not see themselves as a "new religion" and had no intention of cutting loose and creating a different kind of community. They were *part of the same family* and as such were doing what "family" always did—helping one another out as need arose.

Some have suggested yet another motive. According to this view, in Romans 11 Paul was hinting that one day a large number of presently unbelieving Jews would turn to the Messiah and that this event would precipitate the final day, the coming *parousia* of Jesus himself, the resurrection of the dead, the rescue of the old creation from its slavery to decay, the joining into one, in the Messiah, of heaven and earth themselves. "What will their acceptance mean," he had written, "but life from the dead?"[4] Paul did indeed hope for all these things. Did he link them to the collection?

Almost certainly not. He did not say in Romans 15, "I am going to Jerusalem with the collection, so please pray that they will welcome it, so that a great many presently unbelieving Jews will turn to Jesus as Messiah and that Jesus will then return." He asked them to pray simply that he would be delivered from the unbelievers and that the Jerusalem church would welcome what he had done. In any case, he was planning, as soon as he could, to go on to Rome and then Spain. Though we may be sure that all Paul's plans carried the footnote "If the Lord wills" and that all his assessments of God's purposes had the word "maybe" or "perhaps" attached to them, as in Philemon 15, it seems unlikely that he would be thinking that God really wanted him simultaneously to go to Rome and then on to Spain *and* to give money to Jerusalem so that the *parousia* could happen at last. In fact, not only is it very dubious to suggest that he was proposing in Romans 11 a large-scale Jewish conversion that would precipitate the Lord's return, but the suggested link with the collection is one that Paul never made and, granted his other plans, would certainly not have made.

Paul was not the only Jew to collect money for Jerusalem from diaspora communities. The Jewish Temple tax, designed to support the work of the Jerusalem Temple itself, was levied on Jewish communities around the world. The rate was set at two drachmas for every adult male. This was not only a practical necessity for the maintenance of a huge building and its regular round of worship. It meant that even those who could not themselves go to Jerusalem to worship were nevertheless joining in with Temple worship at one remove. There is evidence that under Rome the civic officials took some care for the safe delivery of the money, and pilgrims heading for Jerusalem regularly traveled in sizable groups.[5] Without that, a well-known annual shipment of money would be an obvious target for highway robbery or indeed embezzlement.

Those were problems of which Paul was obviously well aware, but before we address that it is interesting to ask whether he saw his collection as in any sense a Jesus-shaped version of the Jewish tax. He cannot have been unaware of the parallel. Granted that the Jerusalem leaders were known as the "pillars"—however much Paul might raise an eyebrow at the thought!—he must have realized that sending money to support the Jerusalem church was, in a sense, helping to keep the "new Temple" standing. But if he made anything more of this, we do not pick it up in his letters.

More to the point is his careful organization of a group to take responsibility for the money and its safe delivery. We saw earlier the problem when one person was entrusted with delivering money;

in that case, Epaphroditus brought the Philippians' gift to Paul in Ephesus and then was prevented by illness from returning at the expected time, arousing suspicions. So Paul assured the Corinthians, early on in his planning, that he would write formal letters to accompany the people they approved to send to Jerusalem with their gift. At this time, it wasn't clear whether he would himself go with them.[6] By the time he wrote 2 Corinthians, he saw even more clearly the need for complete transparency at every stage of the project. Titus and the unnamed companion would be assisting in the work, Paul said, "both for the Lord's own glory and to show our own good faith," because "we are trying to avoid the possibility that anyone would make unpleasant accusations about this splendid gift which we are administering."[7] Everybody knows today, and everybody knew then, that money is sticky; people who touch it tend to come away with some of it on their hands. Not only must that not happen; it must be seen not to have happened.

Paul had originally intended to sail directly to Syria.[8] That might have made transporting the money a lot easier. But he became aware of a plot against him and decided instead to go by land once more, around northern Greece. By the time they set off (probably in late summer 57), the party had grown. Northern Greece was represented by Sopater (perhaps the Sosipater of Rom. 16:21) from Beroea and by Aristarchus and Secundus from Thessalonica. The churches of Galatia were represented by Gaius from Derbe. Asia, in other words Ephesus and the surrounding country, was represented by Timothy, Tychicus (Paul's messenger to Colossae and Laodicea a year or so earlier), and Trophimus. Aristarchus had been with Paul during his Ephesian imprisonment.[9] Timothy was of course originally from Lystra in Galatia, but he had by this time worked consistently in Ephesus and was able to be regarded as a representative of Asia. We assume, from the "we" in Acts at this point, that Luke was in the party at least from Philippi; perhaps, since nobody else from that important church is mentioned in the list,[10] he is taking that role. We are surprised too that, despite 1 Corinthians 16, there was no official representative from southern Greece. Perhaps they knew some of these men well enough to trust them. The point of having such a sizable group is obvious. Not only would there have been comparative safety in numbers; these seven would have been able to report back to their respective churches that the money had been delivered safely.

But how did they transport it? This is a difficult question. There was no unified banking system in his day that would have allowed Paul and his friends to deposit a large sum in Corinth or Ephesus or elsewhere and then to draw out an equivalent sum in Caesarea or Jerusalem. That might have been possible in Egypt, where a network of royal or state banks had developed branches in local areas. Similar systems were in place in parts of Italy. But even had there been an integrated international system within the larger Roman Empire, banking involved deposits, loans, and credit, not long-distance credit transfers. So how was it done? How did they take the money?

Even supposing that Roman officials, as Josephus suggests, did keep an eye out for the annual transportation of the Temple tax, Paul could hardly rely on them to do the same for his project. If all the money collected were put into large chests or bags—always assuming it could be carried, perhaps on mules—it would be an obvious target in every port, at every wayside inn, on every lonely stretch of road. By traveling as a group (and perhaps recruiting extra traveling companions from the local areas through which they were passing to help guard them for that stretch of the journey) they may have felt sufficiently secure. On board ship, travelers had to sleep on deck and provide their own food, so we may assume that the whole company would form and maintain a tight group. It is possible that friends converted the money into a comparatively small number of high-value coins or bars of gold or silver, which could then be carried less obviously. One way or another, this was a dangerous undertaking even allowing for the normal hazards of ancient travel. They must have been glad when they eventually arrived in Jerusalem, though that is another story to which we must return.

★ ★ ★

The journey was notable for two particular moments. The first is the famous scene, a kind of tragicomedy, that took place when the group had reached Troas. On the eve of their departure for Assos on the next leg of their journey, Paul was speaking at a crowded meeting. He went on and on, later and later into the night, and a young man named Eutychus was sitting by an upstairs window in a warm room . . .

This anecdote was presumably intended to remind Luke's readers of Paul's healing powers, but in its sharp depiction of an otherwise unlikely scene it keeps us on track in our view of Paul himself. He had, we remember, just written Romans, itself a highly compressed account of things he could have spelled out at much more length. We can well imagine his walking through the arguments again: Adam, Abraham, Exodus, David, exile, Isaiah, the Psalms, the Messiah—with the shocking break in the story at this point: nobody expected the Messiah to be crucified and raised from the dead! Then he would go on to the promise of the worldwide inheritance and the bodily resurrection in the ulti- mate new creation; to the need for Jesus's followers to be united, to renounce idols and sexual immorality; to the ways in which Jewish law was both utterly fulfilled and utterly transcended in Jesus and the spirit. And more, and more. Questions would fly to and fro, with his answers ranging across scripture, story, and missionary anecdotes. We can imagine interruptions, discussion, and the vivid debating style he had used in parts of Romans itself ("What shall we say, then?" "But supposing . . ." "Or does God only belong to the Jews?" and so on.) We can imagine the company pausing for prayer, to sing a hymn, or to allow someone to look up one of the scriptural passages Paul had been quoting from memory and read it out loud again for the benefit of the larger group. And then Paul starts up once more . . .

And Eutychus, the young man by the window, is overcome with sleep as Paul goes on and on. He falls out of the window, crashes to the ground below, and appears to be dead. Paul rushes downstairs, stoops over the young man, and picks him up, reviving him. They break bread and eat together. He then carries on with his discourse until dawn, almost as if nothing had happened.[11] Then it is time to go. Some of Luke's readers, pondering this passage, might imagine Paul as a second Socrates, discussing philosophy all night and then going about his normal business.[12]

The second significant moment on the journey came when the party landed at Miletus, south of Ephesus. (Like Ephesus itself, Miletus is now some distance from the sea; the mouths of their respective rivers have silted up over time.) As we saw, Luke explains Paul's decision to bypass Ephesus itself on the grounds that he was eager to be in Jerusalem in time for Pentecost. That may well have been part of the motive, but I think it equally likely that Paul was anxious not be drawn into a difficult or dangerous situation, and that he may also have been concerned about bringing his small party, guarding a substantial sum of money, into a bustling city. These potential dangers are, indeed, reflected in the address he then gave to the elders of the church who had come from Ephesus to meet him. The distance would have been around thirty miles as the crow flies, but longer by road, perhaps two or even three days' journey in each direction.

The speech that Luke ascribes to Paul on this occasion, like the very different address on the Areopagus in Athens, would take less than three minutes to deliver. As with that occasion, we must assume that Paul would have spoken for a good deal longer. If the elders were taking the best part of a week to travel to Miletus and back again, they and Paul would probably have wanted to take at least a full day to talk. This would have included Paul saying the sort of things we find here, only at much more length.

Paul is saying farewell, and the speech has the flavor of a final testament. He is still hoping and praying that he will make it to Rome and then to Spain. But as he contemplates the trip to Jerusalem, he has a strong suspicion, which he takes to be given by the spirit, that he ought to be preparing for trouble in some form or other. It was therefore appropriate to look back at his own work in Ephesus and to look forward to what might now be facing the church there. No doubt Luke, wanting to present a rounded picture of Paul's work, had his own reasons for giving this speech such space. But from it all we get a vivid portrait of Paul at work.

We see in particular Paul the pastor, out and about, visiting the homes of Jesus-followers as well as teaching in public. He remembers the suffering brought upon him because of the plots of the local Jewish community, and he refers to the same torments that had caused him to despair in those dreadful months a year or more earlier. But his message, as ever, is the same, the Jewish message reshaped around Jesus: people should turn from idols and serve the living God now made known in Jesus. That message has not changed from his early days, and it was still what a great pagan city needed to hear. He has been sensitive, ever since the Galatian crisis, to the possible charge that he might have trimmed the message down, might have given them only part of the truth and not the whole thing. No, he says, on that score he is blameless. He had not shrunk from declaring and explaining to them the entire divine plan.

After working our way through the main letters, seeing the way Paul relished laying it all out, making the connections between different biblical themes and tying them all together with Jesus and the spirit, we may find any suggestion that he would be omitting bits and pieces faintly ridiculous. One might as well accuse Gustav Mahler of making his symphonies too short. But it wasn't just a matter of Paul enjoying the big picture and the little details. The way he puts it implies that holding anything back would make him guilty of jeopardizing people's salvation. He was innocent; he had told them the whole story. And, like a refrain, he reminds them of his tireless labors among them and of the way in which he worked with his own hands to support his preaching and teaching. They had had plenty of time to observe him, night and day, and they would know that he had earned his own keep and had not been angling for special treats or favors.

But Paul wasn't simply reflecting on his own time in Ephesus. He was also warning the elders about what might be waiting for them just around the corner. He had, he says, often warned them with tears about the dangers all around them, and now he could see those dangers looming all the larger. The world of idolatry and immorality was powerful and insidious, and there were many, including perhaps some who had once professed Christian faith, who were being drawn into it. It had happened in Corinth, and it would happen again in various places. Paul grieves over any who even start down that road, and he urges them, with powerful emotion, to turn back. In particular, he has given them an example by his own refusal to be drawn into the snares of materialist culture. He wasn't in this preaching and teaching business for money, and nor should they be.

This personal testimony seems designed to rule out, or to head off before it can get going, the kind of criticism he had experienced behind his back after he had left Corinth. But, all the same, Paul knew that difficulties lay ahead. The elders from Ephesus were like shepherds, put there to guard a flock of sheep, and since the flock in question was "the church of God, which he purchased with his very own blood"—one of the most striking early Christian statements of the meaning of Jesus's crucifixion—they must take great care.[13] There would be wolves. There always are. Some of them would be former shepherds themselves—perhaps some among those listening to him right now!—who would distort the truth and draw people away after them. Perhaps half of Paul's letters were written because this sort of thing had already happened, in Galatia, in Corinth, and elsewhere. It wasn't a new problem. It remained acute.

But this farewell address wasn't simply about Paul and about the dangers facing the church. It was about God and about Jesus. It would hardly be true to Paul if these were not the ultimate focal points. "I commit you to God," he says, "and to the word of his grace, which is able to build you up and give you the inheritance among all those whom God has sanctified."[14] God's word of grace was the powerful word of the cross, the life-transforming word of the gospel, the word that started in the ancient scriptures and told the story reaching forward to the explosive new event of Jesus himself. And it was Jesus himself whom Paul invoked at the end. Just as the Jerusalem leaders had urged him to "remember the poor," so Paul urged the Ephesians to "work to help the weak," since Jesus himself had said (in a saying unrecorded elsewhere), "It is more blessed to give than to receive."[15] That was how the church was to be known—as the community that modeled the outgoing, generous grace of God. That was how it would confront the principalities and powers who were all out for their own ends. That was why, no doubt, the wolves would come in to snatch what they could; this kind of community was by its very nature vulnerable, and would always be. Loyalty would be contested. But God's grace and God's word were stronger, and like good wholesome food they would build up the church's strength, nourishing the believers and their leaders so that they would indeed "inherit the kingdom," the worldwide inheritance promised to the Messiah and his people.

Paul explained that this would be his last visit. He had other plans now, and he did not envisage any return to Asia Minor. They were upset, distraught, but his mind was made up. His face, like that of his master, was turned toward Jerusalem, but then, unlike Jesus, toward Rome.

They knelt down to pray. Then, after more embraces, they brought him to his ship.

★ ★ ★

Paul could never say he hadn't been warned. People kept telling him he was in for trouble in Jerusalem. The travelers changed ships at Patara, on the coast of Lycia in southwest Asia, and then headed for Tyre on the Syrian coast. The Jesus-followers there urged Paul not to go to Jerusalem, but he would not be deflected. They continued via Ptolemais, just a little south, and ended up at Caesarea, staying with Philip and his daughters. There Agabus, a prophet from Jerusalem, warned Paul that the Judaeans in Jerusalem would tie him hand and foot and hand him over to the Gentiles. Everyone pleaded with Paul not to go. But we are not surprised, knowing him as we now do, that he resisted. It broke his heart that they were so affectionate and concerned for him, but he was quite prepared not only to be tied up, but to die for the name of Jesus, if that should prove to be God's will. They relented. The travelers moved on. Finally they arrived in Jerusalem at last. It was, most likely, the early autumn of AD 57.

No one who has made that journey, in ancient or in modern times, forgets it. The Holy City. Jerusalem the golden. The place where the living God had promised to put his name, had promised to install his king as ruler of the nations. The place where, Paul believed, these promises had come true—with Jesus enthroned outside the city wall, doing once and for all what only Israel's One God could do and then being exalted as Lord of the world. How could he not go there one more time?

But how could he possibly go to Jerusalem in full public view when so many in the city, including so many Jesus-followers who were "zealous for the law"—as Paul himself had been!—would hear about his coming and react with anger and perhaps violence? This was a problem for the Jerusalem leaders as much as for Paul. One would have hoped that the collection would have provided a welcome sign of mutual acceptance, but to our frustration Luke never mentions it. We simply do not know what happened to the money. Reading Paul's letters, watching him carefully organize the collection and its equally careful transportation, we are like people watching all but the last ten minutes of a great sporting event on television, when a sudden power outage stops us from finding out who won.

Luke was not writing to answer our questions. Perhaps he wanted to distract attention from the whole episode. Perhaps Paul and his friends had presented the money, only to have it refused on the grounds that it came from "tainted" Gentile sources. Or perhaps it was accepted, but made little difference to the public perception of Paul and his missionary activity. Perhaps, as sometimes happens, this unexpected and generous gift divided the local church between those who wanted to receive it in the spirit it was given and those who were afraid they were being bribed into overlooking or colluding with what they saw as Paul's notoriously lax attitude toward the Torah. (Perhaps there were long memories of the earlier visit when Paul and Barnabas had come to Jerusalem with money—and also with Titus, whom some had wanted to circumcise.) In any case, since for this period we are entirely dependent on Luke for information and since he has chosen not to mention the collection at all, we cannot tell. We can only hope. (Nor, for that matter, does Luke mention Titus. That is a well-known problem to which there is no obvious solution, but it is no more problematic than the small-scale puzzles one repeatedly meets in ancient history.)

When Paul and his friends arrived in Jerusalem at last, they stayed with Mnason, who like Barnabas was originally from Cyprus. The Jerusalem leaders, while welcoming the news of what Paul and his colleagues had done in the years since they last met, came up with a plan to quiet any potential anti-Pauline feeling in Jerusalem before it even got going. What they proposed was that Paul join four others who had taken a vow and would undergo a rite of purification in the Temple. This was a variation on the earlier theme where Paul, after his first visit to Corinth, had taken a vow. As before, it is perfectly reasonable to suppose that Paul would have continued, as a Jesus-follower, with various Jewish devotional practices designed to direct the mind and heart toward worship, humility, and service.

The Jerusalem leaders hoped their plan would head off the "zealots" among the local Jesus-followers. Those "zealots," after all, were firmly convinced that, because of Jesus, God was now going to complete his long-term plan to get rid of the hated Gentile rulers and give freedom to Israel once and for all. But if other people claiming to follow Jesus were going soft on their devotion to God and his law, and teaching yet other people to go soft on it as well, then the whole divine purpose would be in jeopardy. So what Paul needed to do was to demonstrate his loyalty to the law by joining a group who had taken a vow of purity. He could share the same vow and actually pay their expenses as well (a good use for some of the collection monies?). Then it would be clear that the rumors and gossip about him, all the accusations that he was teaching people to ignore the law, were untrue.

This plan has the same sense of naïveté about it that we recall from the letter drafted after the Jerusalem Conference nearly a decade earlier. Like a British politician who never stirs out of Westminster or an American banker who never travels away from Wall Street except to visit other banks in Frankfurt or Tokyo, there is a sense of unreality, of the Jerusalem leaders failing to see how the complexities of real life might ruin the neat ideas.

And, indeed, the Jerusalem leaders do now remind Paul that they had written to the Jesus-believing Gentiles about keeping away from anything to do with idolatry and immorality, including meat that had been sacrificed in pagan temples. One can imagine Paul's heart sinking at this reference to the document that had really been designed, like the supposed "division of labor" in Galatians 2:9, as an expedient to allow mutual recognition while things went forward. He knows, from years of facing actual pastoral situations in Corinth, Ephesus, and elsewhere—and from hammering out the first theological principles that related to those situations, particularly in 1 Corinthians 8–10 and Romans 14–15—that things are much more complicated than the "apostolic letter" had allowed. He has remained true to the absolute prohibition on idolatry and immorality. But he has come to the conclusion, on good biblical grounds, that all meat is in fact "clean" and that nothing is "impure" unless someone's bad conscience made it so.[16] The "letter" had been well intentioned, but the realities on the ground meant that it could only ever be a starting position. Was the new plan, Paul must have wondered, going to be a similar mixture of good intentions and unreal expectations?

His own position on the matters covered by the "letter" was not, after all, a mere pragmatic compromise. It was a statement of strong theological principle. Some early Christians would have agreed with him, pointing out that the line he was taking had the backing of Jesus himself, or at least of Mark's view of what Jesus had meant at one point. In Mark, Jesus's cryptic remark about things passing through the stomach and out of the body without causing defilement is taken to indicate that "all foods are clean."[17] Paul had, in any case, moved on a long way since the Jerusalem Conference. His churches had been taught to think theologically at a depth far beyond what was implied in the rather simplistic "letter." He must have felt like a serious musician who, having played in top concert halls around the world, returned home and was invited to admire someone playing a few old tunes in the pub down the road. He could understand and respect what they were saying, but he knew a larger world.

But maybe, just maybe, their new plan might work. He goes ahead with the ritual of purification. He makes the declaration. (Those who suppose that the "real Paul," being a good Protestant, would never have done anything like this have missed the point. Paul's gospel did not make him opposed to the Temple and

its sacrificial system. Just because he believed that Jesus was the ultimate sacrifice, that did not mean that following the Levitical code
was now sinful.) The purificatory ritual takes a week—it must have
seemed a very long week to Paul and his anxious friends—after
which Paul and the other men enter the Temple. Has the ruse
worked? Have they gotten away with it? Will the Jerusalem church
be spared the embarrassment—and more than embarrassment—
of being associated with a notoriously traitorous character? Will
Paul be spared the outcry that might so easily follow?

The answer is no. Only now it's even worse than they had feared.
They had been worried that Paul would be accused of fomenting
lawbreaking among diaspora Jews. The actual charge is one higher.
He is now accused of deliberately defiling the Temple itself. In trying to avoid a road accident, they have stepped on the accelerator
rather than the brake. They would have done better to keep Paul
away from the Temple altogether. The evidence for the charge of
attempted defilement is of course circumstantial and slight, but that
wouldn't stop an angry crowd. The trouble began, Luke explains,
with some Jews from Asia, people who had known of Paul in
Ephesus. (Everybody in Ephesus, we recall, had known who Paul
was.) So much, Paul might have thought grimly, for coming back
for the festival. Lots of other Jews had had the same idea; people
came to Jerusalem from all over the world of the Diaspora. Some
of them, already hostile to him, would think the worst. And so
much for trying to calm people down by coming into the Temple
however carefully, however ritually pure.

These diaspora Jews now formulate the charge that will resonate throughout the next five chapters of Acts. Here he is, they
say; this is the fellow who's been going around the world teaching
everybody to disobey the law and to disregard the Temple! (How
Paul must have longed to explain to them the difference between
abolition and fulfillment. But then, as now, when people are angry, they can read things whichever way they please.) And here
he is in person, they say. Not content with charging around the

world spreading this anti-Jewish heresy, he's come here to Jerusalem and has brought his pagan friends into the Temple so that he can prove his point by polluting our holy place . . .

What had Paul done? Luke explains that these men from Ephesus had seen him in the city with Trophimus, another Ephesian and a Gentile, and assumed that Paul had taken him into the Temple, past the sign that warned Gentiles to keep out. The assumption was false, but the damage was done. Paul, we may assume, braced himself wearily, knowing what to expect, like someone bathing in the sea who, too late, realizes that a huge wave is bearing down on him and there is absolutely nothing he can do about it. With a rush, people in the mob seize him and start to beat him up. He is kicked and punched, slapped and scratched. He only escapes with his life because the Roman tribune on duty, hearing the uproar, quickly intervenes and arrests him. The tribune can't figure out what the problem is (here, as with the riot in Ephesus, most of the crowd has little idea what is really happening), so he gives the order for Paul to be brought into the barracks. The soldiers carry Paul over the heads of the angry crowd. They reach comparative safety. We sense the door being shut, the roar of the mob still audible but now at bay.

How Paul could talk coherently after all this is not clear, but he has come too far to lapse into passivity now. He wants, above all, to be able to speak to the people. They are zealous for God and the law; he is zealous for God and his son—and he remembers only too well the time when he thought just as they do. They are his people, the kind of people over whom he had grieved,[18] for whom he had prayed,[19] the people who, he believed, might not forever "remain in unbelief."[20] If he cannot speak to them, who can? After all, Paul has recently stayed up all night explaining to an eager group in Troas what the scriptures really meant, how it all fitted together, why his own mission was part of the plan stretching back to Adam and Abraham and forward to the ultimate renewal of heaven and earth. He has just written it out, a few weeks before, with great care and artistry, in what he must have known was a work of literary skill as well as theological and pastoral power and passion. He wants, he yearns, he longs above all things at that moment to be allowed to say all this to the angry crowd.

So he asks the tribune for permission. Actually, he begins by asking permission to speak to the tribune himself, which sets in motion an odd little dialogue. The tribune has assumed that Paul is the Egyptian rabble-rouser mentioned by Josephus and other Jewish traditions, the man who had led a band of hopefuls into the desert with promises that he would accomplish God's coming liberation. It isn't quite clear whether, hearing Paul speak Greek, the tribune has his guess confirmed (an Egyptian might be expected to speak Greek) or whether, hearing Paul speak a better standard of Greek, he is now questioning his original assumption. But it gives Paul the opportunity to introduce himself, to say that he is a Jew from Tarsus. No wonder he can speak good Greek. His native city is a place of culture and renown. So, having gotten that sorted out, he requests, and is granted, permission to speak to the crowd who a minute before were baying for his blood.

★ ★ ★

It was a noble effort, but it was doomed to failure. Paul's speech from the steps of the Roman barracks gained attention when the crowd realized he was now speaking in the local language, Aramaic. They listened politely, perhaps in a mixture of suspicion and surprise, as he rehearsed his early life, not least his zeal for the law in Jerusalem itself. The story of his meeting with Jesus is of course spectacular, as is the immediate sequel, in which the devout, law-observant Ananias comes at the Lord's bidding to enable the opening of his eyes. So far, so good.

But then came the critical moment, the moment where Paul needed to expound the fulfillment of the scriptural promises about all nations coming to worship Israel's God. He longed in particular to explain that to them and then to explain the ways

in which this inclusion of Gentiles was the true fulfillment of
the Torah predicted by Moses and the prophets. He was itching
to explain as well how it was that Jesus the Messiah, as promised
by God to King David, was the ultimate means by which the
great Temple promises had come true, how the divine glory was
dwelling bodily in him and by his spirit dwelling also now in
his followers. Paul had not been cynically breaking the law. He
certainly had not been defiling the Temple. He deeply respected
and cherished them both. He had been loyal. But when God sends
Israel a crucified Messiah . . .

That was what Paul wanted to say, but he never got the chance.
He sprang the trap too soon by saying that the risen Jesus had
said he was sending Paul to the Gentiles. That was enough. The
crowd had been ready to see him as a compromiser, and now
their suspicions were confirmed. He was the sort who had given
up the Torah, who had no time for the Temple, who'd made
friends with their enemies, with the monsters who were oppress-
ing God's people. He's polluted himself, they said, and now he
wants to pollute the rest of us. He will get his reward, no doubt,
when God judges the world, but he ought to have it right now!
"Away with him from the face of the earth! Someone like that has
no right to live!"[21]

Faced with a troublesome prisoner, a Roman tribune would
normally use torture to find out what was going on. It was assumed that nobody would tell the truth or the whole truth unless
it was forced out of them. But once again the tribune was in for a
surprise. Just as when he faced down the magistrates in Philippi,
Paul revealed his secret to the officer standing by: "Is it lawful to
flog a Roman citizen without first finding him guilty?"[22]

The question was rhetorical. Paul knew the answer, and so did
the officer. They both also knew that it wasn't just unlawful; it
was very unwise. If a citizen were to report such a thing, the roles
could easily be reversed, and the officers involved would themselves face severe punishment.

This naturally raises another question. How could Paul prove his claim of citizenship? To make a false claim, especially under such circumstances, would be a serious crime, possibly a capital offense. In Rome, citizens would wear a toga, but it is highly unlikely that Paul was doing so on this occasion (even supposing that his clothes were recognizable after his near lynching). The other mark, which we may be sure Paul had kept safe about his person all along, perhaps on a chain or string, was the small wooden badge (known as a *diploma*) that, much like a passport, gave official details of who he was and where his citizenship was registered. The tribune raises an eyebrow: "It cost me a lot of money to buy this citizenship," he said. "Ah," Paul replied, "but it came to me by birth."[23] That was enough. The torturers were told to stand down. But the tribune still had no idea what was actually going on. Having failed to find out either from the crowd or from Paul himself, he called the chief priests and the whole Sanhedrin.

We should know by now what to expect. Paul believed firmly that the One God had created all the power structures of the world—and that when they stepped out of line, they ought to be reminded of the fact. Never one for a soft approach (had he ever really pondered Proverbs 15:1, advising that a gentle answer turns away anger?), he was much more inclined to get his retaliation in first. So, without waiting for anyone to accuse him of anything, he insisted that throughout his life he had kept a clear conscience before the One God of Israel. He had been loyal. At this, the high priest ordered him to be struck on the mouth. As in the trial of Jesus,[24] this was a standard if violent way of saying symbolically "You ought not to be speaking in your own defense, because you are obviously guilty. You should shut your mouth, and if you don't, we'll shut it for you."

Paul wasn't having it. "God will strike you, you whitewashed wall!" he responded. "You're sitting to judge me according to the law, and yet you order me to be struck in violation of the law?"[25] If part of the charge was that he had failed to be sufficiently zealous for the Torah, he would show right from the start that he knew that the Torah required fair play for the accused. What he had not taken into account was that the person addressing him was the high priest himself; the bystanders quickly informed him of this. So now *he* was in the wrong for speaking like that to someone in high office. Paul knew, however, that when you did something wrong without intending to do so—"unwilling" or "unwitting" sin—this required only an apology and ultimately a sin offering. "I didn't know," he said, "he was the high priest."[26] Again, Paul knew as well as they did that scripture required respect for office.[27]

This brought the bizarre back-and-forth of insult and accusation to a standstill, but Paul wasn't going to leave it there. He at once seized the initiative. He had come of age in Jerusalem; he had studied with Gamaliel; he knew very well where the flash points would come. He knew that though the gathering would have liked to present a united front, there were deep ideological differences, represented broadly by the aristocratic Sadducees and the populist pressure group, the Pharisees, with their revolutionary dream of the resurrection hope of Israel. Now was the time to drop a small bomb into this august company. "My brothers," he shouted to the whole assembly. (Brothers! Now, there's a thought.) "I am a Pharisee, the son of Pharisees. This trial is about the hope, about the resurrection of the dead!"

This really put the cat among the pigeons, as he knew it would. At once the Pharisees in the gathering rallied to his defense. They hadn't quite understood what he meant, but if the game was now Pharisees versus Sadducees (rather than Sanhedrin versus heretics), they knew which side they were on. The reason for their confusion goes to the heart of the difference between what the young Saul of Tarsus had believed and what Paul the Apostle had come to believe.

"Resurrection," as far as they were concerned, was something that would happen to everybody at the end of time, but that meant that those who had died were still alive in some form in the interval before that final event. Lacking, just as we do, good, unambiguous language for this intermediate state, they sometimes spoke of the dead as having an "angelic" existence and sometimes of them as now being "spirits"; in both cases, the people were still alive but were *awaiting* a resurrection body on the last day. This enabled the Pharisees to cut Paul some slack; maybe, they thought, when he had spoken of meeting Jesus on the road to Damascus, what he had actually seen and heard was an "angel" or a "spirit," somebody still alive in this intermediate state.

The early Jesus-followers would see in an instant that this wasn't the point. As far as they were concerned, with Paul as their most articulate representative, the whole point was that to their astonishment Jesus had gone on ahead and was already raised from the dead, ahead of everybody else. But Paul's initiative had made it impossible for the meeting to continue. The charges about observing the law and defiling the Temple were forgotten, at least for the moment. The gathering broke up in disorder. Once again the Roman tribune had to rescue Paul from an angry gathering, only this time it was the senior Jerusalem court rather than the city mob.

How does Paul react to that small triumph? We watch as the tribune's men frog-march him back to the barracks and lock him up for the night. Paul is used to this, of course, and at least he and the tribune seem to have established some kind of rapport. Paul might wish that his own fellow Jews would be more sympathetic, but by now he may be getting a sense that, as in Corinth, a Roman official standing outside the immediate controversy might be a better ally. He prays the evening prayers. The bed is hard, but he has had an exhausting day. He sleeps . . .

And the next thing he knows Jesus is standing there beside him. The last time this happened was in Corinth, and Jesus told him to stay there and not be afraid. Now he's telling him he will have to move on. He has given his evidence in Jerusalem. Now he will have to do the same thing in Rome. *So,* Paul thinks, *that's how*

it's going to happen. For the last year or two he has had a strong
sense that he ought to be heading for Rome, but it had looked as
though the Jerusalem visit might put an end to that, and to everything else as well. But now he sees how it might be done. This
wasn't the way he had planned it, but maybe, just maybe, this is
what had to happen. Twice now the tribune has rescued him from
violence. Perhaps that is a sign. Perhaps the Roman system as a
whole, despite its creaky bureaucracy and careless pagan attitude
toward life, will now be the means by which he will be rescued
from the threats that are reaching a crescendo.

If that thought crossed his mind, it was vindicated the next
day by another strange incident. Forty Torah-zealous Jews swore
a solemn oath not to eat or drink until they had killed Paul.
Their plot was simple. They would have Paul brought back to the
Sanhedrin and assassinate him in transit. Unfortunately for them,
news leaked out. To our surprise, since this is the only mention of
Paul's family in the whole narrative, Paul's sister's son heard about
it. (This opens in a flash a window on other questions: How many
relatives did Paul have in Jerusalem? Were some of them Jesus-
followers? We do not know.) The lad came to tell Paul, and Paul
got him to tell the tribune.

The tribune, who must have been wondering what on earth to
do next, knew exactly how to meet this challenge. He ordered
two centurions with a hundred soldiers each, seventy horsemen,
and an additional two hundred light-armed guards to take Paul to
Caesarea, the best part of a hundred miles away, where the governor was based. That night they got as far as Antipatris, roughly
halfway; by then the conspirators must have realized they had lost
their chance. The soldiers then returned to Jerusalem, and the
horsemen and guards took Paul on to Caesarea itself.

The tribune, Claudius Lysias, wrote a cover letter to the governor in which he expressed a view not dissimilar to the one Gallio
had taken in Corinth. This fellow, he said, has been accused in
relation to disputes concerning Jewish law, but he has not been

charged with any crime for which he would deserve to die or to be imprisoned. The Roman viewpoint seems to be that this is all about internal Jewish disputes. Nothing for them to bother about, except insofar as they need to keep the peace, and for whatever reason that seems to become harder when this man is around.

So Paul is handed on to the provincial governor himself. The governor at the time was Antonius Felix. Originally a freedman, Felix had risen quickly up the social scale as a favorite of the emperor Claudius; he was a brother of Pallas, one of Claudius's right-hand men. Felix was a callous, corrupt official who had squashed a rebellion, instigated the murder of a high priest, and, rather like Gallio when the mob beat up Sosthenes in Corinth, stood by as Jews in Caesarea were attacked by a local crowd. He was, however, married to a Jewish princess (his third wife), Drusilla, a daughter of Herod Agrippa. There was at least a small chance that he might listen favorably to a plea from the Jewish hierarchy.

When the Jewish leaders arrive, annoyed no doubt at being made to come to Caesarea, they bring their accusations, using a professional attorney who might be expected to frame things in a way that would get the governor's attention. "We find this fellow," says the attorney, "to be a public nuisance. He stirs up civil strife among all the Jews, all over the world. He is a ringleader in the sect of the Nazoreans. He even tried to defile the Temple!"[28] This is the usual tactic, taking an originally Jewish charge and "translating" it into a charge of public disturbance. The Jewish leaders know there is no point trying to get the governor to adjudicate a specifically Jewish question. Temple defilement, however, is something anyone in the ancient world would understand; people in every city, in every subculture would shudder at the thought.

Paul, of course, is having none of it. He simply denies the basic charge of fomenting civil unrest. He wasn't disputing in the Temple, he wasn't stirring up a crowd. He has in any case been in Jerusalem for less than two weeks. However, they are right that he is a follower of the Way, which they call a "sect"; but this is because he is convinced that what has happened in Jesus is the fulfillment, not the abrogation, of the law and the prophets. There will be a resurrection of both the righteous and the unrighteous (none of Paul's letters make this point, since they focus on the resurrection of the righteous only). But for that reason, as he had said before the Sanhedrin, Paul has always kept his conscience clear before God and all people. He has, though, been a loyal Jew, even though—actually, he would say, precisely because—that loyalty has been reshaped around Israel's Messiah.

So what *had* Paul been doing? What account will he give of himself, not just to rebut the charges, but to explain why he had come to Jerusalem in the first place? He opens with a powerful point. Far from intending to stir up trouble for the Jewish people, his journey was motivated by the desire to help: for years he had been collecting money to bring "to his nation." That had brought him to the city, and that's what took him into the Temple, properly purified and devout, without any crowds or fuss. The trouble was caused, he says, by "some Jews from Asia";[29] as in Philippians 1 and the scene in Ephesus itself, we catch the sense that some of Paul's fiercest and most determined opponents came, for whatever reason, from the Jewish community in Ephesus itself. Paul knows that they would have far more Jewish-specific complaints than the generalized charge of fomenting civil unrest that the attorney had presented, so he proposes that they should come themselves and bring their accusations against him.

Or perhaps, he says as an afterthought, the real problem has to do with what he said in the Sanhedrin. This is a tease, and the Jewish hierarchy will know it but will not be able to do anything about it. Yes, of course, Paul had shouted out to them that what was at stake was the Jewish hope of resurrection. He was claiming the high ground; his whole raison d'être was that this Jewish hope, as seen by the Pharisees at least, had been accomplished in Jesus. He was not, in other words, opposed to the Jews and their way of life. He was celebrating its fulfillment.

Felix defers judgment. He and Drusilla call the battered apostle in and let him talk. He explains one more time—but Paul is not complaining about having another opportunity to announce the good news—who Jesus is, why according to scripture he is Israel's Messiah, and what this means with regard to the coming final judgment, the justice of God, and the gospel challenge to a life of self-control. Felix hasn't exercised self-control for a long time, if ever, and has long considered all ultimate judgment to be a matter of Roman justice, with Roman justice itself being open to manipulation in return for a consideration. Felix stops Paul in his tracks. Quite enough for now, he says. But he is hoping—granted that Paul seems to have access to funds—that he might be good for a bribe. So he calls him in again and again. But after two years there is still no bribe, and Felix comes to the end of his time in office.

At that point he could have released Paul. Although his primary motive had always been self-interest, his hope for a bribe had waned, and his attention had now shifted to the normal anxiety of a provincial governor returning to Rome—he did not want to get into trouble. (His original patron, Claudius, had now been succeeded by Nero.) He therefore wanted a good report from his Jewish subjects. So he left Paul in prison to await the mercy, or otherwise, of the incoming governor, Portius Festus.

Once again Luke has presented all this as a fast-paced drama, action packed and with plenty of colorful characters. We can read it through in a few minutes. But we should not lose sight of the fact that it has all taken two years. Paul had written his letter to Rome in 57 and had arrived in Jerusalem late the same year. It was now 59 (Festus's arrival as governor can be dated to that year). He had, for the moment, escaped death. But Roman custody was still Roman custody, and even though he was clearly allowed to have friends visit him and bring him what he needed, there was a sense of marking time, of an unpleasant and unwanted hiatus. He knew that a belief in providence always constituted a call to patience, but even so, this was getting ridiculous. Jesus had

promised him that he would be going to Rome. He had guessed
that this might mean that Rome would itself take him there. But
how would that happen if Rome kept sending corrupt officials
who were uninterested in moving things along?

The answer came—and Paul must have been pondering this
for quite some time—when the new governor, Festus, held a brief
hearing in Caesarea. Jewish speakers once more hurled all kinds of
accusations at Paul. He responded by insisting once more on the
three all-important points: he had committed no offense against
Jewish law or the Temple: or, for that matter, against Caesar. Why
he mentioned Caesar at that point is not clear, since so far as we
know nobody had suggested that he was guilty of any kind of
treason against the emperor. However, the sequel may show what
Paul had in mind.

But first we see a typical move. Festus, uninterested in justice
but wanting to do the Jews a favor, suggested that they should
hold a trial in Jerusalem. Paul, remembering the earlier plot, knew
perfectly well where that would lead. It was time to play the card
he had held up his sleeve all this time:

> I am standing before Caesar's tribunal, which is where I
> ought to be tried. I have done no wrong to the Jews, as
> you well know. If I have committed any wrong, or if I
> have done something which means I deserve to die, I'm
> not trying to escape death. But if I have done none of
> the things they are accusing me of, nobody can hand me
> over to them. *I appeal to Caesar.*[30]

An appeal of this kind was not an appeal against sentence. No
sentence had been passed, since no verdict had been reached. It
was an appeal that the entire case should be passed up to the highest possible court. It was, of course, a risky move. Caesar might
have all sorts of reasons for wanting the case to go this way or that
and might well not take kindly to a Jew whose reputation as a

world-roving troublemaker would go before him. But if the only alternative was to start again in Jerusalem, with all the attendant risks, then this, however unexpected, was the way by which he would get to Rome at last. Festus consulted his advisers, but he surely knew the answer already. Paul had appealed to Caesar, and to Caesar he would go.

But he could not be sent without an account of the case, a statement of the facts. How then would Festus discover "the facts" in this case? An opportunity presented itself. Herod Agrippa II, a flamboyant character with an equally flamboyant wife, Bernice, was coming to greet Festus as the newly arrived governor. (The relationship between Roman governors and the local aristocracy was complex, but both sides usually realized that it was better to have some kind of mutual understanding. Many ordinary Jews would despise them both, though this particular Herod was less unpopular than most of his family had been.) Festus explained to Agrippa who Paul was and the nature of the problem, including the telling comment: "It turned out to have to do with various wranglings concerning their own religion, and about some dead man called Jesus whom Paul asserted was alive."[31] This sounds very much like Gallio's response to the charges against Paul in Acts 18 and the similar statement by the tribune who had written to Felix in Acts 23: from the Jewish point of view Paul might be introducing dangerous new elements into traditional formulations, but from the Roman point of view this just looked like wrangling over words. At least Festus had grasped the central point at issue, that this all concerned the resurrection of Jesus, though he professed not to understand why Paul wouldn't go to Jerusalem and why, instead, he had appealed to Caesar. So, not unnaturally, Agrippa asked to hear Paul for himself.

One common view is that Luke wrote Acts to provide material in Paul's defense. Whether it was written early enough for his trial before Nero or whether it was written a long time afterward but to make the same point in retrospect does not ultimately affect our understanding of Paul here. This is the last time we see him give his own answer to our overall questions: What made him tick, and in particular what had happened on the road to Damascus to bring it all about? And how, granted all this, might we explain how the movement launched by this strange, enigmatic but energetic man would become so successful so quickly?

Paul's speech before Agrippa, Bernice, Festus, and their retinue is longer than either the Areopagus address or the farewell address to the Ephesian elders. Like them, however, it must be a great deal shorter than what Paul actually said on that occasion. However, this speech presses so many of the buttons that we have seen again and again in Paul's own writings that we can be sure it summarizes fairly accurately what was said. The main upshot of it all—and this is why an earlier generation of readers, determined to stop Paul from being "Jewish," rejected the portrait in Acts!—is that Paul had been a loyal Jew from the start. He was acting as a loyal Jew at the time when he met Jesus on the road; his mission in the wider world had been on behalf of Israel's God, who was now claiming the whole world as his own; and he was simply doing his best to tell the world what Moses and the prophets had been saying all along, namely, "that the Messiah would suffer, that he would be the first to rise from the dead, and that he would proclaim light to the people and to the nations."[32] Paul had always been, and still remained, a loyal Jew. That was the whole point.

It was the point he wanted to make to Herod Agrippa II, who might just have been able to wield some influence on wider Jewish opinion. It was the point he wanted to make in the face of the accusations of disloyalty, of treating the Torah too loosely and plotting to desecrate the Temple. It was the point Luke wanted to make as well whenever he was writing—that despite the repeated accusations, Paul was not trying to overthrow the Jewish tradition, culture, and way of life. It was just that, as other loyal Jews have supposed from time to time, he believed that Israel's

Messiah had appeared, that he knew the Messiah's name and his qualifications, and that this Messiah had done something much more powerful than merely defeating a pagan army. He had over-thrown the dark powers that had kept the nations in captivity; he had built a new "Temple," a worldwide community in which the divine glory had come to dwell by the spirit; and he had now sent out messengers to tell the nations what devout Jews had wanted to tell them all along, that they should turn from idols to serve the living God. All this is built into Paul's account of what Jesus said to him in their first meeting and into Paul's own account of what he had been doing as a result.

The heart of the speech is of course the third and final account in Acts of the appearance of Jesus to Saul of Tarsus on the road to Damascus. This time the story is at its fullest. No doubt Luke, editing all three versions, has arranged them in a crescendo. And this fuller version gives us yet another angle on our underlying questions of what made Paul the man he was, what the Damascus Road event had done to him, and why his work bore fruit beyond his dreams.

The opening challenge has become proverbial. As in the two other versions, Jesus asks Saul why he is persecuting him, but this time he adds a wry comment: "It's hard for you, this kicking against the goads."[33] This is an allusion to a well-known Greek proverb about humans trying to resist the divine will, which is exactly what Saul's teacher, Gamaliel, had warned against.[34] In the mind of Saul of Tarsus at the time, and of Paul in this speech, there is already a profound irony: Jesus, commissioning him to go and tell the polytheistic nations about the One God, is warning him about his present behavior—by using a saying from the very pagan traditions from which people must turn away! The proverb in this context, of course, is designed to show the inner tensions within the "zeal" of young Saul. This moment corresponds ex-actly to what Paul had written in Romans about his fellow Jews in a lament with strong autobiographical echoes:

> I can testify on their behalf that they have a zeal for God;
> but it is not based on knowledge. They were ignorant,
> you see, of God's covenant faithfulness, and they were
> trying to establish a covenant status of their own; so they
> didn't submit to God's faithfulness. The Messiah, you
> see, is the goal of the law, so that covenant membership
> may be available for all who believe.[35]

That passage, like Paul's present speech, goes on at once to indicate that since the One God has unveiled his ultimate covenant
purpose in *this* Messiah—this unexpected, unwanted, and indeed
scandalous crucified Jesus—then the nations are to be summoned
into a new kind of community. His death has defeated the dark
powers that kept the nations captive, so that the stigma of idolatry, uncleanness, and immorality, which formed the wall between
Israel and the Gentiles, can be done away. They can now have
"forgiveness of sins, and an inheritance among those who are
made holy by their faith" in Jesus.[36]

Scholars over the last generation have wrestled with the question
of whether the focus of Paul's gospel was *either* personal forgiveness *or* the inclusion of the Gentiles. This verse, true to what Paul
says in every letter from Galatians right through to Romans, indicates that it is both—and that the two are mutually defining. Since
the pagan powers had been defeated, like Pharaoh at the Exodus,
all people were free to worship the One God. Since the defeat
of the powers had been accomplished by Jesus's death, through
which sins were forgiven (the sins that kept humans enslaved to
the powers in the first place), the barrier to Gentile inclusion in a
new "sanctified" people had gone. "Forgiveness of sins" thus *entails*
"Gentile inclusion," and Gentile inclusion happens precisely *because of* "forgiveness of sins." This is central to Paul's understanding
of the gospel from the Damascus Road experience on, for the rest
of his life. He would say that it was the primary reason behind any
"success" his movement would have.

For the moment, of course, Paul knew how unpopular this was bound to be and how unwelcome it had been in practice. The idea that Gentiles could repent and become true worshippers of the One God—but without becoming Jews by being circumcised, a point implicit here but perhaps wisely left unsaid—was the main reason why he was so often opposed out in the Diaspora. It was, in particular, the reason why the mob went after him in the Temple two years before, setting off the sequence of events that finally brought him face-to-face with Herod Agrippa.

But Paul stood firm. All he was doing was expounding Moses and the prophets. It was they who had said—and if Paul got the chance, he would eagerly give Agrippa chapter and verse—two things in particular. First, the Messiah "would be the first to rise from the dead."[37] There is Paul's theology of the two-stage resurrection, as in 1 Corinthians 15, in a nutshell, in which the Messiah's own resurrection inaugurates a new period of history and the resurrection of all his people follows later. Second, the Messiah "would proclaim light to the people and to the nations."[38]

There may be a distant echo here, in Luke's mind at least, of the song of Simeon, right back at the start of Luke's Gospel, in which Simeon calls Jesus "a light for revelation to the nations, and glory for your people Israel."[39] But the more important echo is Isaiah 49, the text which meant so much for Paul: the Lord's servant will not only "raise up the tribes of Jacob and restore the survivors of Israel"; God will give him "as a light to the nations, that [God's] salvation may reach to the end of the earth."[40] This is a particularly appropriate passage for Paul to have in mind as he stands before Agrippa, since the next verse goes on:

> Thus says the LORD,
>   the Redeemer of Israel and his Holy One,
> to one deeply despised, abhorred by the nations,
>   the slave of rulers,
> "Kings shall see and stand up,

princes, and they shall prostrate themselves,
because of the LORD, who is faithful,
    the Holy One of Israel, who has chosen you."[41]

This too had its obvious resonances in Paul's reflection on his ministry in Romans, written not long before. He quotes the end of Isaiah 52:15:

People who hadn't been told about him will see;
    People who hadn't heard will understand.[42]

But the half verse immediately before declares:

So shall he startle many nations;
    kings shall shut their mouths because of him.

Standing there before Caesar's representative, on the one hand, and the current "king of the Jews," on the other, Paul of all people would have been alive to a sense of scripture coming true, even though the listening nobility couldn't or wouldn't see it.

Caesar's representative, in particular, had no intention of having his mouth shut by Paul's message. Those who know Paul will see that this speech, even in the compressed form Luke provides, presents a clearly thought out, scripturally resourced, and coherent worldview. To Festus, however, it appeared simply a jumble of strange ideas. Paul had always known that his message would be scandalous to Jews and madness to Gentiles. He was challenging Agrippa to look beyond the scandal, and he must have known that Festus would hear nothing but madness. Right on cue, Festus responds.

"Paul," he roars out at the top of his voice, "you're mad! All this learning of yours has driven you crazy!"[43] This is simply one more instance of what had happened in Athens, of what Paul remembered from Corinth and elsewhere. But Paul, calmly informing Festus that he is not at all mad, uses the moment to appeal directly to Agrippa. The king knows about Jesus and his followers—"After all, these things didn't happen in a corner." So Paul puts him on the spot: "Do you believe the prophets, King Agrippa? I know you believe them."[44]

This is a clever move. Agrippa, eager to retain such popularity as he has with the Jewish people, is not going to say he doesn't believe the prophets. But he sees very well what the next move would be: "You reckon you're going to make *me* a Christian, then, and pretty quick, too, by the sound of it!"[45] Whether that was intended as a sneer or as a friendly comment—since Agrippa must have realized, as Festus did not, the deep underlying coherence of all that Paul had said, granted his starting point in the revelation of the resurrected Jesus—Paul responds calmly. It is the last time we see the apostle face-to-face with high authority, and, true to form, he respects the office and appeals to the man: "I pray to God that not only you but also all who hear me today will become just as I am"—and then, with a smile and a gesture to the visible signs of his own status—"apart, of course, from these chains."[46]

The royal and official parties get up to leave. They are seen shaking their heads and commenting that this man doesn't deserve either to die or to be tied up. He could, in fact, have been set free, if only he hadn't gone and appealed to Caesar. Luke is aware of the multiple ironies here. If Paul hadn't appealed to Caesar, Festus would have sent him for trial in Jerusalem, and who knows what might have happened then. Because he had appealed, putting Festus in the position of needing to write an official report on the case (and he still doesn't seem to know what he's going to say), Festus has brought in Agrippa to hear Paul, giving Paul the opportunity to fulfill what Isaiah had said. And the appeal, though it will send Paul to Rome in chains, will at least send him to Rome. He will stand before the ultimate earthly king, and he will do so as a helpless prisoner. When he is weak, then he will be strong.

PART THREE

The Sea, the Sea

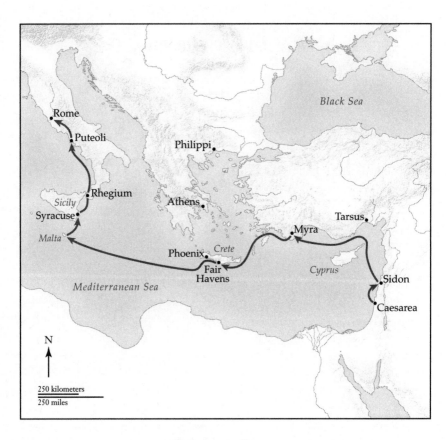

Caesarea to Rome

14

———

From Caesarea to
Rome—and Beyond?

T
HE REALLY STRANGE thing about Paul's voyage to
Rome is the way in which Paul himself appears to take
charge. He is a prisoner under guard. He is neither the
ship's owner nor its captain. He is of course a seasoned traveler
and, according to 2 Corinthians 11, has already been shipwrecked
three times, once ending up adrift at sea for a night and a day.
But that hardly justifies, one would think, his giving advice and
instructions, as he does repeatedly throughout the voyage. I think
Luke intended this to be a positive portrait of Paul. That is not
how it strikes me. He comes across as bossy.

Though Paul had sailed the Mediterranean and the Aegean often enough, he was still the heir to a Jewish tradition in which
the sea represented the dark forces of chaos, which had been overcome by God's good creation, as well as the equally dark force
that had threatened the children of Israel before the Red Sea had
opened up to let them through. Occasional psalms such as Psalm
93 invoked the same idea. In the book of Daniel, one of the most
popular books in the Jewish world of Paul's day, the "monsters,"

representing the wicked pagan empires, come up out of the sea.[1] The sea was the symbol of chaos, the source of danger, the untamable power that might at any moment strike back against the One God and his purposes in creation and new creation. Paul treated it warily, planning journeys so that he did not have to travel during winter.[2] If there were dangers on the land—plots, brigands, whatever—one might choose to go by sea instead. But that was always a calculated risk.

Luke has constructed Acts in such a way that chapter 27, the great voyage and shipwreck, functions as a kind of parallel to the climax of his Gospel, which is obviously the trial and crucifixion of Jesus. That had been the moment when "the power of darkness" did its worst.[3] This, now, is the moment when Paul has to face the worst that the powers can throw at him before he can arrive in Rome to announce Jesus as Lord. His rescue and his arrival in Rome thus have the character of "salvation," a major theme of the chapter; in fact, Greek words related to "saving" occur seven times in quick succession.[4] Luke seems to view the whole episode as a kind of dramatic enactment of the spiritual battle Paul described in Ephesians 6. It is always risky to jump too quickly to the view that Luke and Paul, being close friends and travel companions, must have held the same views on all subjects, but on this point I think they would have been close. Nor will Luke have ignored the fact that the shipwreck, with the entire ship's company in danger of drowning, was like a dramatic though distorted version of the crossing of the Red Sea—a Passover moment, a baptismal image in itself.

Paul was fortunate in the particular officer who was put in charge of him. Julius, a centurion from the imperial cohort, arranged for a ship from Caesarea up the coast to Sidon, where he let Paul visit his friends. He had already realized that this strange prisoner was quite happy to be taken to Rome and was not going to run away. They then sailed around the northeast Mediterranean to Myra on the coast of Lycia. That was the destination of their original vessel, so they found another ship, this time on its way from Alexandria to Italy. There were, Luke tells us later, 276 persons on board, of whom a significant number would have been slaves. Plenty of people wanted to get to Rome. One can only imagine the diversity of human life cooped up in the small space. If there was little privacy in ancient city life, there was none at all on a crowded ship.

It was late in the year for such a voyage. Sailing in the Mediterranean was generally reckoned in antiquity to be dangerous after the middle of September and more or less impossible from November through to February or March. Rome, however, needed a regular and plentiful supply of grain from Egypt, and Claudius had taken special measures to encourage the shipments to continue for as much of the year as possible. It looks as though the ship owner in this case was one of those prepared to take risks in the hope of a bigger profit.

The early part of the voyage was slower than expected. When they finally made it as far as Crete, it was already well into October, getting into the dangerous period. (Luke mentions that this was after the Day of Atonement, which in AD 59 fell on October 5.) They made landfall at Fair Havens, a small fishing settlement on the south side of Crete, a few miles from the town of Lasea. By common consent this was not a good place to spend the winter. The harbor was not secure against storms, and the town itself was too far back from the port to be easily accessible for those who would need to stay on board to guard the ship. So they wanted to press on, knowing that much better accommodation would be available at Phoenix, about fifty miles farther along the coast.

This is the point where Paul—the prisoner!—gave his advice. This is not as unlikely as some might suppose. Paul was a Roman citizen who had not even been formally charged, far less found guilty of any offense. Since he had a small retinue of friends traveling with him and was obviously a man of integrity and intelligence, he must have commanded respect. There is plenty of evidence, anyway, for decisions about travel in such circumstances being made after discussion among interested parties. He warned that the voyage would be nothing but trouble; heavy losses would be likely, not only to the cargo and the ship itself, but quite possibly to human life. This was actually a reasonable assessment. But the centurion, who as the imperial representative seems to have taken ultimate charge over the head of the ship's captain and owner, took their advice instead. They had their vested interests to consider, and they seem to have thought it was worth the risk.

In fact, it wasn't. The well-known northeasterly wind caught them as they were inching along the coast, and apart from a brief stop in the lee of the small island of Cauda, they were forced to run before the storm. We can well imagine the scene. Nearly three hundred people of all sorts were crowded on a small and vulnerable boat, with the winds getting higher and waves more furious. Everybody on board knew the way the decision had been made; there would have been an element of anger as well as anxiety. Staying in the wrong port would have been better than drowning.

The sailors would have been rushing about anxiously, doing all they could to avoid being driven onto the sandbanks some way off the North African shore. They did their best to lighten the vessel, to enable it to ride higher in the vast waves. First they threw the cargo overboard (so much for the goods that had been intended to make someone money when they arrived in Rome), and then they jettisoned the ship's tackle too. The passengers, watching all this going on, would have realized only too well what it meant. If the experienced sailors were taking extreme measures, what hope could there be? The nights would have been terrifying, the stormy days not much better. There they were, wet through, chilled to the marrow, huddled together, eating little or nothing in an attempt to preserve what supplies they had, some no doubt seasick. Misery and fear would have reduced them all, soldiers and slaves, tradesmen and apostles alike, to the same condition.

We imagine Paul and his companions muttering to one another about the book of Jonah. This would only have raised the dark question of who the "Jonah" was on this boat—who got them into this mess anyway? Or perhaps they might have reminded one another about Jesus stilling storms in Galilee; they wondered why he didn't do that now, as they no doubt prayed fervently that he would. On roared the wind, tossing the little craft and its unhappy occupants to and fro, with no letup, no glimpse of the sun by day or the stars by night. Sleep would have been difficult or impossible; the nightmare was real. Dark days turned into even darker nights and back again, as the storm showed no sign of abating. It went on for two whole weeks. There was a good reason, after all, why one would not normally sail the Mediterranean at that time of year. In the end, says Luke, "All hope of safety was finally abandoned."[5] Salvation? Not likely.

But then something happened. Not the lull in the storm for which their bodies and their dizzy minds ached. Not a rescue operation, even had such a thing been possible. Rather, a word—a messenger with encouragement. You might well think, and I expect plenty of those on board did think, that Paul's mind had finally been addled by the storm, but he had received a revelation, and he needed to share it. He did so in his usual tactless way. In our world, saying "I told you so" at such a moment would not have been the best way to retain goodwill and gain a hearing. But this is the Paul we know, never for a moment shrinking from speaking out. Since his whole life had been shaped by extraordinary visions and revelations, why stop now? So he said what he had heard:

> It does seem to me, my good people, that you should
> have taken my advice not to leave Crete. We could have
> managed without this damage and loss. But now I want
> to tell you: take heart! No lives will be lost—only the
> ship. This last night, you see, an angel of the God to

whom I belong, and whom I worship, stood beside me. "Don't be afraid, Paul," he said. "You must appear before Caesar, and let me tell you this: God has granted you all your traveling companions." So take heart, my friends. I believe God, that it will be as he said to me. We must, however, be cast up on some island or other.[6]

That was all very well. But the sailors still had to sail (without the aid of the ship's tackle); decisions still had to be made. They seemed to be getting near land, and the sailors were worried that they were going to be smashed on rocks, so they did what sailors in those days often did: with a prayer for day to come they let down four anchors from the stern. Seabed archaeology has made it clear how this system worked. As a ship was driven by wind and waves, anchors would be let down one by one, to slow the ship down as much as possible. Then, when each in turn threatened to break under the pressure, it would be abandoned and the next one lowered. The ship would lurch forward perhaps fifty yards or so and then be caught with a jerk; then again, then again. They would approach the land bit by bit rather than accelerating toward possible disaster. After this maneuver was completed, the sailors tried a more selfish plan—they would themselves escape in the ship's small boat and leave the rest to their fate. But Paul spotted them—why did it always have to be him?—and told the centurion and the soldiers to stop them. If he had not already acquired a reputation for bossiness, the sailors would have come to that conclusion right then. But he followed this up with a very different proposal.

The whole ship's company had been conserving their food, going without, for two weeks. It was time, he said, to eat. Rescue ("salvation" again, for Luke) was at hand. So Paul broke bread, saying a prayer of thanks in front of them all. They cheered up and ate. Then they lightened the ship even more than before by throwing the rest of the grain over the side. The whole point of the voyage, as far as the ship owner was concerned, had now been lost. But at least they were near to land.

That did not itself assure safety. Many ships have been wrecked, with loss of life, within sight of an apparently welcoming shore. In any case, nobody on board recognized the coastline ahead of them. Nobody, then, knew the possible places where one might bring the ship in, if not to an actual harbor, then at least to a safe landing. We sense the mixture of hope and fear among sailors and passengers alike. They could make out a bay, and perhaps all they would have to do would be to head the boat in that direction! They slipped the anchors, let the tillers go slack, and hoisted a sail for the wind to take them in.

Their reckoning did not include a reef just below the surface. We hear in our mind's ear the horrible grind and crunch as the ship, scudding before the wind, rushes straight onto rock. We feel the shudder and lurch as it suddenly stops, while the wind continues to scream in the sail. We hear the rush of water coming through the broken hull, the shouts of the sailors, the passengers shrieking in panic. The ship has stopped dead, but the waves have not, and the relentless beating of water begins to smash the stern to bits. Then, suddenly, a grim extra element is added to the chaos: in the confusion and noise, the soldiers realize (as the Philippian jailer had realized) what might happen to them if they let their prisoners escape. Wouldn't it be better to kill them rather than risk being blamed for letting them get away? Paul's fate hangs for a horrible moment between the sea and the sword. Has it come to this?

Fortunately, the centurion has learned a deep respect, perhaps even affection, for his brilliant if bossy prisoner. (Perhaps it was moments like that that made Luke, in his writings, give centurions the benefit of the doubt.) In any case, he gives a different order: those who can swim should swim, and those who can't should grab a plank and do their best. The ship, their home for the last few terrifying weeks, is falling apart under the battering of the waves. Two hundred and seventy-six frightened men—merchants, businessmen, ship owners, soldiers, apostles, sailors, slaves, and prisoners alike, in the sudden egalitarianism of emergency—gasp and splash their way to shore. There is no distinction: all are soaked, scared, freezing, and exhausted. Rank and wealth mean nothing as they crawl or stagger onto dry land. But the trial by water is over. All have been saved.

The dark powers have done their worst. Once again Paul has put his faith in the God who raises the dead, the God who wins the victory over the forces of evil, the God of the Exodus. Once again, though he and his companions are just as tired and wet as everybody else, they are at least alive. And, despite everything, they are still on their way to Rome.

But that can hardly have been their first reflection in the initial minutes after dragging themselves onto shore. It was cold and raining, but the local people, seeing a shipwreck, came to help, explaining to anyone who was interested that the island was Malta. The first thing needed was a fire, to warm everybody up, and they set about gathering brushwood. Paul, never idle, lent a hand by collecting a bundle of sticks. As he put them on the fire, a viper wriggled out at speed, escaping from the flames, and, before Paul could get out of its way, sank its fangs into his hand. The sea, the soldiers, and now a snake! Paul, alert as ever for deeper meanings in everyday events, might have been reminded of the ancient prophecy about a man escaping from a lion only to be met by a bear, then darting into a house, leaning against a wall to catch his breath, and being bitten by a snake.[7]

What happened next, however, is more or less the opposite of what had happened to Paul in Lystra. There, the locals had begun by thinking Paul was a god and ended by stoning him. The Maltese inhabitants, by contrast, began by thinking he must be a murderer: he'd been rescued from the sea, they said, but a blind divine "Justice" had caught up with him nonetheless. Paul didn't believe in a blind divine force of "justice," only in the "justice" of the living God; even so, it must have been a nasty moment. His instant reaction was to shake the snake off his hand into the fire, but surely, thought the watchers, the poison would get into his system in a minute or two. We imagine not only the local people but also Paul's friends crowding around him, with Luke the doctor anxiously examining him, to see if there was anything they could do. The pessimists were muttering that he would soon start to swell up or simply collapse. Gradually they realized it wasn't going to happen; he felt fine, no ill effects at all. "Ah," said the locals, "we were wrong. He isn't a murderer. He must be a god."

After things calmed down and arrangements for the travelers were made, Paul and his companions were welcomed by "the leading man of the island," one Publius, whose father was sick with a fever and dysentery. (Publius was not the Roman magistrate in charge of the island; such a person would neither have owned lands in the region nor had his father living with him.) Paul laid his hands on the father and prayed, and the fever and sickness left him. The news of this, predictably, produced a crowd of sick people from all around the island. Paul cured them all, earning an outpouring of gratitude that spilled over to the whole party; the local people now looked after them well and eventually sent them on their way with a liberal supply of provisions.

This scene, as told by Luke, is no doubt compressed and idealized. But it explains what otherwise might be puzzling, namely, how the whole party, presumably now without money or other means to rent accommodation, was able to last through the winter months of 59/60 before it was once again possible to sail. Paul and his friends must have had a sense of marking time, but also a sense of relief, gratitude, and renewed hope.

★ ★ ★

And so to Rome. The travelers spent three months on Malta, from late October or early November 59 to January or February 60. The next leg of the trip, crossing from Malta to Sicily, is short, and from there the journey up the Italian coast is easier than that across the larger expanse of the Mediterranean. As we think of the last stages of Paul's journey, he does not seem like a prisoner on his way to the highest court in the known world. It feels as though he is on some kind of celebratory procession. The ship docks at Puteoli, seven or eight miles north of Naples. An old Roman colony from the Republican days, Puteoli was by this time a harbor of considerable importance for the grain arriving from the East. If the ship owner and his colleagues were still with the party at this stage, they must have thought sadly of what might have been.

In Puteoli Paul and his party find a group of Christians. There is evidence at this time for Christian groups in Pompeii, just inland in the same region. Clearly the gospel had already borne fruit all up this stretch of coast. The travelers were allowed to stop and spend a week there before continuing up the road on their final journey, probably taking inside of a week. Word of their imminent arrival brought fellow Jesus-followers from Rome to Appian Forum, forty miles southeast of Rome, and Three Taverns, ten miles closer. This must have been a great encouragement to Paul. It was now early in AD 60, nearly three years since he had sent Phoebe to Rome with his remarkable letter. Like an artist sending his greatest-ever painting to a far-off gallery for a major exhibition, he must have wondered a thousand times how it had been received. These reception parties would have reassured him. They indicated that, for many in Rome at least, he was seen as an honored and respected guest. It would normally only be nobility or returning generals who would expect people to come miles to meet them and escort them to their destination.

He was, of course, still under guard. But he was not a condemned criminal. It was he, after all, who had initiated the appeal to Caesar. In a strange way, he still held that initiative. He was allowed to lodge privately in the city, with a soldier in charge of him.

Archaeologists think they may have found where he lived at this time. There is a first-century dwelling with decorations that seem to indicate this as a distinct possibility. The house in question, below the modern street level, is just beside the Corso, the main street running northwest to southeast through Rome, roughly halfway between the Forum and the Pantheon. It is underneath a church, in the lower part of the building that now houses the Palazzo Doria Pamphili. If this is right, it would put Paul in the very middle of the ancient city. It is normally assumed that most of the Christian groups lived across the river in the poorer district of Trastevere. But from the indications that there were several house-churches in Rome, which might well not have had much to do with one another, it is quite possible that some were located in the main part of the city and that Paul would have been living close to one or more of them.

As often in ancient history, we now want to know several things on which our sources are silent. First, had the letter to Rome had the desired effect? The local believers had had three years to ponder it. Were they now doing what Paul had urged? Had the largely Gentile Roman church learned to respect the synagogue community and to pray for them, as Paul had prayed in Romans 10? Had the divided house-churches found a way to "welcome one another," so that they could "glorify the God and father of our Lord Jesus the Messiah," as he had put it, "with one mind and one mouth"?[8] Were they, in other words, worshipping and praying together? Were they thus able to support him in any further work? Or had his letter alarmed or even alienated them? The welcome parties indicate that some had been enthusiastic. What about the others? We do not know.

Second, what then happened after Paul's two-year house arrest, when, we assume, he was brought before Nero? Was there another great scene like the one before Festus and Agrippa, only more so? Or was it an anticlimax? Did Nero see the apostle in person, or did he delegate this unsavory and trivial task to a minor official? Again, we do not know.

More specifically, third, was Paul put to death then, or did he have a new lease on life—unrecorded in any contemporary sources—that allowed him more travel and perhaps more writing? If so, when and how did he ultimately die? It may seem strange to modern readers that we know so much about Paul, so much intimate detail of his thoughts, his hopes, his fears, his joys, but not how it all ended. We can, and will, speculate a little, but first we must look at what Luke chooses to tell us instead of all this.

The book of Acts has focused, up to this point, on the way Paul was perceived in Jerusalem and on the charges that were brought against him in relation to undermining the Torah and defiling the Temple. These were, in other words, charges of radical disloyalty to the Jewish world and its ancestral heritage, charges that of course Paul rebutted in both his letters and the various legal hearings. But there was a large synagogue community in Rome. Having returned from the banishment under Claudius, this community might well have been sensitive about someone who might look outwardly as if he spoke for the Jewish people but who might actually be undermining their ancient culture and threatening their national security. Their question would have been one that resonates to this day: Was Paul really a loyal Jew?

Paul made it a priority on his arrival in Rome to address this issue. We assume, of course, that he made contact with his own friends as soon as possible. But the key question, which might in fact determine how everything else including the trial before Nero would turn out, had to do with the Jewish community itself (as opposed to the various Jewish Jesus-followers, some of whom might still be part of the synagogue community, but others of whom might well not be). Just as in one city after another on his earlier travels Paul had made straight for the synagogue or at least the *proseuchē,* and just as in the opening of Romans he had declared that the gospel was "to the Jew first, and also, equally, to the Greek," so now he stuck to his principles and his habits and—assuming he was under house arrest and could not attend a synagogue himself—invited the leaders of the Jewish community to call on him.

The point of their first meeting was not scriptural or theological discussion. Before they could even get to that, Paul wanted to make one thing clear, something we from our distance might not have guessed from the earlier story. He had realized that, after the prolonged legal wrangling in Jerusalem and Caesarea, his appeal to Caesar might have been seen not so much as a way of getting out of trouble himself, but as a way of turning the tables and bringing countercharges against his fellow Jews. And this might have had significant implications in several directions.

The early 60s were, after all, an increasingly tense time for Roman-Jewish relations. Not only was there the bad memory of the expulsion under Claudius. In Judaea itself, a string of inept and corrupt governors, of whom Felix and Festus were simply the most recent, had enraged the locals. Rome had repressed and suppressed potential movements of revolt intermittently over the previous hundred years. But this had succeeded only in clamping down the lid on a pot that, heated to boiling point by scripture-fueled "zeal" of the sort that Paul knew only too well, was now ready to explode. All this would be well known to the Jewish communities in Rome. Might it not look as though he was now part of the problem, coming as a Jew to bear witness against his own kinsfolk?

What's more, if Caesar was now presented with a Roman citizen (who happened to be Jewish) coming to complain of his treatment in Judaea, might that not fuel the Roman desire to deal with those troublesome Jews once and for all? Might it not also awaken echoes of Claudius's decree? Might the Jews once again find themselves unwelcome in Rome, just a few years after returning to their homes and their livelihoods? Might this spark the kind of anti-Jewish backlash we saw when the mob beat up Sosthenes in Corinth or when Alexander tried to speak to the crowd in Ephesus? Paul would be only too aware of this danger. He was eager to head it off before it could begin.

He would not, in fact, have been the first Jew to make a journey to Rome in order to register a protest about the state of affairs back in Judaea. Archelaus, the heir of Herod the Great, had gone to Rome to receive his kingdom sixty years before. Augustus had granted Archelaus his wish, though in a modified form, installing him as "ethnarch" rather than "king." But not long afterward a combined delegation of Jews and Samaritans went to Rome to protest, and in AD 6 Archelaus was banished.[9] That story, with a different twist, is probably reflected in Jesus's parable about a king going away, receiving kingly authority, and coming back to face local opposition, though Jesus was thinking then of a different kind of kingdom and different opposition.[10]

So was there now going to be trouble? Was Paul's appeal to Caesar going to pull down the roof on top of the Jewish community in Rome and Judaea? Might that not undermine all the things he had been trying to accomplish in his letter? He had written what he did in order to prepare carefully for his own arrival in Rome at last. But the delicate balance of what he had said three years earlier might now be jeopardized by the realization that he had come because he had appealed to Caesar.

So Paul insisted to the Jewish elders in Rome, as he had insisted in every speech he had made in Jerusalem and Caesarea, that he was a loyal Jew and that his whole mission was about "the hope of Israel." This fits so securely with the Paul we know from the letters, not least Galatians, 1 Corinthians, Philippians, and of course Romans, that we can be sure we are on solid historical ground. This is exactly the sort of thing he would have wanted to say. Of course, for him "the hope of Israel" meant both the worldwide inheritance (the king of Israel would be king of the world) and the resurrection of the dead. Paul saw both of these in Jesus and therefore saw following Jesus as the way, the only way, by which this ancient national aspiration would be achieved.

To his relief, no doubt, the Jewish elders told him that they had not received any messages about him from Judaea. Nobody had passed on warnings about him. They did, however, know about this messianic sect, perhaps because that had been the cause of their expulsion by Claudius twelve or more years before. All they knew was that everybody was saying rude things about this crazy anti-social new movement. They were indeed. The Roman historian Tacitus, writing about this period and this movement from the safe vantage point of the early second century, says with a sneer that the Christians are a group of people who hate the whole human race. "What can you expect?" he says. "All the filth and folly of the world ends up in Rome sooner or later."[11] Yes, Paul would have thought had he heard that comment: folly to Gentiles, scandal to Jews. Nothing much had changed—though Tacitus still suggests that Nero's persecution went a bit too far. (This is rather like Trajan advising Pliny that, though of course Christians must be killed, one does not want people spying and informing on their neighbors. Standards of civilized behavior must be kept up.)[12]

So the Jewish elders fixed a day where they could meet Paul at more leisure and explore his message. We know the script. The subject would be the hope of Israel: the One God becoming king of all the world. For Paul, this would mean telling the story as we have seen him tell it in city after city: Genesis, Exodus, Numbers (remember Phinehas), Deuteronomy, the Psalms, Isaiah, Jeremiah, Ezekiel, and much, much more. Patriarchs, Moses, David, exile, Messiah. Crucifixion, resurrection. We can guess what is coming next. Some would believe; others would not. Paul saw with sorrow that this too was part of the scriptural promise and warning. He quoted Isaiah 6, as Jesus had done: the heart of the people had grown dull.[13] He had thought all this through and laid it all out in the letter he had written to Rome three years earlier. Now here, in Rome itself, he saw it before his own eyes.

There was still the hope. In his mind's eye, he would recall the prayer he had uttered in the letter ("My prayer to God ... is for their salvation"), the possibility he had held out ("If they do not remain in unbelief, they will be grafted back in"), and the promise to which he had clung ("'all Israel shall be saved' ... when the fullness of the nations comes in").[14] But for the moment the pattern continued, the pattern, that is, of Paul's whole career to date. The gospel was "to the Jew first," but when the Jews rejected it, as most had rejected Jesus himself, "this salvation from God has been sent to the Gentiles." This line, from Acts 28:28, directly echoes Romans 11:11 ("by their trespass, salvation has come to the nations"). Paul may himself have echoed, under his breath or in his heart, the words that end the latter verse, "in order to make them jealous," perhaps going on to 11:14, "so that, if possible, I can make my 'flesh' jealous, and save some of them." But it would be tactless to say this out loud to his visitors, at least on this first occasion. What might make them "jealous," after all, would not be a word of teaching from him, but the sight of non-Jews celebrating the ancient Jewish hope of the kingdom, of the Messiah, of resurrection. That was, in part, why it was important for Paul that the house-churches in Rome should find their way to united worship and community, whatever it took. These issues were all intertwined.

Paul waited two years, under house arrest, for his case to come before the emperor. A strange Jewish prisoner would not have rated highly on Nero's list of priorities. Paul was, however, free to welcome people to his quarters and to go on making the royal announcement, the true "gospel" of which the imperial "good news" was, as he believed, simply a parody. Nobody stopped him; he told anybody and everybody who would listen that the One God of Israel was the world's true king and that he had installed his son Jesus, Israel's Messiah, as Lord of the world. Paul taught, says Luke, "with all boldness."[15] We are not surprised; "boldness" had been the keynote of Paul's self-description, even in the tense and contested atmosphere of 2 Corinthians 3 when the "boldness" of his apostolic proclamation had been a major theme. He had never tried to hide things. He never tried to curry favor. (Here is, no doubt, one root of what comes across in the account of the voyage as bossiness and interfering; Paul was used to saying what he thought.) He was much more afraid of not being true to the gospel than of any consequences a "bold" proclamation might have had. He was loyal to Israel's traditions as he had seen them rushing together in the Messiah. He was loyal, ultimately, to the Messiah himself, faithful to the one who had himself been faithful to the point of death.

But what of Paul's own death? If he arrived in Rome in AD 60, as seems the most likely, these two years of house arrest take us forward to 62. What happened then?

★ ★ ★

Two possible scenarios, very different from one another, follow from this point. In a small way, they integrate with the question of why Acts stops where it does. An early date for Acts places it as a document for use in Paul's trial, meaning that Luke was writing it down during that final two-year period, telling the story of one "hearing" after another. The whole thing would then have been building up toward the coming appearance before Nero, with a heavy emphasis on Paul's innocence, on his standing as a loyal (albeit messianic) Jew, and in consequence on his right as a Jewish citizen of Rome, at least as seen by Gallio in Corinth, to pursue his vocation as he pleased. A later date for Acts might indicate that Luke knew the result of the trial, but did not want to draw attention to it—especially if Paul had after all been condemned right away—because it would have spoiled his story of pagan authorities supporting, to their own surprise perhaps, this strange wandering Jew. Or it might indicate that Luke knew Paul had been released by Nero and had been able to engage in other activity, but that his (Luke's) own purpose had been served; that is, the gospel of God's kingdom had now gone from Jerusalem and Judaea to Samaria and thence to the ends of the earth.[16] The gospel itself, not Paul, is the real hero of Luke's story. That, then, would be enough.

Trying to guess Luke's motives for stopping here does not, then, take us very far. We are left, like some postmodern novelists, with the possibility of writing two or even three endings to the story and leaving readers to decide. There are, of course, traditions that

Paul was martyred in Rome; you can still see his chains, so it is claimed, by the tomb where he is supposed to lie, in the church of St. Paul Outside the Walls. Once, in October 2008, I heard the Vienna Philharmonic Orchestra there, playing Bruckner's magnificent Sixth Symphony as a command performance for Pope Benedict, who sat enthroned in the middle surrounded by a large number of cardinals. The music was impressive, but it provided me no clue, of course, as to whether Paul is really buried there.

So the options divide, and then divide again. The first and most obvious is that Paul was killed in the persecution of Christians that followed the great fire of Rome in AD 64. Since most of the Christians, as we mentioned, lived on the impoverished southwest bank of the river, and since the fire was confined to the wealthier northeast side, they were an easy target—people would say, they must have started it, since their own homes were untouched! (In any case, since they didn't worship the gods, any disaster was probably their fault.) It is perfectly possible that Paul and perhaps Peter as well were among the leaders rounded up and made to suffer the penalty for a disaster whose actual origins have remained unknown from that day to this. Paul, as a citizen, would have been entitled to the quick death of beheading with a sword rather than the slow, appalling tortures that Nero inflicted on many others or the upside-down crucifixion that tradition assigns to Peter. But even then, if Paul were killed in 64, that leaves two more years after the two that Luke mentions. Would that have been enough time for a visit to Spain?

Quite possibly. There was a regular traffic between Rome and Tarraco, quite enough to justify, if not finally to vindicate, the enthusiastic advocacy of some today in the historic Catalan town of Tarragona. (Tarraco was the capital of *Hispania Tarraconensis,* which since the time of Augustus had stretched right across the north of the Iberian Peninsula to the Atlantic coast.) We can see why he might have wished to go. The original temple to Augustus had been replaced in Paul's day with a dramatic terraced complex for the imperial cult, in which the main temple was easily visible from several miles out to sea, as is the present cathedral on the same site. If I am right in suggesting that Paul was eager to announce Jesus as king and Lord in places where Caesar was claiming those titles along with others, then Tarraco, in the province at the farthest reaches of the world, would have been a natural target.

I am inclined now to give more weight than I once did to the testimony of Clement, an early bishop of Rome. Writing about Paul in the late first century, he says:

> After he had been seven times in chains, had been driven into exile, had been stoned, and had preached in the east and in the west, he won the genuine glory for his faith, having taught righteousness to the whole world and having reached the farthest limits of the west. Finally, when he had given his testimony before the rulers, he thus departed from the world and went to the holy place, having become an outstanding example of patient endurance.[17]

"The farthest limits of the west" would of course mean Spain. Clement could have been simply extrapolating from Romans 15, and it would suit his purpose to give the impression of Paul's worldwide reach. But he was a central figure in the Roman church within a generation of Paul's day. He is writing at the most about thirty years after Paul's death. It is far more likely that he knew more solid and reliable traditions about Paul than we, discounting him, can invent on our own.

The other alternative at this point is that Paul, given his freedom at a hearing in 62, changed his mind from what he had said in Miletus (about not showing his face in that region again) and more conclusively in Romans 15:23 (having no more room left for work in the East). This too is possible. Paul makes a great play in 2 Corinthians about having the right to change his mind. Just because he had said before that he would do this or that, he might nevertheless do something else when the time came. He would follow God's leading in the moment. All his plans carried the word "perhaps" about with them.

But to what end? Why go back to the East? If he did make it to Spain, could he not then have gone north? Might we not have had the chance of a Pauline version of Blake's famous poem "Jerusalem" ("And did those feet in ancient time / Walk upon England's mountains green?"). Perhaps on reflection it is as well that we do not. How do we fit together the travel details in those most tricky of Pauline pieces, the so-called Pastoral Letters?

I have kept these back until now because they are, in my judgment, far harder to fit not only into Paul's travel plans, but into Paul's writing style than any of the other relevant material. (Some earlier generations thought that Paul wrote the Letter to the Hebrews. The standard objection to this—that the theology of the letter is so unlike Paul's—is considerably overstated; but there is no evidence that he had any hand in it.) Granted, as I said before, writers may easily change their style between one week and the next, between one work and the next. But the changes required for us comfortably to ascribe to Paul the letters we call 1 Timothy and Titus, especially, are of a different kind to those required for us to accept Ephesians and Colossians; more too than those required for us to recognize those two other very different letters, 1 and 2 Corinthians, as both from the same hand.

However, if we were to make a start, it ought, in my judgment, to be with 2 Timothy. If this were the only "Pastoral" letter we had, I suspect it would never have incurred the same questioning that it has endured through its obvious association with 1 Timothy and Titus. Second Timothy claims to be written from Rome in between two legal hearings; Paul has been lonely and bereft, though Onesiphorus, a friend from his time in Ephesus, has come to Rome, searched for him, and found him.[18] Onesiphorus contrasts sadly with "all who are in Asia," who, Paul says, have turned away from him—presumably to something more like the message urged upon the Galatians in the late 40s. But where is Timothy? He cannot now be in Ephesus if he needs Paul, in Rome, to tell him what is happening there. And where has Paul been?

He speaks of leaving a cloak at Troas.[19] This would fit easily enough with the earlier trip from Corinth to Jerusalem; Paul might well have been absentminded after an all-night preaching session enlivened by someone falling out of a window. But if he had wanted to send somebody to retrieve the cloak, he would have been far more likely to do that from his two-year imprisonment in Caesarea than to wait until he was in Rome. Indeed, had it not been for the mention of Onesiphorus looking for Paul in Rome in 2 Timothy 1:17, a case could have been made for the letter being written from Caesarea, though other details would remain puzzling. He speaks of sending Tychicus to Ephesus, which might work if Ephesians and Colossians were after all written from Rome, not Ephesus itself, though as I said earlier that raises other problems. He sends greetings to Prisca and Aquila; maybe they had moved back one more time from Rome to Ephesus, but if so, they hadn't stayed in Rome very long. He says that Erastus had stayed in Corinth, whereas in Acts 19:22 he goes ahead of Paul to Macedonia. He mentions leaving Trophimus behind, ill, in Ephesus, whereas according to Acts 21:29 he is with Paul in Jerusalem. None of these, individually or taken together, is historically impossible. It may be that the comparatively easy convergence we have seen between Paul's other letters and the narrative of Acts has lulled us into thinking that we know more than we do. But it does seem to me that if 2 Timothy is genuine, then it certainly implies some additional activity back in the East, despite Paul's earlier plans, after an initial hearing in Rome. And it implies that this time, unlike the situation reflected in Philippians 1, Paul really does believe he is facing death at last:

I am already being poured out as a drink-offering; my
departure time has arrived. I have fought the good fight;
I have completed the course; I have kept the faith. What
do I still have to look for? The crown of righteousness!
The Lord, the righteous judge, will give it to me as my
reward on that day—and not only to me, but also to all
who have loved his appearing.[20]

We can easily imagine Paul writing that—as we can the next
passage, where he comes across as tired, anxious, weary of having
people who let him down ("Demas . . . is in love with this present world!"[21]). If 2 Timothy is genuine, then, it reflects a complex
journey—and a return to Rome—of which we know nothing else.

First Timothy seems altogether brighter, somewhat like the contrast we see when we move back from 2 to 1 Corinthians. Timothy
is in Ephesus,[22] and Paul is giving him instructions about his work
there. Much of the instruction in this letter could have been given,
in its basic content, at any time in the first two centuries; there is
little to connect it directly with Paul, or indeed with Timothy either. Hymenaeus and Alexander are mentioned as blasphemers who
have been "handed over to the satan,"[23] as Paul recommended doing with the incestuous man in 1 Corinthians.[24] Hymenaeus then
crops up in 2 Timothy 2:17, this time in company with Philetus,
this time over a more specific charge: "saying that the resurrection
has already happened." We are left looking at small fragments of a
jigsaw puzzle for which we have far too few pieces and no guiding
picture to show us what might belong where.

As for the letter to Titus, the problems are compounded. It is
possible that the journey from Miletus to Jerusalem in Acts 21
took a far more circuitous route than Luke indicates and that the
party went around by Crete, dropping off Titus on the way. Acts
21:1–3 does, however, offer a close description of events, and we
have already been told that Paul was in a hurry because he wanted
to be in Jerusalem for Pentecost.[25] The only other geographical

detail of possible significance is that Paul tells Titus he has decided to winter in Nicopolis, a small town on (with strong Roman imperial associations) the northwest coast of Greece. Again, we have no indication anywhere in Paul or Acts that he was going in that direction, which—to repeat the point yet again—does not mean that it is either impossible or unlikely, merely that we do not have the larger picture within which a small detail like this might fit.

So, as with Paul's putative trip to Spain, I have become more open to the possibility of a return visit to the East after an initial hearing in Rome. The problem might then be that these two, Spain and the East, might seem to cancel one another out. If Paul was to be back in Rome by the time of Nero's persecution, facing additional hearings in difficult circumstances, two years would hardly be enough for the relevant trips, both west and east. But perhaps that is the point. Perhaps the persecution would not need any legal trappings. The emperor had laid the blame for the fire on the Christians, and that would be enough. Perhaps, then, one or both trips might after all be feasible; Paul might have been away either in the East or in the West when Nero was rounding up the Christians. Perhaps Paul came back sometime after 64 to find that it was all over, but that the social mood had changed and that, citizen or not, appealing to Caesar or not, he was straightforwardly on trial as a dangerous troublemaker. Perhaps. Paul had to live with a good many "perhaps" clauses in his life. Maybe it is fitting that his biographers should do so as well.

Before we can look, finally, at how Paul would have approached his oncoming death, it is important to stand back and survey the larger picture of the man and his work.

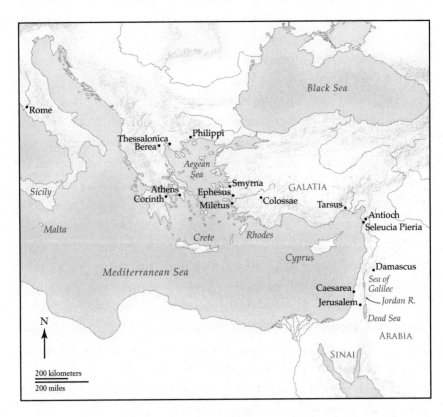

Paul's World

15

The Challenge of Paul

HAT WAS PAUL trying to do? What made him do it?
Why did he keep on going back to the synagogue,
even though they kept on beating him? Why did
he keep on urging his message on non-Jews, even though they
thought he was a crazy Jew and wanted to run him out of town?
Why did he carry on relentlessly, with his apparent desire to be in
three places at once, to write to five churches at once, to explain
and to cajole, to teach and to proclaim, to travel and travel and
travel some more? What was it, both about the initial event on
the road to Damascus and about his subsequent sense of an inner
compulsion flowing from that that kept him going? And, on the
one occasion when even that ran out of steam, what was it that
eventually regenerated his faith and hope? What assessment can we
make of this brilliant mind and passionate heart? What motivated
him in his heart of hearts, and how did the event on the Damascus
Road set that in motion? And finally, out beyond all that, why did
it work? Why did the movement he started, against all the odds,
become in a fairly short time the church we see in the fourth and
fifth centuries? What was it about this busy, vulnerable man that,
despite everything, seems to have been so effective?

It may help a little to explain why Paul has not had an easy ride in the modern church and world if we recall his moment of greatest crisis in Ephesus, where he experienced terrible depression and then the regeneration of faith and hope. Those who like their metaphysics or philosophy simple and clear-cut will find, like Festus in Caesarea, that when they hear Paul, they find it all so complicated and confusing that they want to wave it away angrily—it's just a lot of madness. Festus has had plenty of successors in the modern world. Those who like their religion, or indeed their friendships, served at medium temperature may find Paul's personality hard to take: at once eager and vulnerable, both bold and (in his own words) "in your face" and then liable to serious self-doubt ("Was it all for nothing?"). One might suppose that, as a friend, he was, as we say, high maintenance, though the reward would be high performance.

But are those even the right questions to ask? Why should Paul's ideas and personality be placed on the Procrustean bed of our modern likes and dislikes? He might well have a sharp retort for any such suggestion. Why should *he* not question *our* criteria, our ideas, our preferred personality types? Where does one even start to ask such questions?

For Paul there was no question about the starting point. It was always Jesus: Jesus as the shocking fulfillment of Israel's hopes; Jesus as the genuinely human being, the true "image"; Jesus the embodiment of Israel's God—so that, without leaving Jewish monotheism, one would worship and invoke Jesus as Lord *within,* not alongside, the service of the "living and true God." Jesus, the one for whose sake one would forsake all idols, all rival "lords." Jesus, above all, who had come to his kingdom, the true lordship of the world, in the way that Paul's friends who were starting to write the Jesus story at that time had emphasized: by dying under the weight of the world's sin in order to break the power of the dark forces that had enslaved all humans, Israel included.

Jesus, who had thereby fulfilled the ancient promise, being

"handed over because of our trespasses and raised because of our justification."[1] Jesus, who had been bodily raised from the dead on the third day and thereby announced to the world as the true Messiah, the "son of God" in all its senses (Messiah, Israel's representative, embodiment of Israel's God). Jesus, therefore, as the one in whom "all God's promises find their yes," the "goal of the law," the true seed of Abraham, the ultimate "root of Jesse."[2] Jesus, then, the Lord at whose name every knee would bow. Jesus, who would reappear in a great future event that would combine the sense of a true king coming to claim and establish his kingdom and the sense of the long-hidden God at last being made visible. Jesus, whose powerful message could and did transform lives in the present time ahead of the final moment when he would raise his people from the dead. And, in and with all of this, Jesus not just as the label to put on an idea, a theological fact, if you like, but as the living, inspiring, consoling, warning, and encouraging presence, the one whose love "makes us press on," the one "who loved me and gave himself for me," the one whom to know, Paul declared, was worth more than all the privileges that the world, including the ancient biblical world, has to offer. Jesus was the starting point. And the goal.

The goal? Yes, because Paul never wavered in his sense that Jesus would reappear. He would "descend from heaven," though to get the flavor of that we have to remind ourselves that "heaven" is not "up in the sky," but is rather God's dimension of present reality. Jesus would come *from* heaven *to* earth not—as in much popular fantasy—in order to scoop up his people and take them back to "heaven," but in order to complete the already inaugurated task of colonizing "earth," the human sphere, with the life of "heaven," God's sphere. God's plan had always been to unite all things in heaven and on earth in Jesus, which meant, from the Jewish point of view, that Jesus was the ultimate Temple, the heaven-and-earth place. This, already accomplished in his person, was now being implemented through his spirit. Paul always

believed that God's new creation was coming, perhaps soon. By
the time of his later letters he realized that, contrary to his earlier
guess, he might himself die before it happened. But that the present corrupt and decaying world would one day be rescued from
this state of slavery and death and emerge into new life under
the glorious rule of God's people, God's new humanity—this he
never doubted.

This, moreover, gave his work its particular urgency. Here there
has been a serious misunderstanding throughout the last century.
Insofar as there was a view we might label "apocalyptic" in Paul's
day, he shared it. He believed that Israel's God, having abandoned
the Temple at the time of the Babylonian exile and never having
fulfilled his promise to return in visible and powerful glory, had revealed himself suddenly, shockingly, disruptively, in Jesus, breaking
in upon an unready world and an unready people. Paul believed
that this had happened not only in the events of Jesus's death and
resurrection and the gift of the spirit, but in his own case, and perhaps in other cases, in a moment of blinding and life-transforming
glory. He believed in a new creation already begun and to be completed in the future. He believed that a great transformation *had*
taken place in the entire cosmos when Jesus died and rose again,
and he believed that a coming great transformation *would* take
place at his "return" or his "reappearing," the time when heaven
and earth would come together at last.

The last few generations of students and clergy have often been
taught, however, that Paul, and indeed Jesus and his earliest followers, believed two things about all this: first, that this coming
great event would involve (in some sense or other) the end of the
known world, and, second, that this coming event would take
place within a generation. So, because the world did not end after
the first Christian generation, it has been common coin, particularly among those who have wanted to distance themselves from
early Christian ideas in general and Paul's in particular, to say,
sometimes with kindly and sometimes with patronizing intent,

that "They expected the end of the world and they were wrong, so perhaps they were wrong about a lot of other things too." The irony of this position is that the idea of the "end of the world" is neither biblical nor Jewish nor early Christian. It comes from the secular world of nineteenth-century Europe fueled by dreams of revolutions past and still to come. When, toward the end of that century, some writers began to take seriously the Jewish contexts of the kingdom language of Jesus and his first followers, they were attuned not to the way such language worked in the first-century Jewish world, but to the way such language worked within current European ideologies. They projected that back onto Jesus, Paul, and the rest. It made a good story at the time, particularly when Europe then plunged into a horrendous, "apocalyptic" century with wars, rumors of wars, and worse. But this didn't help with the essentially historical question of what motivated Paul.

What, then, caused the urgent note in Paul's eschatology? The main point is that the long-awaited event could occur *at any time,* not that it had to occur within a specific time frame. The event that *was* to occur within a generation was not the end of the world but, according to Mark 13 and the parallels in Matthew and Luke, *the fall of Jerusalem.* This was woven deep into the structure of early Christianity in a way that until recently, with the rise of contemporary studies of the Jewish world of the time, was not usually appreciated. But Jerusalem, and the Temple specifically, had always been seen as the place where heaven and earth met; so much so that when Isaiah speaks of "new heavens and new earth," some commentators will now say, without the need for much elaboration, that this is referring to the ultimate rebuilding of the Temple, the heaven-and-earth building.[3]

Of course, that would in turn point ahead to heaven and earth themselves being renewed and ultimately united. But the Temple, and before that the Tabernacle in the wilderness, had always had that meaning, a forward-looking signpost to the Creator's ultimate intention. It was clear enough in the gospel traditions: Jesus had warned that the Temple was under judgment; not one stone would be left upon another. That would indeed be "the end of the world"—not in the shallow, modern sense of the collapse of the space-time universe, but in the Jewish sense that the building that had held heaven and earth together would be destroyed. As Jeremiah had warned, chaos would come again.

I have suggested above that in 2 Thessalonians Paul had seen this moment coming, quite possibly through a Roman emperor doing what Caligula had so nearly done. The monsters—presumably the ultimate monster from the sea, Rome itself—would draw themselves up to their full height, demolishing the heaven-and-earth structure that had (according to Jesus) come to embody Jeremiah's "den of robbers." Jesus, as the true Lord, would then set up a kingdom of a different sort, a kingdom that could not be shaken. But if *this* was going to happen within a generation—if Jerusalem was going to fall to the Romans—then Paul had better get busy, because he knew, better perhaps than any of his contemporaries, what reactions such a terrible event would produce.

Gentile Jesus-followers would say that God had finally cut off those Jews, leaving "the church" as a non-Jewish body. Christianity would become "a religion," to be contrasted (favorably, of course) with something called "Judaism." Conversely, Jewish Jesus-followers would accuse their Gentile colleagues—and particularly the followers of that wretched compromiser Paul—of having precipitated this disaster by imagining that one could worship the true God without getting circumcised and following the whole Torah. And Jews who had rejected the message of Jesus would be in no doubt at all. All this happened because of the false prophet Jesus and his wicked followers, especially Paul, who had led Israel astray.

All this is supposition, but it is rooted at every point in what we know about Paul and his gospel. He was therefore determined *to establish and maintain Jew-plus-Gentile communities, worshipping the One God in and through Jesus his son and in the power of the spirit, ahead of the catastrophe*. Only so could this potential split—the destruction of the "new Temple" of 1 Corinthians 3 and Ephesians 2, no less—be averted. This is why Paul insisted, in letter after letter, on *the unity of the church across all traditional boundaries*. This was not about the establishment of a new "religion." It had nothing to do—one still meets this ill-informed slur from time to time—with Paul being a "self-hating Jew." Paul affirmed what he took to be the central features of Jewish hope: One God, Israel's Messiah, and resurrection itself. For him, what mattered was *messianic eschatology* and the community that embodied it. The One God had fulfilled, in a way so unexpected that most of the guardians of the promises had failed to recognize it, not only a set of individual promises, but the entire narrative of the ancient people of God. That, after all, was what Paul had been saying in one synagogue after another. And it was because of that fulfillment that the Gentiles were now being brought into the single family.

People have often written as if Paul believed himself to be living in the *last* days, and in a sense that was true. God had, in the Messiah, brought the old world of chaos, idolatry, wickedness, and death up short, had taken its horror onto himself, and had launched something else in its place. But that meant that, equally, Paul was conscious of living in the *first* days, the opening scenes of the new drama of world history, with heaven and earth now held together not by Torah and Temple, but by Jesus and the spirit, pointing forward to the time when the divine glory would fill the whole world and transform it from top to bottom. You would not find this vision in the non-Jewish world of Paul's day. It is Jewish through and through, including in the fact that it has been reshaped around the one believed to be Israel's Messiah.

Paul's motivation and mindset, then, was shaped centrally and radically by Jesus himself as crucified and risen Messiah and Lord and by the new shape that the Jewish hope had as a result. This is why his loyalty always appeared contested. And this is where we can understand, in its proper context, what he had to say about human beings, their plight, and their rescue. This has been central to most accounts of Paul from the sixteenth century to the present, and as we look back over his life it is important to display this theme in its true colors by placing it in its historical context.

Paul had always believed that the One God would at the last put the whole world right. The Psalms had said it; the prophets had predicted it; Jesus had announced that it was happening (though in a way nobody had seen coming). Paul declared that it *had* happened in Jesus—and that it *would* happen at his return. In between those two, the accomplishment of the putting-right project first in cross and resurrection and then in the final fulfillment at Jesus's return, God had given his own spirit in the powerful and life-transforming word of the gospel. The gospel, incomprehensibly foolish to Greeks and blasphemously scandalous to Jews, nevertheless worked powerfully in hearts and minds. Listeners discovered that it made sense and that the sense it made transformed them from the inside out. This is the great "evangelical" reality for which Paul and his letters are famous.

Our problem has been that we have set that powerful gospel reality in the wrong framework. The Western churches have, by and large, put Paul's message within a medieval notion that rejected the biblical vision of heaven and earth coming together at last. The Middle Ages changed the focus of attention away from "earth" and toward two radically different ideas instead, "heaven" and "hell," often with a temporary stage ("purgatory") before "heaven." Paul's life-changing and world-transforming gospel was then made to serve this quite different agenda, that is, that believing the gospel was the way to escape all that and "go to heaven." But that was not Paul's point. "You have been saved by grace through faith," he writes in Ephesians. "This doesn't happen on your own initiative; it's God's gift. It isn't on the basis of works, so no one is able to boast."[4] As it stands, that statement can easily be fitted into the going-to-heaven scheme of thought, but a glance at the wider context will show that Paul has very different ideas. In the first chapter of Ephesians he insists that the entire divine plan "was to sum up the whole cosmos in the king—yes, everything in heaven and on earth, in him."[5] Here, in the second chapter of the letter, he explains the purpose of "being saved by grace through faith":

> God has made us what we are. God has created us in
> King Jesus for the good works that he prepared, ahead of
> time, as the road we must travel.[6]

God has made us what we are; or, to bring out a different but equally valid flavor of the Greek, *we are God's poetry,* God's artwork. God has accomplished, and will accomplish, the entire new creation in the Messiah and by the spirit. When someone believes the gospel and discovers its life-transforming power, that person becomes a small but significant working model of that new creation.

The point of being human, after all, was never simply to be a passive inhabitant of God's world. As far as Paul was concerned, the point of being human was to be an image-bearer, to reflect God's wisdom and order into the world and to reflect the praises of creation back to God. Humans were therefore made to stand at the threshold of heaven and earth—like an "image" in a temple, no less—and to be the conduit through which God's life would come to earth and earth's praises would rise to God. Here, then, is the point of Paul's vision of human rescue and renewal ("salvation," in traditional language): those who are grasped by grace in the gospel and who bear witness to that in their loyal belief in the One God, focused on Jesus, are not merely beneficiaries, recipients of God's mercy; they are also agents. They are poems in which God is addressing his world, and, as poems are designed to do, they break open existing ways of looking at things and spark the mind to imagine a different way to be human.

That is what Paul's gospel and ethics are, at their heart, all about. *God will put the whole world right* at the last. He has accomplished the main work of that in Jesus and his death and resurrection. And, through gospel and spirit, *God is now putting people right,* so that they can be both examples of what the gospel does and agents of further transformation in God's world.

This is the heart of Paul's famous "doctrine of justification," which is so important in Galatians, Philippians, and Romans, though remarkably inconspicuous (until we realize how it is integrated with everything else) in the other letters. Once again the problem has been the wrong framework. If we come with the question, "How do we get to heaven," or, in Martin Luther's terms, "How can I find a gracious God?" and if we try to squeeze an answer to those questions out of what Paul says about justification, we will probably find one. It may not be totally misleading. But we will miss what Paul's "justification" is really all about. It isn't about a moralistic framework in which the only question that matters is whether we humans have behaved ourselves and so amassed a store of merit ("righteousness") and, if not, where we can find such a store, amassed by someone else on our behalf. It is about the *vocational* framework in which humans are called to reflect God's image in the world and about the rescue operation whereby God has, through Jesus, set humans free to do exactly that.

For Paul, therefore, questions of "sin" and "salvation" are vital, but they function within a worldview different from the one Western Christians have normally assumed. For Paul, as for all devout Jews, the major problem of the world was idolatry. Humans worshipped idols and therefore behaved in ways that were less than fully human, less than fully image-bearing. That was a core Jewish belief, and Paul shared it. What he did not share, as he thought through his tradition in the light of Jesus and the spirit, was the idea that the people of Israel, as they stood, constituted the answer to this problem—as though all one had to do was to become a Jew and try to keep the Torah, and all would be well not only with Israel, but with the world. Paul knew that view, and he firmly rejected it.

Paul believed, not least because he saw it so clearly in the scriptures, that Israel too was in Adam. Israel too had its own brand of idolatry. But the point of Jesus's rescuing death, which Jesus himself had seen as the new Passover, was that the powerful "gods" and "lords" to which humans had given away their own proper authority had been defeated. The resurrection proved it and had thereby launched a new world and a new people to reflect the true God into that new world. That is why Paul's Gentile mission was not a different idea from the idea of "forgiveness of sins" or the "cleansing of the heart." It was *because* the powerful gospel announced and effected those realities that the old barriers between Jew and Greek were abolished in the Messiah. It was *because* in the Messiah the promises of Psalm 2 had come true—that God would set his anointed king over the rulers of the nations, thus extending into every corner of the world the promises made to Abraham about his "inheritance"—that Paul could summon people of every kind of background to "believing obedience." That is why Paul's work must be regarded just as much as "social" or "political" as it is "theological" or "religious." Every time Paul expounded "justification," it formed part of his argument that in the Messiah there was a single family composed of believing Jews and believing Gentiles, a family that demonstrated to the world that there was a new way of being human. Paul saw himself as a working model of exactly this. "Through the law I died to the law, so that I might live to God."[7]

Paul's particular vocation, then, was to found and maintain Jew-plus-Gentile churches on Gentile soil, and to do so while "the restrainer" was still holding back the cataclysm that was coming all too soon. And since he could not in fact be in more places than one and could not write nearly as much, even in his longest letters, as he would ideally have liked (we think again of that long, hot night in Troas and of Eutychus falling out of the window), he realized early on that it was his job not just to teach people *what* to think and believe, but to teach them *how*. How to think clearly, scripturally, prayerfully. How to have the mind renewed and transformed so that believers could work out for themselves the thousand things that he didn't have time to tell them. How to think with "the Messiah's mind," especially as it was shaped around the story of the cross: "This is how you should think among yourselves—with the mind that you have because you belong to the Messiah, Jesus."[8] This is the only way in which the church would be either united or holy, and since both were mandatory—but very difficult—it was vital, Paul recognized, that those "in the Messiah" should acquire the discipline of the Christian mind. In that quest, he drew on all the resources he could find, including ideas and phrases from contemporary philosophy. "We take every thought prisoner," he writes, "and make it obey the Messiah."[9] This, I submit, is part of the reason for the remarkable success of his work.

All this might seem to imply, however, that Paul was primarily, and perhaps only, a "thinker"—a detached brain box, a computer on legs. Not so. As we have seen repeatedly, he defined himself in terms of love: the love of God in the Messiah, the debt of that love which only love could repay, the love that bound him in a rich personal relationship with Jesus himself ("knowing him, knowing the power of his resurrection, and knowing the partnership of his sufferings"[10]). The love that constantly overflowed into what we might call "pastoral" activity but that, for Paul, was simply love in action. We see that powerful but also vulnerable love in his very explicit anxieties over the Thessalonian church in the early days after its founding and in his deeply troubled reaction to the Corinthian church as he made his final journey from Ephesus to confront them once more. We see that love, powerfully and shrewdly in action, in the little letter to Philemon.

It is out of that love and pastoral concern that there flowed simultaneously the constant question of whether he was "running to no good effect" and the constant scriptural answer: *You are my servant.* Isaiah 49 played around and around in his head—

along with many other passages, of course, but this one, and some phrases from it in particular, formed a lifelong mental habit. Isaiah's vision of the servant who would bring God's light to the Gentiles and of the troubles that this servant would have to undergo—including doubt about whether his work was actually doing any good at all—was Paul's constant companion. This was one of the things that made him tick.

It is from within the servant vocation that we can best understand Paul's central concept of *pistis,* which as we have seen means both "faith" (in the various meanings of that English word, all of which come into play at various points) and "loyalty" or "trustworthiness." This helps us to address one of the central questions asked in our own day, as in many earlier days, about Paul: Was he, did he think of himself as, a loyal Jew?

If *pistis* can mean "loyalty" as well as "faith," might one express Paul's most famous doctrine as "justification by loyalty"? That might be too much of a stretch, but for Paul "justification" itself meant something rather different from its normal Western meaning, framed as that has been by a moralistic vision ("Have I done all the things God wants me to do?") linked to a platonic eschatology ("How can I go to heaven?"). For Paul, justification was about God's declaration that this or that person was a member of the single family promised to Abraham—which meant that, though "ungodly" because they were Gentiles, such people had been "justified," declared to be in the right, to be within God's covenant family, by God's overthrow of the enslaving powers, by his forgiveness of sins, and by the powerful cleansing work of the spirit. What was said of Phinehas and before that of Abraham would be said of them: "It will be reckoned to them as righteousness." They will be members of the covenant. The "zeal" of Phinehas, the "zeal" of Saul of Tarsus, had been translated into a zeal for the gospel. The point was that one could then recognize members of the family by their *pistis,* which could be expressed as "believing *in* the God who raised Jesus from the dead" or

confessing Jesus as Lord and believing *that* God raised him from
the dead. Titus shared that *pistis;* that is why Paul and Barnabas
insisted that he should not be circumcised. The Gentile believers
in Antioch shared that *pistis;* that is why Paul confronted Peter
when by his behavior he seemed to suggest otherwise. And so on.

The "faith" in question is thus the response of the whole person to the whole gospel. In traditional Latin tags, it can be *fides
qua,* the faith *by which* one believes, that is, the actual human
trust, the personal response to the message of the gospel. Or it
can be *fides quae,* the faith *that* one believes, that is, the specific
things to which one gives assent. But "assent" is only ever one
part of it. The gospel does not merely produce a mental reaction,
a calculation and a conclusion. That matters but it never happens
alone, and perhaps only a certain type of late medieval philosopher could imagine that it might. Mind and heart are inextricably
linked. And that is why "loyalty" is also a vital part of *pistis.* "Believing obedience"—the obedience of faith, in more common
translations—is the full-hearted, full-person response of loyalty to
the message about Jesus. A contested loyalty, of course, but loyalty
nonetheless.

For the Jews of Paul's day, this "loyalty" was expressed day by
day, indeed several times a day, in the prayer we have seen Paul
use in his younger days and then, in its radically new form, in his
mature following of Jesus. As with several psalms, with the prophets, with the whole style of Jewish worship and liturgy, Paul had
reworked these acts and words around the gospel events. And this
was, and remained, central to his self-perception, his own deep
inner sense of what made him who he was. He was a loyal Jew.

Again and again in the closing chapters of Acts this is reemphasized, and we should resist any attempt to play this picture in Acts
off against the letters of Paul himself. Of course, he had redefined
what that loyalty would mean. It did not mean that, when eating with Gentile friends, he would avoid their type of food. It

did not mean that he would keep the Sabbaths and the festivals the way he had kept them as a young man. When the reality has come, the signposts are no longer needed, not because they were misleading, but because they have done their work. One does not put up a sign saying, "This way to London" outside Buckingham Palace. Paul took the stance he now did neither because he was some kind of a "liberal"—whatever that might have meant in his day!—nor because he was making pragmatic compromises to try to lure Gentiles into his communities, nor, to say it again, because he secretly hated his own culture and identity. It was all because of the Messiah: "I have been crucified with the Messiah. I am, however, alive—but it isn't me any longer; it's the Messiah who lives in me."[11] *If the Messiah has come, and if God has marked him out in his resurrection, then to be a loyal Jew is to be loyal to this Messiah and to the God who has acted in and through him.*

But if the Messiah had been crucified and raised, then the question of what being a loyal Jew actually meant had itself been radically redrawn. It now meant following this pattern of crucifixion and resurrection—reflecting, Paul would have insisted, the pattern of Israel's scriptures themselves. It meant discovering the deep truth of baptism: that one was now "in the Messiah," a member of his extended and multinational family, and that what was true of the Messiah (crucifixion and resurrection) was true of oneself. This is where the act of "calculation" belongs, carrying with it later dogmatic overtones of "imputation." *Calculate yourselves as being dead to sin, he says to those in the churches, and alive to God in the Messiah, Jesus.*[12] What is true of him, Paul would have said, is now true of them, and they must live accordingly. They *have already* been raised "in him"; they *will one day* be raised bodily by his spirit; therefore, their entire life must be lived in this light. This takes faith, in all its usual senses, and when that faith is present, it is in fact indistinguishable from loyalty, loyalty to the Messiah, loyalty to the One God through him. This, ultimately, is what Paul learned on the road to Damascus and in his lifelong reflection on that shattering and blinding event.

★ ★ ★

All this points to the answer I believe Paul would have given and to the answers we ourselves might want to give to our "extra" question: Why did it work? Why was his labor ultimately so fruitful?

There are two quite different ways of approaching this question, and I think Paul would have wanted to have both in play. He would have known all about different levels of explanation. He undoubtedly knew what 2 Kings had said about the angel of the Lord destroying the Assyrians who were besieging Jerusalem, and he may also have known the version in Herodotus, in which mice nibbled the besiegers' bowstrings, forcing them to withdraw.[13] He would certainly have known that one could tell quite different stories about the same event, all equally true in their own way. Luke's account of Paul's appearance before Agrippa and Bernice would be significantly different from what Paul himself might have told his jailer that night, and different too from what Agrippa and Bernice might have said to one another when talking it over the next day.

So what might be said, from different angles, about the reasons for the surprising long-term success of Paul's work? To go a step farther, helping us to get a sense of the significance of the apostle's work, let's ask: How might Paul himself assess this success if he could have seen it?

Paul would probably begin with a theological answer. There is One God, and this God has overcome the powers of darkness through his son; we should expect that by his spirit he will cause the light of the knowledge of his glory to spread throughout the world—through the faithful, suffering, and prayerful witness of Jesus's followers. Or, to put it another way, the One God has already built his new Temple, his new *microcosmos;* the Jew-plus-

Gentile church is the place where the divine spirit already lives in our midst, already reveals his glory as a sign of what will happen one day throughout the whole world. So, sooner or later, this movement is bound to thrive.

Of course, Paul would not expect all this to happen smoothly or easily. Paul is after all a realist. He would never assume that the transformation of small and often muddled communities into a much larger body, forming a majority in the Roman world, would come about without terrible suffering and horrible pitfalls. Yes, he would be saddened, but not surprised, at the mistakes that would be made in the coming centuries and the battles that would have to be fought. But he will insist that what matters is Jesus and the spirit. *Something has happened* in Jesus, he would insist, something of cosmic significance. This movement doesn't just run on its own steam. It isn't just the accidental by-product of energetic work and historical opportunity. God is at work in the midst of his people to produce the will and the energy. This is bound to have its larger effect, sooner or later and by whatever means.

But would Paul think this theological explanation sufficient? In one sense yes and in another sense no. Paul was very much alive to all the factors the historian, as opposed to the theologian, might want to study. He would have been aware of the way Herodotus demythologized the story in 2 Kings. Paul knew that others in his own day were doing the same kind of thing with the stories in Homer.

But just because he would not wish to copy Herodotus and give a purely naturalistic explanation, he certainly wouldn't want instead to ascribe the whole thing to divine or angelic power operating without human agency. Paul believed that when grace was at work, the human agents themselves were regularly called upon to work hard as a result, not least in prayer. He says this of himself.[14] The Creator works in a thousand ways, but one central way is through people—people who think, who pray, who make difficult decisions, who work hard, especially in prayer. That is part of what it means to be image-bearers. The question of divine action and human action is seldom a zero-sum game. If the worlds of heaven and earth have rushed together in Jesus and the spirit, one should expect different layers of explanation to reside together, to reinforce one another.

So what was it about Paul and his work that might, humanly speaking, have made the difference? In particular, what was it about Paul the man that made him—let's face it—one of the most successful public intellectuals of all time? What did he have that enabled him to take advantage of the circumstances (a common language, freedom of travel, Roman citizenship) and establish his unlikely movement not only for the course of his own lifetime but thereafter?

The first thing, coming at us throughout his story, is his sheer energy. We feel it pulsing through the letters. We watch as he responds to violence in one city by going straight on to the next one and saying and doing the same things. He is the kind of person to whom people say, "Don't you ever sleep?" He is working all hours, his hands hardened with his tentmaking, his back stiff from bending at the workbench. But he is ready every moment for the visitor with a question, for the distraught youngster whose parents have thrown him out, for the local official worried about his status if people discover he is following Jesus. He is ready to put down his tools for an hour or two and go from house to house to encourage, to warn, to pray, to weep. He is persistent. People know they won't get rid of him, won't be able to fob him off with glib excuses. He is all the while thinking through what he will say in his afternoon lecture in the house of Titius Justus in Corinth or the hall of Tyrannus in Ephesus. He takes time out to call a scribe and dictate a letter. He is relentless. He pauses to say the evening prayers with his close friends. He works on into the night, praying under his breath for the people he has met, for the city officials, for the Jesus-followers in other cities, for the next day's work, for the next phase of the project.

The second thing, the sharp edge of all this energy, is his blunt, up-front habit of telling it as he sees it no matter who is confronting him. He will say "Boo" to every goose within earshot and to all the swans as well. There is a reason why Saul of Tarsus, in his early days in Damascus, is the one getting into trouble, just as there is a reason why the Jerusalem apostles then decide to pack him off home to Tarsus. He confronts Peter in Antioch. I have suggested that the only reason he doesn't say more at the Jerusalem Conference is because Barnabas would have persuaded him to hold back.

He is the kind of man you want on your side in a debate but who may just alienate more sensitive souls. He confronts the magistrates at Philippi; he is itching to speak to the vast crowd in Ephesus; he tries to explain himself to the Jerusalem mob that had been trying to lynch him; he rebukes the high priest. He knows how to turn the factions in the Sanhedrin against one another. He lectures the Roman governor himself about justice, self-control, and the coming judgment. He tells the ship owner where he should and shouldn't spend the winter, and then says, "I told you so" when it all goes horribly wrong. He spots the sailors who are trying to bolt and tells the centurion to stop them. As a companion, he must have been exhilarating when things were going well and exasperating when they weren't. As an opponent, he could cause some people to contemplate murder as their only recourse.

People today write doctoral dissertations and business books about how successful companies and not-for-profit organizations begin. In ninety-nine cases out of a hundred there is someone like Paul hammering away from the start, getting things off the ground, confronting local authorities, raising money, persuading co-workers about what needs to be done, never losing the vision. Someone who will take the bull by the horns. Someone who will go on and on insisting on what to do and how to do it until it happens.

With all this, there is something disarming about Paul's vulnerable side, which explains why, despite his relentless and in-your-face energy, people loved him, wanted to work with him, and wept when he left. When he says that his heart has been opened wide, that there are no restrictions in his affections for his churches, it rings true.[15] His honesty shines out. With Paul, what you see is what you get, even if it isn't what you wanted. You know where you are. You know he will do anything for you, because (he would say) God has done everything for him in the Messiah.

He will never ask anyone to face anything he hasn't faced himself, up to and including horrible suffering and hardship—which he will then use as a visual aid in proclaiming the gospel. That is why his claims about himself are so credible. When he says he was gentle as a nurse in Thessalonica, we believe him. When he writes the poem about love, we know that the Corinthians would have recognized a self-portrait. When he tells the Philippians, over and over, to rejoice and celebrate, they know that, given half a chance, he would be the life and soul of the party. He modeled what he taught, and what he taught was the utter, exuberant, self-giving love of the Messiah.

People may sometimes have wished he would not give them quite so much of himself—life would not have been dull when he was around, but it would not have been particularly relaxing either—but they would have acknowledged that when they were with him, they saw truth more clearly because they saw it in his face and felt the love of God more warmly because they knew it was what drove him on. He was the sort of person through whom other people are changed, changed so that they will themselves take forward the same work with as much of the same energy as they can muster. If loyalty to the One God and his Messiah was Paul's watchword, one of the reasons why the strange movement he started thrived in the coming days was because his associates were, for the most part, fiercely loyal to Paul himself. He loved them, and they loved him. That is how things get done. It is how movements succeed.

All this helps to explain at one level why things happened the way they did. But within two or three generations (as happens with the founders of companies and charities) this personal memory would have faded. What kept Paul's influence alive then and thereafter was, obviously, his letters. The flow of words in his daily teaching, arguing, praying, and pastoral work is captured for us in these small, bright, and challenging documents. They (the conclusion is hardly original, but it's important nonetheless) are the real answer to the question, drawing readers as they do into Paul's lecture room, into his crowded little shop, into his inner circle, into his heart. It isn't just their content, strikingly original and powerful though that is. He wasn't just, as many have wrongly suggested, synthesizing the worlds of Israel, Greece, and Rome; his was a firmly *Jewish* picture, rooted in Israel's ancient story, with Israel's Messiah in the center and the nations of the world and their best ideas brought into new coherence around him. Nor was he simply teaching a "religion" or a "theology"; if we were to do Paul justice today we ought to teach him in departments of politics, ancient history, economics, and/or philosophy just as much as in divinity schools and departments of religion.

What matters, I think, is the way in which the letters cover so many moods and situations, the way in which, like the great music of our own classical tradition, they can find you at every stage of life, in every joy and sorrow, chance and challenge. I am reminded of one of the finest British journalists of the last generation, Bernard Levin, who spoke of how the great composers had accompanied him through his life: "Beethoven first, for the boy who wanted to put the world to rights; Wagner next, for the man unable to put himself to rights; Mozart at last, as the shadows lengthen, to confirm the growing belief that there is a realm 'where everything is known and yet forgiven.'"[16]

Thus, for Paul one might say: Galatians, for the young reformer eager to defend the gospel and attack the heretics; 2 Corinthians, for the adult sadly aware that things are more complicated and disturbing than he had thought; Romans at last, to remind us, despite everything, that nothing "will be able to separate us from the love of God in King Jesus our Lord."[17] Like the psalms he knew so well, Paul's letters wait for us just around the corner, to take our arm and whisper a word of encouragement when we face a new task, to remind us of obligations and warn us of snakes in the grass, to show us from one angle after another what it might mean to live in the newly human way, the newly Jewish way, the way of Jesus, to unveil again and again the faithful, powerful love of the creator God.

When we ask why Paul, with seventy or eighty pages of text to his name in the average Bible, has succeeded far beyond the other great letter writers of antiquity—the Ciceros, the Senecas—and for that matter the great public intellectuals and movement founders of his day and ours, this range of writing, from the urgent to the winsome, from the prophetic to the poetic, from intellectual rigor to passionate advocacy, must be central to the answer. The man who could write Philemon and Romans side by side was a man for all moments.

Yes, within a generation people were grumbling that he was sometimes hard to understand and that some folk were taking him the wrong way. That happens. But it is no accident that many of the acknowledged great moments in church history—think of Augustine, Luther, Barth—have come about through fresh engagement with Paul's work. Even those who think that those great men too partially misunderstood Paul will acknowledge the point. Paul had insisted that what mattered was not just *what* you thought but *how* you thought. He modeled what he advocated, and generation after generation has learned how to think in the new way by struggling to think his thoughts after him. His legacy has continually generated fresh dividends. It is a challenge that keeps on challenging.

All this is at the heart of who Paul was and why he succeeded. Of course, Paul himself would say that the One God was behind it all. Of course, skeptics might retort that since Alexander had made Paul's world speak Greek and the Romans had made travel easier than ever before, conditions were right. "So what?" Paul would have said. If the Messiah was sent "when the fullness of time arrived,"[18] perhaps Greece and Rome were part of the preparation as well as part of the problem. I do not think, however, that Paul would so readily have agreed with those who have said that people were getting tired of the old philosophies and pagan religions and were ready for something new. The problem in Ephesus was not that people had stopped worshipping Artemis and so were ready for Paul's message, but that Paul's message about the One God had burst on the scene and stopped the worship of Artemis. Social and cultural conditions can help to explain the way things worked out, but they cannot explain it away.

A better explanation may be found in the new way of life, the new kind of community, that Paul was not only advocating, but making possible through his writings. Paul emphasizes, in letter after letter, the family life of believers, what he begins to call, and subsequent generations will usually call, "the church," the *ekklēsia*. Not for nothing does he repeatedly emphasize the *unity* and the *holiness* of the church. Nor is it irrelevant that he highlights, and even apparently celebrates, the suffering that he and others would and did endure because of their loyalty to Jesus. These tell a different story from the idea of bored ex-pagans looking for something different to do with their "religious" side. This is about a new kind of community, a new kind, we dare to say, of "politics."

Politics is about the *polis*—the city, the community—and how it works, how it runs. Sophisticated theories had been advanced in Paul's day, often by theoreticians (like Cicero and Seneca) who were also hands-on members of the ruling elite. The main feature of Paul's political landscape was of course Rome. Rome had united the world—or so it claimed. But that unity, a top-down uniformity in which diversity was welcomed as long as it didn't threaten the absolute sovereignty of Caesar, was always creaky, and often ugly. The "diversity" was, after all, still seen in strictly hierarchical terms: men over women, free over slaves, Romans over everybody else. Rebels were ruthlessly suppressed. "They make a wilderness," sighed the Briton Calgacus, "and they call it 'peace.'"[19]

In this imperial world there appeared, in groups of six here and a dozen or two there, through the energetic work of this strange man Paul, a vision of a different kind of community owing allegiance to a different *Kyrios,* offering a different vision of unity, hosting a different kind of diversity. Unity and diversity were the pressure points for Paul, both for the individual communities (such as the church in Corinth, challenged by Paul's vision of the Messiah's single but very diverse "body") and for the worldwide "family" (such as the churches of Gentiles and Jews, both challenged by Paul's collection project). But what Paul had been doing was undoubtedly "political" in the sense that he was founding and maintaining an interrelated network of communities for which the only analogies, as we saw earlier, were the synagogue communities, on the one hand, and the Roman army and civil service, on the other. But Paul's communities were very different from either.

However, they had—and Paul's work and lasting achievement is unthinkable without this—the deepest of roots. Paul's Messiah communities were not simply a freestanding innovation. Rome traced its story back nearly a thousand years; Augustus had been careful to have his court poets and historians explain that his innovatory rule was the appropriate climax to Rome's long history and noble traditions. The synagogue told and retold the still longer story that went back to Abraham, Isaac, and Jacob, to Moses and Joshua, to David and Solomon. Paul told that story too and regularly explained to his communities that *they had been grafted into that great tradition.* His communities may have been a novelty in one respect. In other respects, they were claiming—he was teaching them to claim—that they were Abraham's family. This, in Paul's work, was as much a social and communal strength as it was a theological one.

There may, in other words, have been a different kind of vacuum into which the Jesus message made its way. It was not so much a matter of people giving up an old "religion" and then finding a new one. Nor was it explicable as dissatisfaction with existing philosophies and the discovery of the new one that Paul was teaching. Rather, people who were used to one kind of political reality, albeit with its own history and variations, were glimpsing a vision of a larger united though diverse world—and then, as they looked around them, they were discovering at the same time that Rome, after all, could not really deliver on its promises. When the new communities spoke of a different *Kyrios,* one whose sovereignty was gained through humility and suffering rather than wealth and conquest, many must have found that attractive, not simply for what we would call "religious" reasons, but precisely for what they might call "political" ones. This looked like something real rather than the smoke and mirrors of imperial rhetoric.

Paul did not, of course, have the time or the need to develop his picture of the differentiated unity of the Messiah's body into a larger exposition of the church as a whole. He had not articulated a political theory to match that of Aristotle or his successors. But it was that kind of social experiment—developing a new way of living together—that the churches of the second and third century were attempting. And when you ask what inspired them to do what they were doing, the lines go back to Paul. Paul's stress on unity, to be sure, stemmed from his theological vision. It was not mere pragmatism. But it also had, and Paul probably realized that it had, the power to generate an alternative social and cultural reality, to announce to the watching world that Jesus was Lord and Caesar wasn't. What Paul was articulating in his letters, often in haste and to meet particular crises, was being reused to encourage Jesus-followers to glimpse and practice a refreshingly new kind of human society.

If the fact of a different kind of cross-cultural social diversity-in-unity had a powerful appeal, the same is true of holiness. This is counterintuitive for modern Westerners, who generally resent from an early age the fussy moralisms of home, school, and church: How could a new and demanding standard of behavior ever be attractive? In the ancient world, however, this was good news for many, especially for those—women, the poor, ethnic minorities, slaves, children—who were most vulnerable to the normal patterns of pagan behavior. This perception seems to lie behind the sneaking admiration (mixed, to be sure, with bemusement) that came from the famous second-century doctor Galen. In his only mention of the Christian movement, he comments on two points that to him made the followers of this strange new cult appear to be crazy: they believed in the resurrection of the body, and they didn't sleep around.[20] The two went together. The human body was attaining a new dignity, a new valuation. Nobody had imagined that kind of way of life. Paul taught it; the early Christians were modeling it.

In particular, those who have studied the life of the church in the second, third, and fourth centuries have emphasized that, again against the expectations of our own day, the Christian message provided a much better prospect for women than the pagan world could. For a start, there would be more of them. Pagans routinely practiced infanticide for unwanted children in general and girls in particular, but the Christians followed the Jews in renouncing such behavior. The consequent shortage of marriageable girls in the pagan world and the surplus of them among the Christians resulted in many marriages between Christian women and pagan men, who might then either convert or at least give consent for the children to be brought up as Christians. And, once again against the common perceptions of our age, the fresh evaluation of the role of women, though it came ultimately from Jesus himself, was mediated not least through Paul—the Paul who listed several women among his colleagues and fellow workers (including one "apostle"), who saw early on that in the Messiah's family there was ultimately no "male and female," and who entrusted Phoebe with the responsibility of delivering and almost certainly expounding the letter to the Romans.

Now we must pursue a parallel train of thought. If we simply focus on unity and holiness we may miss the fact that Paul's communities were essentially *outward looking* and that the face they turned outward was the face of active care. Medicine in the ancient world was almost entirely reserved for those who could afford it; within a few generations, the Christians were setting up hospitals and caring for all within reach. When a plague struck a town or village and the rich and respectable retreated to their country houses away from the risk of infection, the Christians would stay and nurse the sick, often at the risk of their own lives. Nobody had ever dreamed of living like that before. Paul doesn't mention this kind of social imperative, but it belongs with the work of healing, which characterized his own ministry, at least from time to time, and it flows directly from the things he says about the life of the community whose members were like shining lights in a dark world.

In the same way, education in the ancient world was almost entirely for the elite. Jewish boys were taught to read and write; they would, after all, need to study the Torah. But a great many ordinary pagans were either functionally illiterate or able only to read what was required for daily tasks. Some estimates put the level of literacy at between 20 and 30 percent; some of the older Greek cities and islands had a tradition of elementary education for citizens, but for many people, again especially for women and slaves, this would have been minimal. The early Christians, however, were enthusiastic about education, and particularly reading. When we ask ourselves what the "teachers" in Paul's communities were teaching, I suspect that part of the answer was "reading," since if they were teaching the converts (as they surely were) the scriptures of ancient Israel, this would have involved basic skills that many of those converts had hitherto lacked.

As we know, the early Christians were technological pioneers when it came to books, abandoning the scroll with its natural limitations and developing instead the codex, the ancestor of the modern bound book. They would only have been doing that if they wanted more and more people to be able to read the books the community was producing. This insistence on education and particularly reading can be traced directly back to Paul. It is Paul, after all, who tells his churches to be grown-up in their thinking, to be transformed by the renewing of their minds. He wanted Jesus-followers not only to think the right things, but to think in the right *way*. Though he did not himself (so far as we know) found what we today would call "schools," when such things came about, they would have him to thank for their underlying impetus.

All this comes down to the basic imperative that we see as the assumed norm in Paul's very first letters and that then becomes a major and attractive feature of the church in subsequent centuries. "Remember the poor," the Jerusalem apostles had urged Paul. "Yes," he replied, "that is precisely what I am most eager to do." For Paul this eventually took one particular focus, namely, the collection for Jerusalem, but all the signs are that each local Jesus community had the same priority, presumably of course because of Jesus himself. Paul congratulated the Thessalonians on their practical "love," *agapē,* and urged them to work at it more and more. "Do good to everyone," he wrote to the Galatians, "and particularly to the household of the faith." "Celebrate with those who are celebrating, mourn with the mourners." "Shine like lights in the world." The gospel itself was designed to generate a new kind of people, a people "who would be eager for good works"; in fact, the new kind of humanity that was brought to birth through the gospel was created for the specific purpose of "good works."[21] This point has often been missed when people have read the phrase "good works" as meaning simply "the performance of moral rules," especially when that in turn has been played off against "justification by faith alone." Morals matter, faith matters, but that isn't the point here. Paul's emphasis here is all about communities through whose regular practice the surrounding world is made a better place.

A glance at the second and third centuries is enough to confirm that all these things, particularly when we see them together, offer good explanations for the spread of the Christian communities. These Jesus-followers, strange though their views might have seemed to those around, antisocial though some might have supposed them to be, were doing things that really did transform the wider society. By the end of the second century, Roman officials were not particularly aware of the nuances of Christian teaching, but they did know what the word "bishop" meant—it meant someone who kept on agitating about the needs of the poor. And at point after point these strands of community life went back to Paul. He had planted these seeds. He died long before most of them began to sprout, but when they did, a community came into being that challenged the ancient world with a fresh vision and possibility. The vision was of a society in which each worked for all and all for each. The possibility was that of escaping the crushing entail of the older paganism and its social, cultural, and political practices and finding instead a new kind of community, a *koinōnia,* a "fellowship." A family.

As the historical question invites the theological one back into the room, no wonder the theologians of the second and third centuries often emphasized, when speaking about the crucifixion of Jesus, their belief that on the cross he won the victory over all the dark powers. That wasn't just a theological theory about an abstract "atonement." It was the necessary foundation for the lives of the communities in which they lived and worked. The communities could exist only because the old gods, much as they might try to strike back, really had been overthrown. Mammon, Mars, and Aphrodite had been shown up as impostors. Caesar himself was not the ultimate Lord. The theology was hiding under the historical reality, the political reality. These communities were demonstrating, on the street, in the home, in the marketplace, what it meant to follow a different Lord, to worship the One God.

It was Paul too who provided some of the major intellectual infrastructure for this community. Here again this was not because the other major intellectual constructs of the ancient world had run out of steam. The Stoics, the Epicureans, and the up-and-coming Middle Platonists had serious, articulate, and in many ways attractive spokespeople. With hindsight, however, Paul's Jesus-focused vision of the One God, creator of all, was able to take on all these philosophies and beat them at their own game. They were all, in the last analysis, ways of understanding the world and ways of finding a coherent and meaningful human path within it. When later generations wanted to articulate the Christian version of the same thing (which was, to say it once more, the Jewish version with the Jesus-based reframing), it was to Paul that they looked for help. Of course, other sources remained vital. The prologue to the Gospel of John, a piece of writing that I think would have had Paul himself on his knees, is an obvious example. But it was Paul's robust engagements with the triple traditions of Israel, Greece, and Rome and his translation of them all into the shape of Jesus and the spirit (Jesus as Israel's Messiah and the spirit as the agent of resurrection, the ultimate hope of Israel) that offered a platform for the great thinkers of subsequent generations.

Although the thinkers were seldom the people who made the gospel spread—that accolade belongs to the local communities that were living out the gospel imperatives, often under the threat or the reality of persecution—the church would not have survived or thrived without their work. Theology is the backbone of a healthy church. The body still needs limbs and organs, joints and tissue. Paul, with his own image of the Messiah's body, would have been the first to insist on that. But without a backbone the body will not survive. The survival and flourishing of the church of subsequent centuries look back to Paul's achievement in teaching his followers not only what to think, but how to think. He knew only too well what that would cost, but he believed it was the genuinely human way, a way that would win out precisely by the power of that genuine humanness. And with that, we have our answer.

There are, then, several lines of explanation that converge on Paul himself. His was the vision of the united, holy, and outward-facing church. He pioneered the idea of a suffering apostleship through which the message of the crucified Jesus would not only be displayed, but be effective in the world. He could not have foreseen the ways in which these communities would develop. He might well not have approved of all that was done. But the historian and biographer can look back and discern, in Paul's hasty and often contested work, the deep roots of a movement that changed the world. This is not the book to address the next question, as to what difference it might make if the church in our own day were to reassess its policies and priorities in the light of Paul's work. We, after all, have seen the electronic revolution produce a global situation just as dramatically new, in its way, as the one the first-century world had experienced with the sudden rise of Rome. What might the church's response and responsibility be at such a time?

But Paul's vision of a united and holy community, prayerful, rooted in the scriptural story of ancient Israel, facing social and political hostility but insisting on doing good to all people, especially the poor, would always be central. His relentless personal energy, his clarity and vulnerability, and his way with words provided the motor to drive this vision, and each generation will need a few who can imitate him. His towering intellectual achievement, a theological vision of the One God reshaped around Jesus and the spirit and taking on the wider world of philosophy, would provide the robust, necessary framework for it all. When the church abandons the theological task, with its exegetical roots in the work of Paul and his colleagues, we should not be surprised if unity, holiness, and the care for the poor are sidelined as well.

★ ★ ★

There is one more thing on which Paul and his successors would insist, and that is prayer. We return, as we now probe cautiously into the last days of Paul, to the pattern of prayer he had learned from childhood and then developed in the light of Jesus and the spirit.

Paul always knew that his labors might cost him his life. He did not expect to die at home in his own bed, even supposing that after leaving Antioch in the late 40s he ever had a place he could call "home." Whether he faced death after the two years of his house arrest at the end of Acts or whether he made subsequent journeys before a second arrest and a final trial, I think we must see his preparation for death and the event itself when it came in relation to the life he lived, and particularly the prayers he had prayed all throughout.

There is a famous story of how Rabbi Akiba, one of the greatest Jewish teachers of all time, went on praying the *Shema*, declaring his loyalty to the One God and his determination to stand for his kingdom, as the Roman torturers, catching up with Jewish rebels after the Bar-Kochba revolt in AD 135, ran steel combs through his flesh until he died a horrible and lingering death.[22] He continued to pray: "*Shema Yisrael*, Hear, O Israel: the LORD our God, the LORD is one. You shall love the LORD your God with all your heart, and with all your soul, and with all your might . . ." ("soul" here means "life"). His disciples, standing by like Socrates's friends as he drank the hemlock, asked him in awe and horror how he could go on praying that prayer even now. His answer, recorded much later but reflecting what we know of the man, is a model of wise, humble Jewish thought. All his life long, he explained, he had been troubled by the words in the prayer "and with all your soul." He wondered what that meant and if he would ever have the opportunity to fulfill *that* part of the prayer. Now that he finally had the opportunity, he declared, he was going to seize it. This, then, was what it meant to love the One God with one's *life*. Akiba died with the word *echad*, "one," on his lips: "Hear, O Israel, the LORD our God, the LORD is *one*." *Echad*. A statement of loyalty. Of loyalty even to the death.

In my mind's eye I see Paul, perhaps also surrounded by friends, awaiting the executioner. He too will be praying, and it might well be the prayer of loyalty and love, of Jewish-style loyalty, of Messiah-shaped loyalty, the monotheism of the inaugurated kingdom: "For us there is One God (the father, from whom are all things, and we to him); and One Lord (Jesus the Messiah, through whom are all things and we through him), *and you shall love him . . .*" It flows better in Greek than in English:

> *Heis theos, ho patēr, ex hou ta panta kai hēmeis eis auton,*
> *Kai heis kyrios, Iēsous Christos, di'hou ta panta kai hēmeis*
> *di' autou.*

This is what made him who he was. This is the reality that burst upon him on the road to Damascus. This, he would have said, is the ultimate explanation for why his work, so contested, so agonizing, so demanding, so inevitably open to misunderstanding, would not go to waste, but would grow, would produce not just "a religion," but a new kind of humanity—new people, a new community, a new world. A new *polis*. A new kind of love. It would do things he could hardly have dared to imagine.

He prays the prayer, over and over. He prays it with the rhythm of his breathing. He prays it with the spirit's breath in his innermost self. He declares his *pistis,* his loyalty, his love one more time. One God, one Lord. One. His life's work has been to bear witness, openly and unhindered, to the kingdom of God and the lordship of Jesus, and that is what he now does in prayer as the executioner draws his sword. Loving this One God with his heart, his mind, and his strength. And, finally, with his life.

CHRONOLOGICAL TABLE

As with all ancient history, most dates are approximations. At several points these rely on particular arguments reflected in the text. Main journeys are in bold text; letters are in capitals.

?4 BC	Birth of Jesus of Nazareth
?AD 5–10	Birth of Saul of Tarsus
30	Crucifixion and resurrection of Jesus of Nazareth
?33	Revelation of Jesus to Saul on the road to Damascus
33–36	Paul in Damascus, Arabia, Damascus again
36	Paul's first post-Damascus visit to Jerusalem (Gal. 1:18–24)
36–46	Paul in Tarsus; brought to Antioch by Barnabas
40	Caligula's plans to erect his statue in Jerusalem
41	Assassination of Caligula; accession of Claudius
46/47	"Famine visit" to Jerusalem (Acts 11:30; Gal. 2:1–10)
47–48	Paul and Barnabas on **first missionary journey: Cyprus and South Galatia**
48	Peter in Antioch (Gal. 2:11–21); Crisis in Galatia
48	GALATIANS
48/49	Jerusalem Conference (Acts 15)
?49	Claudius's expulsion of Jews from Rome
49	Paul and Silas on **second missionary journey: Greece**
50/51	1 and 2 THESSALONIANS

51 (early)–52 (late)	Paul in Corinth
52/53	Paul in Jerusalem, Antioch; **third missionary journey: Ephesus**
53–56	Paul in Ephesus
?53	1 CORINTHIANS
53/54	Short, painful visit to Corinth
54	Death of Claudius; accession of Nero
?55–56	Imprisonment in Ephesus
?55	PHILIPPIANS
?55/56	PHILEMON, COLOSSIANS, EPHESIANS
56	Release from prison; **travel from Ephesus to Corinth**
56	2 CORINTHIANS
57	ROMANS
57	**Travel from Corinth to Jerusalem**
57–59	"Hearings" and imprisonment in Jerusalem and Caesarea
59, autumn	**Voyage to Rome; shipwreck on Malta**
60, early	**Arrival in Rome**
60–62	House arrest in Rome
?62–64	Further travels, either to Spain or to the East, or both?
?after 62	1 and 2 TIMOTHY, TITUS?
64	Fire in Rome; persecution of Christians
?64 or later	Death of Paul
66–70	Roman-Jewish war
68	Death of Nero
70	Fall of Jerusalem

NOTES

Preface

1. All published by SPCK in London and by Fortress Press in Minneapolis.
2. Stephen Mitchell, *Anatolia: Land, Men, and Gods in Asia Minor,* vol. 2, *The Rise of the Church* (Oxford: Clarendon, 1993).
3. George S. Duncan, *Paul's Ephesian Ministry: A Reconstruction* (London: Hodder and Stoughton, 1929).
4. *The New Testament for Everyone* (London: SPCK, 2011); *The Kingdom New Testament* (San Francisco: HarperOne, 2011).

Introduction

1. Gal. 1:14.
2. Gal. 1:14; Phil. 3:6.
3. Phil. 3:20.
4. Rom. 8:30.
5. Gal. 4:4.
6. Deut. 6:4.
7. Phil. 4:8, NRSV.
8. Deut. 30.
9. See Ezra 9:9; Neh. 9:36.
10. Lev. 25.
11. Exod. 40; 1 Kings 8.
12. Isa. 52:7–12.
13. Phil. 3:6.
14. Gal. 1:14.
15. Gal. 4:17–18.

Chapter 1: Zeal

1. Num. 22–24.
2. Num. 25:6.
3. Ps. 106:30–31.
4. Gen. 15:6.

5.   1 Macc. 2:51–60.
6.   1 Kings 18–19.
7.   1 Macc. 2:49–68.
8.   2 Macc. 7.
9.   Acts 5:34–39.
10.   Acts 7:56.

Chapter 2: Damascus

1.   John Betjeman, *Uncollected Poems* (London: John Murray, 1982), 68.
2.   John Shelton Lawrence and Robert Jewett, *The Myth of the American Superhero* (Grand Rapids: Eerdmans, 2002); Robert Jewett and John Shelton Lawrence, *Captain America and the Crusade Against Evil: The Dilemma of Zealous Nationalism* (Grand Rapids: Eerdmans, 2004).
3.   See, e.g., Margaret MacMillan, *The War That Ended Peace* (London: Profile Books), 2013, esp. chap. 9.
4.   Isa. 40:1.
5.   Isa. 40:4–5, my paraphrase.
6.   Isa. 52:8.
7.   Ezek. 43:1–5; Exod. 40:34–38.
8.   Mal. 3:1.
9.   Gen. 15:7–21.
10.   Gen. 28:10–22.
11.   Gen. 40–42.
12.   Dan. 2:17–49; 7:1–28.
13.   Ezek. 1:26.
14.   2 Cor. 4:6.
15.   Gal. 3:28.
16.   Gal. 1:17.

Chapter 3: Arabia and Tarsus

1.   Gal. 1:15–17.
2.   Gal. 1:12.
3.   1 Kings 19:1–9.
4.   1 Kings 19:10–15.
5.   1 Kings 19:15.
6.   1 Kings 19:18.
7.   Rom. 11:3–4.
8.   Gal. 1:15; Jer. 1:5.
9.   Gal. 1:16.
10.   Gal. 1:24, echoing Isa. 49:3.
11.   Gal. 2:2, echoing Isa. 49:4.
12.   2 Cor. 11:30–33.
13.   2 Cor. 12:1–10.

14. 2 Cor. 1:20.
15. Ps. 2:7–9.
16. Ps. 47:8–9.
17. Ps. 72:8.
18. 2 Cor. 10:5.
19. Phil. 4:8.
20. Rom. 9:1–5.
21. 1 Cor. 7:7.
22. 1 Cor. 7:8.
23. 1 Cor. 9:6.
24. 1 Cor. 7:15.
25. Gal. 3:28.
26. 1 Cor. 9:26–27.

Chapter 4: Antioch

1. Rom. 9:2.
2. Acts 11:26.
3. Acts 26:28; 1 Pet. 4:16.
4. Gal. 2:10.
5. Gal. 2:2.
6. 1 Thess. 2:1; 3:5; Phil. 2:16.
7. 1 Cor. 9:26–27.
8. 1 Cor. 9:20.
9. Rom. 1:16.

Chapter 5: Cyprus and Galatia

1. Phil. 1:23.
2. Luke 23:43.
3. Acts 26:16–18.
4. Acts 13:7.
5. Luke 13:12.
6. Acts 13:9.
7. Rom. 11:1–2, quoting 1 Sam. 12:22.
8. Acts 13:16–41.
9. Pss. 2; 16; Isa. 55.
10. Isa. 49:6, my translation.
11. Acts 13:51; see Luke 10:11.
12. Acts 13:52.
13. Gal. 3:5.
14. Acts 14:5.
15. Acts 14:19.
16. Gal. 4:13.
17. Gal. 4:15.

18. Gal. 4:14.
19. 2 Cor. 4:7–12; 6:3–10; 11:21–12:10.
20. Ovid, *Metamorphoses* 8.618–724.
21. Acts 13:38–39.
22. 2 Cor. 11:25.
23. Acts 14:22.

Chapter 6: Antioch and Jerusalem

1. Acts 10–11.
2. Acts 21:27–22:22.
3. Acts 13:38–39.
4. 1 Macc. 2:46; Josephus, *Antiquities* 13.257–58, 318.
5. Acts 11:9.
6. Gal. 2:13.
7. Gal. 2:11, 14.
8. Gal. 2:15–16a.
9. Phil. 2:8.
10. Gal. 2:16b–c.
11. Gal. 2:17–18.
12. Gal. 2:19–20.
13. Gal. 2:21.
14. Acts 18:22.
15. Gal. 1:4–5.
16. Gal. 6:15.
17. Gen. 15:6 as quoted in Gal. 3:6.
18. 1 Macc. 2:52, 54.
19. Gal. 4:8–11.
20. Gal. 3:28.
21. Gal. 4:6.
22. Gal. 4:26.
23. Gal. 6:15.
24. Gal. 4:25.
25. Acts 15:16–17, quoting Amos 9:11–12.
26. Gal. 2:19–20.
27. Gal. 1:15–16.
28. 2 Pet. 3:16.

Chapter 7: Into Europe

1. Gal. 4:20.
2. Col. 4:10; Philem. 23; 2 Tim. 4:11.
3. 1 Cor. 9:6.
4. Esther 6:1, my translation.
5. Acts 16:3.

6.   Gal. 2:3–5.
7.   1 Cor. 9:20.
8.   Acts 16:10.
9.   Acts 16:14.
10. Acts 16:17.
11. Acts 16:20–21.
12. Acts 16:28.
13. Acts 16:30.
14. Acts 16:31.
15. Acts 16:37.
16. 1 Thess. 1:9.
17. Acts 17:6–7.
18. 1 Thess. 2:7–8.
19. 1 Thess. 2:17.
20. 1 Thess. 3:6.
21. 1 Thess. 2:1; 3:5.
22. 1 Cor. 1:26.
23. 1 Thess. 2:8.

Chapter 8: Athens

1.   1 Thess. 3:2.
2.   Acts 17:21.
3.   Aeschylus, *Eumenides* 647–48.
4.   Acts 17:19–20.
5.   2 Cor. 10:5.
6.   John 19:11.
7.   Col. 2:15.
8.   Ps. 50:12.
9.   Acts 17:27–28.
10. Acts 17:31.
11. 1 Cor. 4:3–4; see Rom. 2:14–16.
12. Ps. 2:10.
13. Acts 17:33.

Chapter 9: Corinth I

1.   1 Cor. 2:3.
2.   1 Cor. 15:3–5.
3.   1 Cor. 2:1–2.
4.   1 Cor. 1:22–25.
5.   1 Thess. 1:9.
6.   Rom. 2:8–9.
7.   1 Thess. 2:10–12.
8.   1 Thess. 2:19–20.

9. 1 Thess. 1:5; 2:13.
10. 1 Thess. 4:1–8.
11. Gal. 6:10.
12. 1 Thess. 4:12.
13. 1 Thess. 4:13–14.
14. Eph. 1:10.
15. 1 Thess. 4:16.
16. 1 Thess. 5:2–3.
17. Jer. 6:14.
18. 1 Thess. 5:4–10.
19. Isa. 13:10.
20. Jer. 4:23–28.
21. 2 Thess. 2:6–7.
22. 2 Thess. 2:13–14.
23. 2 Thess. 3:10.
24. 2 Thess. 3:7–9, 12.
25. Acts 18:9–10.
26. Acts 18:13.
27. 1 Cor. 8:6.
28. Acts 18:15.
29. Acts 18:17.
30. 1 Thess. 5:17.
31. 1 Cor. 8:6.
32. Acts 18:22.

Chapter 10: Ephesus I

1. 2 Cor. 1:8.
2. Pausanias 4.31.8; 7.5.4.
3. 2 Cor. 1:8–9.
4. 2 Cor. 1:9.
5. 2 Cor. 4:8–9.
6. 2 Cor. 4:10.
7. 2 Cor. 1:3–7.
8. 2 Cor. 1:13–14.
9. 2 Cor. 2:16–17, literally translated.
10. 1 Cor. 15:32.
11. 1 Cor. 16:8–9.
12. Acts 23–26.
13. Acts 20:25, 38; Rom. 15:24, 28.
14. Acts 20:16.
15. Acts 19:19.
16. 1 Cor. 5:9–10.
17. Acts 19:1–7.

18. 2 Cor. 2:1.
19. 2 Cor. 11:24.
20. 1 Cor. 15:32.
21. Col. 1:8.
22. Col. 1:6.
23. Acts 19:12.
24. Acts 19:15.
25. Acts 19:18–20.
26. Acts 20:21.
27. Acts 19:22.
28. Acts 20:1.
29. 1 Cor. 3:10–17.
30. 1 Cor. 3:21–23.
31. 1 Cor. 4:18–21.
32. 1 Cor. 1:18, 25; 2:5; 4:20.
33. 1 Cor. 5:7–8.
34. 1 Cor. 15:23–28.
35. 1 Cor. 8:6.
36. 1 Cor. 10:26.
37. 1 Cor. 9:19–22.
38. Gal. 2:19–21.
39. 1 Cor. 10:27.
40. 1 Cor. 13:9–13.
41. 1 Cor. 15:17.
42. 1 Cor. 15:17, 2, 58.
43. 1 Cor. 15:25, quoting Ps. 110:1.
44. 1 Cor. 15:23.
45. 2 Cor. 1:15–16.
46. 2 Cor. 1:15–17.
47. Acts 19:26.
48. Acts 19:28.
49. Rom. 16:4.
50. Matt. 10:28; Luke 12:4–5.
51. 2 Cor. 1:9.
52. 1 Cor. 8:6.
53. 2 Cor. 4:7.

Chapter 11: Ephesus II

1. Phil. 1:20.
2. Phil. 1:15–18, 21–26, 23.
3. Phil. 2:25–30.
4. Phil. 2:1–4; Phil. 2:12–18.
5. Phil. 2:6–11.

6. Phil. 2:15.
7. Phil. 2:16.
8. Phil. 3:21.
9. Isa. 45:23.
10. Phil. 3:2–3.
11. Phil. 3:7–11.
12. Phil. 3:10.
13. 2 Cor. 1:9.
14. Phil. 3:13.
15. Phil. 3:17.
16. Phil. 3:19.
17. Phil. 4:11–13.
18. 2 Cor. 4:7.
19. Rom. 8:21.
20. Pliny, *Letters* 9.21.
21. Gal. 3:28; 1 Cor. 12:12.
22. Eph. 4:15.
23. 2 Cor. 5:19.
24. Col. 1:9–11.
25. Col. 2:2.
26. Col. 2:3.
27. Sir. 28.
28. 1 Kings 8.
29. Col. 1:15–20.
30. John 1:14.
31. Col. 1:27.
32. Col. 2:9–10.
33. Col. 2:11–12.
34. Col. 2:13–15.
35. Col. 2:9–19.
36. Col. 2:8.
37. Col. 3:1–4.
38. Col. 3:17.
39. Eph. 1:22, echoing Ps. 8.
40. Eph. 1:21.
41. Eph. 3:18–19.
42. Eph. 1:10; 2:11–22.
43. Eph. 4:1–16; 5:21–33.
44. Col. 2:9.
45. Eph. 3:10.
46. Eph. 6:10–20.

Chapter 12: Corinth II

1. 2 Cor. 2:12.
2. Phil. 4:6.

3. 2 Cor. 7:5.
4. 2 Cor. 7:6–7.
5. 2 Cor. 7:7–9, 13–16.
6. 2 Cor. 5:21–6:2, with Isa. 49:8.
7. 2 Cor. 3:3.
8. 2 Cor. 4:4–6.
9. 2 Cor. 4:7–10.
10. 1 Cor. 15:51–52; also 1 Thess. 4:17.
11. Phil. 1:21–23.
12. 2 Cor. 1:12.
13. 2 Cor. 5:11–15.
14. 2 Cor. 5:17–18.
15. 2 Cor. 6:4–10.
16. 2 Cor. 11:7–11.
17. 1 Cor. 9:18.
18. 2 Cor. 11:11.
19. 2 Cor. 11:23–33.
20. 2 Cor. 12:2–4.
21. 2 Cor. 12:8.
22. 2 Cor. 12:9–10.
23. 2 Cor. 13:10.
24. Rom. 1:16.
25. 2 Cor. 5:14.
26. John 19:11; Rom. 13:1–7; Col. 1:15–20; 1 Pet. 2:13–17.
27. Rom. 1:1–5, 16–17.
28. Rom. 15:8–12.
29. Rom. 15:7.
30. Rom. 8:3.
31. Exod. 40.
32. Rom. 8:17–30.
33. Rom. 8:26.
34. Rom. 8:37.
35. Rom. 8:39.
36. Rom. 10:4.
37. Rom. 9:2.
38. John 1:11.
39. Rom. 10:1.
40. Rom. 10:9.
41. Rom. 10:14–15.
42. Rom. 11:23.
43. Rom. 10:1–3.
44. Rom, 11:18.
45. Rom. 11:11–15.
46. Rom. 11:14; note the similarity with "some" in 1 Cor. 9:22.
47. Rom. 11:32.

48. Rom. 12:2.
49. Rom. 13:8–10, 11–14.
50. Rom. 13:1–7.
51. Rom. 10:2.
52. Rom. 15:4–6.
53. Rom. 15:19.
54. Acts 20:2.
55. Rom. 15:31.
56. Rom. 16:22.
57. Rom. 16:25–27.

Chapter 13: Jerusalem Again

1. Gal. 2:10; 3:28.
2. 2 Cor. 8:9.
3. Rom. 15:27.
4. Rom. 11:15.
5. See Josephus, *Antiquities* 14.190–216; 17.313.
6. 1 Cor. 16:3–4.
7. 2 Cor. 8:19–20.
8. 2 Cor. 1:16; Acts 20:3.
9. Col. 4:10; Philem. 24.
10. Acts 20:4.
11. Acts 20:7–12.
12. Plato, *Symposium* 223D.
13. Acts 20:28.
14. Acts 20:32.
15. Acts 20:35.
16. Rom. 14:14, 20.
17. Mark 7:19.
18. Rom. 9:1–5.
19. Rom. 10:1.
20. Rom. 11:23.
21. Acts 22:22.
22. Acts 22:25.
23. Acts 22:28.
24. John 18:22.
25. Acts 23:3.
26. Acts 23:5.
27. In this case Exod. 22:7.
28. Acts 24:5–6.
29. Acts 24:19.
30. Acts 25:10–11.
31. Acts 25:19.
32. Acts 26:23.
33. Acts 26:14.

34. Acts 5:39.

35. Rom. 10:2–4.

36. Acts 26:18.

37. Acts 26:23.

38. Acts 26:23.

39. Luke 2:32; see also 1:78–79.

40. Isa. 49:6.

41. Isa. 49:7.

42. Isa. 52:15, quoted in Rom. 15:21.

43. Acts 26:24.

44. Acts 26:27.

45. Acts 26:28.

46. Acts 26:29.

Chapter 14: From Caesarea to Rome—and Beyond?

1. Dan. 7:3.

2. 1 Cor. 16:5–8; see also 2 Tim. 4:21.

3. Luke 22:53.

4. Acts 27:20, 31, 34, 43, 44; 28:1, 4.

5. Acts 27:20.

6. Acts 27:21–26.

7. Amos 5:19.

8. Rom. 15:6–7.

9. Josephus, *Antiquities* 17.219–49; *Jewish War* 2.80–100.

10. Luke 19:11–27.

11. Tacitus, *Annals* 15.44.

12. Pliny, *Letters* 10.97.

13. Acts 28:27.

14. Rom. 10:1; 11:23, 25–26.

15. Acts 28:31.

16. Acts 1:8.

17. *1 Clement* 5:6–7.

18. 2 Tim. 1:16–18.

19. 2 Tim. 4:13.

20. 2 Tim. 4:6–8.

21. 2 Tim. 4:10.

22. 1 Tim. 1:3.

23. 1 Tim. 1:20.

24. 1 Cor. 5:5.

25. Acts 20:16.

Chapter 15: The Challenge of Paul

1. Rom. 4:25.

2. 2 Cor. 1:20; Rom. 10:4; Gal. 3:16; Rom. 15:12.

3.　Isa. 65:17; 66:22.

4.　Eph. 2:8–10.

5.　Eph. 1:10.

6.　Eph. 2:10.

7.　Gal. 2:19.

8.　Phil. 2:5.

9.　2 Cor. 10:5.

10.　Phil. 3:10.

11.　Gal. 2:19–20.

12.　Rom. 6:11.

13.　2 Kings 19:35; Herodotus, *Histories* 2.141.

14.　1 Cor. 15:10; Col. 1:29.

15.　2 Cor. 6:12.

16.　Bernard Levin, *Enthusiasms* (New York: Crown, 1983), 195.

17.　Rom. 8:39.

18.　Gal. 4:4.

19.　Tacitus, *Agricola* 30.6.

20.　Galen, *Summary of Plato's Republic*, in Mary Beard, John North, and Simon Price, *Religions of Rome* (Cambridge: Cambridge Univ. Press, 1998), 2.338.

21.　Gal. 2:10; 1 Thess. 4:9–10; Gal. 6:10; Rom. 12:15: Phil. 2:15; Titus 2:14; Eph. 2:10.

22.　Babylonian Talmud Berakoth 61b; Jerusalem Talmud Berakoth 9:14b.

SCRIPTURE INDEX

APOSTOLIC FATHERS

SUBJECT INDEX

Paul (*cont.*)

239, 241; letter to Philippi, 244, 264, 271–80; letter to Romans, 138, 317–19, 327–37; letter to Thessalonians, 238, 244; letter to Titus, 218, 396–97; loyalty to God, 150–51; loyalty to the hope of Israel, 10; in Lystra, 122–24; marriage and, 80–82; meeting with Barnabas in Jerusalem, 163–66; meeting with Jewish elders in Rome, 387–90; message of radical messianic eschatology, 130–31; ministry of, 308–9, 366; monotheism of, 76; motivation and mindset, 405–6; multilingual ability, 15–16; name change, 115–16; opposition to mission, 244–45, 275–76; parallel with Elijah, 63–65; parody of imperial boasting, 314–16; personal knowledge of Jesus, 277–79; in Pisidian Antioch, 111, 113–14, 117–21; plot to kill, 360; poem about Jesus, 272–75; practice of meditation, 51–54, 69, 298–300; practice of prayer, 51–52, 55–56, 69–70, 80, 267, 298, 412, 430–32; Prison Letters, 241, 265, 268, 271; proclaiming foreign divinities, 199; proclamation of Jesus as Messiah, 65–67, 104–5; proclamation of Jesus as "son of God," 58; purificatory ritual with Jerusalem leaders, 350–53; reading of the Bible, 16, 18; reasons for long-term success of, 414–30; returns to Damascus, 64–65; return to Ephesus, 259–69; return to Tarsus, 66, 68–83; rift between Barnabas and, 294; role as world changer, 4; before the Sanhedrin, 355–59, 362; schooling in Jewish thought, 2, 12, 15, 27–28; second letter to Corinth, 67, 220,

237–39, 250, 307–8; second letter to Thessalonica, 218, 223–25; self-discipline, 96–97; sent from Syrian Antioch to Jerusalem with a gift of money for Jerusalem believers, 95–97, 350; servant vocation of, 410–11; shipwreck on Malta, 183, 314–15, 375–83; speech before Herod Agrippa, 107; stoning of, 123, 127–28, 211; study of ancient scriptures, 27–30, 70–71; in Syrian Antioch, 92–100, 231, 233, 244, 267; teacher in Jerusalem, 35–36; telling of Israel's story, 331–34; tentmaking, 11, 15, 68–69; theological principle, 252; theology of two-stage resurrection, 369; theories on conversion of, 41–47; in Thessalonica, 185–89; transfer to Caesarea, 360–61; trial before Felix, 361–63; trial before Festus, 363–65; "To an Unknown God" altar inscription, 202–5; view of God's future, 310–11; vision of different kind of community, 421–22; vision of Jesus, 227, 339–40; vision of kingdom, 106–7; visit from Ananias in Damascus, 55–58; visits to Jerusalem, 34–35, 66–68, 92, 138, 175, 229–33, 267, 289, 301, 349–71; vocation as "the ministry of reconciliation," 171; voyage to Rome, 375–86; vulnerable side of, 418–19; zealous behavior of, 23, 33–36, 44, 62, 64, 69, 73, 77–78, 134, 277–79, 328

Pauline "Gentile Christianity," 249
Pelagianism, 152
Pentecost, 20, 345
Peres, Shimon, 36
peritomē, 276, 292
"personality cults," 242
Peter (Cephas), 61, 67, 98–99, 100,

Also by N. T. Wright

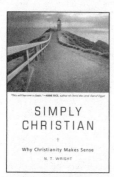

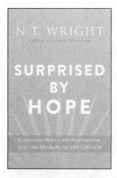

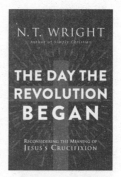

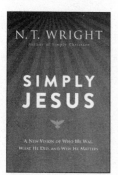

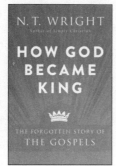

HarperOne
An Imprint of HarperCollinsPublishers